# Land Rover Owners Workshop Manual

## by J H Haynes
Member of the Guild of Motoring Writers

## and M S Daniels

GW00660404

**Models covered**
Land Rover Series II, IIA & III with four-cylinder petrol engine; 2286 cc
All short & long wheelbase models including County; 88 & 109 in

*Does not cover Diesel engine, six- or eight-cylinder petrol engines, 90 & 110 Series, forward-control models or 24V electrical systems*

**ISBN 1 85010 182 5**

© Haynes Publishing Group 1977, 1978, 1984, 1985, 1987

Printed in England *(314-1N4)*

ABC

**Haynes Publishing Group**
Sparkford Nr Yeovil
Somerset BA22 7JJ England

**Haynes Publications, Inc**
861 Lawrence Drive
Newbury Park
California 91320 USA

| British Library Cataloguing in Publication Data |
| --- |
| Daniels, Marcus S. |
|   Land Rover (4 cyl. petrol) series II, IIA, & III. |
|   —(Owners workshop manual). |
| 1. Land-Rover truck |
| I. Title     II. Series |
| 629.28'722     TL230.5.L3 |
| ISBN 1-85010-182-5 |

# Acknowledgements

Thanks are due to the Leyland Company for the provision of technical information and certain illustrations. Castrol Limited supplied information on lubrication, and the Champion Sparking Company supplied the illustrations showing the various spark plug conditions.

The Land Rover (XHR 539) used as the project vehicle for the compilation of this manual was kindly loaned to us for this purpose by Mr Gordon Knott.

Lastly, we thank all of those people at Sparkford who helped in the preparation of this manual.

# About this manual

## Its aim

The aim of this manual is to help you get the best value from your vehicle. It can do so in several ways. It can help you decide what work must be done (even should you choose to get it done by a garage), provide information on routine maintenance and servicing, and give a logical course of action and diagnosis when random faults occur. However, it is hoped that you will use the manual by tackling the work yourself. On simpler jobs it may even be quicker than booking the car into a garage and going there twice, to leave and collect it. Perhaps most important, a lot of money can be saved by avoiding the costs a garage must charge to cover its labour and overheads.

The manual has drawings and descriptions to show the function of the various components so that their layout can be understood. Then the tasks are described and photographed in a step-by-step sequence so that even a novice can do the work.

## Its arrangement

The manual is divided into thirteen Chapters, each covering a logical sub-division of the vehicle. The Chapters are each divided into Sections, numbered with single figures, eg 5; and the Sections into paragraphs (or sub-sections), with decimal numbers following on from the Section they are in, eg 5.1, 5.2, 5.3 etc.

It is freely illustrated, especially in those parts where there is a detailed sequence of operations to be carried out. There are two forms of illustration: figures and photographs. The figures are numbered in sequence with decimal numbers, according to their position in the Chapter — eg Fig. 6.4 is the fourth drawing/illustration in Chapter 6. Photographs carry the same number (either individually or in related groups) as the Section or sub-section to which they relate.

There is an alphabetical index at the back of the manual as well as a contents list at the front. Each Chapter is also preceded by its own individual contents list.

References to the 'left' or 'right' of the vehicle are in the sense of a person in the driver's seat facing forwards.

Unless otherwise stated, nuts and bolts are removed by turning anti-clockwise, and tightened by turning clockwise.

Vehicle manufacturers continually make changes to specifications and recommendations, and these, when notified, are incorporated into our manuals at the earliest opportunity.

**Whilst every care is taken to ensure that the information in this manual is correct, no liability can be accepted by the authors or publishers for loss, damage or injury caused by any errors in, or omissions from, the information given.**

# Introduction to the Land Rover

First introduced in 1948 at the Amsterdam motor show, the Land Rover was primarily designed for use by farmers as a combined tractor/pick-up truck and only a limited production volume was anticipated. However, the vehicle was a phenomenal success and by 1951 it was outselling the Rover saloon cars.

The Land Rover's great strength lay in the short, rigid box-section chassis and simple rugged construction, the problem of corrosion and weight was overcome by the use of aluminium for the bodywork. The original model was fitted with the existing Rover P3 1.6 litre engine and gearbox. A new transfer box obviously then had to be designed and built, and such was the success of this unit that the basic design has remained virtually unchanged to the present day.

In 1952 the 1.6 litre engine, which featured the overhead inlet side exhaust valve layout designed by Rover, was bored out to a 2 litres capacity. In 1958 the Series II model was introduced with a new 2,286 cc overhead valve engine which is still fitted on current models. The waistline body panels were rounded off and the wheelbase had been standardised to 88 inches for the short wheelbase model and 109 inches for the long wheelbase model.

The Series III model was produced in 1971 and incorporated an all-synchromesh gearbox and a full-width instrument panel. The front grille was also modified.

One of the greatest moments in the Land Rover success story came in 1976 when the one millionth vehicle was delivered.

# Contents

SWB Land Rover - the project vehicle used for this manual

LWB Land Rover Station Wagon

# Use of English

*As this book has been written in England, it uses the appropriate English component names, phrases, and spelling. Some of these differ from those used in America. Normally, these cause no difficulty, but to make sure, a glossary is printed below. In ordering spare parts remember the parts list may use some of these words:*

| English | American | English | American |
|---|---|---|---|
| Accelerator | Gas pedal | Leading shoe (of brake) | Primary shoe |
| Aerial | Antenna | Locks | Latches |
| Anti-roll bar | Stabiliser or sway bar | Methylated spirit | Denatured alcohol |
| Big-end bearing | Rod bearing | Motorway | Freeway, turnpike etc |
| Bonnet (engine cover) | Hood | Number plate | License plate |
| Boot (luggage compartment) | Trunk | Paraffin | Kerosene |
| Bulkhead | Firewall | Petrol | Gasoline (gas) |
| Bush | Bushing | Petrol tank | Gas tank |
| Cam follower or tappet | Valve lifter or tappet | 'Pinking' | 'Pinging' |
| Carburettor | Carburetor | Prise (force apart) | Pry |
| Catch | Latch | Propeller shaft | Driveshaft |
| Choke/venturi | Barrel | Quarterlight | Quarter window |
| Circlip | Snap-ring | Retread | Recap |
| Clearance | Lash | Reverse | Back-up |
| Crownwheel | Ring gear (of differential) | Rocker cover | Valve cover |
| Damper | Shock absorber, shock | Saloon | Sedan |
| Disc (brake) | Rotor/disk | Seized | Frozen |
| Distance piece | Spacer | Sidelight | Parking light |
| Drop arm | Pitman arm | Silencer | Muffler |
| Drop head coupe | Convertible | Sill panel (beneath doors) | Rocker panel |
| Dynamo | Generator (DC) | Small end, little end | Piston pin or wrist pin |
| Earth (electrical) | Ground | Spanner | Wrench |
| Engineer's blue | Prussian blue | Split cotter (for valve spring cap) | Lock (for valve spring retainer) |
| Estate car | Station wagon | Split pin | Cotter pin |
| Exhaust manifold | Header | Steering arm | Spindle arm |
| Fault finding/diagnosis | Troubleshooting | Sump | Oil pan |
| Float chamber | Float bowl | Swarf | Metal chips or debris |
| Free-play | Lash | Tab washer | Tang or lock |
| Freewheel | Coast | Tappet | Valve lifter |
| Gearbox | Transmission | Thrust bearing | Throw-out bearing |
| Gearchange | Shift | Top gear | High |
| Grub screw | Setscrew, Allen screw | Trackrod (of steering) | Tie-rod (or connecting rod) |
| Gudgeon pin | Piston pin or wrist pin | Trailing shoe (of brake) | Secondary shoe |
| Halfshaft | Axleshaft | Transmission | Whole drive line |
| Handbrake | Parking brake | Tyre | Tire |
| Hood | Soft top | Van | Panel wagon/van |
| Hot spot | Heat riser | Vice | Vise |
| Indicator | Turn signal | Wheel nut | Lug nut |
| Interior light | Dome lamp | Windscreen | Windshield |
| Layshaft (of gearbox) | Countershaft | Wing/mudguard | Fender |

# Buying spare parts
# and vehicle identification numbers

*For modifications, and information applicable to later models, see Supplement at end of manual*

## Buying spare parts

Spare parts are available from many sources, for example: Leyland garages, other garages and accessory shops, and motor factors. Our advice regarding spare part sources is as follows:

**Officially appointed Leyland garages** - This is the best source of parts which are peculiar to your vehicle and are otherwise not generally available (eg; complete cylinder heads, internal gearbox components, badges, interior trim etc). It is also the only place at which you should buy parts if your vehicle is still under warranty - non-Leyland components may invalidate the warranty. To be sure of obtaining the correct parts it will always be necessary to give the storeman your vehicle's engine and chassis number, and if possible, to take the old part along for positive identification. Remember that many parts are available on a factory exchange scheme - any parts returned should always be clean! It obviously makes good sense to go straight to the specialists on your vehicle for this type of part, for they are best equipped to supply you.

**Other garages and accessory shops** - These are often very good places to buy materials and components needed for the maintenance of your vehicle (eg; oil filters, spark plugs, bulbs, fan belts, oils and greases, touch-up paint, filler paste etc). They also sell general accessories, usually have convenient opening hours, charge lower prices and can often be found not far from home.

**Motor factors** - Good factors will stock all of the more important components which wear out relatively quickly (eg; clutch components, pistons, valves, exhaust systems, brake cylinders/pipes/hoses/seals/shoes and pads etc). Motor factors will often provide new or reconditioned components on a part exchange basis - this can save a considerable amount of money.

## Vehicle identification numbers

The chassis number will be found on a plate attached to the dash-panel. The plate also displays information on the vehicle's maximum laden weight and the maximum front and rear axle loads.

The engine number is stamped on the front left-hand side of the engine block.

The transmission number will be found on the rear, right-hand side of the gearbox (see photo).

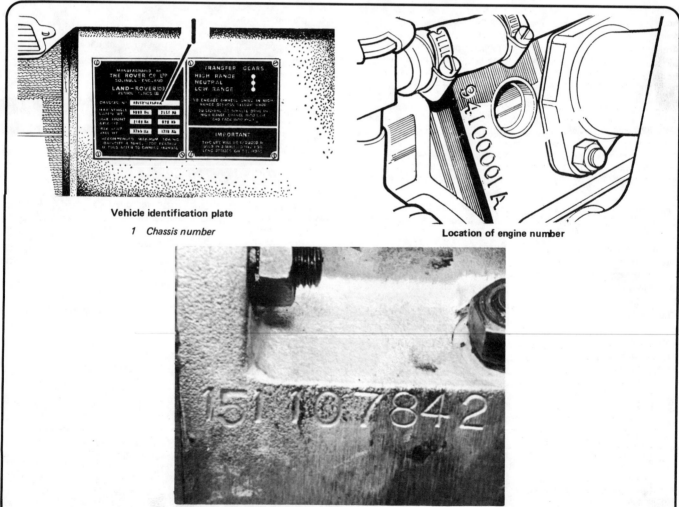

Vehicle identification plate

1   Chassis number

Location of engine number

Transmission number

# Tools and working facilities

## Introduction

A selection of good tools is a fundamental requirement for anyone contemplating the maintenance and repair of a motor vehicle. For the owner who does not possess any, their purchase will prove a considerable expense, offsetting some of the savings made by doing-it-yourself. However, provided that the tools purchased are of good quality, they will last for many years and prove an extremely worthwhile investment.

To help the average owner to decide which tools are needed to carry out the various tasks detailed in this manual, we have compiled three lists of tools under the following headings: Maintenance and minor repair, Repair and overhaul, and Special. The newcomer to practical mechanics should start off with the 'Maintenance and minor repair' tool kit and confine himself to the simpler jobs around the vehicle. Then, as his confidence and experience grows, he can undertake more difficult tasks, buying extra tools as, and when, they are needed. In this way, a 'Maintenance and minor repair' tool kit can be built-up into a 'Repair and overhaul' tool kit over a considerable period of time without any major cash outlays. The experienced do-it-yourselfer will have a tool kit good enough for most repair and overhaul procedures and will add tools from the 'Special' category when he feels the expense is justified by the amount of use these tools will be put to.

It is obviously not possible to cover the subject of tools fully here. For those who wish to learn more about tools and their use there is a book entitled 'How to Choose and Use Car Tools' available from the publishers of this manual.

## Maintenance and minor repair tool kit

The tools given in this list should be considered as a minimum requirement if routine maintenance, servicing and minor repair operations are to be undertaken. We recommend the purchase of combination spanners (ring one end, open-ended the other); although more expensive than open-ended ones, they do give the advantages of both types of spanner.

*Combination spanners - 3/8 in, 7/16 in, 1/2 in, 9/16 in, 5/8 in. AF (and/or 8 to 19 mm on later models)*
*Adjustable spanners - 9 inch*
*Engine sump/gearbox/rear axle drain plug key (where applicable)*
*Spark plug spanner (with rubber insert)*
*Spark plug gap adjustment tool*
*Set of feeler gauges*
*Brake adjuster spanner (where applicable)*
*Brake bleed nipple spanner*
*Screwdriver - 4 in long x ¼ in dia (plain)*
*Screwdriver - 4 in long x ¼ in dia (crosshead)*
*Combination pliers - 6 inch*
*Hacksaw, junior*
*Tyre pump*
*Tyre pressure gauge*
*Grease gun (where applicable)*
*Oil can*
*Fine emery cloth (1 sheet)*
*Wire brush (small)*
*Funnel (medium size)*

## Repair and overhaul tool kit

These tools are virtually essential for anyone undertaking any major repairs to a motor vehicle, and are additional to those given in the Basic list. Included in this list is a comprehensive set of sockets. Although these are expensive they will be found invaluable as they are so versatile - particularly if various drives are included in the set. We recommend the ½ inch square-drive type, as this can be used with most proprietary torque wrenches. If you cannot afford a socket set, even bought piecemeal, then inexpensive tubular box spanners are a useful alternative.

The tools in this list will occasionally need to be supplemented by tools from the Special list.

*Sockets (or box spanners) to cover range in previous list*
*Reversible ratchet drive (for use with sockets)*
*Extension piece, 10 inch (for use with sockets)*
*Universal joint (for use with sockets)*
*Torque wrench (for use with sockets)*
*'Mole' wrench - 8 inch*
*Ball pein hammer*
*Soft-faced hammer, plastic or rubber*
*Screwdriver - 6 in long x 5/16 in dia (plain)*
*Screwdriver - 2 in long x 5/16 in square (plain)*
*Screwdriver - 1½ in long x ¼ in dia (crosshead)*
*Screwdriver - 3 in long x 1/8 in dia (electricians)*
*Pliers - electricians side cutters*
*Pliers - needle nosed*
*Pliers - circlip ( internal and external)*
*Cold chisel - ½ inch*
*Scriber (this can be made by grinding the end of a broken hacksaw blade)*
*Scraper (this can be made by flattening and sharpening one end of a piece of copper pipe)*
*Centre punch*
*Pin punch*
*Hacksaw*
*Valve grinding tool*
*Steel rule/straight edge*
*Allen keys*
*Selection of files*
*Wire brush (large)*
*Axle stands*
*Jack (strong scissor or hydraulic type)*

## Special tools

The tools in this list are those which are not used regularly, are expensive to buy, or which need to be used in accordance with their manufacturers instructions. Unless relatively difficult mechanical jobs are undertaken frequently, it will not be economic to buy many of these tools. Where this is the case, you could consider clubbing together with friends (or a motorists club) to make a joint purchase, or borrowing the tools against a deposit from a local garage or tool hire specialist.

The following list contains only those tools and instruments freely available to the public, and not those special tools produced by the vehicle manufacturer specifically for its dealer network. You will find occasional references to these manufacturers special tools in the text of this manual. Generally, an alternative method of doing the job without the vehicle manufacturers special tool is given. However, sometimes, there is no alternative to using them. Where this is the case and the relevant tool cannot be bought or borrowed you will have to entrust the work to a franchised garage.

Valve spring compressor
Piston ring compressor
Ball joint separator
Universal hub/bearing puller
Impact screwdriver
Micrometer and/or vernier gauge
Carburettor flow balancing device (where applicable)
Dial gauge
Stroboscopic timing light
Dwell angle meter/tachometer
Universal electrical multi-meter
Cylinder compression gauge
Lifting tackle
Trolley jack
Light with extension lead

## Buying tools

For practically all tools, a tool factor is the best source since he will have a very comprehensive range compared with the average garage or accessory shop. Having said that, accessory shops often offer excellent quality tools at discount prices, so it pays to shop around.

Remember, you don't have to buy the most expensive items on the shelf, but it is always advisable to steer clear of the very cheap tools. There are plenty of good tools around, at reasonable prices, so ask the proprietor or manager of the shop for advice before making a purchase.

## Care and maintenance of tools

Having purchased a reasonable tool kit, it is necessary to keep the tools in a clean and serviceable condition. After use, always wipe off any dirt, grease and metal particles using a clean, dry cloth, before putting the tools away. Never leave them lying around after they have been used. A simple tool rack on the garage or workshop wall, for items such as screwdrivers and pliers is a good idea. Store all normal spanners and sockets in a metal box. Any measuring instruments, gauges, meters, etc., must be carefully stored where they cannot be damaged or become rusty.

Take a little care when the tools are used. Hammer heads inevitably become marked and screwdrivers lose the keen edge on their blades from time-to-time. A little timely attention with emery cloth or a file will soon restore items like this to a good serviceable finish.

## Working facilities

Not to be forgotten when discussing tools, is the workshop itself. If anything more than routine maintenance is to be carried out, some form of suitable working area becomes essential.

It is appreciated that many an owner mechanic is forced by circumstances to remove an engine or similar item, without the benefit of a garage or workshop. Having done this, any repairs should always be done under the cover of a roof.

Wherever possible, any dismantling should be done on a clean flat workbench or table at a suitable working height.

Any workbench needs a vice: one with a jaw opening of 4 in (100 mm) is suitable for most jobs. As mentioned previously, some clean dry storage space is also required for tools, as well as the lubricants, cleaning fluids, touch-up paints and so on which become necessary.

Another item which may be required, and which has a much more general usage, is an electric drill with a chuck capacity of at least 5/16 in (8 mm). This, together with a good range of twist drills, is virtually essential for fitting accessories such as wing mirrors and reversing lights.

Last, but not least, always keep a supply of old newspapers and clean, lint-free rags available, and try to keep any working area as clean as possible.

*Spanner jaw gap comparison table*

| Jaw gap (in) | Spanner size |
|---|---|
| 0.250 | $\frac{1}{4}$ in AF |
| 0.276 | 7 mm |
| 0.313 | $\frac{5}{16}$ in AF |
| 0.315 | 8 mm |
| 0.344 | $\frac{11}{32}$ in AF; $\frac{1}{8}$ in Whitworth |
| 0.354 | 9 mm |
| 0.375 | $\frac{3}{8}$ in AF |
| 0.394 | 10 mm |
| 0.433 | 11 mm |
| 0.438 | $\frac{7}{16}$ in AF |
| 0.445 | $\frac{3}{16}$ in Whitworth; $\frac{1}{4}$ in BSF |
| 0.472 | 12 mm |
| 0.500 | $\frac{1}{2}$ in AF |
| 0.512 | 13 mm |
| 0.525 | $\frac{1}{4}$ in Whitworth; $\frac{5}{16}$ in BSF |
| 0.551 | 14 mm |
| 0.563 | $\frac{9}{16}$ in AF |
| 0.591 | 15 mm |
| 0.600 | $\frac{5}{16}$ in Whitworth; $\frac{3}{8}$ in BSF |
| 0.625 | $\frac{5}{8}$ in AF |
| 0.630 | 16 mm |
| 0.669 | 17 mm |
| 0.686 | $\frac{11}{16}$ in AF |
| 0.709 | 18 mm |
| 0.710 | $\frac{3}{8}$ in Whitworth; $\frac{7}{16}$ in BSF |
| 0.748 | 19 mm |
| 0.750 | $\frac{3}{4}$ in AF |
| 0.813 | $\frac{13}{16}$ in AF |
| 0.820 | $\frac{7}{16}$ in Whitworth; $\frac{1}{2}$ in BSF |
| 0.866 | 22 mm |
| 0.875 | $\frac{7}{8}$ in AF |
| 0.920 | $\frac{1}{2}$ in Whitworth; $\frac{9}{16}$ in BSF |
| 0.938 | $\frac{15}{16}$ in AF |
| 0.945 | 24 mm |
| 1.000 | 1 in AF |
| 1.010 | $\frac{9}{16}$ in Whitworth; $\frac{5}{8}$ in BSF |
| 1.024 | 26 mm |
| 1.063 | $1\frac{1}{16}$ in AF; 27 mm |
| 1.100 | $\frac{5}{8}$ in Whitworth; $\frac{11}{16}$ in BSF |
| 1.125 | $1\frac{1}{8}$ in AF |
| 1.181 | 30 mm |
| 1.200 | $\frac{11}{16}$ in Whitworth; $\frac{3}{4}$ in BSF |
| 1.250 | $1\frac{1}{4}$ in AF |
| 1.260 | 32 mm |
| 1.300 | $\frac{3}{4}$ in Whitworth; $\frac{7}{8}$ in BSF |
| 1.313 | $1\frac{5}{16}$ in AF |
| 1.390 | $\frac{13}{16}$ in Whitworth; $\frac{15}{16}$ in BSF |
| 1.417 | 36 mm |
| 1.438 | $1\frac{7}{16}$ in AF |
| 1.480 | $\frac{7}{8}$ in Whitworth; 1 in BSF |
| 1.500 | $1\frac{1}{2}$ in AF |
| 1.575 | 40 mm; $\frac{15}{16}$ in Whitworth |
| 1.614 | 41 mm |
| 1.625 | $1\frac{5}{8}$ in AF |
| 1.670 | 1 in Whitworth; $1\frac{1}{8}$ in BSF |
| 1.688 | $1\frac{11}{16}$ in AF |
| 1.811 | 46 mm |
| 1.813 | $1\frac{13}{16}$ in AF |
| 1.860 | $1\frac{1}{8}$ in Whitworth; $1\frac{1}{4}$ in BSF |
| 1.875 | $1\frac{7}{8}$ in AF |
| 1.969 | 50 mm |
| 2.000 | 2 in AF |
| 2.050 | $1\frac{1}{4}$ in Whitworth; $1\frac{3}{8}$ in BSF |
| 2.165 | 55 mm |
| 2.362 | 60 mm |

# Routine maintenance

The maintenance schedules listed in this Section are based on those recommended by Leyland and apply to a Land Rover that is being used in the conventional manner, ie; normal roadwork, trailer towing and light cross-country duties.

If the vehicle is used in rough terrain and is constantly working in mud and dust, the oil should be changed more frequently and the aircleaner should be cleaned daily. In exceptionally harsh conditions or if the vehicle is used for deep wading, the engine oil should also be changed daily.

The gearbox, transfer box, differential and swivel pin oils should also be changed more frequently if the vehicle is being used in the conditions described in the previous paragraph. In particular the propeller shaft sliding joints should be lubricated frequently if driving through sand.

If the vehicle is driven constantly with the low transfer ratio engaged or as a stationary power source then obviously the mileage reading cannot be used for deciding the frequency of service intervals. When used in these conditions the engine and transmission service periods must be based on hours running time or fuel consumption and for this purpose a conversion chart is given at the end of this Section.

## Maintenance intervals - later models

From 1981 the maker's recommended maintenance interval for all Series III models is increased from 4,000 to 6,000 miles (6,000 to 10,000 kms), or the equivalent in hours of running time or fuel consumed.

## Weekly, (or daily if operating under severe conditions)

### Steering
Check the tyre pressures, including the spare wheel.
Examine tyres for wear or damage.

### Brakes
Check reservoir fluid level.
Is there any fall off in braking efficiency?
Try an emergency stop. Is adjustment necessary?

### Lights, wipers and horns
Do all bulbs work at the front and rear?
Are the headlamp beams aligned properly?
Do the wipers and horns work?
Check windscreen washer fluid level.

### Engine
Check the sump oil level and top-up if required.
Check the radiator coolant level and top-up if required.
Check the battery electrolyte level and top-up to the level of the plates with distilled water as needed.

## At the first 1,000 miles (1,500 kms) - New vehicles only

Take the vehicle to an authorised Leyland Dealer and have the free service carried out, and any faults rectified.

## Every 4,000 miles (6,000 kms)

1  Change the engine oil and renew the oil filter element.
2  On vehicles fitted with the oil bath type air cleaner, empty out the oil, clean out the casing and refill.
3  Check the carburettor slow running speed and adjust if necessary.
4  Clean and adjust the spark plugs.
5  Check the contact breaker points and adjust if necessary.
6  Lubricate the contact breaker cam and centrifugal advance mechanism.
7  Check the fan belt tension and adjust if necessary.
8  Top up the radiator water level if required.
9  Check the gearbox and transfer box oil levels and top up if necessary.
10 If a drain plug has been fitted in the flywheel housing, remove it and allow any oil present to drain out.
11 Check the fluid level in the clutch and brake reservoir(s) and top-up if necessary.
12 Check the battery electrolyte level.
13 Check the oil levels in the front and rear differentials and top up if necessary.
14 Check the oil levels in the front swivel pin housings and top-up if necessary.
15 Examine the front wheel hubs for any sign of oil leakage.
16 Check the steering box and steering damper oil levels, topping-up if necessary.
17 Examine the rubber boots on all steering joints and renew them if torn.
18 Have the front wheel alignment checked at the local garage.
19 Check and adjust the brake shoes, (do not forget the handbrake shoes).
20 Examine tyres for wear and damage and check the pressures.
21 Lubricate the propeller shaft sleeves and, if grease nipples are fitted, lubricate the universal joints.
22 Road test the vehicle and rectify any faults that are found.

## Every 8,000 miles (12,000 kms)

Carry out the checks listed under the heading 4,000 miles (6,000 kms), plus the following:
1  Remove the engine breather filters and wash them out in petrol.
2  Fit a new set of spark plugs.
3  Check the tappet clearances and adjust if necessary.
4  Clean the battery terminals and coat them with petroleum jelly.
5  Take the vehicle to the local garage and have them check the headlamp beam alignment.
6  Check all lights and instruments for correct operation.
7  Lightly oil the door locks, hinges, handbrake and throttle linkages.

## Every 12,000 miles (18,000 kms)

Carry out the checks listed under the heading 4,000 miles (6,000 kms), plus the following:
1 Clean out the fuel sediment bowl adjacent to the fuel pump.
2 Lubricate the dynamo rear bearing.
3 Drain and refill the gearbox and transfer box.
4 Drain and refill the front and rear differentials.
5 Drain and refill the front axle swivel pin housings.
**Note:** the above last three checks replace the oil level checks listed in the 4,000 miles (6,000 kms) service.
6 Check all body bolts for tightness.
7 Check the tightness of the road spring 'U' bolts and spring clips.
8 Check all the propeller shaft bolts for tightness and the universal joints for wear.

## Every 16,000 miles (24,000 kms)

Carry out the checks listed under the headings 4,000 miles (6,000 kms) and 8,000 miles (12,000 kms).

## Every 20,000 miles (30,000 kms)

Carry out the checks listed under the heading 4,000 miles (6,000 kms), plus the following:
1 Clean the emission control flame-trap, if fitted.

## Every 24,000 miles (36,000 kms)

Carry out the checks listed under the headings 4,000 miles (6,000 kms), 8,000 miles (12,000 kms) and 12,000 miles (18,000 kms), plus the following:
1 Lubricate the propeller shaft sliding joints.
2 **IMPORTANT:** The brake fluid should be renewed every eighteen months, and if the vehicle is going to be used for touring in mountainous terrain it must be renewed within a period of nine months prior to the tour.

All the rubber seals in the braking system should be renewed every three years or 40,000 miles (64,000 kms), whichever occurs first.

### Conversion chart

The following chart can be used to convert hours running time or fuel consumption into an equivalant mileage.

| | | Fuel consumption | | |
| Kilometres | Miles | Litres | Gallons | Hours' running time |
| --- | --- | --- | --- | --- |
| 6,000 | 4,000 | 900 | 200 | 160 |
| 12,000 | 8,000 | 1,800 | 400 | 320 |
| 18,000 | 12,000 | 2,700 | 600 | 480 |
| 24,000 | 16,000 | 3,600 | 800 | 640 |
| 30,000 | 20,000 | 4,500 | 1,000 | 800 |
| 36,000 | 24,000 | 5,400 | 1,200 | 960 |

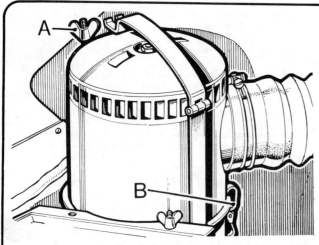

**Air cleaner assembly**

A  *Clamp wing-nut*        B  *Securing clips (3 off)*

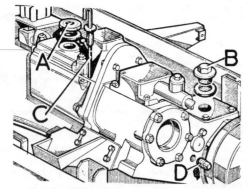

**Transmission oil filler and level plugs (earlier models)**

A  *Filler cap, main gearbox section*    C  *Oil level dipstick, main gearbox*
B  *Filler plug, transfer box section*      D  *Oil level plug, transfer box*

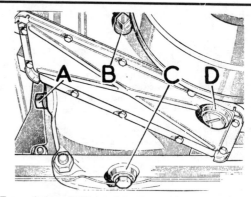

**Transmission oil filler and drain plugs (later models)**

A  *Filler level/plug main gearbox section*
B  *Filler level/plug, transfer box section*
C  *Drain plug, main gearbox section*
D  *Drain plug, transfer gearbox section*

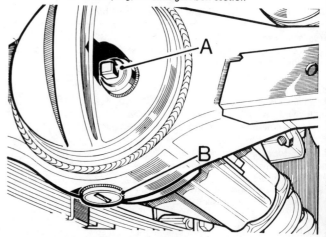

**Front differential oil level and drain plugs**

A  *Filler/level plug*            B  *Drain plug*

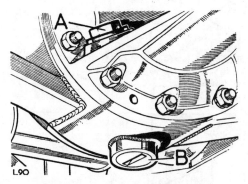

**Rear differential oil level and drain plugs**

A  *Filler/level plug*          B  *Drain plug*

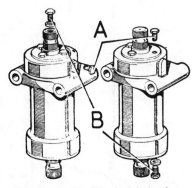

**Steering damper filler and drain plugs**

A  *Oil filler hole and plug*
B  *Breather hole and plug on early type*
   *Drain plug on latest type*

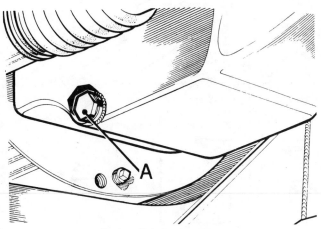

**Engine oil drain plug 'A'**

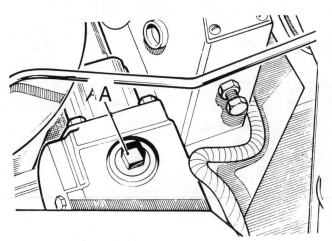

**Steering box filler plug 'A'**

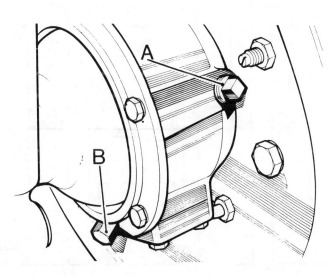

**Swivel pin housing oil level and drain plugs**

A  *Filler/level plug*          B  *Drain plug*

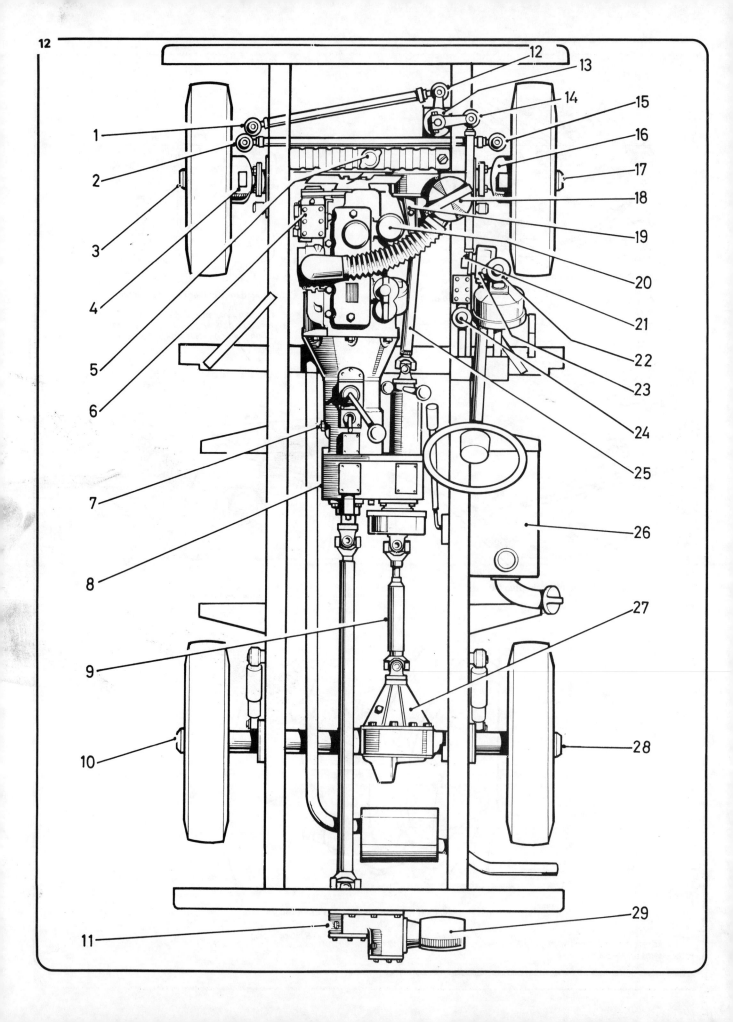

# Recommended lubricants and fluids

| Diagram number | Component or system | Lubricant type or specification |
|---|---|---|
| 6 | Governor | |
| 18 | Air cleaner | Multigrade engine oil, viscosity range from 10W/40 |
| 20 | Engine | to 20W/50, to API SE or SF |
| | | |
| 4 | Swivel housing, LH | |
| 7 | Main gearbox | |
| 8 | Transfer box | |
| 11 | Rear power take-off | |
| 13 | Steering relay | |
| 16 | Swivel housing, RH | Gear oil, SAE 90EP or 85W/140, to API GL |
| 19 | Front differential | |
| 23 | Steering box | |
| 27 | Rear differential | |
| 29 | Pulley unit | |
| | | |
| 1 | Drag link balljoint, LH | |
| 2 | Track rod balljoint, LH | |
| 3 | Front hub, LH | |
| 9 | Rear propeller shaft | |
| 10 | Rear hub, LH | |
| 12 | Drag link balljoint, RH | |
| 14 | Longitudinal arm balljoint, front | Multi-purpose lithium based grease |
| 15 | Track rod balljoint, RH | |
| 17 | Front hub, RH | |
| 21 | Longitudinal arm balljoint, rear | |
| 25 | Front propeller shaft | |
| 28 | Rear hub, RH | |
| | | |
| 5 | Radiator | Ethylene glycol based antifreeze solution to BS3152 |
| | | |
| 22 | Brake fluid reservoir | |
| 24 | Clutch fluid reservoir | Brake and clutch fluid (J1703 or DOT 3) |
| | | |
| 26 | Fuel tank | |

*These recommendations apply to temperate climates where operation temperatures are above −10°C (14°F). If in doubt consult an authorised Land-Rover dealer.*

# Chapter 1 Engine

*For modifications, and information applicable to later models, see Supplement at end of manual*

## Contents

## Specifications

### Engine, general

| | |
|---|---|
| Capacity (piston displacement) ... ... ... ... ... | 2286 cc (140 cu in) |
| Number of cylinders ... ... ... ... ... ... ... | 4 |
| Bore ... ... ... ... ... ... ... ... ... ... | 3.562 in (90.47 mm) |
| Stroke ... ... ... ... ... ... ... ... ... | 3.5 in (88.8 mm) |
| Compression ratio ... ... ... ... ... ... ... | 7 : 1 or 8 : 1 |
| BHP at 4,250 rpm ... ... ... ... ... ... ... | 77 (7 : 1) 81 (8 : 1) |
| BMEP ... ... ... ... ... ... ... ... ... | 7 : 1 134 lb/in$^2$ (9.4 kg/cm$^2$) at 2,500 rpm |
| | 8 : 1 137 lb/in$^2$ (9.6 kg/cm$^2$) at 2,500 rpm |
| Maximum torque ... ... ... ... ... ... ... | 7 : 1 124 lb/ft (17 mkg) at 2,500 rpm |
| Firing order ... ... ... ... ... ... ... ... | 1 - 3 - 4 - 2 |
| Piston speed at 4,280 rpm ... ... ... ... ... | 2,500 ft/min (12.6 m/sec) |
| Compression pressure (at starter motor cranking speed, with engine hot) | 7 : 1 145 lb/in$^2$ (10.2 kg/cm$^2$) |
| | 8 : 1 160-170 lb/in$^2$ (11.2-11.9 kg/cm$^2$) |

### Camshaft

| | |
|---|---|
| Journal diameter ... ... ... ... ... ... ... ... | 1.842 in − 0.001 (26.70 mm − 0.025) |
| Clearance in bearing ... ... ... ... ... ... ... | 0.001 to 0.002 in (0.02 to 0.05 mm) |
| Endfloat ... ... ... ... ... ... ... ... ... | 0.0025 to 0.0055 in (0.06 to 0.14 mm) |
| Cam lift - inlet ... ... ... ... ... ... ... ... | 0.257 in (6.53 mm) |
| Cam lift - exhaust ... ... ... ... ... ... ... | 0.257 in (6.53 mm) |

### Camshaft bearings

| | |
|---|---|
| Type ... ... ... ... ... ... ... ... ... ... | Split, steel backed, white metal lined |
| Internal diameter (line-reamed in position) ... ... ... | 1.843 in + 0.0005 (46.8 mm + 0.012) |

### Connecting rods

| | |
|---|---|
| Bearing fit on crankpin ... ... ... ... ... ... ... | 0.001 to 0.0025 in (0.025 to 0.063 mm) |
| Bearing nip ... ... ... ... ... ... ... ... ... | 0.002 to 0.004 in (0.05 to 0.10 mm) |
| Endfloat at big-end ... ... ... ... ... ... ... | 0.007 to 0.011 in (0.20 to 0.30 mm) |
| Gudgeon pin bush, fit in small-end ... ... ... ... ... | 0.001 to 0.003 in (0.02 to 0.76 mm) interference |
| Gudgeon pin bush internal diameter - reamed in position ... ... | 1.000 in + 0.0003 (25.4 mm + 0.008) |
| Fit of gudgeon pin in bush ... ... ... ... ... ... | 0.0003 to 0.0005 in (0.007 to 0.012 mm) clearance |

## Crankshaft

| | |
|---|---|
| Journal diameter ... ... ... ... ... ... ... ... | 2.5 in − 0.0005 (63.5 mm − 0.012) |
| Crankpin diameter: | |
|     Early models ... ... ... ... ... ... ... ... | 2.126 in − 0.001 (53.9 mm − 0.025) |
|     Late models ... ... ... ... ... ... ... ... | 2.312 in (58.7 mm) |
| Endfloat (controlled by thrust washers at centre bearing) ... ... ... | 0.002 to 0.006 in (0.05 to 0.15 mm) |
| Regrind sizes: | |

| Undersize | Journal dia. | Crankpin dia. |
|---|---|---|
| 0.010 in | 2.490 in | 2.302 in |
| (0.25 mm) | (63.24 mm) | (58.47 mm) |
| 0.020 in | 2.480 in | 2.292 in |
| (0.50 mm) | (62.99 mm) | (58.22 mm) |
| 0.030 in | 2.470 in | 2.282 in |
| (0.76 mm) | (62.73 mm) | (57.96 mm) |
| 0.040 in | 2.460 in | 2.272 in |
| (1.01 mm) | (62.48 mm) | (57.70 mm) |

## Flywheel

| | |
|---|---|
| Number of teeth ... ... ... ... ... ... ... ... | 97 |
| Thickness at pressure face ... ... ... ... ... ... | 1.250 to 1.226 in (31.75 to 31.14 mm) |
| Maximum permissible run-out on flywheel face ... ... ... ... | 0.002 in (0.05 mm) |
| Primary pinion bush - fit in flywheel ... ... ... ... ... | 0.001 to 0.003 in (0.02 to 0.07 mm) |
| Internal diameter - reamed in position ... ... ... ... ... | 0.878 in + 0.0005 in (22.3 + 0.013 mm) |
| Fit of shaft in bush ... ... ... ... ... ... ... | 0.001 to 0.003 in (0.025 to 0.076 mm) |
| Maximum refacing depth ... ... ... ... ... ... | 0.030 in (0.76 mm) |
| Minimum overall thickness after grinding ... ... ... ... | 1.485 in (37.7 mm) |

## Engine timing markings

| | |
|---|---|
| Early engines ... ... ... ... ... ... ... ... ... | Timing marks and pointer at flywheel |
| Later engines ... ... ... ... ... ... ... ... ... | Valve timing marks at timing chain wheels |
| | Ignition timing mark on crankshaft pulley, timing pointer at engine front cover |
| TDC (74-76 octane fuel) ... ... ... ... ... ... ... | When opposite pointer, No. 1 piston is at top dead centre (TDC) |
| 3º BTDC (80-85 octane fuel) } ... ... ... ... ... ... | When opposite pointer, indicates firing point of No. 1 cylinder |
| 6º BTDC (90-96 octane fuel) } | when both valves are closed |

## Gudgeon pin

| | |
|---|---|
| Fit in piston ... ... ... ... ... ... ... ... ... | Zero to 0.0002 in (0.005 mm) interference |
| Fit in connecting rod bush ... ... ... ... ... ... | 0.0003 to 0.0005 in (0.007 to 0.012 mm) clearance |

## Main bearings

| | |
|---|---|
| Clearances on crankshaft journal ... ... ... ... ... ... | 0.001 to 0.0025 in (0.02 to 0.06 mm) |
| Bearing nip ... ... ... ... ... ... ... ... ... | 0.004 to 0.006 in (0.10 to 0.15 mm) |

## Cylinder bores

| | |
|---|---|
| Nominal diameter (new) ... ... ... ... ... ... ... | 3.562 in (90.47 mm) |
| Rebore sizes ... ... ... ... ... ... ... ... ... | + 0.020 and 0.040 in (0.50 and 1.01 mm) |

## Pistons

| | |
|---|---|
| Type ... ... ... ... ... ... ... ... ... ... | Light alloy, tin plated, flat top |
| Clearance in bore, measured at bottom of skirt at right angles to gudgeon pin ... ... ... ... ... ... ... ... | 0.0019 to 0.0023 in (0.048 to 0.058 mm) |
| Clearance in bore, measured at top of skirt at right angles to gudgeon pin ... ... ... ... ... ... ... ... | 0.003 to 0.004 in (0.08 to 0.10 mm) |
| Fit of gudgeon pin in piston ... ... ... ... ... ... | Zero to 0.0002 in (0.005 mm) interference |
| Gudgeon pin bore ... ... ... ... ... ... ... ... | 0.9998 in + 0.0002 (25.37 mm + 0.005) |

## Piston rings

| | |
|---|---|
| Compression (2): | |
|     Type ... ... ... ... ... ... ... ... ... | Taper periphery |
|     Gap in bore ... ... ... ... ... ... ... ... | 0.015 to 0.020 in (0.38 to 0.50 mm) |
|     Clearance in groove ... ... ... ... ... ... ... | 0.0018 to 0.0038 in (0.046 to 0.097 mm) |
| Scraper: | |
|     Type ... ... ... ... ... ... ... ... ... | Slotted, square friction edge |
|     Gap in bore ... ... ... ... ... ... ... ... | 0.015 to 0.020 in (0.38 to 0.50 mm) |
|     Clearance in groove ... ... ... ... ... ... ... | 0.0015 to 0.0035 in (0.038 to 0.089 mm) |

## Rocker gear

| | |
|---|---|
| Bush internal diameter, reamed in position ... ... ... ... | 0.53 in + 0.001 (13.4 mm + 0.02) |
| Shaft clearance in rocker bush ... ... ... ... ... ... | 0.0005 to 0.0015 in (0.013 to 0.038 mm) |

## Tappet clearance ... ... ... ... ... ... ... ...

0.010 in (0.25 mm) hot or cold

## Timing chain tensioner

| | |
|---|---|
| Fit of bush in cylinder ... ... ... ... ... ... ... | 0.003 to 0.005 in (0.07 to 0.12 mm) interference |
| Fit of bush in idler wheel ... ... ... ... ... ... | 0.001 to 0.003 in (0.02 to 0.07 mm) interference |
| Fit of idler wheel on steel shaft ... ... ... ... ... | 0.001 to 0.003 in (0.02 to 0.07 mm) clearance |
| Fit of piston in cylinder bush ... ... ... ... ... ... | 0.0003 to 0.0013 in (0.008 to 0.033 mm) clearance |

## Thrust bearings, crankshaft

| | |
|---|---|
| Type   ...   ...   ...   ...   ...   ...   ...   ...   ... | Semi-circular, steel back, tin plated on friction surface |
| Standard size, total thickness   ...   ...   ...   ...   ...   ... | 0.093 in − 0.002 (2.362 mm − 0.05) |
| Oversizes   ...   ...   ...   ...   ...   ...   ...   ... | 0.0025 in (0.06 mm); 0.005 in (0.12 mm); |
| | 0.0075 in (0.18 mm); 0.010 in (0.25 mm) |

## Valves

| | |
|---|---|
| Inlet valve: | |
|     Diameter (stem)   ...   ...   ...   ...   ...   ...   ...   ... | 0.3112 in − 0.0005 (7.9 mm − 0.013 mm) |
|     Face angle   ...   ...   ...   ...   ...   ...   ...   ... | 30° − ¼ |
| Exhaust valve: | |
|     Diameter (stem)   ...   ...   ...   ...   ...   ...   ... | 0.3415 − 0.0005 in (8.67 mm − 0.013) |
|     Face angle   ...   ...   ...   ...   ...   ...   ... | 45° − ¼ |
| Fit of inlet valves in guide   ...   ...   ...   ...   ...   ... | 0.001 to 0.003 in (0.02 to 0.07 mm) |
| Fit of exhaust valves in guide   ...   ...   ...   ...   ... | 0.0023 to 0.0038 in (0.058 to 0.096 mm) |

## Valve seat

| | |
|---|---|
| Seat angle - inlet ...   ...   ...   ...   ...   ...   ...   ... | 30° |
| Seat angle - exhaust   ...   ...   ...   ...   ...   ... | 45° |

## Valve guides

| | |
|---|---|
| Inlet guide bore size, after fitting   ...   ...   ...   ...   ... | 0.3125 in + 0.0015 (7.93 mm + 0.04) |
| Exhaust guide bore size, after fitting ...   ...   ...   ...   ... | 0.3435 in + 0.0015 (8.73 mm + 0.04) |

## Valve springs

| | |
|---|---|
| Early type: | |
|     Inner: | |
|        Length - free   ...   ...   ...   ...   ...   ...   ... | 1.61 in (40.89 mm) |
|        Length under 17.5 lb (7.9 kg) load   ...   ...   ...   ... | 1.38 in (35.1 mm) |
|     Outer: | |
|        Length - free   ...   ...   ...   ...   ...   ... | 1.76 in (44.9 mm) |
|        Length under 46 lb (21 kg) load   ...   ...   ...   ... | 1.50 in (38.3 mm) |
| Later type: | |
|     Inner: | |
|        Length - free   ...   ...   ...   ...   ...   ...   ... | 1.680 in (42.67 mm) |
|        Length under 17.7 lb (8.0 kg) load   ...   ...   ...   ... | 1.462 in (37.13 mm) |
|     Outer: | |
|        Length - free   ...   ...   ...   ...   ...   ... | 1.822 in (46.28 mm) |
|        Length under 46 lb (21 kg) load   ...   ...   ...   ... | 1.587 in (40.3 mm) |

## Valve timing

| | |
|---|---|
| Inlet opens   ...   ...   ...   ...   ...   ...   ...   ...   ... | 6° BTDC |
| Inlet closes   ...   ...   ...   ...   ...   ...   ...   ... | 52° ABDC |
| Inlet peak   ...   ...   ...   ...   ...   ...   ...   ... | 113° |
| Exhaust opens   ...   ...   ...   ...   ...   ...   ... | 34° BBDC |
| Exhaust closes   ...   ...   ...   ...   ...   ...   ... | 24° ATDC |
| Exhaust peak   ...   ...   ...   ...   ...   ...   ... | 95° |

## Vertical driveshaft gear

| | |
|---|---|
| Backlash   ...   ...   ...   ...   ...   ...   ...   ... | 0.006 to 0.010 in (0.15 to 0.25 mm) |
| Internal diameter of bush   ...   ...   ...   ...   ...   ... | 1.063 in + 0.001 (27.0 mm + 0.02) |
| Fit of gear in bush   ...   ...   ...   ...   ...   ...   ... | 0.001 to 0.003 in (0.02 to 0.07 mm) clearance |

## Oil capacity (with new filter) ...   ...   ...   ...   ...   ...

11.5 Imp pints (6.5 litres)

## Oil pump, early type

| | |
|---|---|
| Type   ...   ...   ...   ...   ...   ...   ...   ...   ... | Spur gear |
| Drive   ...   ...   ...   ...   ...   ...   ...   ...   ... | Splined shaft from camshaft skew gear |
| Endfloat of gears   ...   ...   ...   ...   ...   ...   ... | 0.002 to 0.005 in (0.025 to 0.12 mm) |
| Radial clearance of gears   ...   ...   ...   ...   ...   ... | 0.002 to 0.005 in (0.050 to 0.012 mm) |
| Backlash of gears   ...   ...   ...   ...   ...   ...   ... | 0.004 to 0.008 in (0.10 to 0.20 mm) |

## Oil pump, late type

| | |
|---|---|
| Type   ...   ...   ...   ...   ...   ...   ...   ...   ... | Skew gear |
| Drive   ...   ...   ...   ...   ...   ...   ...   ... | Splined shaft from camshaft skew gear |
| Endfloat of gears: | |
|     Steel gear   ...   ...   ...   ...   ...   ...   ... | 0.002 in (0.05 mm) to 0.005 in (0.12 mm) |
|     Aluminium gear   ...   ...   ...   ...   ...   ... | 0.003 in (0.07 mm) to 0.006 in (0.15 mm) |
| Radial clearance of gears   ...   ...   ...   ...   ...   ... | 0.001 to 0.004 in (0.02 to 0.102 mm) |
| Backlash of gears   ...   ...   ...   ...   ...   ...   ... | 0.006 to 0.012 in (0.14 to 0.28 mm) |

## Oil pressure, engine warm

| | |
|---|---|
| 2,000 rpm   ...   ...   ...   ...   ...   ...   ...   ... | 45 to 65 lb/in$^2$ (3.16 to 4.57 kg/cm$^2$) |

## Oil pressure relief valve

| | |
|---|---|
| Type   ...   ...   ...   ...   ...   ...   ...   ...   ... | Non-adjustable |
| Relief valve spring: | |
|     Free length   ...   ...   ...   ...   ...   ...   ... | 2.670 in (67.82 mm) |
|     Compressed length at 5.7 lb (2.58 kg) load   ...   ...   ... | 2.45 in (61.23 mm) |

## Torque wrench settings

| | | | | | | | | | lb f ft | kg f m |
|---|---|---|---|---|---|---|---|---|---|---|
| Connecting rod cap nuts | ... | ... | ... | ... | ... | ... | ... | | *25 | 3.5 |
| Main bearing cap bolts | ... | ... | ... | ... | ... | ... | ... | | 85 | 11.5 |
| Cylinder head bolts | ... | ... | ... | ... | ... | ... | ... | | 65 | 8.9 |
| Rocker shaft bolts: | | | | | | | | | | |
| ½ in UNF bolts | ... | ... | ... | ... | ... | ... | ... | | 65 | 8.9 |
| 5/16 in UNF bolts | ... | ... | ... | ... | ... | ... | ... | | 18 | 2.4 |
| Flywheel bolts | ... | ... | ... | ... | ... | ... | ... | ... | 60-65 | 8.5-9 |
| Starter dog (crankshaft pulley) | | ... | ... | ... | ... | ... | ... | ... | 150 | 20.5 |
| Clutch housing bolts | ... | ... | ... | ... | ... | ... | ... | | 40 | 5.5 |
| Camshaft sprocket bolt | ... | ... | ... | ... | ... | ... | ... | | 30 | 4.15 |

*35 lb f ft (4.9 kg f m) if the bolts have machined threads, (ie. threaded portion is same diameter as bolt shank).*

## 1 General description

The Land Rover engine covered in this manual is the 2¼ litre, four cylinder overhead valve type. Optional compression ratios of 7 : 1 or 8 : 1 are available.

The crankshaft is supported by three shell-type replaceable bearings. The crankshaft endfloat is limited by the centre bearing.

The camshaft runs in four bearings and is chain driven from the crankshaft sprocket. Chain tension is controlled by an idler sprocket operated by the engine oil pressure.

The roller-type cam followers act directly on bronze slides which operate the valves via pushrods and rocker arms. The valves operate in guides which are an interference fit in the cylinder head.

On earlier models the crankcase ventilation is achieved by washable filters in the oil filler cap and engine breather filter. Later models have a crankcase emission control system which ensures that the engine fumes are drawn back into the combustion chamber via the air-intake.

A pump located inside the crankcase sump provides a pressurised oil feed to all the important engine bearing components and an external full flow oil filter is fitted. The oil pump, which is shaft driven from the camshaft incorporates a pressure relief valve.

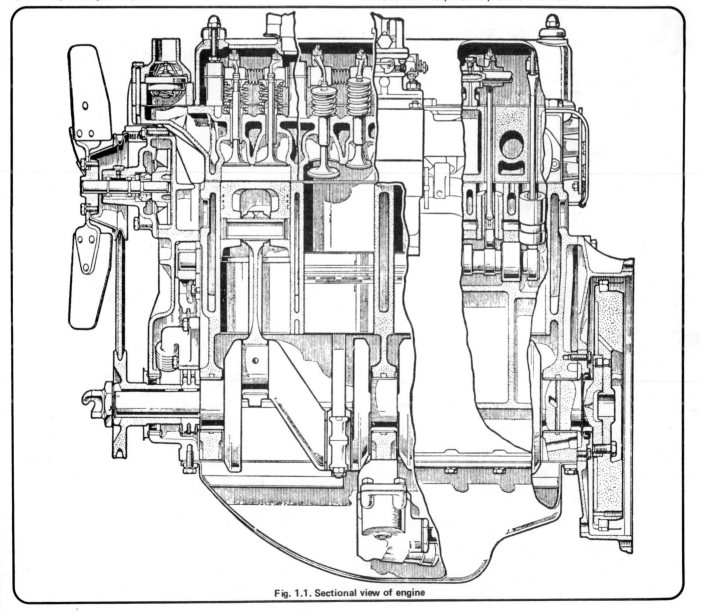

Fig. 1.1. Sectional view of engine

## 2  Major operations possible with the engine in the vehicle

The following components can be removed from the engine for inspection or overhaul without having to lift the engine out of the vehicle:

1   The cylinder head.
2   Oil sump.
3   Oil pump (after removing sump).
4   Timing cover and oil seal.
5   Timing sprockets, tensioner and chain.
6   Pistons and connecting rods (through top of cylinder bores after removing sump and cylinder head).
7   Camshaft and followers.
8   Crankshaft rear oil seal (necessitates the removal of gearbox).

## 3  Major operations only possible after removal of the engine from the vehicle

The Land Rover engine is very accessible; however, removal of the crankshaft, replacing the camshaft bearings, or re-boring the cylinder block requires the removal of the engine from the vehicle.

## 4  Method of engine removal

Before the engine can be removed it is necessary to detach it from the clutch housing. It is not possible to remove the engine complete with transmission.

## 5  Engine removal

1   To remove the engine, it is first necessary to remove the floor panels to enable the clutch housing to be detached from the rear of the engine.
2   Remove the knob and locknut from the transfer lever and remove the screws from the dust cover at the base of the lever.
3   Remove the knob and locknut from the four-wheel drive selector lever and lift off the spring and sleeve.
4   Referring to Fig. 1.2, remove the securing screws from the two front floor panels and remove the panels from the vehicle.
5   Remove the screws from the transmission tunnel cover and lift off the cover.
6   Remove the bolts from the transmission front cover and lift away the cover.
7   Open the bonnet and disconnect the bonnet support rod.
8   Remove the split-pins from the bonnet hinges, and with the help of a friend, raise the bonnet and slide it off the hinges.
9   Remove the three nuts securing the exhaust pipe to the manifold.
10  Remove the complete air cleaner assembly, (refer to Chapter 3 if necessary).
11  Disconnect the battery leads, remove the battery clamp and lift out the battery.
12  Drain the coolant into a suitable container and then, referring to Chapter 2, remove the radiator grille and the radiator and cowl assembly.
13  Disconnect the heater hoses from the rear of the engine (photo).
14  Remove the choke and throttle cables from the carburettor.
15  Disconnect the ignition HT lead from the coil and the LT wire from the distributor.
16  Remove the engine earthing strap from the right-hand side chassis member.
17  Disconnect the fuel inlet pipe from the fuel pump.
18  Remove the clips retaining the battery lead cable, speedometer cable and electrical harness from the right-hand side of the engine block.
19  Remove the starter motor lead from the switch on the rear bulkhead (photo).
20  Detach the electrical leads from the rear of the dynamo or alternator (refer to Chapter 10 if necessary).
21  Using a suitable hoist, attach lifting slings or chains to the engine and raise the hoist until the weight of the engine is just being supported.

22  Remove the bottom retaining nut from the left-hand side engine mounting (Fig. 1.3).
23  Remove the two nuts securing the right-hand side engine mounting bracket to the chassis.
24  Slowly raise the engine until there is just enough room to remove the left-hand side engine mounting and the right-hand side mounting and bracket. Now lower the engine back to its original position.
25  Place a jack or block beneath the front of the gearbox to support its weight.
26  Remove all the bolts securing the clutch housing to the rear of the engine (see Fig. 1.4).
27  Pull the engine forward on the hoist just sufficiently to disengage the gearbox input shaft from the engine and clutch assembly.
28  Check carefully that all cables, pipes and wires have been detached, then slowly lift the engine out of the vehicle (photo).

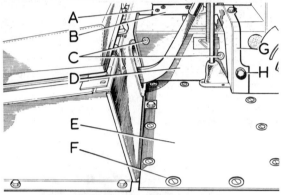

**Fig. 1.2. Floor and transmission panels**

A   Screws (9 off), left-hand floor board
B   Floor board, left-hand
C   Screws (4 off), tunnel cover
D   Gearbox tunnel cover
E   Floor board, right-hand
F   Screws (12 off), right-hand floor board
G   Front panel for gearbox tunnel cover
H   Bolts (4 off), front panel

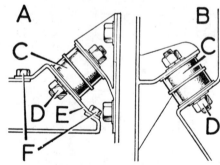

**Fig. 1.3. Engine mountings**

A   RH side mounting          D   Lower centre bolt
B   LH side mounting          E   Support bracket at RH
C   Suspension rubbers        F   Support bracket bolts

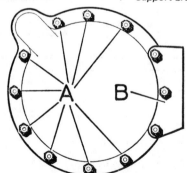

**Fig. 1.4. Clutch housing**

A   Clutch housing to engine bolts
B   Clutch slave cylinder mounting bolts

5.13 Heater hoses at rear of engine

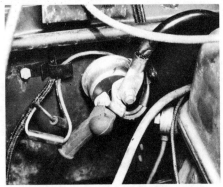
5.19 Starter motor cable attachment point

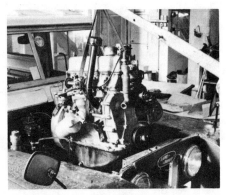
5.28 Hoisting out the engine

## 6 Engine - dismantling general

1 It is best to mount the engine on a dismantling stand but if one is not available, then stand the engine on a strong bench so it is at a comfortable working height. Failing this, the engine can be stripped down on the floor.

2 During the dismantling process the greatest care should be taken to keep the exposed parts free from dirt. As an aid to achieving this, it is sound advice to thoroughly clean down the outside of the engine, removing all traces of oil and congealed dirt.

3 Use paraffin or a good grease solvent. The latter will make the job much easier, as, after the solvent has been applied and allowed to stand for a time, a vigorous jet of water will wash off the solvent and all the grease and filth. If the dirt is thick and deeply embedded, work the solvent into it with a wire brush.

4 Finally wipe down the exterior of the engine with a rag and only then, when it is quite clean should the dismantling process begin. As the engine is stripped, clean each part in a bath of paraffin or petrol.

5 Never immerse parts with oilways in paraffin, ie: the crankshaft, but to clean, wipe down carefully with a petrol dampened rag. Oilways can be cleaned out with wire. If an air line is present all parts can be blown dry and the oilways blown through as an added precaution.

6 Re-use of old engine gaskets is false economy and can give rise to oil and water leaks, if nothing worse. To avoid the possibility of trouble after the engine has been reassembled **always** use new gaskets throughout.

7 Do not throw old gaskets away as it sometimes happens that an immediate replacement cannot be found and the old gasket is then very useful as a template. Hang up the old gaskets as they are removed on a suitable hook or nail.

8 To strip the engine it is best to work from the top down. The sump provides a firm base on which the engine can be supported in an upright position. When the stage is reached where the sump must be removed, the engine can be turned on its side and all other work carried out with it in this position.

9 Wherever possible, replace nuts, bolts and washers fingertight from wherever they were removed. This helps avoid later loss and muddle. If they cannot be replaced then lay them out in such a fashion that it is clear from where they came.

## 7 Ancilllary components - removal

1 With the engine removed from the car and separated from the gearbox, the externally mounted anvillary components should now be removed before dismantling begins.

2 The following is a suggested sequence of removal, detailed descriptions are to be found in the relevant Chapter of this manual.

*Dynamo or alternator (Chapter 10)*
*Clutch assembly (Chapter 5)*
*Manifolds and carburettor (Chapter 3)*
*Flywheel (eight bolts) (Section 15, Chapter 1)*
*Engine mounting brackets (Section 5, Chapter 1)*
*Oil filter (Section 11, Chapter 1)*
*Distributor and spark plugs (Chapter 4)*

*Fuel pump (Chapter 3)*
*Fan assembly (Chapter 2)*
*Water pump/thermostat assembly (Chapter 2)*
*Starter motor (Chapter 10)*

## 8 Cylinder head - removal

1 If the head is to be removed with the engine still in the vehicle, first carry out the following operations:

    a) *Remove the bonnet.*
    b) *Remove the air cleaner.*
    c) *Disconnect both battery leads.*
    d) *Drain the cooling system*
    e) *Disconnect the throttle and choke controls and fuel inlet pipe from the carburettor.*
    f) *Remove the hoses from the thermostat housing.*
    g) *Disconnect the exhaust pipe from the manifold.*
    h) *Remove the oil feed pipe at rear right-hand side of the engine (photo).*
    i) *Disconnect the HT leads from the spark plugs.*

2 Remove the three rocker cover securing nuts and lift off the cover.

3 Undo the large and small bolts retaining the rocker shaft brackets to the cylinder head, but do not attempt to remove the rocker shaft at this stage.

4 As the rocker shaft will tend to spring apart while being removed, great care must be taken to note the assembly order of the rocker springs and spacers on the shaft (see Fig. 1.8).

**Note:** A good method of removal is to turn the rocker cover upside down and secure it to the three rocker shaft studs using the cover nuts. The complete rocker shaft assembly can then be lifted off without any risk of it coming apart.

5 Lift out the pushrods and keep them in the correct order to ensure that each pushrod is replaced in its original position. Punch eight holes in a piece of cardboard, number them one to eight and place the pushrods in order through the card.

6 Unscrew each of the cylinder head bolts a half turn at a time in the reverse order to that shown in Fig. 1.5.

7 With all the bolts removed, lift the cylinder head from the block. If it is stuck, tap it upwards using a block of wood and a hammer. On no account insert any lever into the gasket joint.

8 Remove the cylinder head gasket.

## 9 Cylinder head - dismantling

1 The valves can be removed from the cylinder head by the following method. Compress each spring in turn with a valve spring compressor until the two halves of the collets can be removed. Release the compressor and remove the spring and spring retainer.

2 If, when the valve spring compressor is screwed down, the valve spring retaining cap refuses to free, to expose the split collet, do not continue to screw down on the compressor as there is a likelihood of damaging it.

3   Gently tap the top of the tool directly over the cap with a soft-faced mallet. This will free the cap. To avoid the compressor jumping off the valve spring retaining cap when it is tapped, hold the compressor firmly in position with one hand.
4   Slide the rubber oil control seal off the top of each valve guide and valve and then drop out each valve through the combustion chamber.
5   It is essential that the valves are kept in their correct sequence unless they are so badly worn that they are to be renewed. Numbering from the front of the engine, exhaust valves are 1-4-5-8 and inlet valves 2-3-6-7.

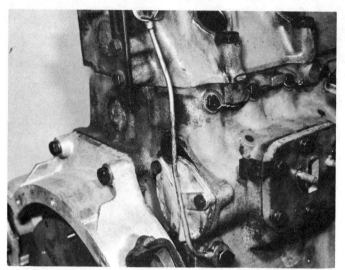

8.1(h) Oil feed pipe to cylinder head

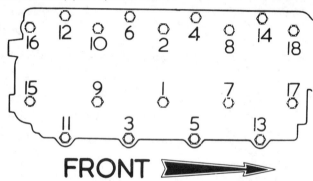

**FRONT** ➤
Fig. 1.5. Tightening sequence for cylinder head bolts

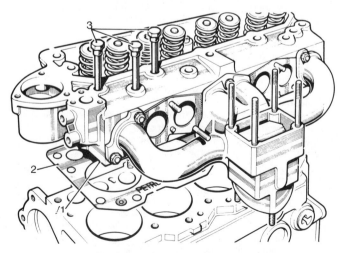

Fig. 1.6. Cylinder head and gasket

1   *Cylinder head*    2   *Head gasket*    3   *Cylinder head bolts*

## 10 Sump - removal

1   The sump can be removed quite easily with the engine still in the vehicle.
2   First drain the engine oil into a suitable container.
3   The Land Rover has considerable ground clearance and it is possible to remove the sump without raising the vehicle. However, if it is decided to jack the vehicle up, ensure that it is securely supported on heavy duty axle stands before working beneath it.
4   Unscrew and remove all the sump bolts, releasing them only one half turn at a time in a diagonal sequence to avoid distortion.
5   If the sump is stuck tight, run a blunt knife round the gasket to release it.

## 11 Oil pump and oil filter - removal

1   If the oil pump is to be removed with the engine still in the vehicle, first remove the sump as described in the previous Section.
2   Remove the two securing bolts and withdraw the pump complete with drive shaft.
3   The oil filter is simply removed by unscrewing the centre bolt. As the oil filter body is withdrawn, a loss of oil trapped within it will occur so have a suitable container at the ready to drop the oil into.
4   Discard the internal filter element. The new element will be supplied complete with new sealing rings.
5   To remove the oil filter housing, first detach the oil pressure switch lead and then remove the two retaining bolts and prise the housing away from the cylinder block (photo).
6   When refitting the housing, a new gasket must be used.

## 12 Timing cover, gears and chain - removal

If the timing cover, gears and chain are being removed with the engine in the car, then the following operations must first be carried out:

*Drain the cooling system.*
*Remove the radiator and fanbelt.*
*Remove the water pump pulley and fan.*
*Remove the dynamo adjusting arm.*
*Separate the by-pass hose from the thermostat housing.*

1   Unscrew and remove the crankshaft starter dog. If the sump has been removed, place a block of wood between a crankshaft web and the internal wall of the crankcase to prevent the crankshaft rotating as the bolt is unscrewed. If the engine is in the car or the sump has not yet been removed, withdraw the starter motor and jam the flywheel starter ring gear with a large screwdriver or cold chisel. The crankshaft starter dog can then be unscrewed.
2   Withdraw the crankshaft pulley. If this is tight, use two levers placed behind the pulley at opposite points to extract it.
3   Unscrew and remove all the nuts and bolts securing the timing cover and water pump to the cylinder block, including the front sump bolts and lift off the cover and pump assembly.
4   Before the chain or tensioner is removed, the following method should be used to ensure correct engine timing during reassembly.
5   On earlier engines, remove the inspection plate from the flywheel housing and rotate the engine until the TDC mark is in line with the pointer (see Fig. 1.8).
6   Using a scriber and steel rule, scratch an alignment mark on the camshaft and camshaft sprocket and a matching mark on the cylinder block timing casing (photo).
7   As an additional precaution make a similar mark on the crankshaft sprocket and cylinder block.
8   On later engines with the timing pointer on the front of the timing case, rotate the crankshaft until the keyway in the crankshaft is in the position shown in Fig. 1.9 (vertical position) and then check that the 'P' marks on the camshaft sprocket are aligned as shown in Fig. 1.10.
**Note:** If the camshaft timing marks do not line up, rotate the crankshaft 360°. The marks should then be aligned.
9   Remove the nut and two bolts and withdraw the complete chain tensioner assembly.

10 Remove the camshaft securing bolt and washer and using a gear puller tool, remove the camshaft sprocket complete with chain.

## 13 Camshaft and tappets - removal

1 It is possible to remove the camshaft with the engine still in the vehicle, but first the cylinder head, timing cover and chain must be removed as described in the previous Sections.
2 Remove the distributor and adaptor plate from the cylinder block (Fig. 1.11).
3 Lift out the distributor drive shaft (earlier engines), or the drive shaft coupling (later engines).
4 Unscrew the grubscrew from oil filter housing face (Fig. 1.12) and lift out the distributor and oil pump drive assembly using a pair of thin-nose pliers.
5 Using a piece of wire bent into a hook, lift out the tappet slides and rollers and keep them in the correct order of removal.
6 Remove the camshaft drive chain and sprocket as described previously and remove the camshaft thrust plate, located behind the sprocket.
7 The camshaft can now be withdrawn from the front of the engine. Take care not to damage the camshaft bearings as the shaft passes through them. **Note:** The tappet guides can be removed if required by undoing the retaining bolts from the side of the block (photo) and pulling out the guides using a slide hammer.

## 14 Pistons and connecting rods - removal

1 The pistons and connecting rods can be removed with the engine still in the vehicle or with the engine on the bench.
2 With the cylinder head and sump removed undo the big-end retaining nuts.
3 The connecting rods and pistons are lifted out from the top of the cylinder block.

4 Remove the big-end caps one at a time, taking care to keep them in the right order and the correct way round. Also ensure that the shell bearings are kept with their correct connecting rods and caps unless they are to be renewed.
5 It is a good idea to mark the side face of each rod and cap with identification marks using a centre punch and light hammer, unless the caps are already marked (photo). Use a single dot for No. 1 connecting rod, two dots for No. 2 and so on. This will ensure there is no mix-up on reassembly, as it is very important that the caps are refitted to the connecting rods from which they were removed.
6 If the big-end caps are difficult to remove they may be gently tapped with a soft-faced mallet.
7 To remove the shell bearings, press the bearing opposite the groove in both the connecting rod, and the connecting rod caps and the bearings will slide out easily.
8 Withdraw the pistons and connecting rods upwards and ensure they are kept in the correct order for replacement in the same bore.

## 15 Flywheel, flywheel housing and rear crankshaft oil seal - removal

1 These components can be removed with the engine still in the vehicle if preferred, but first the transmission must be removed (see Chapter 6), and also the sump.
2 Bend back the locking tabs, remove the eight securing bolts and lift off the flywheel.
3 Remove the bolts securing the flywheel housing to the rear of the cylinder block and lift off the housing. Note that there is an O-ring type seal fitted in the housing aperture (photos).
4 Remove the two retaining bolts and tap out the rear main bearing cap using a soft alloy drift.
5 Using a socket, undo the bolts retaining the upper half of the seal retainer to the rear of the cylinder block. Prise the retainer rearwards until it clears the dowels and then lift it off.
6 Remove the coil spring from around the rear main bearing oil seal and pull the seal off the crankshaft.

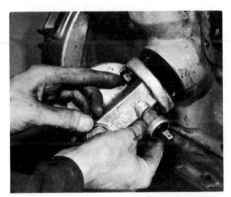

11.5 Removing the oil filter housing

12.6 Timing marks scribed across the camshaft sprocket and front face of cylinder block

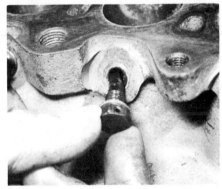

13.7 Removing a tappet guide securing bolt

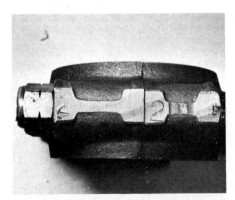

14.5 Identification marks on connecting rod and bearing cap

15.3a Flywheel housing prior to removal

15.3b Location of flywheel housing oil seal

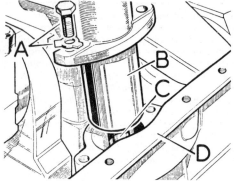

**Fig. 1.7. Removing the oil pump**

A  Securing bolts          C  Driveshaft
B  Pump                    D  Crankcase

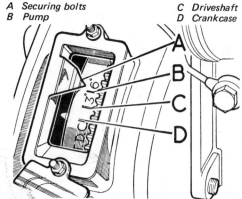

**Fig. 1.8. Timing marks on the flywheel (earlier engines)**

A  Timing pointer
B  6º mark, align when using 90-96 octane fuel
C  3º mark, align when using 80-85 octane fuel
D  TDC mark, align when using 74-76 octane fuel

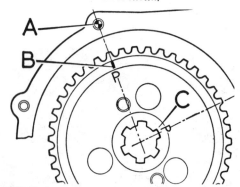

**Fig. 1.9. Crankshaft positioned for engine timing (the keyway 'A' must be vertical as shown)**

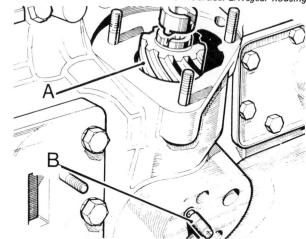

**Fig. 1.10. Timing marks on camshaft sprocket (later engines)**

A  Bolt hole on top, front of engine
B  Mark on sprocket perimeter
C  Mark on sprocket that must line up with master spline on camshaft

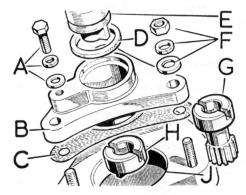

**Fig. 1.11. Distributor adaptor plate and coupling**

A  Distributor bolts          F  Adaptor nuts
B  Distributor adaptor        G  Top driveshaft, early engines
C  Joint washer               H  Driveshaft coupling, later
D  Cork washer                   engines
E  Distributor                J  Vertical drivegear housing

**Fig. 1.12. Distributor drivegear and securing screw**

A  Drivegear                  B  Grubscrew

## 16 Crankshaft and main bearings - removal

1   To remove the crankshaft and bearings, the engine must be lifted from the vehicle and placed on a bench.

2   Drain the engine oil and remove the timing gears, flywheel and housing, sump, connecting rod bearings, and the oil pump, as described in the previous Sections.

3   Mark the main bearing caps and cylinder block faces to ensure the caps are replaced the correct way round.

4   Undo and remove the bolts retaining the three bearing caps to the cylinder block.

5   Remove the main bearing caps and the bottom half of each bearing shell, taking care to keep the bearing shells in the right caps.

6   When removing the centre bearing cap, note the bottom semi-circular halves of the thrust washers, one half lying on either side of the main bearing. Lay them with the centre bearing along the correct side.

7   Slightly rotate the crankshaft to free the upper halves of the bearing shells and thrust washers which can be lifted away and placed over the correct bearing cap when the crankshaft has been lifted out.

8   Remove the crankshaft by lifting it away from the crankcase.

9   Lift away the bearing shells.

## 17 Examination and renovation - general

With the engine stripped down and all parts thoroughly cleaned, it is now time to examine everything for wear. The following items should be checked and where necessary renewed or renovated as described in the following Sections.

## 18 Oil pump - examination and renovation

1 Remove the oil pump as described in Section 11. Undo the four securing bolts and detach the cover plate and driveshaft housing (photo).

2 Lift out the two gears and unscrew the relief valve from the pump housing. Withdraw the valve spring, plunger and steel ball.

3 Clean all the components in petrol and blow dry with an airline, if available.

4 Refit the gears and measure the clearance between the top of the gears and the pump housing face using a steel rule and a feeler gauge, (photo). For the clearance dimensions refer to the Specifications given at the beginning of this Chapter.

5 Using the feeler gauges, check the clearance between the gears and the pump body (photo), and also the backlash between the gears themselves. Again refer to the specifications for the correct dimensions.

6 If the gear endfloat, clearance, or backlash dimensions are not within those given in the specifications, the best policy is to replace the complete pump assembly with a new or reconditioned unit. Although it is possible to renew the gear bushes, they require reaming and drilling and this is a specialist job.

7 Check the relief valve ball for grooving or wear and if evident, renew it. Examine the ball seating inside the pump body for similar signs of wear. The seat can be lapped using a steel ball soldered to a length of tube, and using very fine grinding paste, but if any doubt exists the most sensible decision is to renew the complete pump.

8 Reassemble the pump noting that the drive gear fits into the pump body with the plain section of the bore uppermost.

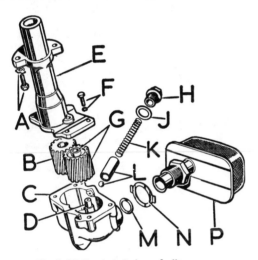

**Fig. 1.13. Exploded view of oil pump**

| | |
|---|---|
| A | Bolt, oil pump to cylinder block |
| B | Rump drivegear |
| C | Pump body |
| D | Idler gear spindle |
| E | Pump cover and shaft housing |
| F | Bolt, cover to body |
| G | Idler gear and bush assembly |
| H | Threaded plug |
| J | Washer |
| K | Spring |
| L | Relief valve ball and plunger |
| M | Sealing ring |
| N | Lockwasher |
| P | Oil filter |

## 19 Crankcase ventilation system

On earlier Land Rover engines, crankcase ventilation is achieved by a breather filter on the rocker cover and an additional one on the oil filter tube, (see Fig. 1.14).

Later models are fitted with a closed-circuit ventilation system, comprising a hose, connecting the rocker cover breather directly into the aircleaner, and a second hose leading from the oil filler tube into the carburettor body via a non-return valve.

The hoses should be periodically checked for perishing or damage and the clips checked for security. The breather filters should be cleaned at the intervals given in the Routine Maintenance section at the front of this Manual.

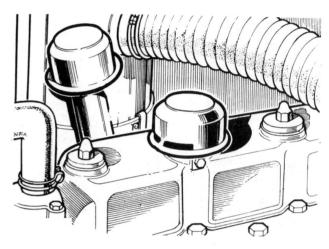

**Fig. 1.14. Crankcase ventilation breathers**

## 20 Crankshaft and main bearings - examination and renovation

1 Remove the crankshaft rear oil seal and discard it.

2 Examine the bearing surfaces of the crankshaft for scratches or scoring and, using a micrometer, check each journal and crankpin for out of round. Where this is found to be in excess of 0.001 in (0.0254 mm) the crankshaft will have to be reground and undersize bearings fitted.

3 The crankshaft can be reground to a maximum of 0.040 in (1.016 mm) undersize, but your Leyland dealer will decide how much is required and supply the matching undersize main and big-end shell bearings.

4 Crankshaft endfloat, with main bearing caps fully tightened, should be between 0.002 and 0.006 in (0.05 and 0.15 mm). The endfloat is controlled by the thrust flanges on the centre main bearing shells.

5 If the gearbox input shaft spigot bush needs renewal, extract it by tapping a thread in it. The new bush requires no lubrication.

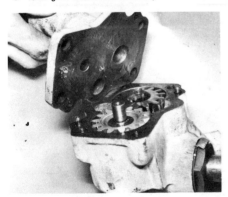

18.1 Removing oil pump cover plate

18.4 Checking the pump gear endfloat

18.5 Checking the clearance between the oil pump gears and the body

## 21 Cylinder block and crankcase - examination and renovation

1   The cylinder bores must be examined for taper, ovality, scoring and scratches. Start by carefully examining the top of the cylinder bores. If they are at all worn a very slight ridge will be found on the thrust side. This marks the top of the piston ring travel. The owner will have a good indication of the bore wear prior to dismantling the engine, or removing the cylinder head. Excessive oil consumption accompanied by blue smoke from the exhaust is a sure sign of worn cylinder bores and piston rings.

2   Measure the bore diameter just under the ridge with a micrometer and compare it with the diameter at the bottom of the bore, which is not subject to wear. If the difference between the two measurements is more than 0.008 in (0.2032 mm), then it will be necessary to fit special pistons and rings or have the cylinders rebored and fit oversize pistons.

3   If the bores are slightly worn but not so badly worn as to justify reboring them, then special oil control rings and pistons can be fitted which will restore compression and stop the engine burning oil. Several different types are available and the manufacturer's instructions concerning their fitting must be followed closely.

4   If the cylinders have already been bored out to the maximum of +0.040 in (1.016 mm), it is possible to have cylinder liners fitted. This is obviously a specialist job and should be entrusted to your Leyland dealer.

5   If new pistons are being fitted and the bores have not been rebored, it is essential to slightly roughen the hard glaze on the sides of the bores with fine glass paper so the new piston rings will have a chance to bed in properly.

6   Examine the crankcase for cracks and leaking core plugs. To renew a core plug, drill a hole in its centre and tap a thread in it. Screw in a bolt and using a distance piece, tighten the bolt and extract the core plug. When installing the new plug, smear its outer edge with gasket cement.

7   Probe oil galleries and waterways with a piece of wire to make sure that they are quite clear.

## 22 Piston/connecting rod assemblies - examination and renovation

1   Remove the circlip from the piston and slide out the gudgeon pin from the piston and small-end bearing. If the piston crown is marked with an 'X' on one side, the pin should be withdrawn from that side.

2   If the gudgeon pin is tight in the piston immerse the piston in hot water and heat it to approximately 55°C (131°F). The gudgeon pin should then slide out quite easily.

3   To remove the piston rings, slide them carefully over the top of the piston taking care not to scratch the aluminium alloy of the piston. Never slide them off the bottom of the piston skirt. It is very easy to break piston rings if they are pulled off roughly so this operation should be done with extreme caution. It is helpful to use an old 0.020 inch feeler gauge to facilitate their removal.

4   Lift one end of the piston ring to be removed, out of its groove and insert the end of the feeler gauge under it.

5   Turn the feeler gauge slowly round the piston and as the ring comes out of its groove it rests on the land above. It can then be eased off the piston with the feeler gauge stopping it from slipping into any empty grooves, if it is any but the top piston ring that is being removed.

6   Piston ring wear can be checked by first removing the rings from the pistons as described previously. Then place the rings in the cylinder bores from the top, pushing them down about 1.5 inches (38.1 mm) with the head of a piston (from which the rings have been removed) so that they rest square in the cylinder. Then measure the gap at the ends of the ring with a feeler gauge. If it exceeds the limits specified at the beginning of this Chapter then they will need renewal.

7   The grooves in which the rings locate in the piston can also become enlarged in use. The clearance between ring and piston, in the groove should not exceed the limits specified at the beginning of this Chapter.

8   Check that the fit of the gudgeon pin in the connecting rod small-end bush is within the limits given in the Specifications at the begining of this Chapter.

9   If new small-end bushes are required, the job should be entrusted to a specialist as the new bushes have to be reamed to fit the gudgeon pins.

10  When refitting the piston to the con-rod, note that the 'X' on the piston crown faces towards the front of the engine and the oil spray hole in the side of the connecting rod faces towards the camshaft (photos).

11  The two compression rings must be fitted with the 'T' or 'TOP' uppermost on the piston (photo). The scraper ring may be fitted either way up.

12  Refitting the gudgeon pin is a reversal of the removal procedure, but ensure that the connecting rod is the correct way round.

## 23 Camshaft and tappets - examination and renovation

1   Examine the camshaft bearing surfaces, cam lobes and gearteeth for wear or scoring. Renew the shaft if evident.

2   If the camshaft bearings require renewal the cylinder block should be taken to your local Leyland dealer or engineering works who will have the special tools for fitting the bearings and reaming them.

3   Check the tappet rollers for pitting or scoring and the tappet slides for excessive wear and renew them if necessary.

**Fig. 1.15. Piston and connecting rod assembly**

1  *Piston rings*         2  *Circlips*         3  *Gudgeon pin*

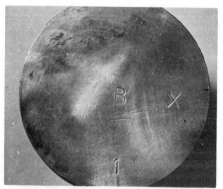

22.11a Piston identification marks

22.11b Oil hole in the side of a connecting rod

22.12 'TOP' identification of compression ring

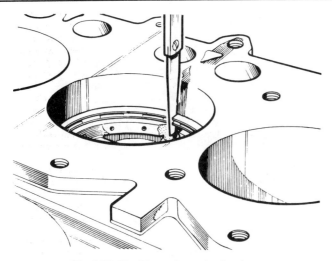

**Fig. 1.16. Checking a piston ring in a bore**

## 24 Timing gears and chain - examination and renovation

1   Examine the teeth on the camshaft, crankshaft and tensioner sprockets. If they are worn or hooked in appearance they must be renewed.

2   Check the tensioner piston and cylinder for wear, also check the sprocket bush and ratchet bush. Renew the components where necessary.

3   Inspect the rubber strip on the chain damper attached to the cylinder block, and if badly grooved, renew it.

4   Examine the timing chain. If it has been in operation for a considerable time or if when held horizontally (link plates facing downwards) it takes on a deeply bowed appearance, renew it.

## 25 Cylinder head - decarbonising, valve grinding, renovation

1   This operation will normally only be required at comparatively high mileages due to the improvements in fuel and oil quality and to the better design of engine breathing systems. However, when persistent 'pinking' occurs and engine performance has badly deteriorated, but it is in perfect tune, then decarbonising and valve grinding will be required.

2   With the cylinder head removed, use a blunt scraper to remove all trace of carbon and deposits from the combustion spaces and ports. Scrape the cylinder head free from scale or old pieces of gasket or jointing compound. Clean the cylinder head by washing it in paraffin and take particular care to pull a piece of rag through the ports and cylinder head bolt holes. Any grit remaining in these recesses may well drop onto the gasket or cylinder block mating surface as the cylinder head is lowered into position and could lead to a gasket leak after reassembly is complete.

3   If the engine is in the vehicle, clean the tops of the pistons and the upper edges of the cylinder bores. It is essential that great care is taken to ensure that no carbon gets into the cylinder bores as this could scratch the cylinder walls or cause damage to the piston and rings. To ensure this does not happen, first turn the crankshaft so that two of the pistons are at the top of their bores. Stuff rag into the other two bores or seal them off with paper and masking tape. The waterways should also be covered with small pieces of masking tape to prevent particles of carbon entering the cooling system and damaging the water pump.

4   Press a little grease into the gap between the cylinder walls and the two pistons which are to be worked on. With a blunt scraper carefully scrape away the carbon from the piston crown, taking great care not to scratch the aluminium. Also scrape away the carbon from the surrounding lip of the cylinder wall. When all the carbon has been removed, scrape away the grease which will now be contaminated with carbon particles, taking care not to press any into the bores. To assist prevention of carbon build-up the piston crown can be polished with a metal polish. Remove the rag or masking tape from the other two cylinders and turn the crankshaft so that the two pistons which were at the bottom are now at the top. Place rag or masking tape in the cylinders which have been decarbonised and proceed as just described.

5   Examine the heads of the valves for pitting and burning, especially the heads of the exhaust valves. The valve seatings should be examined at the same time. If the pitting on valve and seat is very slight the marks can be removed by grinding the seats and valves together with coarse, and then fine, valve grinding paste.

6   Where bad pitting has occurred to the valve seats it will be necessary to recut them and fit new valves.

7   Valve grinding is carried out as follows: Smear a trace of coarse carborundum paste on the seat face and apply a suction grinder tool to the valve head. With a semi-rotary motion, grind the valve head to its seat, lifting the valve occasionally to redistribute the grinding paste. When a dull matt even surface finish is produced on both the valve seat and the valve, wipe off the paste and repeat the process with fine carborundum paste, lifting and turning the valve to redistribute the paste as before. A light spring placed under the valve head will greatly ease this operation. When a smooth unbroken ring of light grey matt finish is produced, on both valve and valve seat faces, the grinding operation is completed.

8   Clean away every trace of grinding paste and if available, use an airline to blow out the ports and valve guides.

9   Insert the valves into their respective guides and check that the amount of wear does not exceed the dimensions given in the Specifications.

10   If the clearance is excessive the guides can be removed by driving them out using a suitable sized stepped drift, (see Fig. 1.17) from the combustion chamber side of the cylinder head.

11   Special drifts are available from the manufacturers for this job, and it is recommended that they are used, when refitting, to avoid damaging the new guides.

12   If the original valve springs have been in use for more than 20,000 miles (32,000 kms), they should be renewed together with new valve stem oil seals (the latter are included in the de-coke set).

## 26 Rockers and rocker shaft - examination and renovation

1   Thoroughly clean the rocker shaft and then check the shaft for straightness by rolling it on a flat surface. It is most unlikely that it will deviate from normal, but, if it does, then a judicious attempt may be made to straighten it. If this is not successful purchase a new shaft. The surface of the shaft must be free from any worn ridges caused by the rocker arms. If any wear is present renew the shaft.

2   Check the rocker arms for wear of the bushes, for wear at the rocker arm face which bears on the valve stem, and for wear of the adjusting ball ended screws. Wear in the rocker arm bush can be checked by gripping the rocker arm tip and holding the rocker arm in place on the shaft, noting if there is any lateral rocker arm shake. If the shake is present, and the arm is very loose on the shaft a new rocker arm must be fitted.

3   Check the pushrods for straightness by rolling them on the bench. Renew any that are bent.

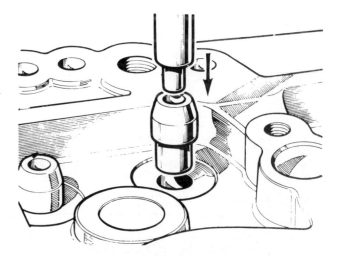

**Fig. 1.17. Driving in a new valve guide**

**Fig. 1.18. Rocker gear components**

A  Rocker brackets. Front, centre and rear brackets carry studs for
    top cover fixings
B  Exhaust valve rockers (4 off)
C  Rocker shaft springs (4 off)
D  Inlet valve rockers (4 off)
E  Spacing washers (6 off)

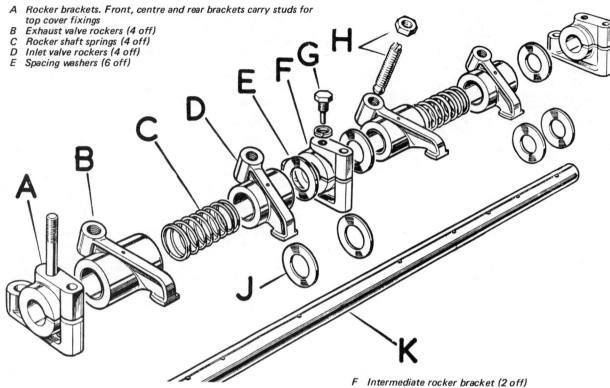

F  Intermediate rocker bracket (2 off)
G  Locating screw for rocker shaft (2 off on early models)
H  Tappet screws adjacent to larger fixing holes in brackets
J  Spacing washers for diesel models. Not applicable for
    petrol models
K  Valve rocker shaft (2 off on early models)

### 27 Flywheel - examination and renovation

1  Examine the clutch driven plate mating surface of the flywheel. If
this is scored or shows signs of many small cracks, then it should either
be renewed or refaced (see Specifications).
2  Examine the teeth of the flywheel starter ring gear. If they are
chipped or worn, the ring must be renewed. To do this, split the ring
with a cold chisel.
3  Heat the new ring to 392°F (200°C) in an electric oven and then
quickly fit it to the flywheel so that the chamfered side of the teeth is
towards the engine side of the flywheel.
4  Allow the ring to cool naturally without quenching.

### 28 Engine reassembly - general

To ensure maximum life with minimum trouble from a rebuilt
engine, not only must everything be correctly assembled, but everything must be spotlessly clean, all the oilways must be clear, locking
washers and spring washers must always be fitted where indicated and
all bearing and other working surfaces must be thoroughly lubricated
during assembly.
Before assembly begins renew any bolts or studs, the threads of
which are in any way damaged, and whenever possible use new spring
washers.
Gather together a torque wrench, oil can and clean rag, also a set of
engine gaskets, crankshaft front and rear oil seals and a new oil filter
element.

### 29 Crankshaft, oil seal and main bearings - refitting

1  Clean the backs of the bearing shells and the bearing recesses in both
the crankcase and the caps.
2  Make sure that the centre thrust washers are located in the crankcase and then fit the remaining shells (photo).

3  Oil the bearings liberally.
4  It will be found easier to fit the rear oil seal before refitting the
crankshaft. First loop the oil seal coil spring around the rear oil seal
journal on the crankshaft. Open the split in the seal just enough to
pass it over the crankshaft journal with the recess in the seal facing
forwards.
5  With the spring ends hooked together, carefully push the spring
into the seal recess using a small screwdriver (Fig. 1.19).
6  Make sure the join in the spring is positioned 90° away from the
split in the seal.
7  Smear a trace of sealing compound on the inner recess of the upper
half (cylinder block side) of the seal retainer and bolt into place.
8  With the split in the seal facing vertically towards the top of the
engine, lower the crankshaft into position. Make sure that the seal fits
snugly into the upper seal retainer without distortion (photo).
9  Fit the 'T' seals onto either side of the rear main bearing cap and
bolt the lower seal retainer onto the cap (Fig. 1.20).
10 Smear a trace of sealing compound on the inner recess of the lower
seal retainer and fit the rear main bearing cap and shell onto the
cylinder. Great care must be taken to ensure that the 'T' seals are not
pushed out of place and the rear oil seal does not get distorted (photo).
Fit the bearing cap bolts but do not tighten at this stage.
11 Fit the front and centre main bearing caps, not forgetting to fit the
thrust washers on either side of the centre cap.
12 Tighten all the bearing cap bolts to the specified torque and check
that the crankshaft rotates smoothly without any tight spots (photo)
13 Check the crankshaft endfloat using a dial gauge or feeler blade
(photo). Refer to the Specifications for the permissible limit.

### 30 Piston/connecting rod - refitting

1  The assemblies must be prepared as described in Sections 21 and
22.
2  Apply engine oil liberally to the cylinder bores and to the piston
rings.
3  Fit a piston ring compressor to No. 1 piston and then insert the
connecting rod into the cylinder bore nearest the front of the block.

Check that the 'X' mark on the piston crown faces the front of the engine.

4   With the piston skirt having entered the cylinder bore and the compressor resting squarely against the block, place the wooden handle of a hammer on the centre of the piston crown and then tap the head of the handle sharply to drive the piston assembly into the bore (photo).

5   With the crankpin at its lowest point, carefully pull the connecting rod downward and connect it to the crankshaft. Make sure that the big-end bearing shell has not become displaced.

6   Install the big-end bearing cap complete with the bearing shell, making sure that the matching marks on the rod and cap are in alignment and are on the correct side of the engine. This will be automatic, provided the piston and connecting rod have been correctly assembled and the mark on the piston crown is correctly positioned.

7   Screw on the big-end nuts and tighten to the specified torque (photo).

8   Repeat the foregoing operations on the remaining three piston assemblies.

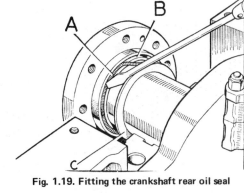

Fig. 1.19. Fitting the crankshaft rear oil seal

A   Coil spring                          B   Seal

29.2a Location of centre main bearing thrust washers and upper shell bearing

29.2b Fitting a shell bearing to one of the main bearing caps

29.2c Location of the rear, upper main bearing shell

29.8 Crankshaft installed in the engine block

29.10 Fitting the rear main bearing cap using a feeler gauge to avoid damaging the 'T' seal

29.12 Tightening the main bearing cap bolts

29.13 Checking the crankshaft endfloat using feeler gauges

30.4 Inserting a piston into the cylinder block

30.7 Tightening the big-end bearing nuts

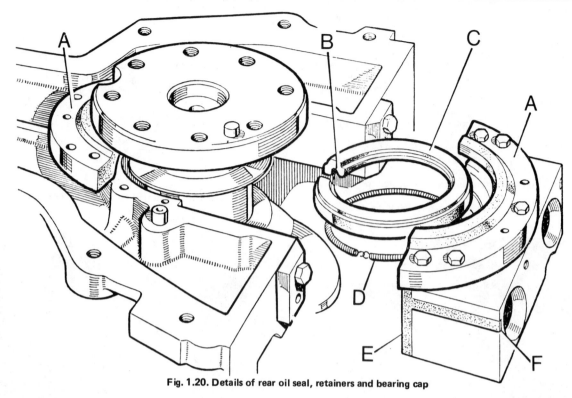

**Fig. 1.20. Details of rear oil seal, retainers and bearing cap**

A   Retainer halves
B   Split line of seal to be towards top of engine when fitted
C   Split oil seal

D   Garter spring, hook and eye to be midway between split and
    hinge of oil seal when fitted
E   'T' seal
F   These ends should protrude 1/32 in (0.8 mm)

### 31 Camshaft and tappets - refitting

1   Lubricate the camshaft bearings with engine oil and carefully install
the camshaft from the front of the engine (photo).
2   Fit the camshaft thrust plate and check that the camshaft endfloat
is within 0.0025 in to 0.0055 in (0.06 to 0.14 mm). If the endfloat
exceeds this limit a new thrust plate must be fitted (photo).
3   Oil the tappet rollers and fit them into the guides followed by the
tappet slides. Make sure that the rollers and slides are correctly seated.
Note that the tappet slides are marked 'FRONT' and this side must
face towards the front of the engine. The chamfered side of the rollers
also faces the front of the engine (photos).

### 32 Timing components - refitting

1   First rotate the crankshaft until the TDC mark on the flywheel is
aligned with the pointer or, on engines with the timing pointer on the
front cover, rotate the crankshaft until the keyway is in a vertical
position (Fig. 1.9).
2   Refit the camshaft sprocket making sure that the alignment marks
described in Section 12 are lined up.
3   Loop the timing chain over the crankshaft and camshaft sprockets
taking care that neither sprocket moves from its set position. Make
sure that the slack in the chain is on the tensioner sprocket side (photo).
4   Re-check that, with the chain correctly fitted, all timing marks
described in Section 12 are lined up.
5   Assemble the chain tensioner complete with sprocket. Lift up the
ratchet arm and compress the piston into the cylinder as far as it will
go. Refit the tensioner onto the engine making sure that the dowels
are correctly located in the piston housing and the spigot fits into the
slot on the front of the engine.
6   Refit the ratchet arm, spring and securing bolt, and release the
cylinder allowing the sprocket to take up the timing chain slack. Refit
the other retaining bolt and nut and tighten all three (photo).
7   Fit the timing chain vibration damper and adjust it so there is a
clearance of 0,010 in (0.25 mm) between the rubber strip and the

chain.
8   Carry out a last check to make sure all the timing positions and
marks are still correctly aligned and then tighten the camshaft securing
bolt and bend over the locking tab (photo).
9   Remove the timing cover oil seal and drive in a new one, using a
piece of tubing as a drift. Apply engine oil to the seal lips and then
install the timing cover, using a new gasket. Tighten the bolts only
finger-tight at this stage.
10  Install the crankshaft pulley and tighten its securing bolt to the
specified torque (photo).
11  Finally tighten the timing cover bolts.

### 33 Distributor and oil pump drive gear - refitting

1   It is essential that the distributor drive gear engages the camshaft gear
in the correct position otherwise the ignition timing will be completely
out of phase.
2   Firstly, the crankshaft must be positioned so that the No. 1 (front)
piston is at the top-dead-centre (TDC) position on the compression
stroke.
3   To do this, rotate the crankshaft until, with the No. 1 piston
approaching TDC, both the No. 1 cylinder tappets are resting on the
heel of the cam, (fully down). This can be checked by lightly pressing
the tappet slides with the fingers and feeling them rise and fall as the
crankshaft is rotated.
4   If work is being carried out with the engine in the vehicle and the
cylinder head is still attached, remove the No. 1 cylinder spark plug
and with a finger pressed over the plug hole, rotate the engine until
pressure is felt. This indicates that No. 1 piston is rising on the
compression stroke.
5   On engines with the timing marks on the flywheel, rotate the
engine in the necessary direction until the TDC mark lines up with the
pointer. If using a higher octane fuel than 74-76 turn the flywheel to
the 3 or 6 mark as required (see Fig. 1.24).
6   If the engine is fitted with a timing pointer on the front cover,
align the notch on the pulley with the required octane tongue as
shown in Fig. 1.25.

7 Position the distributor drive gear bush so that the small hole is facing towards the oil filter mounting face at the point where the grub-screw is located (Fig. 1.12).

8 Insert the drive gear into the block (photo), and turn the gear so that when it is fully engaged with the camshaft gear, the largest (master) spline is facing rowards the No. 1 cylinder as shown in Fig. 1.26.

9 When the drive gear is correctly positioned, insert the grubscrew into the threaded hole in the oil filter mounting face (photo).

10 Insert the distributor drive coupling so that when it is fully seated in the drive gear the narrow segment faces towards the right-hand side of the engine and the slot towards the No. 1 cylinder (see Fig. 1.27).

11 If the engine has been removed from the vehicle, do not refit the distributor until just prior to refitting the engine in the vehicle. This will avoid the possibility of damaging it whilst refitting the cylinder head etc.

12 For information on refitting and adjusting the distributor, refer to Chapter 4.

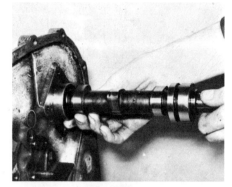

31.1 Sliding the camshaft into the block

31.2 Camshaft thrust plate in position

31.1a Inserting a tappet roller into the block ...

31.3b ... followed by a tappet slide

32.3 Refitting the camshaft timing chain

32.6 Timing chain tensioner installed

32.8 Refitting the camshaft sprocket securing bolt

32.10 Installing the crankshaft pulley and securing bolt

33.8 Inserting the distributor/oil pump drivegear

33.9 Refitting the distributor drivegear securing screw

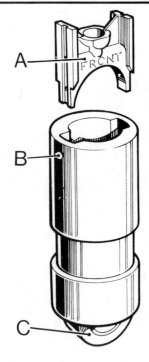

Fig. 1.21. Tappet assembly

A Slide          B Guide          C Roller

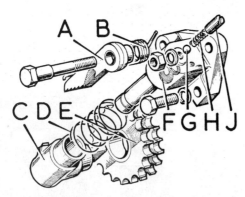

Fig. 1.22. Chain tensioner components

A Ratchet              F Piston
B Ratchet spring       G Non-return ball valve
C Cylinder             H Spring for ball valve
D Chain tensioner spring   J Spring retainer plug
E Idler wheel

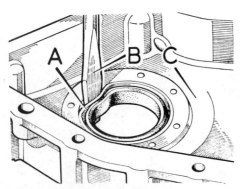

Fig. 1.23. Removing the timing cover oil seal

A Seal          B Screwdriver          C Inner side of cover

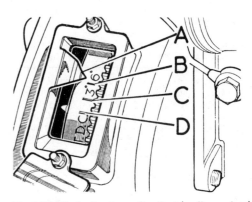

Fig. 1.24. Timing marks on flywheel (earlier engines)

A Timing pointer
B 6° mark, align when using 90-96 octane fuel
C 3° mark, align when using 80-85 octane fuel
D TDC mark, align when using 74-76 octane fuel

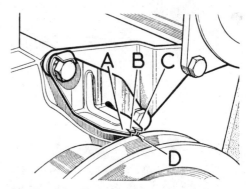

Fig. 1.25. Timing pointer on front cover

A 6° tongue, align when using 90-96 octane fuel
B 3° tongue, align when using 80-85 octane fuel
C TDC tongue, align when using 74-76 octane fuel
D Mark on crankshaft pulley, align with appropriate tongue

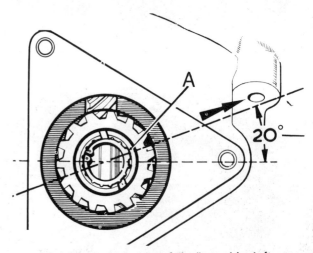

Fig. 1.26. Correct position of distributor driveshaft

A Master spline

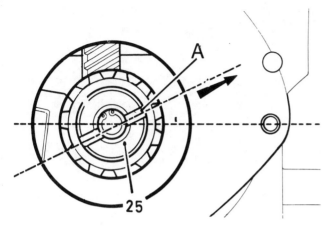

**Fig. 1.27. Correct position of distributor drive coupling**

*A  Coupling slot*

## 34 Oil pump and sump - refitting

1    Fit the oil pump driveshaft into the pump housing, making sure that the shaft spline engages fully with the pump gear.
2    Carefully insert the driveshaft and pump into its location in the crankcase, ensuring that the top splines on the shaft engage fully with the drive gear (photo).
3    Refit the securing bolts, tighten them and bend over the locking tabs (photo).
4    Clean the mating surfaces of the sump and the crankcase and stick the gasket in position on the sump using a light smear of grease.
5    Fit the sump to the crankcase and tighten the bolts in a diagonal sequence. Be careful not to overtighten them (photo).

## 35 Cylinder head - reassembly and refitting

1    Lay the cylinder head on its side, lubricate the valve stems and insert them into the guides they were removed from (photo).
2    Fit the oil seals over the valve stems ensuring the lip fits into the groove in the valve guide. **Note:** On earlier engines the oil seals fit in a groove inside the valve guides, and these must be fitted prior to inserting the valves.
3    Fit the valve spring, the retaining cap and then compress the valve spring and locate the split collets in the cut-out of the valve stem. Release the compressor. Repeat these operations on the remaining seven valves (photos).
4    When all the valves have been installed, place the cylinder head flat on the bench and using a hammer and a block of wood as an insulator, tap the end of each valve stem to settle the components.
5    Make sure that the faces of the cylinder head and the cylinder block are perfectly clean and then lay a new gasket on the cylinder block so that the word 'Front' or 'petrol' is visible from above and correctly located. Do not use any kind of jointing compound (photos).
6    Lower the cylinder head into position, insert the cylinder head bolts and tighten them to the specified torque and in the sequence shown in Fig. 1.15 (photo).
7    Insert each pushrod into the hole from which it was originally removed. Make sure that the pushrod end seats correctly on the tappet slide (photo).
8    With the rocker shaft assembly held together by means of the inverted rocker cover as described in Section 8, lower it into place, making sure the spigots are correctly located in the cylinder head.
9    Make sure that rocker arms are correctly seated on the pushrods and then tighten the securing bolts evenly to the torque wrench setting given in the Specifications.

34.2 Installing the oil pump and driveshaft

34.3 Securing the oil pump bolts with the lockwashers

34.5 Replacing the engine sump

35.1 Insert a valve into the cylinder head

35.3a Fit the valve spring ...

35.3b ... followed by the retaining cap

35.3c Compress the spring and fit the collets

35.5a Refit the head gasket with the word 'PETROL' uppermost

35.5b Correct installation of head gasket

35.6a Lowering the cylinder head into position on the block

35.6b Tightening the cylinder head bolts

35.7 Inserting a pushrod

## 36 Valve - adjustment

1    The valve adjustments should be made with the engine hot. The importance of correct rocker arm/valve stem clearances cannot be overstressed as they vitally affect the performance of the engine. If the clearances are set too wide, the efficiency of the engine is reduced as the valves open late and close earlier than was intended. If, on the other hand the clearances are set too close there is a danger that the stems will expand upon heating and not allow the valves to close properly which will cause burning of the valve head and seat and possible warping. If the engine is in the vehicle, access to the rockers is by removing the four holding down screws from the rocker cover, and then lifting the rocker cover and gasket away (photo).

2    It is important that the clearance is set when the tappet of the valve being adjusted is on the heel of the cam, (ie opposite the peak). This can be ensured by carrying out the adjustments in the following order (which also avoids turning the crankshaft more than necessary):

| Valves fully open | Check and adjust |
|---|---|
| *Valve No. 8* | *Valve No. 1* |
| *Valve No. 6* | *Valve No. 3* |
| *Valve No. 4* | *Valve No. 5* |
| *Valve No. 7* | *Valve No. 2* |
| *Valve No. 1* | *Valve No. 8* |
| *Valve No. 3* | *Valve No. 6* |
| *Valve No. 5* | *Valve No. 4* |
| *Valve No. 2* | *Valve No. 7* |

The correct feeler gauge clearance between valve stem and rocker arm pad with the engine hot is 0.010 in (0.25 mm).

3    Working from the front of the engine (No. 1 valve) the correct clearance is obtained by slackening the hexagon locknut with a spanner while holding the ball pin against rotation with a screwdriver. Then, still pressing down with the screwdriver, insert a feeler gauge in the gap between the valve stem head and the rocker arm and adjust the ball pin until the feeler gauge will just move in and out without

nipping (photo). Then, still holding the ball pin in the correct position, tighten the locknut.

4    When reassembling the cylinder head after a major overhaul or de-coke, the valve clearances should be set to 0.010 in (0.25 mm) with the engine cold and then re-checked after the engine has been started and warmed up to reach its normal operating temperature.

## 37 Ancillary components - refitting

1    This is a reversal of the removal sequence given in Section 7 of this Chapter.

2    Full details of component installation are given in the relevant Chapters of this manual, but the following points should be noted.

3    Always install a new oil filter sealing ring in the cylinder block groove. Tighten the centre-bolt only to specified torque (photo).

4    When refitting the flywheel housing, the O-ring type oil seal located in a groove around the inner aperture of the housing should be renewed (see Fig. 1.28).

5    Tighten the flywheel bolts to the specified torque and bend the locking tabs over (photo).

6    Adjust the fanbelt tension as described in Chapter 2.

## 38 Engine - refitting

Basically the installation of the engine is the reverse procedure to the removal operation, however, mating the engine to the gearbox can be difficult unless the following method is used.

1    Make sure the clutch is centralised on the flywheel as described in Chapter 5.

2    Carefully lower the engine into the engine compartment using a suitable hoist until the flywheel housing is straight and level with the clutch housing.

3    Push the engine rearwards ensuring the gearbox input shaft enters the clutch assembly in a straight line and not at an angle.

4   If the engine begins to mate up and then stops with a couple of inches still to go, fit a spanner onto the crankshaft starter dog and turn it slowly while pushing the engine rearwards.

5   As soon as the flywheel and clutch housings touch, insert a bolt finger-tight to hold them together, and then refit all the bolts and tighten them in a diagonal sequence to the specified torque.

6   Refit the engine mountings using the reverse procedure to that described in Section 5.

7   Finally, lower the hoist completely and remove the engine slings and the jack or blocks from beneath the transmission. Reconnect all the carburettor controls, electrical leads, fuel pipes, exhaust pipe etc., checking each item against the sequence given in Section 5.

8   Do not forget to refill the cooling system, and refill the engine with the recommended grade and quantity of oil.

### 39 Engine - adjustment after major overhaul

1   With the engine refitted to the vehicle, give a final visual check to see that everything has been reconnected and that no loose rags or tools have been left within the engine compartment.

2   Turn the engine slow running screw in about ½ turn (to increase slow running once the engine is started) (Chapter 3). This faster slow-running will be needed due to the tightness of the new engine components.

3   Pull the choke fully out and start the engine. This may take a little longer than usual as the fuel pump and carburettor bowl will be empty and need initial priming.

4   As soon as the engine starts, push the choke in until the engine runs at a fast tickover and examine the engine for leaks. Check particularly the water hoses, oil filter and fuel hose unions.

5   Allow the engine to idle until the normal operating temperature is reached.

6   Switch off the engine, remove the rocker cover and re-check the valve clearances as described in Section 36.

7   Refit the rocker cover and check the engine oil level; approximately ½ pint (.3 litre) will be required to fill the filter casing. Check the radiator water level and top-up if necessary. **Note:** Cover the cap with a cloth to avoid being scalded.

8   Re-start the engine and adjust the throttle stop screw to the required idling speed.

9   Where new internal components have been installed, the engine speed should be restricted for the first 500 miles (800 km) and at this mileage, the engine oil should be renewed, the cylinder head bolts checked for correct torque (unscrew each bolt one ¼ turn and then tighten to specified torque and in recommended sequence). Finally, check and adjust the valve clearances.

36.1 Removing the rocker cover

36.3 Setting the valve clearances

37.3 Refitting the oil filter

37.5 Tightening the flywheel securing bolts

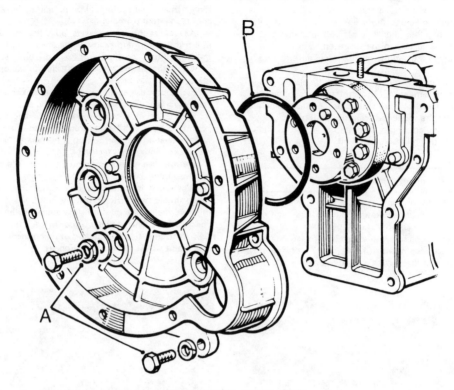

**Fig. 1.28. Flywheel housing assembly**

*A  Retaining bolts*                                                    *B  Seal*

---

**40 Fault diagnosis - engine**

| Symptom | Reason |
| --- | --- |
| Engine fails to start | Discharged battery. |
| | Loose battery connection. |
| | Disconnected or broken ignition leads. |
| | Moisture on spark plugs, distributor or leads. |
| | Incorrect contact points gap, cracked distributor cap or rotor. |
| | Incorrect spark plug gap. |
| | Dirt or water in carburettor jets. |
| | Empty fuel tank. |
| | Faulty fuel pump. |
| | Faulty starter motor. |
| | Faulty carburettor choke mechanism. |
| Engine idles erratically | Air leak at intake manifold. |
| | Leaking cylinder head gasket. |
| | Worn timing sprockets. |
| | Worn camshaft lobes. |
| | Overheating. |
| | Faulty fuel pump. |
| Engine 'misses' at idling speed | Incorrect spark plug gap. |
| | Uneven compression between cylinders. |
| | Faulty coil or condenser. |
| | Faulty contact points. |
| | Poor connections or condition of ignition leads. |
| | Dirt in carburettor jets. |
| | Incorrectly adjusted carburettor. |
| | Worn distributor cam. |
| | Air leak at carburettor flange gasket. |
| | Faulty ignition advance mechanism. |
| | Sticking valves. |
| | Incorrect valve clearance. |
| | Low cylinder compression. |

| Symptom | Reason |
| --- | --- |
| Engine 'misses' throughout speed range | Dirt or water in carburettor or fuel lines.<br>Incorrect ignition timing.<br>Contact points incorrectly gapped.<br>Worn distributor.<br>Faulty coil or condenser.<br>Spark plug gaps incorrect.<br>Weak valve spring.<br>Overheating. |
| Engine stalls | Incorrectly adjusted carburettor.<br>Dirt or water in fuel.<br>Ignition system incorrectly adjusted.<br>Sticking choke mechanism.<br>Faulty spark plugs or incorrectly gapped.<br>Faulty coil or condenser.<br>Incorrect contact points gap.<br>Exhaust system clogged.<br>Distributor advance inoperative.<br>Air leak at intake manifold.<br>Air leak at carburettor mounting flange.<br>Incorrect valve clearance.<br>Sticking valve.<br>Overheating.<br>Low compression.<br>Poor electrical connections on ignition system. |
| Engine lacks power | Incorrect ignition timing.<br>Faulty coil or condenser.<br>Worn distributor.<br>Dirt in carburettor.<br>Spark plugs incorrectly gapped.<br>Incorrectly adjusted carburettor.<br>Faulty fuel pump.<br>Weak valve springs.<br>Sticking valve.<br>Incorrect valve timing.<br>Incorrect valve adjustment.<br>Blown cylinder head gasket.<br>Low compression.<br>Brakes dragging.<br>Clutch slipping.<br>Overheating. |

# Chapter 2 Cooling system

**Contents**

**Specifications**

| | |
|---|---|
| **Type of system** ... ... ... ... ... ... ... ... | Pressurised system, assisted by pump and fan with thermostat temperature control |

**Thermostat**

| | |
|---|---|
| Type .. .. ... ... ... ... ... .. .. ... | Ethyl-alcohol or wax filled |
| Location ... ... ... ... ... ... ... .. .. | Front of cylinder head |
| Initial opening temperature ... . ... ... ... ... .. | 159°F - 173°F ( 70°C - 78°C) |
| Fully open temperature .. ... ... ... ... ... .. | 194°F (90°C) |

**Radiator**

| | |
|---|---|
| Type ... ... ... ... ... ... ... ... ... | Corrugated fin |
| Cap opening pressure ... ... ... ... ... ... ... ... | 9 or 10 lb/in$^2$ (0.6 or 0.7 kg/cm$^2$) |
| Capacity ... ... ... ... ... ... ... ... ... | 18 Imp. pints (10.25 litres) |

## 1 General description

The coolant circulates around the engine using the thermo-syphon principle, assisted by an impeller type water pump. A four-bladed cooling fan is fitted to the pump and both items are belt-driven from the crankshaft pulley.

A thermostat is located under the water outlet pipe at the front of the cylinder head. Earlier engines were fitted with an Ethyl-alcohol filled thermostat that was replaced on later models with the more efficient wax-filled type.

The cooling system functions in the following manner. Cold water from the bottom of the radiator is drawn up the lower radiator hose to the water pump which forces it through the passages in the cylinder block, cooling the cylinders and indirectly, the pistons.

The water then travels up into the cylinder head and circulates round the combustion spaces and valve seats absorbing more heat, and then, when the engine is at its correct operating temperature, travels out of the cylinder head, past the open thermostat into the upper radiator hose and so into the radiator header tank.

The water travels down the radiator where it is rapidly cooled by the in-rush of cold air through the radiator core, which is created by both the fan and the motion of the vehicle. The water, now much cooler reaches the bottom of the radiator when the cycle is repeated.

When the engine is cold the thermostat (which is a valve which opens and closes according to the temperature of the water) maintains the circulation of the same water in the engine.

Only when the correct minimum operating temperature has been reached, as shown in the Specifications, does the thermostat begin to open, allowing water to return to the radiator.

## 2 Cooling system - draining

With the vehicle on level ground drain the system as follows:
1 If the engine is cold, remove the filler cap from the radiator by turning it anticlockwise. If the engine is hot, turn the filler cap very slightly until the pressure in the system has had time to disperse. Use a rag over the cap to protect your hand from escaping steam. If, with the engine very hot, the cap is released suddenly, the drop in pressure can cause the water to boil. With the pressure released the cap can be removed.
2 If antifreeze is in the cooling system, drain it into a clean bowl for re-use. A wide bowl will be necessary to catch all the coolant.
3 If a heater is fitted, close the heater supply tap on the engine to avoid air-locks forming in the heater matrix.
4 Open the tap or plug located at the bottom of the radiator and allow the coolant to drain out into the bowl. Repeat the process with the tap located on the left-hand side of the cylinder block. When the water has finished running, probe the taps with a piece of short wire to dislodge any particles of rust or sediment which may be causing a blockage and preventing all the coolant from draining out.

## 3 Cooling system flushing

1 With time the cooling system will gradually lose its efficiency as the radiator becomes choked with rust scale, deposits from the water and other sediment. To clean the system out, first drain it - leaving the drain taps open. Then remove the radiator cap and leave a hose running in the radiator cap orifice for ten to fifteen minutes.

2   In very bad cases the radiator should be reverse flushed. This can
be done with the radiator in position. A hose must be arranged to feed
water into the lower radiator outlet pipe. Water, under pressure, is then
forced up through the radiator and out of the header tank filler orifice.
3   The hose is removed and placed in the filler orifice and the radiator
washed out in the usual manner.

## 4   Cooling system - filling

1   Close the radiator and cylinder block drain taps.
2   Move the heater control to the 'hot' position and fill the system
slowly to ensure that air locks are minimised.
3   Do not fill the system higher than within 0.5 in (13.0 mm) of the
filler cap orifice. Overfilling will merely result in wastage, which is
especially to be avoided when antifreeze is in use.
4   On later models fitted with an overflow reservoir, fill the container
with sufficient coolant to cover the end of the overflow pipe from the
radiator.
5   Only use antifreeze mixture with an ethylene glycol base. See
Section 9 for further information.
6   Replace the radiator cap and run the engine at a fast idle speed for
approximately half a minute and remove the filler cap slowly. Top-up
as necessary  and finally refit the filler cap turning it clockwise firmly
to lock it in position.

## 5   Radiator - removal, inspection, cleaning and refitting

1   Refer to Section 2 and drain the cooling system.
2   Remove the top hose connecting the radiator to the thermostat
housing.
3   Remove the earth lead from the battery.
4   Undo the screws securing the fan shroud to the radiator and lift the
shroud rearwards over the fan.
5   Undo the screws retaining the 'Land-Rover' badge to the radiator
grille and lift the grille away from the vehicle.
6   Remove the bottom radiator hose.
7   Undo the nuts and bolts securing the radiator assembly to the
front grille panel. Access to these are gained through the grille
aperture.
8   Carefully lift the radiator out of the vehicle taking care not to
damage the radiator core on the fan blades. If difficulty is experienced
in clearing the fan blades, lower the radiator and remove the fan and
pulley as described in Section 7 of this Chapter.
9   With the radiator away from the vehicle any leaks can be soldered or
repaired with a suitable kit. Clean out the inside of the radiator by
flushing as described earlier in this Chapter. When the radiator is out of
the vehicle it is advantageous to turn it upside down and reverse flush.
Clean the exterior of the radiator by carefully using a compressed air
jet or a strong jet of water to clear away any road dirt, flies etc.
10  Inspect the radiator hoses for cracks, internal or external perishing
and damage by overtightening of the securing clips. Also inspect the
overflow pipe. Renew the hoses if suspect. Examine the radiator hose
clips and renew them if they are rusted or distorted.
11  Refit the radiator using the reverse sequence to the removal
procedure. Refill the cooling system as described in Section 4.

Fig. 2.1. Coolant drain points

1   Cylinder block drain tap
2   Radiator drain plug (tap on some models)

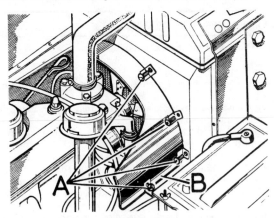

Fig. 2.3. Radiator cowl location

A   Retaining screws and nuts          B   Cowl

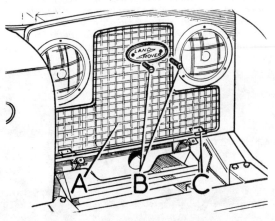

Fig. 2.4. Radiator grille attachment points

A   Grille            B   Securing screws      C   Bottom clips

Fig. 2.2. Location of reservoir bottle on later models

### 6  Thermostat  removal, testing, and refitting

1   The thermostat is located in the alloy housing on the top and at the front of the cylinder head (Fig. 2.5).
2   First undo the radiator drain tap (or plug) and drain off approximately 6 pints (3.75 litres) of coolant.
3   Slacken the clips and remove the top hose from the thermostat outlet pipe and radiator.
4   Remove the three bolts and lift off the outlet pipe exposing the top of the thermostat (photo).
5   Carefully prise out the thermostat from the housing. If difficulty is experienced, remove the housing and push the thermostat out.
6   Examine the thermostat for damage and if it is stuck open, renew it. To test a thermostat, use the following procedure.
7   Suspend it by a piece of string together with a thermometer in a saucepan of cold water. Neither the thermostat nor the thermometer should touch the sides or bottom of the saucepan or a false reading could be obtained.
8   Heat the water  stirring it gently with the thermometer to ensure temperature uniformity, and note when the thermostat begins to open. Note the temperature and this should be comparable with the figure given in the Specifications Section at the beginning of this Chapter.
9   Continue heating the water until the thermostat is fully open. Now let it cool down naturally and check that it closes fully. If the thermostat does not fully open or close then it must be renewed.
10 Refitting the thermostat is the reverse of the removal procedure. Always clean the mating faces thoroughly and use new gaskets.
**Note:** A wax-type thermostat cannot be fitted in place of the ethyl-alcohol type unless a modified water outlet pipe is fitted (obtainable from your Leyland dealer).

### 7  Water pump - removal and refitting

1   Refer to Section 2 and drain the cooling system.
2   Refer to Section 5 and remove the radiator.
3   Refer to Section 10 and remove the fan belt.
4   Slacken the bottom hose clip and carefully detach the hose from the water pump.
5   Slacken the water bypass hose clip and carefully detach the bypass hose from the water pump.
6   If a dynamo is fitted (earlier models) remove the adjusting arm to gain access to the pump retaining bolts.
7   Undo and remove the four bolts securing the fan and hub assembly to the water pump spindle flange and lift away the fan assembly (photo).
8   Undo and remove the bolts securing the water pump body to the cylinder block. Lift away the water pump and recover the old gasket (photo).
9   Refitting the water pump is the reverse sequence to removal, but the following additional points should be noted:
   a) Make sure the mating faces of the pump body and cylinder block are clean. Always use a new gasket.
   b) Refer to Section 10 and adjust the fan belt tension. If the belt is too tight, undue strain will be placed on the water pump and alternator (or dynamo) bearings. If the belt is too loose, it will slip and wear rapidly as well as giving rise to possible engine overheating and low alternator (or dynamo) output.

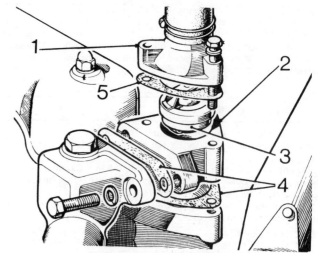

**Fig. 2.5. Thermostat housing assembly**

1   Water outlet pipe          3   Thermostat
2   Thermostat housing         4   Housing gaskets
                               5   Water outlet gasket

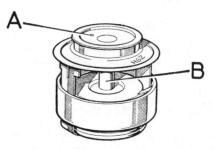

**Fig. 2.6. Ethyl-alcohol type thermostat**

A   Bleed hole                 B   Operating valve

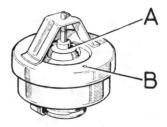

**Fig. 2.7. Wax-type thermostat**

A   Operating valve            B   Bleed hole

6.4 Location of thermostat

7.7 Lifting off the cooling fan

7.8 Removing the water pump

## 8 Water pump - dismantling, overhaul and reassembly

1   Before dismantling the water pump check the economics of overhaul compared with the cost of a guaranteed new unit. Then make quite sure all the spare parts required are to hand.

2   Referring to Fig. 2.8, remove the bearing retaining bolt and with the pump body held in a soft-jawed vice, drift out the impeller, bearing and spindle assembly from the pump body and flange.

3   Cut through the seal and discard it. Support the impeller between two large blocks of wood and drive the spindle and bearing out of the impeller.

4   Examine the bearing for wear and the impeller and spindle for excessive corrosion, if either are evident renew the components affected.

5   On later models fitted with a deflector washer, check that there is a clearance of 0.018 in (0.46 mm) between the washer and the bearing housing face.

6   Before reassembling, insert a few drops of thick oil into the location hole in the bearing.

7   Mark a line on the pump body and the bearing assembly to enable the retaining bolt holes to be lined up during reassembly.

8   Insert the spindle and bearing assembly into the pump body and fit the retaining bolt.

9   Press the pulley flange onto the spindle until the dimension 'A' in Fig. 2.8 is achieved.

10  Fit the carbon ring and seal into the bore of the pump body ensuring the carbon ring is towards the rear of the pump.

11  Press the impeller onto the spindle until there is 0.025 in (0.63 mm) clearance between the impeller and pump body (see Fig. 2.8). The clearance can be checked using feeler gauges.

12  Refit the pump to the engine as described in Section 7, ensuring that a new gasket is used between the mating surfaces.

## 9 Antifreeze coolant solution

1   Where temperatures are likely to drop below freezing point (0°C, 32°F) the cooling system must be adequately protected by the addition of antifreeze. It is still possible for water to freeze in the radiator with the engine running in very cold conditions - particularly if the engine cooling is being adequately dealt with by the heater radiator. The thermostat will remain closed and the coolant in the radiator will not circulate.

2   Before refilling the coolant system with antifreeze solution it is best to drain and flush the system as described in Sections 2 and 3 of this Chapter.

3   Because antifreeze has a greater searching effect than water make sure that all hoses and joints are in good condition.

4   The table below gives the details of the antifreeze percentage to be used:

| % | complete protection | |
|---|---|---|
| 25 | −11°C | 12.2°F |
| 30 | −14°C | 6.8°F |
| 35 | −19°C | −2.2°F |
| 40 | −23°C | −9.4°F |
| 45 | −29°C | −20.0°F |
| 50 | −35°C | −31.0°F |

5   Mix the equal quantity of antifreeze with 4 pints (2.27 litres) of water and pour into the cooling system. Top-up with water and check the level as described in Section 4.

## 10 Fan belt - removal, refitting and adjustment

1   If the fan belt is worn or has stretched unduly it should be renewed. A common reason for renewal is breakage in use, so always carry a spare.

2   Even though the belt may have broken and fallen off, go through the removal routine. First loosen the dynamo or alternator securing bolts and push it towards the engine and lift off the old belt.

3   Position the new belt over the pulleys.

4   The dynamo or alternator must now be used as a tensioner, in effect, by pulling it away from the engine and locking in the required position. This can call for some sustained effort unless the pivot bolts are slackened only a little so that the dynamo or alternator is quite stiff to move. A lever between the dynamo or alternator and cylinder block will help. However, avoid applying pressure to the rear end-cover or it may break. Always tighten the front end-cover securing bolts first.

5   The movement of the belt under finger pressure of the belt, midway between the water pump and dynamo or alternator pulleys, should be set to 0.5 in (13 mm). If in doubt it is better for it to be a little too slack rather than too tight. Only slipping will occur if it is too slack. If too tight, damage can be caused by excessive strain on the pulley bearing (photo).

6   When the adjustment is correct tighten the dynamo or alternator mountings fully.

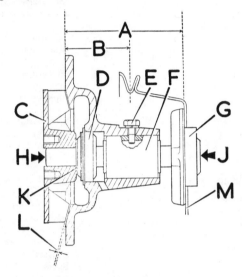

**Fig. 2.8. Cross sectional view of water pump**

A   Dimension, 3.510 in (89.15 mm)
B   Dimension, 1.930 in (49.0 mm)
C   Impeller
D   Carbon ring and seal assembly
E   Locating bolt
F   Pump spindle and bearing assembly
G   Fan hub
H   Support here when fitting hub
J   Support here when fitting impeller
K   Carbon seal faced toward impeller
L   Dimension, 0.025 in (0.63 mm)
M   Fan belt pulley

10.5 Checking the fan belt tension

## 11 Fault diagnosis - cooling system

| Symptom | Reason/s | Remedy |
|---|---|---|
| Overheating | Insufficient water in cooling system | Top-up radiator. |
| | Fan belt slipping (accompanied by a shrieking noise on rapid engine acceleration) | Tighten fan belt to recommended tension or renew if worn. |
| | Radiator core blocked or radiator grille restricted | Reverse flush radiator, remove obstructions. |
| | Water hose collapsed, impeding flow | Remove and fit new hose. |
| | Thermostat not opening properly | Remove and fit new thermostat. |
| | Ignition advance and retard incorrectly set (accompanied by loss of power, and perhaps, misfiring) | Check and reset ignition timing. |
| | Carburettor incorrectly adjusted (mixture too weak) | Tune carburettor. |
| | Exhaust system partially blocked | Check exhaust pipe for constrictive dents and blockages. |
| | Oil level in sump too low | Top-up sump to full mark on dipstick |
| | Blown cylinder head gasket (water/steam being forced down the radiator overflow pipe under pressure) | Remove cylinder head, fit new gasket. |
| | Engine not yet run-in | Run-in slowly and carefully |
| | Brakes binding | Check and adjust brakes if necessary. |
| Underheating | Thermostat jammed open | Remove and renew thermostat. |
| | Incorrect thermostat fitted allowing premature opening of valve | Remove and replace with new thermostat which opens at a higher temperature. |
| | Thermostat missing | Check and fit correct thermostat. |
| Loss of cooling water | Loose clips on water hoses | Check and tighten clips if necessary. |
| | Top, bottom, or bypass water hoses perished and leaking | Check and renew any faulty hoses. |
| | Radiator core leaking | Remove radiator and repair. |
| | Thermostat gasket leaking | Inspect and renew gasket. |
| | Radiator pressure cap spring worn or seal ineffective | Renew radiator pressure cap. |
| | Blown cylinder head gasket (pressure in system forcing water/steam down overflow pipe) | Remove cylinder head and fit new gasket. |
| | Cylinder wall or head cracked | Dismantle engine, despatch to engineering works for repair. |
| | Core plug leaking | Renew faulty core plug. |

# Chapter 3 Carburation:
# fuel exhaust and emission control system

*For modifications, and information applicable to later models, see Supplement at end of manual*

## Contents

## Specifications

**Fuel pump** ... ... ... ... ... ... ... ... ... AC mechanical

**Carburettor (Solex)**

| | |
|---|---|
| Choke size ... ... ... ... ... ... ... ... ... | 28 mm |
| Main jet ... ... ... ... ... ... ... ... ... | 125 |
| Correction jet ... ... ... ... ... ... ... ... | 185 |
| Pilot jet ... ... ... ... ... ... ... ... ... | 50 |
| Pump jet ... ... ... ... ... ... ... ... ... | 65 |
| Economy jet ... ... ... ... ... ... ... ... | Blank |
| Air bleed jet ... ... ... ... ... ... ... ... | 1.5 |
| Starter air jet ... ... ... ... ... ... ... ... | − |
| Starter petrol jet ... ... ... ... ... ... ... | 145 |
| Economy system - petrol jet ... ... ... ... ... | 100 |
| Petrol level ... ... ... ... ... ... ... ... | 5/8 in ± 1/8 in (16 mm ± 3 mm) below float chamber joint face |

Jet sizes to be used when operating at high altitudes:

| | |
|---|---|
| Main jet (120) ... ... ... ... ... ... ... ... | 5,000 ft to 7,000 ft (1.524 m to 2.134 m) |
| Main jet (117.5) ... ... ... ... ... ... ... ... | 7,000 ft to 9,000 ft (2.134 m to 2.740 m) |
| Main jet (115) } Pilot jet (45) } ... ... ... ... ... ... ... | 9,000 ft to 12,000 ft (2.740 m to 3.655 m) |
| Main jet (112.5) } Pilot jet (45) } ... ... ... ... ... ... ... | 12,000 ft to 14,000 ft (3.655 m to 4.268 m) |

**Carburettor (Zenith)**

| | |
|---|---|
| Choke size ... ... ... ... ... ... ... ... ... | 27 mm |
| Main jet ... ... ... ... ... ... ... ... ... | 125 |
| Enrichment jet ... ... ... ... ... ... ... ... | 150 |
| Slow running jet (ball type) ... ... ... ... ... ... | 60 |
| Pump jet (short stroke outer hole) ... ... ... ... ... | 65 |
| Part throttle air bleed ... ... ... ... ... ... ... | 3.0 |
| Full throttle air bleed ... ... ... ... ... ... ... | 1.5 drilled |
| Slow running air bleed ... ... ... ... ... ... ... | 1.4 |
| Spring loaded ball valve in pump circuit ... ... ... ... | 105 |
| Fast idle ... ... ... ... ... ... ... ... ... | 1.20 |
| Needle valve ... ... ... ... ... ... ... ... | 1.75 |
| Needle valve washer ... ... ... ... ... ... ... | 2.00 |
| Fuel level ... ... ... ... ... ... ... ... ... | 1.22-1.23 in (31-32 mm) |

**Fuel filters** ... ... ... ... ... ... ... ... One integral with fuel pump plus in-line cartridge type on models fitted with emission control system

**Fuel tank capacity** ... ... ... ... ... ... ... 10 Imp. gals, 12 US gals (45 litres)

**Torque wrench settings**

| | lb f ft | kg f m |
|---|---|---|
| Manifold to cylinder head nuts ... ... ... ... ... ... | 17 | 2.3 |
| Inlet manifold to exhaust manifold nuts ... ... ... ... ... | 17 | 2.3 |

## 1  General description

Basically the fuel system comprises a fuel tank located beneath the drivers seat, (or at the rear right-hand side on station wagon models), a mechanical fuel pump driven from the camshaft and either the Zenith 36 IV or the Solex 40 PA carburettor. Air is drawn into the carburettor intake via an oil bath type filter.

Certain export models are fitted with various emission control features to comply with the air pollution laws in different countries (mainly the USA). Section 16 describes the emission control systems used.

## 2  Air cleaner - removal, servicing and refitting

1   The air cleaner on the Land Rover is the oil bath and wire mesh type. It is essential to service it at the intervals stated in the Routine Maintenance Section at the beginning of this Manual, especially when operating in dusty conditions.
2   To service the air cleaner, it is necessary to remove the complete assembly from the vehicle (photo).
3   Slacken the clip and remove the intake hose from the top of the carburettor.
4   Undo the wingnut from the retaining strap and lift up the hinged section of the strap. Remove the complete air cleaner assembly.
5   Keep the cleaner in an upright position. Release the clips at the base and withdraw the bottom oil container section.
6   Remove the seal and lift out the wire mesh element.
7   Drain off the old oil and wash the wire mesh and container in clean petrol. Refill the bottom container with fresh engine oil until it is level with the groove (approximately 1.5 Imp. pints, 0.85 litre).
8   Refit the air cleaner to the vehicle using the reverse procedure to removal.

## 3  Carburettor - description

The Zenith and Solex carburettors are similar in design and operation; both being the single barrel downdraught type with mechanically operated chokes.

The main difference between the two types of carburettor is the choke, or cold starting mechanism. On the Solex model a rotating valve and duct is fitted with the option of an electrical heater element, while the Zenith has the more conventional flap valve. The accelerator pump on the Zenith is the piston type as opposed to the diaphragm operated type on the Solex.

The use of fixed diameter jets for the idling, slow running and full power modes ensure smooth running throughout the engine speed range combined with maximum economy.

The only adjustments necessary at the specified service intervals are the mixture control and slow running screw settings.

## 4  Carburettor - removal and refitting

1   The procedure for removing the Zenith and the Solex carburettor is virtually the same.
2   Undo the clip holding the air cleaner hose to the top of the carburettor and remove it.
3   Disconnect the choke inner and outer cables and the throttle control rod (photo).
4   Disconnect the distributor vacuum control pipe at the carburettor end.
5   Disconnect the fuel inlet pipe from the carburettor union and tape over the end to prevent dirt ingress.
6   Undo the two nuts securing the carburettor to the inlet manifold and lift it away from the engine. Push some clean rag into the manifold aperture to prevent any dirt getting in.
7   Refitting the carburettor is the reverse sequence to removal, however, it will be necessary to check the carburettor adjustments as described later in this Chapter.

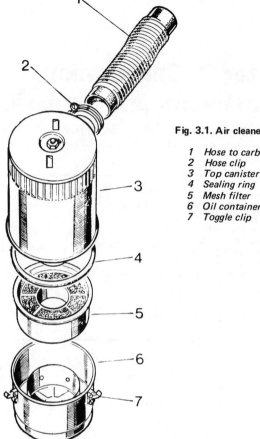

Fig. 3.1. Air cleaner assembly

1   Hose to carburettor
2   Hose clip
3   Top canister
4   Sealing ring
5   Mesh filter
6   Oil container
7   Toggle clip

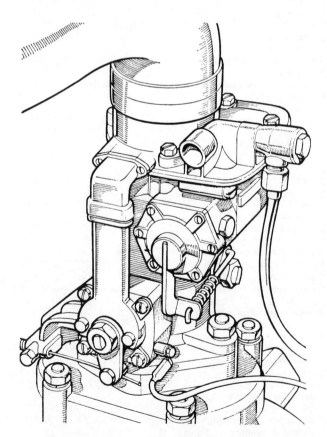

Fig. 3.2. General view of Solex carburettor

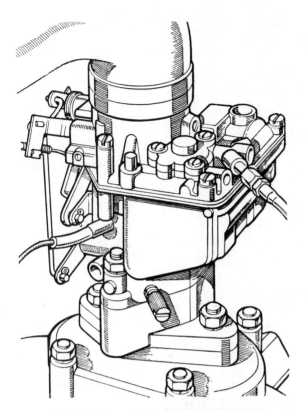

**Fig. 3.3. General view of Zenith carburettor**

## 5 Solex carburettor - dismantling, inspection and reassembly

1  Undo the screws securing the top cover to the carburettor body and lift off the cover complete with the cold start elbow. Do not lose the rubber seal located between the cold start elbow and duct.

2  Unscrew the needle valve assembly from the inside of the top cover.

3  Disconnect the operating rod from the accelerator pump lever, taking care not to lose the small washers and spring.

4  Undo the volume control screw, remove the four securing screws and detach the lower throttle chamber from the main carburettor body. Recover the gasket.

5  If it is intended to remove the throttle flap and control rod, carefully scratch a mark on the flap, rod and side of the venturi as shown in Fig. 3.5. to ensure correct reassembly.

6  Undo the four retaining screws and withdraw the cold start unit from the side of the throttle chamber.

7  Remove the operating lever from the cold start unit, taking care not to lose the small steel ball and spring.

8  Remove the cold start unit from the outer cover and duct assembly and recover the rubber seal.

9  If a heating element is fitted, remove the circlip and withdraw the element from the cold start valve unit.

10 Lift the starter valve out of the valve casing.

11 To dismantle the carburettor main body assembly, first undo the securing bolt and lift out the float assembly.

12 Undo the retaining screws and remove the accelerator pump assembly from the side of the body.

13 Unscrew the air correction jet from inside the choke tube and withdraw the emulsion tube.

14 Referring to Fig. 3.4, unscrew and remove the economy jet, the pilot jet, the starter jet and the accelerator pump jet. Remove the main jet holder and the main jet and then the non-return valve, complete with filter.

15 To dismantle the accelerator pump assembly, first undo the retaining screws and remove the outer cover.

16 Withdraw the pump membrane assembly and coil spring.

17 Twist the economy valve washer and remove the washer, spring and valve (Fig. 3.6).

18 The carburettor is now completely dismantled and all the compon-

ents should be washed in clean petrol and blown dry with compressed air.

19 Check that all the jet size numbers are the same as those given in the Specifications.

20 Examine the throttle spindle bushes for wear, and, if wear is evident, the complete throttle chamber will have to be renewed.

21 Check the float for leaks and the accelerator diaphragm for splitting or perishing. Renew the components if any damage is evident.

22 Before reassembling the carburettor, obtain a new set of gaskets and seals from your Leyland dealer.

23 Reassembly is basically the reverse procedure to dismantling. Commence by rebuilding the accelerator pump and refit it to the side of the carburettor body (Fig. 3.7). Reassemble the cold start valve into the cover as shown in Fig. 3.8 and refit to the carburettor. When refitting the throttle flap and spindle, ensure that the location marks made previously are lined up and the throttle linkage components are refitted in the correct sequence (Fig. 3.9).

24 Continue to reassemble the carburettor components referring to the associated illustrations where necessary. When refitting the accelerator pump operating rod, ensure that the throttle flap is fully closed with the slow running screw slackened right off. Add washers to the end of the rod up to the nearest split pin hole until there is 0.020 in (0.5 mm) clearance between the pump operating arm and the first washer, when the split pin is inserted (see Fig. 3.10). Compress the coil spring and fit the inner split pin.

25 After refitting the carburettor to the engine, it must be adjusted as described in Section 7.

2.2 Air cleaner assembly

4.3 Throttle operating rod

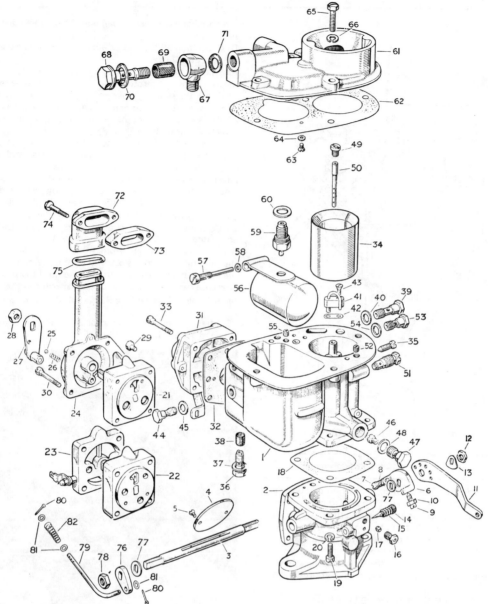

**Fig. 3.4. Exploded view of Solex carburettor**

1  Carburettor body
2  Throttle chamber
3  Spindle for throttle
4  Butterfly for throttle
5  Special screw securing butterfly
6  Plate, throttle abutment
7  Special screw  -} For slow running
8  Spring  -}  adjustment
9  Special screw  }
10  Locknut  -}  For throttle stop
11  Throttle lever
12  Nut securing throttle lever
13  Lockwasher for nut
14  Special screw  -}
15  Spring  -}  For mixture control
16  Screwed union  -}
17  Olive  -}  For suction pipe
18  Joint washer for throttle chamber
19-20  Screw and washer chamber to carburettor body
21  Starter body and valve, without starter heater element
22  Starter body and valve complete with starter heater element
23  Heater element for starter
24  Cover for starter
25  Ball  -}
26  Spring  -}  For starter valve

27  Lever for starter
28  Nut securing starter lever
29  Special bolt fixing starter cable
30  Special screw fixing starter body
31  Accelerator pump complete
32  Joint washer for pump
33  Special screw securing pump
34  Choke tube
35  Special screw securing choke tube
36  Non-return valve
37  Fibre washer for valve
38  Filter gauze for non-return valve
39  Jet, accelerator pump
40  Fibre washer for jet
41  Pump injector
42  Joint washer for pump injector
43  Special screw securing injector
44  Economy jet (blank)
45  Joint washer for blank jet
46  Main jet
47  Main jet carrier
48  Fibre washer for carrier
49  Correction jet
50  Emulsion tube
51  Pilot jet
52  Jet air bleed
53  Starter jet, petrol

54  Fibre washer for jet
55  Economy jet
56  Float
57  Spindle for float
58  Copper washer for spindle
59  Needle valve completer
60  Fibre washer for valve
61  Top cover for carburettor
62  Joint washer for top cover
63-64  Screw - joint washer to top cover
65-66  Screws - top cover to body
67  Banjo union
68  Special bolt for union
69  Filter gauze for union
70  Fibre washer, large
71  Fibre washer, small
72  Elbow for top cover
73  Distance piece, elbow to top cover
74  Screw fixing elbow to top cover
75  Rubber sealing washer, elbow to starter cover
76  Lever for accelerator pump rod
77  Special washer for lever
78  Nut securing lever to spindle
79  Control rod for accelerator pump
80  Split pin  -}
81  Plain washer  }  For control rod
82  Spring  -}

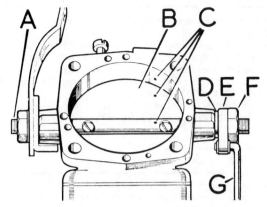

Fig. 3.5. Throttle butterfly flap and spindle

A  Spindle for throttle
B  Butterfly for throttle
C  Markings inserted as required
D  Special washer for lever

E  Lever for accelerator pump
F  Nut fixing lever to spindle
G  Control rod for accelerator
   pump

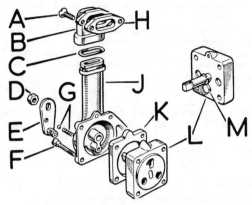

Fig. 3.8. Cold start valve and cover assembly

A  Screw for elbow
B  Elbow
C  Rubber sealing washer
D  Nut securing starter lever
E  Lever for starter
F  Screw securing starter body

G  Ball and spring for starter valve
H  Distance piece for elbow
J  Starter top cover
K  Heater element for starter
L  Starter body
M  Locator

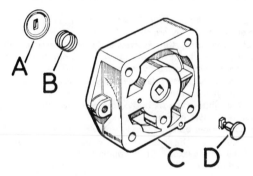

Fig. 3.6. Accelerator pump body and valve assembly

A  Economy valve washer
B  Economy valve spring

C  Pump body
D  Economy valve

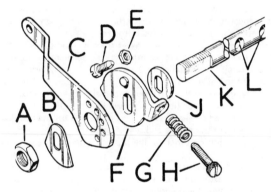

Fig. 3.9. Throttle linkage assembly

A  Spindle nut
B  Spindle nut tab washer
C  Throttle lever
D  Screw    -} Throttle stop
E  Nut      -}
F  Abutment plate

G  Spring   -} Slow running
H  Screw    -}
K  Throttle spindle
L  Countersunk screw holder
J  Special washer

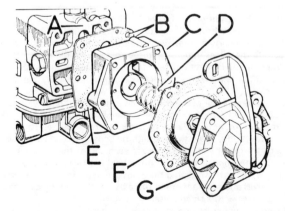

Fig. 3.7. Assembling the accelerator pump

A  Carburettor body
B  Location peg and hole for pump
   body to gasket
C  Pump body

D  Pump spring
E  Pump body gasket
F  Pump membrane assembly
G  Top pump cover

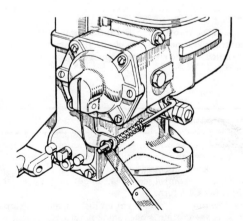

Fig. 3.10. Setting the accelerator pump clearance

## 6   Zenith carburettor - dismantling, inspection and reassembly

1   As most of the important parts of the carburettor are located in the top cover it is usually not necessary to remove the carburettor from the engine for cleaning purposes.

2   Withdraw the split pins and detach the pump linkage and choke control road (Fig. 3.12).

3   Undo and remove the four screws and spring washers that secure the top cover to the main body. Note the location of these screws as they are of different lengths.

4   Carefully lift the cover from the main body so as not to tear the gasket or bend or damage the delicate float assembly which is attached to the cover.

5   To gain access to the jets and accelerator pump, the emulsion block must be removed from the underside of the cover (Fig. 3.13).

6   Withdraw the float arm pivot pin and lift away the float assembly. Lift out the small needle valve.

7   Using a suitable size box spanner unscrew the needle valve seat and lift away together with the special washer.

8   Unscrew the two screws that secure the emulsion block to the cover. Lift the emulsion block upwards and take care to prevent the accelerator pump and spring dropping out. Recover the sealing ring.

9   The economy device is held on the top cover by three screws and spring washers which should next be removed. Lift away the cover, diaphragm and spring.

10   Unscrew the jets in the top cover and put in a safe place. The pump jet may be removed from the emulsion block after removing the plug located on the side.

11   Wash the top cover in petrol and blow out the drillings using compressed air. Inspect the economy device diaphragm for signs of damage and, if evident, obtain a new one ready for reassembly.

12   Reassembly starts with the refitting of the emulsion block to the cover. Refer to Fig. 3.14 and make sure that the accelerator pump inlet ball and circlip are installed in the bottom of the cylinder. Refit the jets to the top cover.

13   Fit the new gasket to the top cover and ensure that the accelerator pump lever is correctly positioned as shown in Fig. 3.15.

14   Examine the needle valve for any signs of ridging on the bevelled face and renew both the needle and seat if in doubt.

15   Position the emulsion block on the top cover and secure with the two screws.

16   Refit the needle valve seating and special washer. Insert the needle.

17   Refit the float assembly and retain in position with the spindle. Hold the cover upside down and measure the distance from the bottom of the float to the face of the cover gaskets. It should be 1 5/16 in (33 mm). Make any adjustments necessary by carefully bending the float arm centre tag which contacts the needle. This setting is important (Fig. 3.16).

18   Before replacing the cover onto the body check that the sealing ring located as shown in Fig. 3.17 is in good order. A bad seal will result in fuel leaking from the float chamber. Secure the cover with the four screws and spring washers. Take care because these are of different lengths.

19   Reconnect the accelerator pump linkage noting that the pin should always be fitted to the upper hole in the pump spindle lever.

20   The choke control rod is not provided with any obvious adjustment. With the choke flap held shut there should be a 0.040 in (1 mm) gap down the side of the throttle flap. For this a number 61 drill is useful. Bend the control rod if necessary to obtain this setting.

21   The choke flap spindle return spring must engage the first notch on the lever.

## 7   Carburettor - setting and adjustment (both types)

1   Before adjusting the carburettor controls ensure that the spark plug gaps and valve clearances are correctly set and the ignition static timing is set up as described in Chapter 4.

2   Screw the mixture control screw right in but do **not** overtighten. Then slacken it back 1½ turns.

3   Turn the slow running screw in until it just touches the stop on the carburettor body then rotate it one complete turn.

4   Operate the accelerator pedal and check that the linkage moves freely and the throttle operating rod has full travel.

5   Start the engine and allow it to run until normal working temperature is reached.

6   Turn the mixture control screw in the required direction until the engine speed increases and runs smoothly. Now adjust the slow running screw until the idling speed is approximately 500 rpm.

**Note:** On vehicles fitted with emission control the idling speed should be between 750 and 800 rpm (see Section 16).

7   Dab the throttle fully open and close it to check that the engine does not stall. If it does, slightly increase the idling speed.

## 8   Fuel pump - removal and refitting

1   Remove the air cleaner as described in Section 2 of this Chapter.

2   Undo and remove the inlet and outlet fuel pipe unions from the pump body.

3   Remove the two securing nuts and withdraw the pump and gasket. If difficulty is experienced in removing the two nuts, undo the four bolts and remove the pump complete with side cover plate and gasket, (see Fig. 3.18).

4   Refitting is a reversal of this procedure but ensure that a new gasket is fitted.

## 9   Fuel pump - dismantling

1   Clean the outside of the pump and wipe dry using a dry non-fluffy rag.

2   Using a file make a mark on the flanges of the upper and lower body to ensure that they are correctly reassembled.

3   Unscrew the stirrup thumb screw and swing the stirrup out of the way. Hold the glass bowl to ensure that it does not drop. Lift away the sediment bowl followed by the cork seal and gauze filter. Inspect the cork gasket for signs of damage or flattening and obtain a new one ready for reassembling.

4   Undo and remove the six body securing screws and spring washers and separate the two halves.

5   Invert the upper body and undo the two valve retaining plate screws and lift away the screws, retaining plate, the two valve assemblies and the valve gasket from the upper body.

6   Note the position of the lip on the diaphragm relative to the lower body to ensure correct reassembly and remove the diaphragm by rotating through 90° in an anti-clockwise direction and lifting it away from the lower body and the link.

7   It is recommended that the lower body parts are not dismantled unless either the seal, hand priming lever or the link assembly require attention.

## 10   Fuel pump - examination and reassembly

1   Check the condition of the cork sediment bowl sealing washer and if it has hardened or broken it must be renewed. The diaphragm should be checked similarly and renewed if faulty. Clean the pump thoroughly and agitate the valves in paraffin or petrol to clean them out. This will also improve the contact between the valve seat and the valve. It is unlikely that the pump body will be damaged but check for fractures and cracks.

2   To reassemble the pump proceed as follows. If the lower body has been dismantled refit the rocker arm assembly comprising the operating link, rocker arm, anti-rattle spring and washers in their relative positions in the lower body. Align the holes in the body and insert the pivot pin.

3   Refit the circlips to the grooves in each end of the pivot pin.

**Note:** On later models the pivot pin is held in place by two retainers (see Fig. 3.19). After refitting the pivot pin, tap the retainers into their grooves and secure them in place by lightly peening over the ends of the grooves with a small chisel.

4   Invert the upper body and replace the gasket, valves, valve retaining plate and tighten the two plate retaining screws. The two valves are interchangeable so care must be taken to ensure they are fitted the correct way round. The inlet valve should be fitted into the offset and shallower part with its spring facing the diaphragm, whilst the outlet valve is fitted to the centre part with its spring facing away from the diaphragm.

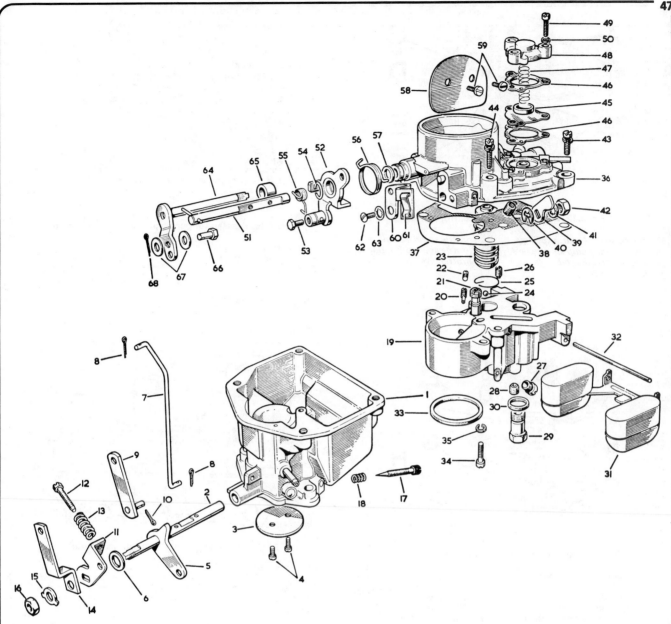

**Fig. 3.11. Exploded view of Zenith carburettor**

| | |
|---|---|
| 1 Carburettor main body | 25 Circlip for piston |
| 2 Throttle spindle | 26 Slow running jet |
| 3 Butterfly for throttle | 27 Main jet |
| 4 Special screw securing butterfly | 28 Enrichment jet |
| 5 Floating lever on throttle spindle | 29 Needle valve |
| 6 Plain washer on spindle for floating lever | 30 Special washer (2 mm) |
| 7 Interconnecting link, throttle to choke | 31 Float |
| 8 Split pin fixing link to levers | 32 Spindle for float |
| 9 Relay lever, throttle to accelerator pump | 33 'O' ring, emulsion block to body |
| 10 Split pin securing relay lever to floating lever | 34 Special screw - } Securing emulsion |
| 11 Throttle stop and fast idle lever | 35 Spring washer - } block to body |
| 12 Special screw - } For throttle stop | 36 Top cover for carburettor |
| 13 Spring - } | 37 Gasket for top cover |
| 14 Throttle lever | 38 Ventilation screw (3.0 for choke) |
| 15 Lockwasher - } Securing | 39 Pump lever, internal |
| 16 Special nut - } throttle levers | 40 Retaining ring for pump lever |
| 17 Volume control screw | 41 Shakeproof washer - } Securing |
| 18 Spring for control screw | 42 Special nut - } pump lever |
| 19 Emulsion block | 43 Screw and spring washer, short - } |
| 20 Pump jet | 44 Screw and spring washer, long - } Securing top cover to main body |
| 21 Pump discharge valve | 45 Diaphragm for carburettor |
| 22 Plug for pump jet | 46 Gasket for diaphragm |
| 23 Piston for accelerator pump | 47 Spring for diaphragm |
| 24 Ball for piston | 48 Cover for diaphragm |
| | 49 Screw - } Securing |
| | 50 Spring washer - } diaphragm cover |
| | 51 Spindle and pin for choke lever |
| | 52 Lever and swivel for choke |
| | 53 Screw for choke lever swivel |
| | 54 Circlip securing choke lever to top cover |
| | 55 Spring, small - } For choke lever |
| | 56 Spring, large - } |
| | 57 Plain washer for choke spindle |
| | 58 Butterfly for choke |
| | 59 Special screw securing butterfly |
| | 60 Bracket and clip for choke cable |
| | 61 Clip for choke bracket |
| | 62 Special screw - } Securing choke |
| | 63 Shakeproof washer - } bracket to top cover |
| | 64 Spindle and lever for accelerator pump |
| | 65 Spacing washer for pump spindle |
| | 66 Pin - } Securing relay lever |
| | 67 Plain washer - } to pump lever |
| | 68 Split pin |

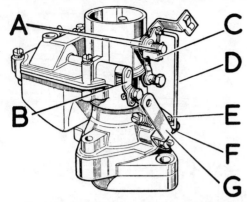

**Fig. 3.12. Zenith carburettor control linkage**

A  Choke linkage return springs
B  Accelerator pump spindle lever
C  Choke operating tab
D  Interconnecting link
E  Throttle spindle relay lever
F  Throttle spindle floating lever
G  Throttle lever

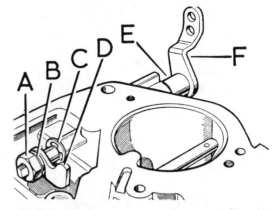

**Fig. 3.15. Accelerator pump spindle assembly (Zenith)**

A  Securing nut
B  Shakeproof washer
C  Circlip
D  Accelerator pump arm
E  Distance piece oilite bush
F  Spindle and lever for accelerator pump

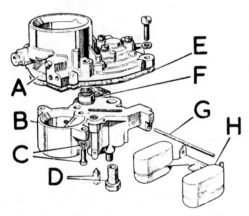

**Fig. 3.13. Zenith carburettor top cover and emulsion block**

A  Carburettor top cover
B  Emulsion block
C  Emulsion block attachment screws and washers
D  Needle valve and housing
E  Top cover gasket
F  Accelerator pump piston assembly
G  Hinge pin
H  Float assembly

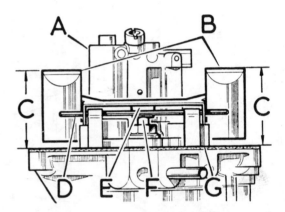

**Fig. 3.16. Checking the float setting (Zenith)**

A  Emulsion block
B  Highest points on floats
C  Dimension to be 1 5/16 in (33 mm)
D  Hinge pin
E  Central tongue on float carrier
F  Needle valve
G  Gasket

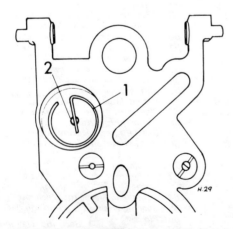

**Fig. 3.14. Location of accelerator pump ball and spring clip**

1  Retaining clip
2  Ball

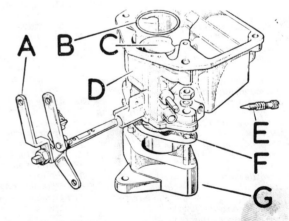

**Fig. 3.17. Carburettor body and adaptor (Zenith)**

A  Throttle control
B  'O' ring seal
C  Venturi barrel
D  Carburettor body
E  Volume control screw
F  Adaptor gasket
G  Adaptor body

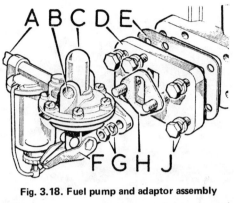

**Fig. 3.18. Fuel pump and adaptor assembly**

A Fuel inlet pipe
B Fuel outlet pipe
C Fuel pump
D Side cover
E Joint washer for side cover

F Hand prime lever
G Pump nuts
H Joint washer
J Bolts for side cover

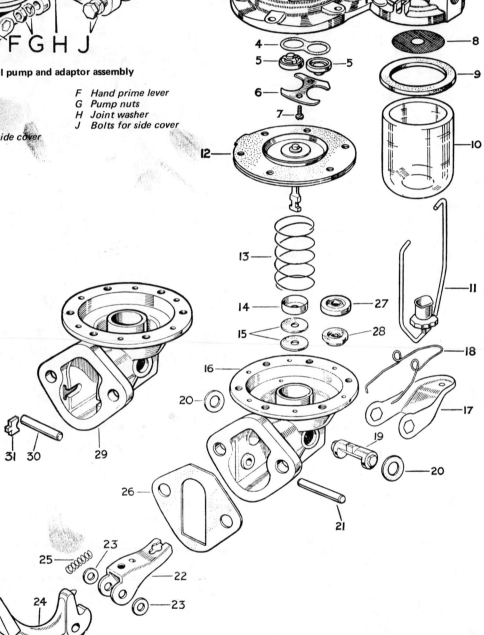

**Fig. 3.19. Exploded view of fuel pump**

| | | |
|---|---|---|
| 1 Top cover | 9 Lock sealing gasket | 17 Hand priming lever | 24 Rocker arm |
| 2 Securing screws | 10 Sediment bowl | 18 Return spring for hand lever | 25 Return spring |
| 3 Spring washer | 11 Bowl retainer | 19 Hand rocker | 26 Joint washer |
| 4 Valve gasket | 12 Diaphragm assembly | 20 Cork washers | 27 Oil seal retainer |
| 5 Valves | 13 Diaphragm spring | 21 Rocker arm pivot pin, early type | 28 Oil seal |
| 6 Retainer for valves | 14 Oil seal retainer | 22 Operating link | 29 Pump body |
| 7 Screw for retainer | 15 Sealing washers | 23 Plain washers | 30 Rocker arm pivot pin |
| 8 Gauge filter disc | 16 Pump body | | 31 Retainer for pivot pin |

5   Place the seal and retainer in the lower body and place the diaphragm spring over them.

6   Refit the diaphragm and pullrod assembly with the pullrod downwards and ensure the small tab on the diaphragm lines up to the previously noted position which should have been adjacent to the centre of the flange and rocker arm.

7   With the body of the pump held so that the rocker arm is facing away, press down the diaphragm, turning it a quarter of a turn to the left at the same time. This engages the slot on the pullrod with the operating lever. The small tab on the diaphragm should now be at an angle of 90º to the rocker arm and the diaphragm should be firmly located.

8   Move the rocker arm until the diaphragm is level with the body flanges and hold the arm in this position. Reassemble the two halves of the pump ensuring that the previously made marks on the flanges are adjacent to each other.

9   Insert the six screws and lockwashers and tighten them down finger tight.

10  Move the rocker arm up and down several times to centralise the diaphragm, and then with the arm held down, tighten the screws securely in a diagonal sequence.

11  Replace the gauze filter, cork washer and sediment bowl and refit the stirrup thumbscrew to the base of the sediment bowl. Tighten lightly only to ensure a fuel tight joint as overtightening will crack the bowl.

11.1 Removing the fuel pump filter bowl

## 11  Fuel filters - general

All models have a wire gauze filter in the glass bowl attached to the fuel pump. This should be removed as described in the previous Section and cleaned at the recommended service intervals (photo).

The Solex carburettor has a filter in the banjo union on the top cover (see photo). This should be removed and cleaned at periodic intervals.

On vehicles equipped with emission control (export models) a renewable fuel filter is fitted in the outlet pipe from the fuel pump. When fitting a new filter unit, ensure the end marked 'IN' is facing towards the fuel pump. If the filter is marked with an arrow this must point away from the pump.

## 12  Fuel gauge and sender unit

The fuel gauge and sender unit are integrated into the electrical system of the vehicle and therefore the description and all notes regarding the fuel sensor system are included in Chapter 10.

11.2 Filter in carburettor inlet pipe union

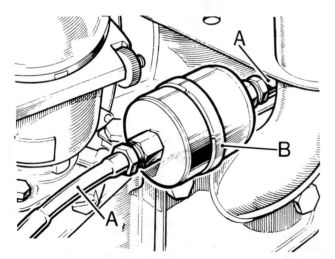

Fig. 3.20. Disposable fuel filter (models fitted with emission control)

A  Inlet and outlet fuel pipes          B  Securing clip

## 13  Fuel tank - description, removal and refitting

1   On the standard models the fuel tank is located on the right-hand side below the seat base. The station wagon models are fitted with a fuel tank at the rear right-hand side of the vehicle.

2   Always work on the fuel system in a well ventilated building or, preferably, outside. Pick a time when the tank is almost empty. Disconnect the battery earth lead before draining the petrol from the tank into a suitable container.

### Front mounted tank

3   Remove the right-hand side seat cushion and fold the seat squab forward.

4   Slacken the clips and pull the filler hose and breather hose off the tank unions.

5   Remove the cover panel and disconnect the fuel supply pipe union and the sender unit wire terminal (photo).

6   Support the weight of the tank, remove the securing bolts and carefully lower the tank and remove it from beneath the vehicle.

7   Refitting the tank is the reverse of the removal procedure. Do not forget to tighten the drain plug.

*Rear mounted tank*

8 Slacken the clip securing the filler hose to the tank and detach the hose.

9 Support the weight of the tank, remove the securing bolts and then lower the tank just enough to give access to the pipes and leads on the top of the tank.

10 Disconnect the fuel supply pipe, breather pipe, air balance pipe and the sender unit wire terminal.

11 Lower the tank to the ground and remove it from beneath the vehicle.

12 Refit the tank using the reverse of the removal procedure. Check the drain plug is tight and before attempting to start the engine, prime the carburettor with fuel using the priming lever on the pump.

## 14 Accelerator linkage - removal and refitting

1 Referring to Fig. 3.22, remove the throttle return spring and detach the ends of the two control rods from the cross-shaft, running across the rear engine compartment bulkhead.

**Note:** Two types of control rod end fittings are used, either the ball and socket type or the spring clip type.

2 Slacken the pinch bolt securing the operating lever to the accelerator pedal shaft and remove the lever. Undo the two bolts securing the shaft to the bulkhead and remove the pedal and shaft assembly from inside the vehicle.

3 Undo the bolts securing the cross-shaft to the rear bulkhead and remove the shaft complete with levers.

4 Examine the control rod ends for wear and the holes in the levers for ovality. If renewal is necessary, mark the position of the levers on the cross-shaft to ensure they are refitted at the correct angle. If adjustable socket type control rods are fitted mark the threads adjacent to the locknut before unscrewing the socket. This will enable the rod to be adjusted to the correct length when reassembling.

5 Refit the pedal and linkage using the reverse procedure to removal. With the linkage correctly installed check that the throttle flap in the carburettor is fully open when the accelerator pedal is pressed down onto the stop and fully closed when the pedal is released. Adjust the linkage as necessary.

6 Finally, run the engine until it is warm and adjust the carburettor controls as described in Section 7.

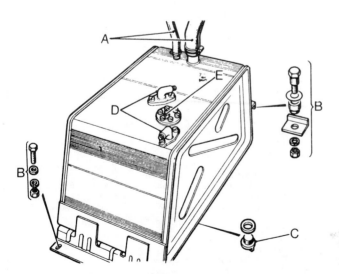

Fig. 3.21. Front mounted fuel tank

A  Filler and breather hoses    D  Fuel supply union (one only)
B  Securing bolts    E  Sender unit
C  Drain plug

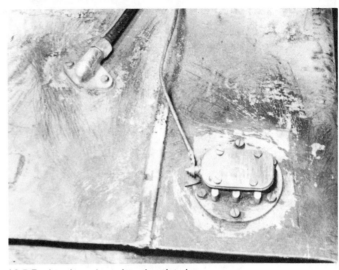

13.5 Fuel tank sender unit and outlet pipe

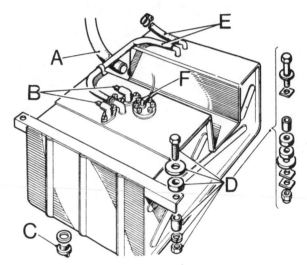

Fig. 3.22. Rear mounted fuel tank

A  Filler hose    D  Securing bolts
B  Fuel supply union (one only)    E  Breather and balance pipes
C  Drain plug    F  Sender unit

## 15 Exhaust system - general

The exhaust system on the 4-cylinder Land Rovers comprises basically of a front pipe clamped to the exhaust manifold, an intermediate pipe section leading into the silencer and tailpipe assembly. On models prior to 1961 the front pipe was fitted with two heat shields. Some models are fitted with a heat shield around the exhaust manifold (see Fig. 3.24).

The exhaust system should be examined periodically for corrosion and, when using the vehicle in rough terrain, damage. If any defects are found, the effected section of pipe (or the silencer) should be renewed.

The task of removing the exhaust system is straightforward as the pipe sections are connected by flanged joints, which are considerably easier to dismantle than the more common sleeve connections.

If any of the flange or bracket nuts are seized, try soaking them overnight in penetrating oil. If this fails they will have to be cut off with a hacksaw or cold chisel.

The exhaust and inlet manifolds are attached to the cylinder head by studs and nuts. Some of the lower nuts will require a socket and extension bar to remove them (photo).

On earlier models the manifold gasket is in one piece while on later models only the inlet manifold is fitted with gaskets. Always use new gaskets when refitting the manifolds.

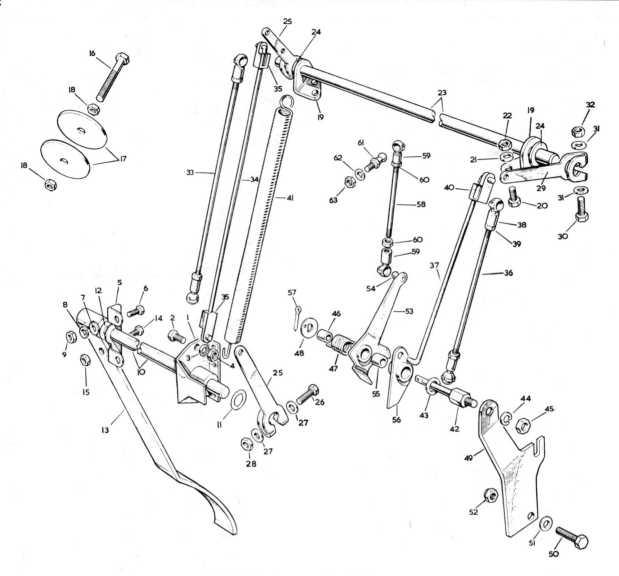

**Fig. 3.23. Accelerator pedal and linkage**

1 Housing for accelerator shaft and pedal stop
2 Bolt (¼ in UNF x ½ in long) -⎫ Securing housing and
3 Spring washer -⎬ pedal stop to dash
4 Nut (¼ in UNF) -⎭
5 Bracket for accelerator pedal shaft
6 Bolt (¼ in UNF x 5/8 in long) -⎫
7 Plain washer -⎬ Securing bracket
8 Spring washer -⎬ to dash
9 Nut (¼ in UNF) -⎭
10 Shaft for accelerator pedal
11 Special washer -⎫ On accelerator shaft
12 Plain washer -⎭
13 Accelerator pedal
14 Bolt (5/16 in UNF x 7/8 in long) -⎫ Securing pedal
15 Nut (5/16 in UNF) -⎭ to shaft
16 Bolt (5/16 in UNF x 1 1/8 in long) -⎫ Pedal stop
17 Plain washer -⎬ in floor
18 Nut (5/16 in UNF) -⎭
19 Bracket for accelerator cross-shaft, 'L' shaped
20 Bolt (¼ in UNF x 5/8 in long) -⎫
21 Spring washer -⎬ Securing bracket to dash
22 Nut (¼ in UNF) -⎭
23 Cross-shaft for accelerator
24 Distance washer for lever
25 Lever for accelerator
26 Bolt (¼ in UNF x 1¼ in long) -⎫
27 Plain washer -⎬ Securing levers to shaft
28 Nut (¼ in UNF) -⎭
29 Lever for cross-shaft
30 Bolt (¼ in UNF x 1¼ in long) -⎫ Securing lever to
31 Plain washer -⎬ cross-shaft
32 Nut (¼ in UNF) -⎭

33 Control rod, pedal shaft to cross-shaft
34 Control rod, pedal shaft to cross-shaft
35 Linkage clip for control rod
36 Control rod, cross-shaft to engine
37 Control rod, cross-shaft to engine
38 Balljoint socket for rods
39 Locknut for socket
40 Linkage clip for control rod, cross-shaft to engine
41 Return spring for pedal
42 Spindle for carburettor bell crank
43 Plain washer -⎫
44 Spring washer -⎬ Securing spindle
45 Nut (3/8 in UNF) -⎭
46 Spacer for spindle
47 Torsion spring for bell crank
48 Special washer for torsion spring
49 Bracket for accelerator controls
50 Bolt (3/8 in UNF x 1 in long) -⎫ Securing bracket to
51 Plain washer -⎬ steering column
52 Self-locking nut (3/8 in UNF) -⎭ support bracket
53 Carburettor bell crank lever assembly
54 Ball end for lever
55 Bush for bell crank
56 Carburettor relay lever
57 Split pin securing levers to spindle
58 Control rod, bell crank to carburettor
59 Balljoint -⎫ For control rod
60 Locknut (2 BA) -⎭
61 Ball end for carburettor lever
62 Spring washer -⎫ Securing ball end to
63 Nut (¼ in UNF) -⎬ carburettor lever

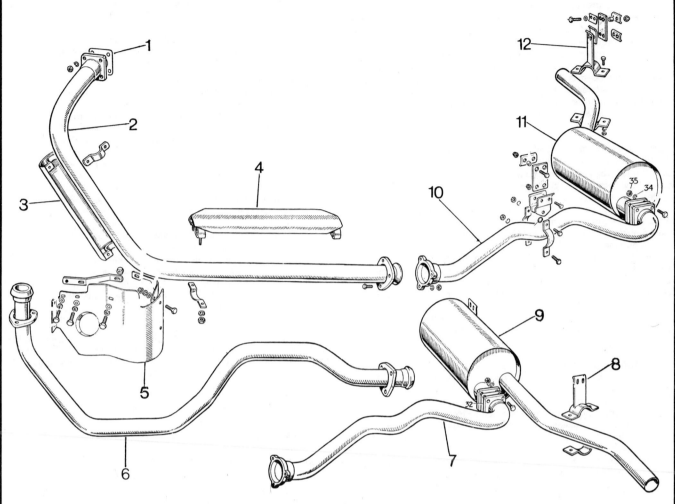

**Fig. 3.24. Exhaust system components**

| | | |
|---|---|---|
| 1   Gasket | 4   Rear heat shield | 7   Intermediate pipe ('88' models)    10   Intermediate pipe ('109' models) |
| 2   Front pipe (prior to 1961) | 5   Manifold heat shield assembly | 8   Bracket    11   Silencer (right-hand drive |
| 3   Front heat shield | 6   Front pipe (1961 onwards) | 9   Silencer (left-hand drive models)      models) |
| | | 12   Support bracket |

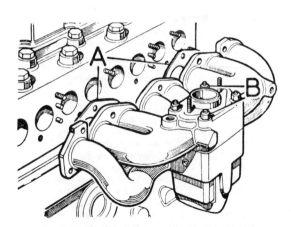

**Fig. 3.25. Inlet and exhaust manifold assembly**

A   Gaskets, late type shown. Position gaskets with raised rings
     towards cylinder head
B   Nuts, inlet manifold to exhaust manifold

15.5 A socket will be required to remove these exhaust manifold
securing nuts

## 16 Emission control systems - general

Export models of the Land Rover, (primarily for the USA) are fitted with various devices to reduce air pollution. Three separate systems can be fitted and these comprise; crankcase ventilation, fuel evaporation control and exhaust emission control. While the servicing procedures described in this Section can be carried out by the home mechanic, any alterations or major adjustments to the systems must be left to an authorised dealer to avoid contravening the pollution laws, which in certain countries are very strict.

### Crankcase emission control

This system consists of a hose connected between the sealed crankcase oil filler tube and the inlet manifold via a non-return valve. A second hose connects the breather on top of the rocker cover to the air cleaner elbow (see Fig. 3.26).

When the engine is running the fumes which collect in the crankcase are drawn into the combustion chambers via the inlet manifold. These are reburnt while clean air is admitted through the breather to assist in purging.

1 Every 12,000 miles (20,000 km), remove the clip securing the non-return valve cover, lift out the diaphragm and spring and clean the cover and the inside of the valve body with methylated spirits, taking care not to allow any of the methylated spirits to come into contact with the diaphragm.

2 Check the diaphragm for damage and renew if necessary. Refit the valve components and secure the cover with the spring clip.

### Fuel evaporation control

The purpose of this system is to prevent fuel vapour from the petrol tank escaping into the atmosphere.

A special filler cap is fitted to prevent loss of vapour and a breather pipe leads from the main fuel tank through an expansion tank into a charcoal canister in the engine compartment. A second pipe connects the top of the charcoal canister to the air cleaner. As fuel vapour builds up in the expansion tank it is fed into the canister and absorbed by the charcoal. When the engine is running the vapour in the charcoal is drawn into the combustion chambers via the air cleaner and inlet manifold. Air is drawn into the canister through a renewable filter.

3 Every 12,000 miles (20,000 km) the filter should be renewed. The canister is located at the rear of the engine compartment on the right-hand side. Note the respective positions of the two hoses and then remove them.

4 Remove the bolts securing the canister to the bracket and lift the canister away from the vehicle.

5 Unscrew the base of the canister and withdraw the filter (see Fig. 3.28). Fit the new filter with the smooth side facing inward.
**WARNING:** Do not attempt to clean the inside of the canister with compressed air as this may cause the charcoal filling to self-ignite.

6 Fit a new sealing ring, screw on the base and refit the canister into the engine compartment ensuring the pipe on the side of the canister faces towards the rear of the engine compartment.

### Exhaust emission control

Exhaust emission control is achieved by modifications to the carburettor and ignition system. In the case of the carburettor, the normal jets are replaced with ones having special flow characteristics and can be identified by their cadmium plated finish. To improve combustion on the overrun, a small servo unit is connected to a throttle prop lever on the carburettor and when the inlet manifold depression is high, (on the overrun) a trigger switch connected to the manifold actuates the servo unit, which causes the throttle prop lever to open the throttle flap a small amount thus improving the fuel/air mixture in the carburettor.

The engine idle speed on vehicles equipped with emission control has been increased to 750-800 rpm. To prevent running-on due to this high idle speed the idle by-pass drilling and progression chambers within the carburettor are cut off by a solenoid operated needle valve, whenever the ignition switch is turned off. The valve, which is located next to the mixture control screw (see Fig. 3.29) is preset and must not be adjusted.

7 The carburettor slow running adjustment is very important on vehicles equipped with emission control and should be checked every 6,000 miles (10,000 km) using the following procedure:

a) *Before adjusting the carburettor, ensure the valve clearances and ignition timing are correctly set and that the throttle linkage is free to move.*

b) *With the engine throughly warmed up, unlock the mixture control screw and turn it gently clockwise until it is fully in. Then screw it out for ¾ of a turn.*

c) *Adjust the throttle stop screw to obtain an idling speed of 800 rpm. A suitable tachometer must be used to obtain this setting.*

d) *Turn the mixture control either in or out as necessary to get the highest engine idle speed, and reset the idle speed to 800 rpm using the throttle stop screw.*

e) *Turn the mixture control screw clockwise until the idling speed drops to 750 rpm and then enrich the mixture slightly by turning the screw ¼ turn anticlockwise. Lock the mixture control screw.*

f) *Reset the idling speed to 800 rpm using the throttle stop screw and then lock it. Remove the tachometer and switch off the engine.*

Some changes were made to the ignition system of vehicles which have emission control systems. These are, a special distributor, and a throttle controlled vacuum switch. When the throttle is closed the switch opens the vacuum line to the distributor and retards the ignition. The purpose of this is to retard the ignition when the throttle is closed at high engine speeds.

8 To adjust the switch plunger position in relation to the cam on the throttle linkage, proceed as follows:

a) *First check that the throttle linkage is in the correct idle position.*

b) *Push the switch plunger right down into the switch and measure the clearance between the cam and the plunger. This should be 0.030 in (0.76 mm).*

c) *Adjust the clearance if necessary by slackening the nuts securing the switch mounting bracket to the inlet manifold. Move the switch and bracket assembly in the required direction. When the clearance is correct tighten the bracket securing nuts.*

The correct ignition timing on vehicles fitted with the exhaust emission control system is absolutely essential and the static timing method described in Chapter 4 is not accurate enough. It is strongly recommended that the vehicle is taken to a Leyland dealer, or engine tuning specialist who will have the electronic equipment necessary to do the job properly.

9 However, for the home mechanic who has a strobe lamp and tachometer, the ignition timing can be checked using the following procedure:

a) *Set the engine idling speed as close as possible to 800 rpm without exceeding this speed.*

b) *Set the vernier adjustment nut on the side of the distributor to the fully advanced position. This is to prevent the ignition being subsequently advanced beyond the correct setting.*

c) *Slacken the distributor clamping bolt and rotate the distributor until the flash of the strobe light, (which must be connected to No 1 plug lead) is synchronised with the 6⁰ ATDC timing pointer on the front engine cover and the mark on the crankshaft pulley (see Fig. 3.31).*

d) *Tighten the distributor clamping bolt and recheck the timing.*

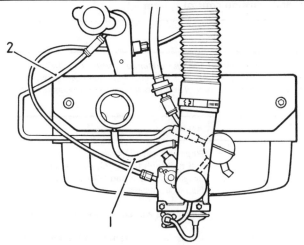

**Fig. 3.26. Crankcase emission control system**

1 Hose connecting breather to air cleaner hose
2 Hose and valve connecting oil filler pipe and inlet manifold

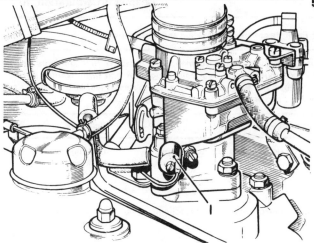

**Fig. 3.29. Fuel cut-off valve**

1 Location of valve

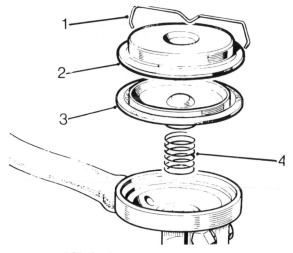

**Fig. 3.27. Crankcase emission valve components**

| 1 | Retaining clip | 3 | Diaphragm |
| 2 | Top cover | 4 | Coil spring |

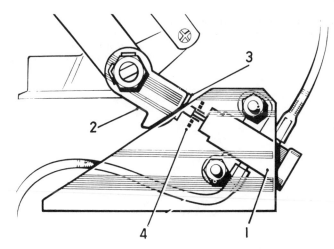

**Fig. 3.30. Throttle controlled vacuum switch**

| 1 | Vacuum switch | 3 | Switch plunger extended |
| 2 | Throttle linkage cam | 4 | Switch plunger retracted |

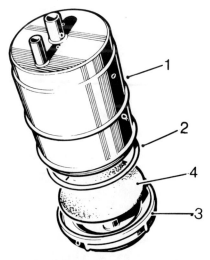

**Fig. 3.28. Charcoal filter canister**

| 1 | Main body | 3 | End cap |
| 2 | Sealing ring | 4 | Filter |

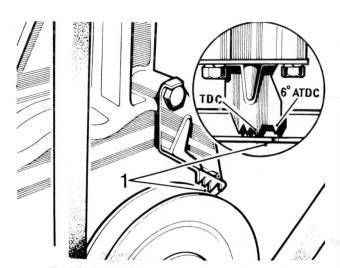

**Fig. 3.31. Timing pointer location (strobe lamp timing)**

1 Correct alignment of timing marks

## 17 Fault diagnosis - fuel system and carburation

*Unsatisfactory engine performance and excessive fuel consumption are not necessarily the fault of the fuel system or carburettor. In fact they more commonly occur as a result of ignition and timing faults. Before acting on the following it is necessary to check the ignition system first. Even though a fault may lie in the fuel system it will be difficult to trace unless the ignition is correct. The faults below therefore, assume that this has been attended to first (where appropriate).*

| Symptom | Reason/s | Remedy |
| --- | --- | --- |
| Smell of petrol when engine is stopped | Leaking fuel lines or unions<br>Leaking fuel tank | Repair or renew as necessary.<br>Fill fuel tank to capacity and examine carefully at seams, unions and filler pipe connections. Repair as necessary. |
| Smell of petrol when engine is idling | Leaking fuel line unions between pump and carburettor<br>Overflow of fuel from float chamber due to wrong level setting, ineffective needle valve or punctured float | Check line and unions and tighten or repair.<br>Check fuel level setting and condition of float and needle valve, and renew if necessary. |
| Excessive fuel consumption for reasons not covered by leaks or float chamber faults | Worn jets<br>Over-rich jet settings<br>Sticking mechanism | Renew jets or carburettor body if not removable.<br>Adjust jet.<br>Check correct movement of mechanism. |
| Difficult starting, uneven running, lack of power, cutting out | One or more jets blocked or restricted<br>Float chamber fuel level too low or needle valve sticking<br>Fuel pump not delivering sufficient fuel | Dismantle and clean out float chamber and jets.<br>Dismantle and check fuel level and needle valve.<br>Check pump delivery and clean or repair as required. |

# Chapter 4 Ignition system

*For modifications, and information applicable to later models, see Supplement at end of manual*

**Contents**

---

**Specifications**

### Distributor
| | |
|---|---|
| Contact breaker gap ... ... ... ... ... ... ... ... | 0.014 - 0.016 in (0.36 - 0.40 mm) |
| Rotation of rotor ... ... ... ... ... ... ... ... | Anti-clockwise |
| Centrifugal advance ... ... ... ... ... ... ... ... | Crankshaft angle      Engine rev/min |

| Crankshaft angle | Engine rev/min |
|---|---|
| $38^\circ$ to $42^\circ$ | 4500 |
| $30^\circ$ to $34^\circ$ | 3500 |
| $22^\circ$ to $26^\circ$ | 2500 |
| $12^\circ$ to $16^\circ$ | 1200 |
| $4^\circ$ to $12^\circ$ | 900 |
| $0^\circ$ to $4^\circ$ | 600 |
| No advance below | 450 |

**Vacuum advance:**
| | |
|---|---|
| Starts ... ... ... ... ... ... ... ... ... | 89 mm (3.5 in) Hg |
| Finishes ... ... ... ... ... ... ... ... ... | 635 mm (25.0 in) Hg |

### Static ignition timing
| | |
|---|---|
| 8.0 : 1 compression ratio ... ... ... ... ... ... ... | TDC using 90 octane fuel |
| | $3^\circ$ ATDC using 85 octane fuel |
| 7.0 : 1 compression ratio ... ... ... ... ... ... ... | $6^\circ$ BTDC using 90 octane fuel |
| | $3^\circ$ BTDC using 83 octane fuel |

### Firing order  ... ... ... ... ... ... ... ...   1 - 3 - 4 - 2

### Spark plugs
Type:
| | |
|---|---|
| 8.0 : 1 compression ratio ... ... ... ... ... ... | Champion UN12Y |
| 7.0 : 1 compression ratio ... ... ... ... ... ... | Champion N8 |
| Gap ... ... ... ... ... ... ... ... ... | 0.029 to 0.032 (0.75 to 0.80 mm) |

### Torque wrench setting
| | lb f ft | kg fm |
|---|---|---|
| Spark plugs ... ... ... ... ... ... ... ... | 25 | 3.5 |

---

## 1  General description

In order that the engine may run correctly it is necessary for an electrical spark to ignite the fuel/air mixture in the combustion chamber at exactly the right moment in relation to engine speed and load. The high tension voltage generated by the ignition system is powerful enough to jump the spark plug gap in the combustion chambers many times a second under high compression pressure, providing that the ignition system is in good working order and that all adjustments are correct.

The ignition system comprises two individual circuits known as the low tension circuit and the high tension circuit.

The low tension circuit (sometimes known as the primary circuit) comprises the battery, lead to ignition switch, lead to the low tension or primary coil windings and the lead from the low tension coil windings to the contact breaker points and condenser in the distributor.

The high tension circuit (sometimes known as the secondary circuit) comprises the high tension or secondary coil windings, the heavily insulated ignition lead from the centre of the coil to the centre of the distributor cap, the rotor arm, the spark plug leads and the spark plugs.

The complete ignition system operation is as follows:

Low tension voltage from the battery is changed within the ignition coil to high tension voltage by the opening and closing of the contact breaker points in the low tension circuit. High tension voltage is then fed via a contact in the centre of the distributor cap to the rotor arm of the distributor. The rotor arm revolves inside the distributor cap, and each time it comes in line with one of the four segments in the cap (these being connected to the spark plug leads) the opening and closing of the contact breaker points causes the high tension voltage to build up, jump the gap from the rotor arm to the appropriate segment and so, via the spark plug lead, to the spark plug where it finally jumps the gap between the two spark plug electrodes, one being connected to the earth system.

The ignition timing is advanced and retarded automatically to ensure the spark occurs at just the right instant for the particular load at the prevailing engine speed.

The ignition advance is controlled both mechanically and by a vacuum operated system. The mechanical governor mechanism comprises two weights which move out under centrifugal force from the central distributor shaft as the engine speed rises. As they move outwards they rotate the cams relative to the distributor shaft, and so advance the spark. The weights are held in position by two light springs, and it is the tension of the springs which is largely responsible for correct mechanical advancement.

The vacuum control comprises a diaphragm, one side of which is connected via a small bore tube to the carburettor, and the other side to the contact breaker plate. Depressions in the induction manifold and carburettor, which varies with engine speed and throttle opening, causes the diaphragm to move, so moving the control breaker plate and advancing or retarding the spark. A fine degree of control is achieved by a spring in the vacuum assembly.

## 2  Contact breaker points - adjustment

1   To adjust the contact breaker points so that the correct gap is obtained; first, release the two clips securing the distributor cap to the distributor body, and lift away the cap. Clean the inside and outside of the cap with a dry cloth. It is unlikely that the four segments will be badly burnt or scored, but if they are the cap should be renewed. If only small deposits are on the segments they may be scraped away using a small screwdriver.

2   Push in the carbon brush, located in the top of the cap, several times to ensure that it moves freely. The brush should protrude by at least 0.25 in (6.35 mm).

3   Gently press the contact breaker points open to examine the condition of their faces. If they are rough, pitted or dirty it will be necessary to remove them for resurfacing, or for new points to be fitted.

4   Presuming the points are satisfactory, or that they have been cleaned or renewed, measure the gap between the points by turning the engine over using the starting handle until the contact breaker arm is on the peak of one of the four cam lobes. A 0.014 - 0.016 in (0.36 - 0.41 mm) feeler gauge should now just fit between the points.

5   If the gap is either too wide or too small, slacken the screw securing the contact plate and adjust the gap by inserting a screwdriver in the notches shown in Fig. 4.1 and twist it in the appropriate direction until the gap is correct. Tighten the securing screw and re-check the gap (photo).

6   Refit the rotor arm and clip the distributor cap back into position.

2.5 Setting the contact breaking gap using a feeler gauge

## 3  Contact breaker points - renovation or renewal

1   If the contact breaker points are burnt, pitted or badly worn, they must be removed and either renewed or their faces must be filed smooth.

2   To remove the points first detach the distributor cap and rotor arm. Unscrew the terminal nut and remove it together with the washer under its head. Remove the flanged nylon bush, the condenser lead and the low tension lead from the terminal pin. Lift off the contact breaker arm and remove the large fibre washer from the terminal pin.

3   The adjustable contact breaker plate is removed by unscrewing one screw and then withdrawing the plate.

4   To reface the points, rub the faces on a fine carborundum stone, or on fine emery paper. It is important that the faces are rubbed flat and parallel to each other so that there will be complete face to face contact when the points are closed. One of the points will be pitted and the other will have deposits on it.

5   It is necessary to completely remove the built up deposits, but unnecessary to rub the pitted point right to the stage where all the pitting has disappeared, though obviously, if this is done it will prolong the time before the operation of refacing the points has to be repeated.

6   If the points are badly pitted or worn they should be renewed.

7   To refit the points: first, position the adjustable contact breaker plate and secure it with its screw, spring and flat washer. Fit the fibre washer to the terminal pin and fit the contact breaker arm over it. Insert the flanged nylon bush with the condenser lead immediately under its head, and the low tension lead under that, over the terminal pin. Fit the steel washer and screw on the securing nut.

8   The points are now reassembled and the gap should be set as detailed in Section 2.

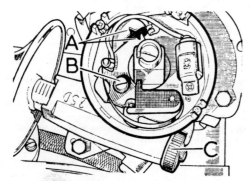

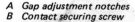

### Fig. 4.1. Contact breaker adjustment

A  Gap adjustment notches        C  Vernier advance adjusting nut
B  Contact securing screw

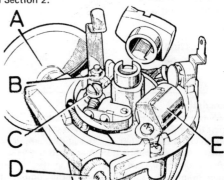

### Fig. 4.2. Distributor components

A  Vacuum advance unit           D  Advance adjusting nut
B  Contact breaker terminal      E  Condenser
C  Securing screw

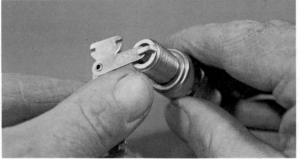

**Measuring plug gap.** A feeler gauge of the correct size (see ignition system specifications) should have a slight 'drag' when slid between the electrodes. Adjust gap if necessary

**Adjusting plug gap.** The plug gap is adjusted by bending the earth electrode inwards, or outwards, as necessary until the correct clearance is obtained. Note the use of the correct tool

**Normal.** Grey-brown deposits, lightly coated core nose. Gap increasing by around 0.001 in (0.025 mm) per 1000 miles (1600 km). Plugs ideally suited to engine, and engine in good condition

**Carbon fouling.** Dry, black, sooty deposits. Will cause weak spark and eventually misfire. Fault: over-rich fuel mixture. Check: carburettor mixture settings, float level and jet sizes; choke operation and cleanliness of air filter. Plugs can be re-used after cleaning

**Oil fouling.** Wet, oily deposits. Will cause weak spark and eventually misfire. Fault: worn bores/piston rings or valve guides; sometimes occurs (temporarily) during running-in period. Plugs can be re-used after thorough cleaning

**Overheating.** Electrodes have glazed appearance, core nose very white — few deposits. Fault: plug overheating. Check: plug value, ignition timing, fuel octane rating (too low) and fuel mixture (too weak). Discard plugs and cure fault immediately

**Electrode damage.** Electrodes burned away; core nose has burned, glazed appearance. Fault: pre-ignition. Check: as for 'Overheating' but may be more severe. Discard plugs and remedy fault before piston or valve damage occurs

**Split core nose (may appear initially as a crack).** Damage is self-evident, but cracks will only show after cleaning. Fault: pre-ignition or wrong gap-setting technique. Check: ignition timing, cooling system, fuel octane rating (too low) and fuel mixture (too weak). Discard plugs, rectify fault immediately

## 4 Condenser - testing, removal and refitting

1   The purpose of the condenser (sometimes known as a capacitor) is to ensure that when the contact breaker points open there is no sparking across them which would waste voltage and cause excessive wear.
2   The condenser is fitted in parallel with the contact breaker points. If it develops a short circuit, it will cause ignition failure, as the points will be prevented from interrupting the low tension circuit.
3   If the engine becomes very difficult to start, or begins to misfire after several miles running, and the breaker points show signs of excessive burning, then the condition of the condenser must be suspect. A further test can be made by separating the points by hand with the ignition switched on. If this is accompanied by a flash it is indicative that the condenser has failed.
4   Without special test equipment, the only sure way to diagnose condenser trouble is to replace a suspected unit with a new one and note if there is any improvement.
5   To remove the condenser from the distributor, remove the distributor cap and rotor arm. Unscrew the contact breaker arm terminal nut, remove the nut, washer, and flanged nylon bush and release the condenser (photo).
6   Undo and remove the condenser securing screw and lift away the condenser.
7   Refitting the condenser is simply a reversal of the removal procedure. Take particular care that the condenser lead does not short circuit against any portion of the breaker plate.

## 5 Distributor - lubrication

1   Periodically the distributor cam, spindle and advance mechanism should be lubricated to prevent possible seizure.
2   Remove the distributor cap and rotor arm, and inject a few drops of thin oil into the top of the cam spindle (photo). Apply a few more drops onto the side of the cam and allow it to run down through the contact breaker base plate, thus lubricating the advance mechanism beneath it (photo).
3   Lightly oil the moving contact pivot point. Wipe off any excess oil and refit the rotor arm and cap.

## 6 Distributor - removal and refitting

1   Disconnect the HT leads from the spark plugs and the centre terminal of the coil.
2   Disconnect the LT lead from the terminal on the side of the distributor.
3   Undo the pipe from the vacuum advance control.
4   To avoid altering the timing, use a scriber to mark the position of the bolt in the slotted plate that secures the distributor to the engine block.
5   Remove the bolt and lift out the distributor from its recess. **Do not** slacken the securing plate pinch bolt otherwise it will be necessary to re-set the ignition as described in Section 8.
6   To refit the distributor, line up the offset lugs on the distributor shaft with the offset slot in the top of the driveshaft visible in the engine recess (see Fig. 4.3).

7   With the distributor correctly installed in the cylinder block, insert the securing bolt and tighten it, making sure that the line scribed on the distributor plate is in its original position against the bolt head.

## 7 Distributor - dismantling and reassembly

1   Remove the distributor from the engine as described in Section 6.
2   Referring to Fig. 4.4, unhook the vacuum advance spring from the baseplate, remove the two securing screws and lift out the complete contact breaker and baseplate assembly, sliding the LT terminal from the distributor body at the same time.
3   Remove the small circlip from the end of the vernier adjusting nut and rotate the nut until the vacuum control assembly can be withdrawn from the distributor body; take care not to lose the small spring and ratchet.
4   Drive out the pin from the drive dog and remove the dog from the end of the shaft. Pull the shaft out from the top of the distributor complete with the advance mechanism.
5   To dismantle the centrifugal advance mechanism, remove the two springs from the counter-weights, after noting which spring fits which post. Undo the screw from the centre of the cam. Make a careful note of the slot above the cam in relation to the drive dog (temporarily refit the dog onto the shaft) and then remove the cam and plate assembly from the shaft. Note the distance collar on the shaft.
6   Examine all the components for wear or breakage. If the distributor is in a poor condition due to high mileage, it is best to renew it.
7   If a new driveshaft bush is to be fitted, the new bush must be left to soak in engine oil for 24 hours before installation. Drill an oil hole in the new bush using the old bush as a guide to its correct location.
8   Reassemble the distributor using the reverse procedure to dismantling. Lubricate the driveshaft before refitting, and if a new bush has been fitted, ensure that the shaft rotates freely. When fitting the centrifugal advance springs, take care not to stretch them any more than absolutely necessary.
9   Note that one of the baseplate screws is also used to secure the earthing wire.
10 Check the contact breaker gap as described in Section 2 and refit the distributor to the engine (see Section 6).

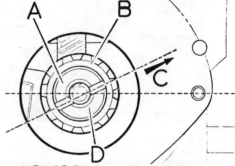

**Fig. 4.3. Distributor drive coupling**

A   Top drive coupling          C   No. 1 cylinder
B   Vertical drive gear          D   Narrow segment of coupling

4.5 Removing the condenser lead

5.2a Lubricating the cam spindle
Centrifugal advance mechanism

5.2b Contact breaker base plate removal

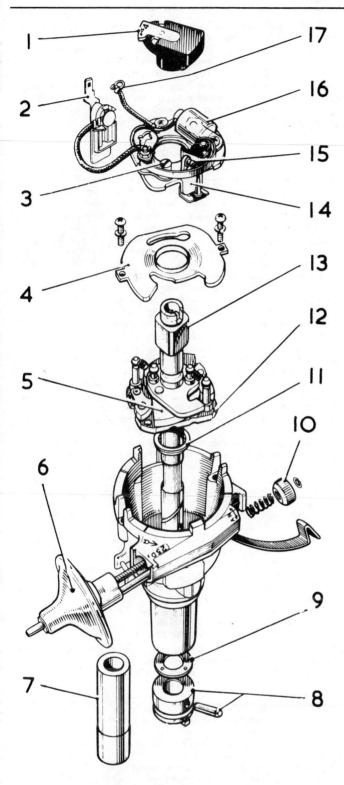

Fig. 4.4. Exploded view of distributor

| | | | |
|---|---|---|---|
| 1 | Rotor arm | 9 | Thrust washer |
| 2 | LT terminal | 10 | Vernier adjustment nut |
| 3 | Fixed contact plate securing | 11 | Distance collar |
| | screw | 12 | Baseplate |
| 4 | Contact breaker baseplate | 13 | Cam |
| 5 | Centrifugal advance control | 14 | Contact breaker moving plate |
| | weights and mechanism | 15 | Contacts |
| 6 | Vacuum advance control unit | 16 | Condenser |
| 7 | Bearing bush | 17 | CB earth connector |
| 8 | Driving dog and pin | | |

## 8 Ignition timing - adjustment

1 The first procedure is to ascertain that the No. 1 piston is on its compression stroke. To do this, remove the front cylinder spark plug and with a finger held over the plug hole, have a friend turn the engine over with the starting handle, until pressure is felt on the finger.

2 On earlier engines, remove the small plate on the right-hand side of the flywheel housing and continue to rotate the engine until the appropriate TDC or octane mark on the flywheel is aligned with the pointer (see Fig. 4.5).

3 On later engines the TDC marks are on a pointer attached to the front timing cover and a notch on the crankshaft pulley. These should be lined up as shown in Fig. 4.6.

4 Remove the distributor cap and connect a test lamp between the coil LT lead to the distributor and a good earth.

5 Slacken the distributor clamp pinch bolt.

6 Switch on the ignition and turn the distributor body in the required direction until the test lamp just lights up, indicating the points have just opened.

7 Tighten the pinch bolt taking care not to alter the position of the distributor. Switch off the ignition and remove the test lamp.

8 Refit the distributor cap.

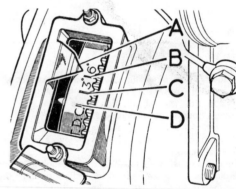

4.5 Timing pointer on flywheel housing (earlier engines)

A    Timing pointer
B    6° mark, align when using 90 - 96 octane fuel
C    3° mark, align when using 80 - 85 octane fuel
D    TDC mark, align when using 74 - 76 octane fuel

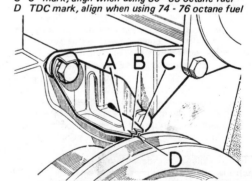

Fig. 4.6. Timing pointer on front timing chain cover (later engines)

A    6° tongue, align when using 90 - 96 octane fuel
B    3° tongue, align when using 80 - 85 octane fuel
C    TDC tongue, align when using 74 - 76 octane fuel
D    Mark on crankshaft pulley, align with appropriate tongue

## 9 Coil - general

The coil is located inside the engine compartment and attached to the rear bulkhead by two screws (photo).

Periodically check that the centre HT lead is firmly in place and the two LT terminals are clean and tight.

If the coil is suspect, the best method of checking it is to temporarily exchange for one that is known to be good and then check if there is any improvement in engine efficiency.

9.1 Location of ignition coil

## 10 Spark plugs and HT leads

The correct functioning of the spark plugs is vital for the proper running and efficient operation of the engine.

At regular intervals the plugs should be removed, examined, cleaned, and if worn excessively, renewed. The condition of the spark plugs can also tell much about the general condition of the engine.

If the insulator nose of the spark plug is clean and white, with no deposits, this is indicative of a weak mixture, or too hot a plug (a hot plug transfers heat away from the electrodes slowly - a cold plug transfers heat away quickly).

If the insulator nose is covered with hard black looking deposits, then this is indicative that the mixture is too rich. Should the plug be black and oily then it is likely that the engine is worn, as well as the mixture being too rich.

If the insulator nose is covered with light tan to greyish brown deposits, then the mixture is correct, and it is likely that the engine is in good condition.

If there are any traces of long brown tapering stains on the outside of the white portion of the plug, then the plug will have to be renewed, as this shows that there is a faulty joint between the plug body and the insulator and compression is being allowed to leak away.

Plugs should be cleaned by a sand blasting machine, which will free them from carbon completely. The machine will also test the condition of the plugs under compression. Any plug that fails to spark at the recommended pressure should be renewed.

The spark plug gap is of considerable importance, as, if it is too large, or too small, the size of spark and its efficiency will be seriously impaired. The spark plug gap should be set as recommended in the 'Specifications' Section at the beginning of this Chapter.

1   To set it, measure the gap with a feeler gauge, and then bend open, or close, the outer plug electrode until the correct gap is obtained. The centre electrode must never be bent as this will crack the insulation and cause plug failure if nothing worse.

2   When refitting the plugs, remember to use new washers and refit the leads from the distributor cap in the correct firing order, which is 1 3 4 2 - number 1 cylinder being the one nearest the fan.

3   The plug leads require no maintenance other than being kept clean and wiped over regularly. At regular intervals, however, pull each lead off the plug in turn and remove them from the distributor cap. Water can seep down their joints giving rise to a white corrosive deposit which must be carefully removed from the end of each cable.

## 11 Fault diagnosis - ignition system (general)

By far the majority of breakdowns and running troubles are caused by faults in the ignition system either in the low tension or high tension circuits.

There are two main symptoms indicating ignition faults. Either the engine will not start or fire, or the engine is difficult to start and misfires. If it is a regular misfire, ie. the engine is running on only two or three cylinders, the fault is almost certain to be in the secondary or high tension circuit. If the misfiring is intermittent, the fault could be in either the high or low tension circuits. If the vehicle stops suddenly, and will not start at all, it is likely that the fault is in the low tension circuit. Loss of power and overheating, apart from faulty combustion settings, are normally due to faults in the distributor or to incorrect ignition timing.

## 12 Fault diagnosis - engine fails to start

1   If the engine fails to start and the car was running normally when it was last used, first check there is fuel in the petrol tank. If the engine turns over normally on the starter motor and the battery is evidently well charged, then the fault may be in either the high or low tension ignition circuits. First check the HT circuit. **Note:** If the battery is known to be fully charged, the ignition light comes on, and the starter motor fails to turn the engine, **check the tightness of the leads on the battery terminals** and also the secureness of the earth lead at its **connection to the body.** It is quite common for the leads to have worked loose, even if they look and feel secure. If one of the battery terminal posts gets very hot when trying to work the starter motor this is a sure indication of a faulty connection to that terminal.

2   One of the more common reasons for bad starting is wet or damp spark plug leads and/or distributor. Remove the distributor cap and if condensation is visible internally dry the cap with a rag and also wipe over the leads. Replace the cap.

3   If the engine still fails to start, check that current is reaching the plugs, by disconnecting each plug lead in turn at the spark plug end, and holding the end of the cable about 3/16 inch (5 mm) away from the cylinder block. Spin the engine on the starter motor.

4   Sparking between the end of the cable and the block should be fairly strong with a strong regular blue spark. (Hold the lead with rubber to avoid electric shocks). If current is reaching the plugs, then remove them, and clean and regap them. The engine should now start.

5   If there is no spark at the plug leads take off the HT lead from the centre of the distributor cap and hold it to the block as before. Spin the engine on the starter once more. A rapid succession of blue sparks between the end of the lead and the block indicates that the coil is in order and that the distributor cap is cracked, the rotor arm faulty, or the brush in the top of the distributor cap is not making good contact with the rotor arm. Possibly the points are in bad condition. Clean and reset them as described in Sections 2 and 3 of this Chapter.

6   If there are no sparks from the end of the lead from the coil, check the connection at the coil end of the lead. If it is in order start checking the low tension circuit.

7   Use a 12v voltmeter or a 12v bulb and two lengths of wire. With the ignition switched on and the points open, test between the low tension wire to the coil (it is marked SW) and earth. No reading indicates a break in the supply from the ignition switch. Check the connections at the switch to see if any are loose. Refit them and the engine should run. A reading shows a faulty coil or condenser, or broken lead between the coil and the distributor.

8   Take the condenser wire off the points assembly terminal and with the points open test between the moving point and earth. If there now is a reading, then the fault is in the condenser. Fit a new one and the fault should be cleared.

9   With no reading from the moving point to earth, take a reading between the earth and CB terminal of the coil. A reading here shows a broken wire which will need to be renewed between the coil and distributor. No reading confirms that the coil has failed and must be renewed, after which the engine will run once more. Remember to refit the condenser wire to the points assembly terminal. For this test it is sufficient to separate the points with a piece of thin, dry, card while testing with the points open.

## 13 Fault diagnosis - engine misfires

1   If the engine misfires regularly run it at a fast idling speed. Pull off each of the plug caps in turn and listen to the note of the engine. Hold the plug cap in a dry cloth or with a rubber glove as additional protection against a shock from the HT supply.

2   No difference in engine running will be noticed when the lead from the defective circuit is removed. Removing the lead from one of the good cylinders will accentuate the misfire.

3   Remove the plug lead from the end of the defective plug and hold it about 3/16 inch (5 mm) away from the block. Re-start the engine. If the sparking is fairly strong and regular the fault must lie in the spark plug.

4   The plug may be loose, the insulation may be cracked, or the points may have burnt away giving too wide a gap for the spark to jump. Worse still, one of the points may have broken off. Either renew the plug, or clean it, reset the gap and then test it.

5   If there is no spark at the end of the plug lead, or if it is weak and intermittent, check the ignition lead from the distributor to the plug. If the insulation is damaged renew the lead. Check the connections at the distributor cap.

6   If there is still no spark, examine the distributor cap carefully for tracking. This can be recognised by a very thin black line running between two, or more, electrodes; or between an electrode and some other part of the distributor cap. These lines are paths which now conduct electricity across the cap thus letting it run to earth. The only answer is a new distributor cap.

7   Apart from the ignition timing being incorrect, other causes of misfiring have already been dealt with under the section dealing with the failure of the engine to start. To recap, these are:

a)   *The coil may be faulty giving an intermittent misfire.*
b)   *There may be a damaged wire or loose connection in the low tension circuit.*
c)   *The condenser may be short circuiting.*
d)   *There may be a mechanical fault in the distributor (broken driving spindle or contact breaker spring).*

8   If the ignition timing is too far retarded, it should be noted that the engine will tend to overheat, and there will be quite a noticeable drop in power. If the engine is overheating and the power is down, and the ignition timing is correct, then the carburettor should be checked, as it is likely that this is where the fault lies.

# Chapter 5 Clutch

**Contents**

**Specifications**

| | |
|---|---|
| **Clutch type** ... ... ... ... ... ... ... ... ... | Borg and Beck single dry plate with coil spring pressure plate (diaphragm-type pressure plate optional) |
| **Operation** ... ... ... ... ... ... ... ... ... | Hydraulically actuated by a clutch mounted slave cylinder |
| **Diameter** ... ... ... ... ... ... ... .. ... ... | Coil spring type, 9 in (230 mm). Diaphragm spring type, 9½ in (241 mm) |
| **Driven plate** | |
| Lining thickness when new ... ... ... ... ... ... ... | 0.330 in (8.38 mm) |
| Maximum permissible thickness ... ... ... ... ... ... | 0.120 in (3.0 mm) |
| **Pressure plate** | |
| Re-grinding limit ... ... ... ... ... ... ... ... | 0.10 in (0.25 mm) undersize |
| Minimum thickness ... ... ... ... ... ... ... ... | 1.531 in (39 mm) |
| **Master cylinder** | |
| Type ... ... ... ... ... ... ... ... ... ... | Girling, with integral or separate reservoir |
| Bore ... ... ... ... ... ... ... ... ... ... | 0.75 in (19 mm) |
| Stroke ... ... ... ... ... ... ... ... ... ... | 1.375 in (35 mm) |
| **Slave cylinder** | |
| Type ... ... ... ... ... ... ... ... ... ... | Girling |
| Bore ... ... ... ... ... ... ... ... ... ... | 0.875 in (22 mm) |

| **Torque wrench setting** | lb f ft | kg f m |
|---|---|---|
| Clutch cover bolts ... ... ... ... ... ... ... ... | 22 - 25 | 3 - 3.5 |

## 1 General description

The Series II and IIA Land Rovers are fitted with either the 9 inch (230 mm) diameter clutch (standard), or the 9.5 inch (241 mm) diameter clutch (optional). The pressure plate on the 9 inch (230 mm) clutch is actuated by coil springs while the 9.5 inch (241 mm) type is fitted with a diaphragm type spring.

The Series III models are equipped with the 9.5 inch (241 mm) clutch as standard.

The clutch is hydraulically operated by a master cylinder connected to the clutch pedal. A single pipe line from the master cylinder supplies hydraulic fluid to a slave cylinder attached to the clutch bellhousing.

When the clutch pedal is pushed down, the slave cylinder actuating linkage partially rotates the clutch release shaft located in a casting at the rear of the clutch bellhousing. A fork attached to the shaft then pushes the clutch release sleeve and bearing forward against the thrust plate forks (coil spring type) on the centre of the diaphragm (later types). This causes the pressure plate to move rearwards, releasing its grip on the drive plate and enabling it to turn freely on the input

shaft without transmitting drive to the gearbox.

When the clutch pedal is released slowly, the pressure plate moves forward and progressively clamps the drive plate against the flywheel face, thus transmitting engine power to the gearbox.

## 2 Clutch pedal - height adjustment

1 The height of the clutch pedal from the floor is correctly set at the factory and should not normally require adjustment. However, if it is suspected that the pedal height is incorrect, it can be checked using the following method.

2 Refer to Fig. 5.2 and measure the distance between the bottom of the clutch pedal and the floor. If adjustment is necessary, slacken the locknut on the pedal stop bolt (Fig. 5.2) and screw it in or out until the correct pedal height is achieved; then tighten the locknut.

3 On models fitted with an adjustable master cylinder pushrod, the clearance between the pushrod end and the master cylinder piston should be 1/16 in (1.5 mm). To adjust the clearance, slacken the two nuts securing the rod to the clutch pedal and rotate the rod until the specified clearance is obtained. Then tighten the locknuts.

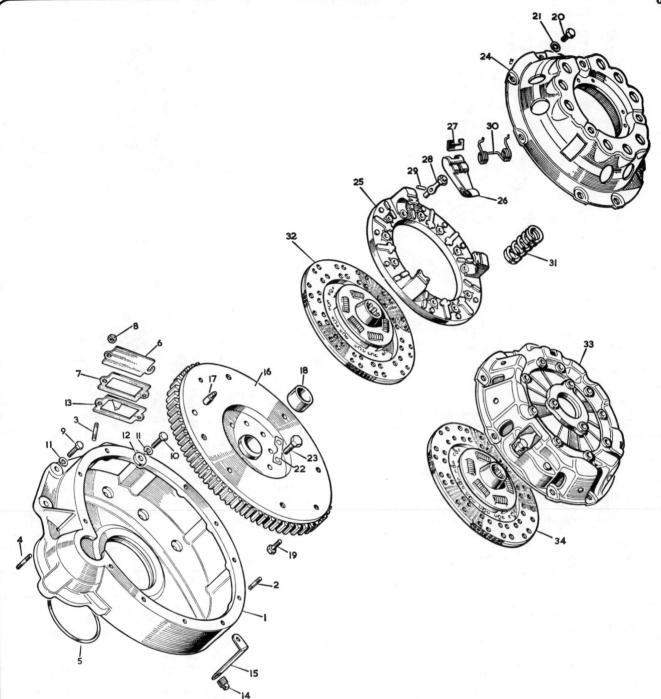

**Fig. 5.1. Exploded view of early and later type clutch assemblies**

1  Flywheel housing
2  Stud fixing flywheel housing to bellhousing
3  Stud for inspection cover
4  Stud for starter motor
5  Sealing ring for flywheel housing
6  Inspection cover plate (early type engines)
7  Joint washer for cover plate
8  Nut for cover plate
9  Bolt                    ⎫ Fixing
10 Bolt                    ⎬ flywheel
11 Spring washer           ⎪ housing to
12 Plain washer            ⎭ cylinder block
13 Indicator for engine timing (early type engines)
14 Drain plug for housing
15 Stowage bracket for drain plug. On later engines the plug is
   stowed in a blind tapping in the flywheel housing
16 Flywheel assembly
17 Dowel locating clutch cover plate

18 Bush for primary pinion
19 Special fitting bolt fixing clutch cover plate, applicable to certain
   models only
20 Set bolt
21 Spring washer
22 Lock tab
23 Special set bolt
24 Cover plate for coil spring type clutch
25 Pressure plate
26 Release lever
27 Strut for release lever
28 Eyebolt and nut for release lever
29 Pin for release lever
30 Anti-rattle spring for release lever
31 Clutch coil spring (9 off)
32 Clutch driven plate
33 Diaphragm spring type clutch
34 Clutch driven plate

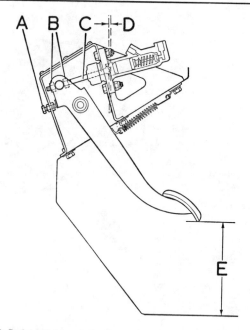

**Fig. 5.2. Pedal height and clutch master cylinder push rod adjustments**

A  *Pedal position setting bolt*
B  *Master cylinder push rod locknuts*
C  *Master cylinder push rod*
D  *Free-play 1/16 in (1.5 mm)*
E  *Models with non-hydrostatic clutch mechanism: 6¼ in (158 mm)*
   *Models with hydrostatic clutch mechanism: 5½ in (140 mm)*

### 3  Clutch - adjustment

1   On earlier models the clutch thrust bearing clearance is adjusted by altering the length of the slave cylinder operating rod, while later models are fitted with a self-adjusting clutch mechanism. This system only requires adjustment when a new drive plate is fitted. The earlier adjustable type slave cylinder can be identified by the support bracket which partially encloses it (see Fig. 5.3).
2   To adjust the earlier type clutch, slacken the locknut on the slave cylinder pushrod, (Fig. 5.4) and rotate the pushrod in the required direction to obtain 1.5 in (38 mm) free movement on the clutch pedal, i.e. the pedal can be pushed down freely for 1.5 in before the resistance of the clutch release mechanism is felt.
3   As stated previously, the later type clutch release mechanism only requires setting up after fitting a new clutch plate.
4   Referring to Fig. 5.5, slacken locknut 'E' and, holding the clutch operating lever down to eliminate any backlash, rotate the pushrod in the required direction until the dimension 'C' is obtained. Hold the push rod firmly and tighten the locknut.
5   There is no adjustment on the Series III slave cylinder pushrod. However, the clutch pedal height, and master cylinder pushrod should be adjusted as described in Section 2.

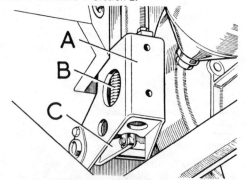

**Fig. 5.3. Earlier type slave cylinder location**

A  *Support bracket enclosing slave cylinder*
B  *Return spring for operating lever*
C  *Straight operating lever*

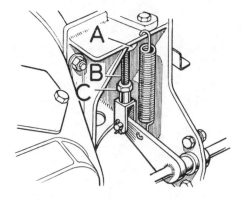

**Fig. 5.4. Clutch adjustment - earlier type**

A  *Slave cylinder*            C  *Locknut for push rod*
B  *Push rod*

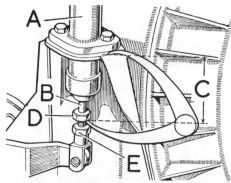

**Fig. 5.5. Hydrostatic type clutch adjustment (later Series II and IIA models)**

A  *Slave cylinder*
B  *Push rod*
C  *2 7/8 in (73.4 mm). Check dimension with calipers as shown*
D  *Nut must be at end of push rod thread*
E  *Lock nut for push rod*

### 4  Clutch hydraulic system - bleeding

1   Obtain a clean glass jar, a length of rubber/plastic tubing which fits tightly over the bleed nipple on the slave cylinder, and a tin of the correct type of hydraulic brake fluid. You will also need the help of an assistant.
2   Check that the master cylinder reservoir is full. If it is not, fill it and also fill the bottom two inches of the jar with hydraulic fluid.
3   Remove the rubber dust cap from the bleed nipple on the slave cylinder, and, with a suitable spanner, open the bleed nipple approximately three-quarters of a turn.
4   Place one end of the tube over the nipple and insert the other end in the jar so that the tube orifice is below the level of the fluid.
5   The assistant should now depress the pedal and hold it down at the end of its stroke. Close the bleed screw and allow the pedal to return to its normal position.
6   Continue this series of operations until clean hydraulic fluid, without any trace of air bubbles, emerges from the end of the tubing. Be sure that the reservoir is checked frequently to ensure that the hydraulic fluid does not drop too far, thus letting air into the system.
7   When no more air bubbles appear, tighten the bleed nipple during a downstroke.
8   Refit the rubber dust cap over the bleed nipple.

### 5  Clutch pedal - removal and refitting

1   The clutch pedal can only be removed complete with the master cylinder and mounting bracket and reference should be made to Section 6 of this Chapter which describes the removal procedure.
2   To remove the clutch pedal from the mounting bracket assembly, first remove the top plate from the bracket, remove the nut securing

the pushrod to the pedal and push the rod into the master cylinder until it is clear of the pedal trunnion.
3  Using a small pin punch, drive out the pin from the end of the pedal shaft (see Fig. 5.6).
4  Tap out the pedal shaft from the bracket and remove the pedal.
5  Examine the pedal shaft and bushes for wear and renew if necessary.
6  Refit the pedal, bracket and master cylinder assembly using the reverse procedure to removal.

## 6  Clutch master cylinder - removal and refitting

1  Two types of master cylinder are fitted to the Land Rover. The earlier type has a separate reservoir clamped to the master cylinder bracket (photo), while the later type has an integral reservoir. The internal components of both types of master cylinder are the same. **Note:** On vehicles with left-hand drive it is necessary to remove the left-hand front wing before the master cylinder assembly can be removed, (see Chapter 12).
2  If a separate reservoir is fitted, first undo the brake and clutch outlet pipe unions and allow the fluid to drain into a suitable container. Remove the nut retaining the reservoir clamp to the bracket and lift off the reservoir and clamp. Take care not to spill any fluid onto the paintwork as it acts as a solvent.
3  Remove the clutch fluid outlet pipe from the master cylinder body (also the inlet pipe if a separate reservoir is fitted).
4  On left-hand drive models, remove the bolts securing the master cylinder bracket to the bulkhead and disconnect the pedal return spring (see Fig. 5.7). The complete master cylinder, bracket and pedal assembly can now be removed from the vehicle.
5  In the case of right-hand drive vehicles, remove the top cover plate from the master cylinder bracket, undo the retaining nut and push the operating rod back into the master cylinder, until it is clear of the clutch pedal trunnion.
6  Remove the two bolts securing the master cylinder to the bracket and lift out the master cylinder.
7  Refitting is the reverse of the removal procedure, however, make sure that the pedal height and pushrod clearance dimensions are adjusted as described in Section 2.
8  Do not forget to bleed the system (Section 4).

## 7  Clutch master cylinder - dismantling, examination and reassembly

1  Before dismantling the master cylinder, spread a clean sheet of paper on the workbench and lay each component out in the order of removal from the cylinder.
2  Pull the rubber boot off the end of the cylinder and remove the circlip from inside the cylinder. The pushrod and retaining washer can now be withdrawn (see Fig. 5.9).
3  Tap the cylinder body gently on a wooden surface until the piston emerges from the end of the cylinder. Withdraw the complete piston, spring and valve assembly.
4  To remove the piston from the spring and valve assembly, prise up the locking tag on the spring retainer until it is clear of the piston shoulder and pull off the spring and retainer from the piston (see Fig. 5.10).
5  Make a note of the correct way the seal is fitted to the piston and then ease it off using the fingers only.
6  Disengage the valve stem from the spring retainer by compressing the spring and positioning the stem so that it can pass through the larger hole in the retainer (see Fig. 5.11).
7  Slide the valve spacer and spring washer off the stem and remove the seal from the valve assembly (see Fig. 5.12).
8  Thoroughly wash all parts with hydraulic fluid or methylated spirit and wipe dry.
9  Carefully examine all parts, especially the piston cups, for signs of distortion, swelling, splitting or other wear and check the piston and cylinder for wear or scoring. Renew any parts that are suspect. It is recommended, that, whenever a master cylinder is dismantled, new rubber seals are always fitted.
10 When reassembling the components to the master cylinder all components to be fitted must be lubricated with clean hydraulic fluid.

11 Fit a new seal onto the valve head and slide the spring washer and valve spacer onto the valve stem (Fig. 5.13).
12 Refit the piston return spring centrally on the spacer, insert the retainer into the spring and depress it until the valve stem engages in the keyhole of the retainer.
13 Ensure that the spring is central on the spacer before fitting a new piston seal onto the piston.
14 Insert the reduced end of the piston into the retainer until the leaf engages under the shoulder of the plunger, and press home the leaf.
15 Check that the master cylinder bore is clean and smear with clean hydraulic fluid. With the piston suitably wetted with hydraulic fluid, carefully insert the assembly into the bore, valve end first. Ease the lips of the piston seal carefully into the bore.
16 Refit the pushrod and the circlip into the groove in the cylinder bore. Smear the sealing areas of the dust cover with a little rubber grease and pack the cover with the rubber grease so as to act as a dust trap. Fit the cover to the master cylinder body. The master cylinder is now ready for refitting to the vehicle.

## 8  Clutch slave cylinder - removal and refitting

1  Wipe the top of the clutch master cylinder, unscrew the cap and place a piece of polythene sheet over the top to stop hydraulic fluid syphoning out when the slave cylinder is removed. Refit the cap.

### Series II and IIA
2  Remove the right-hand side front floor panel as described in Chapter 1.
3  Undo the hydraulic fluid pipe union from the slave cylinder and tape over the end to prevent dirt ingress.
4  Undo the two retaining nuts and withdraw the slave cylinder from the bracket and pushrod.

### Series III
5  Access to the slave cylinder on Series III vehicles is gained from beneath the clutch bellhousing; if it is necessary to jack the vehicle up, make sure it is firmly supported on heavy duty axle stands.
6  Disconnect the bleed pipe and fluid pipe from the slave cylinder and tape over the ends to prevent dirt ingress.
7  Release the plastic clip from the clutch release lever and slide it back along the slave cylinder pushrod.
8  Remove the two securing bolts and lift the slave cylinder away from the clutch housing.
9  Refitting both types of slave cylinder is the reverse procedure to removal. In the case of the Series II and IIA type, make sure the pushrod is correctly located in the slave cylinder piston and adjusted as described in Section 3. Bleed the clutch hydraulic system on both types as described in Section 4.

6.1 Combined clutch and brake reservoir, (earlier models)

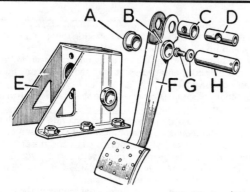

Fig. 5.6. Clutch pedal components

A  Pedal bush
B  Locating pin
C  Trunnion distance piece
D  Pedal trunnion

E  Pedal bracket
F  Clutch pedal
G  Oil plug and joint washer
H  Pedal shaft

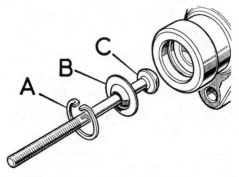

Fig. 5.9. Master cylinder push rod assembly

A  Circlip              C  Push rod
B  Retaining washer

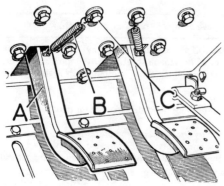

Fig. 5.7. Location of clutch pedal bracket retaining bolts and return spring

A  Clutch pedal          C  Bracket bolts (6 off)
B  Pedal return spring

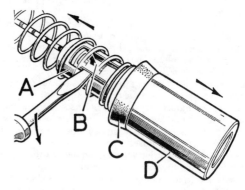

Fig. 5.10. Releasing the return spring from the piston

A  Spring retainer       C  Seal
B  Locking tag           D  Piston

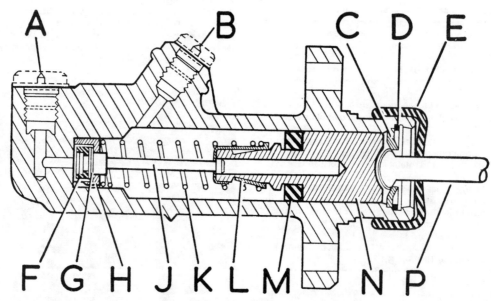

Fig. 5.8. Cross-section of clutch master cylinder

A  Inlet port
B  Outlet port
C  Spring washer
D  Circlip

E  Dust cover
F  Valve seal
G  Spring washer

H  Valve spacer
J  Valve stem
K  Return spring

L  Spring retainer
M  Piston seal
N  Piston
P  Push rod

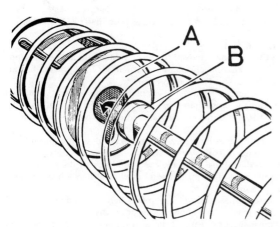

**Fig. 5.11. Location of valve stem in spring retainer**

A   Retainer                              B   Valve stem

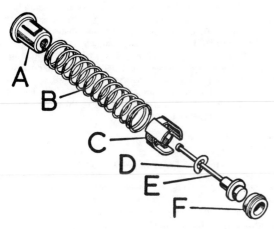

**Fig. 5.12. Valve and spring components**

A   Spring retainer          D   Spring washer
B   Spring                   E   Valve stem
C   Valve spacer             F   Valve seal

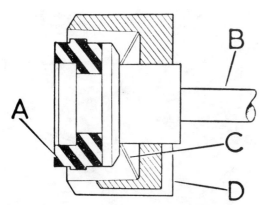

**Fig. 5.13. Correct assembly of master cylinder valve**

A   Valve seal               C   Spring washer
B   Stem                     D   Spacer

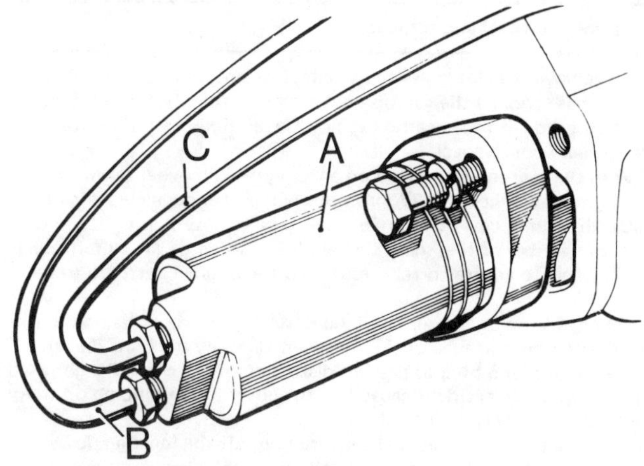

**Fig. 5.14. Later type slave cylinder**

A   Cylinder body            C   Bleed pipe
B   Inlet pipe

## 9  Slave cylinder - dismantling, examination and reassembly

1   Clean the exterior of the slave cylinder using a dry non-fluffy rag.
2   Carefully ease back the dust cover from the body and lift away.
3   Using a pair of circlip pliers, remove the piston retaining circlip (if fitted).
4   Gently tap the open end of the slave cylinder on a wooden surface to extract the piston and spring.
5   Inspect the inside of the cylinder for score marks caused by impurities in the hydraulic fluid. If any are found a new slave cylinder will be necessary.
6   If the cylinder is sound, thoroughly clean it out with fresh hydraulic fluid.
7   Remove the old seal and smear the new one with hydraulic fluid before fitting it to the piston. Note that the raised lip of the seal must face towards the rear of the piston (see Fig. 5.15).
8   Smear some hydraulic fluid on the cylinder bore and refit the spring, (wider end first) and then the piston, taking care not to damage the seal.
9   Push the seal down the bore with the piston and retain the piston assembly in the bore with the circlip (if fitted).
10  Smear the sealing areas of the new dust cover with hydraulic fluid or rubber grease and refit to the slave cylinder.

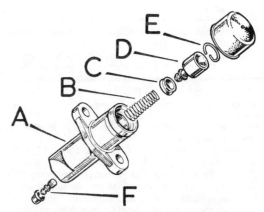

**Fig. 5.15. Exploded view of slave cylinder (all models)**

A   Slave cylinder           D   Piston
B   Spring                   E   Circlip
C   Piston seal              F   Bleed union

## 10 Clutch - removal and refitting

1   To remove the clutch assembly only, it is **not** necessary to remove the seat base and lift the gearbox out of the vehicle. Refer to Chapter 6 and proceed with the gearbox removal operations with the exception of seat base removal.

2   With the gearbox supported on a trolley jack, move it rearwards approximately 5 inches (127 mm); this will give enough clearance to enable the clutch cover and drive plate to be removed.

3   With a scriber or file, mark the relative position of the clutch cover and flywheel to ensure correct refitting if the original parts are to be reused.

4   Remove the clutch assembly by unscrewing the six bolts holding the cover to the rear face of the flywheel. Unscrew the bolts diagonally half a turn at a time to prevent distortion of the cover flange, also to prevent an accident caused by the cover flange binding on the dowels and suddenly flying off.

5   With the bolts removed, lift the assembly off the locating dowels. The driven plate or clutch disc will fall out at this stage, as it is not attached to either the clutch cover assembly or flywheel. Carefully note which way round it is fitted.

6   It is important that no oil or grease gets on the clutch disc friction linings, or the pressure plate and flywheel faces. It is advisable to handle the parts with clean hands and to wipe down the pressure plate and flywheel faces with a clean dry rag before inspection or refitting commences.

7   To refit the clutch plate, place the clutch disc against the flywheel with the larger end of the hub away from the flywheel. On no account should the clutch disc be refitted the wrong way round as it will be found impossible to operate the clutch (photo).

8   Refit the clutch cover assembly loosely on the dowels. Refit the six bolts and tighten them finger tight so that the clutch disc is gripped but can still be moved.

9   The clutch disc must now be centralised so that when the engine and gearbox are mated, the gearbox input shaft splines will pass through the splines in the centre of the hub.

10 Centralise the clutch disc by inserting a short bar through the centre of the clutch and into the input shaft bearing in the flywheel, using a mirror and a good light. Move the bar in the appropriate direction until the clutch disc is centralised.(photo). If difficulty is experienced a special centralisation tool, part number 605022 is available from your Leyland dealer.

11 Tighten the clutch cover bolts evenly in a diagonal sequence to avoid distortion of the cover flange. Finally, use a torque wrench to tighten them to the setting given in the Specifications at the beginning of this Chapter.

12 Refit the gearbox using the method described in Chapter 6.

## 11 Clutch - inspection

1   In the normal course of events, clutch dismantling and reassembly is the term used for simply fitting a new clutch pressure plate and friction disc. Under no circumstances should the diaphragm spring clutch unit be dismantled. If a fault develops in the pressure plate assembly, an exchange replacement unit, must be fitted.

2   If a new clutch disc is being fitted it is false economy not to renew the release bearing at the same time. This will preclude having to renew it at a later date when wear on the clutch linings is very small.

3   Examine the clutch disc friction linings for wear or loose rivets and the disc for rim distortion, cracks and worn splines.

4   It is always best to renew the clutch disc as an assembly to preclude further trouble, but, if it is wished to merely renew the linings, the rivets should be drilled out, and not knocked out with a centre punch. The manufacturer's do not advise that the linings only are renewed and personal experience dictates that it is far more satisfactory to renew the clutch disc complete than to try to economise by fitting new friction linings only.

5   Check the machined faces of the flywheel and the pressure plate. If either is badly grooved it should be machined until smooth, or replaced with a new item. If the pressure plate is cracked or split it must be renewed.

6   Examine the hub splines for wear and also make sure that the centre hub is not loose.

## 12 Clutch release bearing - removal and refitting

1   To remove the release bearing on all models, it is necessary to first remove the gearbox from the vehicle as described in Chapter 6.

### Series II and IIA

2   With the gearbox removed from the vehicle, undo the securing nuts and withdaw the clutch release assembly from the bellhousing studs (see Fig. 5.16). Remove the gasket.

3   Undo the screws from the cover plate on the side of the housing and drift out the cross-shaft from right to left. The operating fork, thrust washer and spring can now be removed from the housing (Fig 5.17).

4   Support the housing on wooden blocks and, using a suitable sized piece of tubing, drift the withdrawal sleeve from the bearing.

5   Remove the oil seal from the right-hand side of the housing and examine the cross-shaft bushes and withdrawal sleeve bush for wear. Renew as necessary.

**Note:** These bushes have to be reamed when renewed, and this task should be entrusted to an engineering company.

6   The cross-shaft oil seal and thrust bearing should be renewed as a matter of course unless the latter is in perfect condition. When refitting the cross-shaft oil seal, ensure the knife-edge of the seal faces in towards the housing.

7   Refit the withdrawal sleeve into the housing and drift the thrust bearing onto the sleeve shoulder using a large piece of tubing (photo).

8   Place the release fork, spring and spacer into the housing in the order shown in Fig. 5.18. Ensure the withdrawal sleeve is protruding from the housing 7/16 in (11 mm), by placing a steel bar of this diameter between the sleeve and housing and with the hole in the cross-shaft in line with the sleeve (Fig. 5.19) drive in the cross-shaft through the housing and release fork assembly (photo).

9   Refit the cross-shaft cover plate and gasket and, after checking the release assembly for correct operation, refit it to the clutch bellhousing using a new gasket (photo).

### Series III

10 The clutch release mechanism on the later models is a much simpler design than the earlier type (see Fig. 5.20).

11 With the gearbox out of the vehicle, remove the retaining clip and withdraw the thrust bearing and sleeve from the release fork.

12 Inspect the thrust bearing for wear and, unless in perfect condition, it should be driven off the sleeve using a suitable sized piece of tubing and wooden support blocks or a vice.

13 Press on the new bearing using a vice and packing pieces. Note that the domed side of the bearing faces towards the engine.

14 Apply some high melting point grease to the contact surfaces of the release lever and pivot point.

15 Refit the bearing and carrier, using the reverse sequence to the removal procedure.

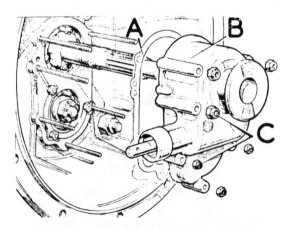

**Fig. 5.16. Location of clutch release mechanism**

A   Gasket                       C   Retaining nuts
B   Housing

10.7 Refitting the clutch plate and cover

10.10 Centralising the clutch disc with the flywheel bush

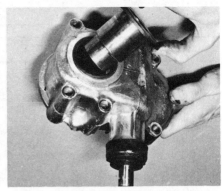

12.7 Inserting the clutch withdrawal sleeve into the housing (Series II and IIA)

12.8 Correct location of thrust bearing and cross-shaft in the housing (Series II and IIA)

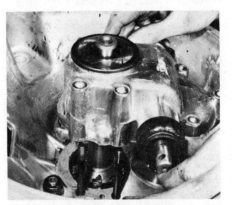

12.9 Refitting the clutch release assembly into the bell housing (Series II and IIA)

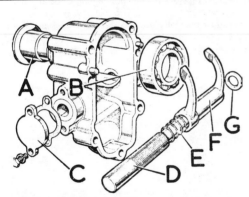

Fig. 5.17. Exploded view of clutch release components

A  Clutch withdrawal sleeve
B  Thrust bearing for withdrawal sleeve
C  Cover plate for cross-shaft
D  Cross-shaft
E  Spring for operating fork
F  Operating fork
G  Thrust washer for cross-shaft

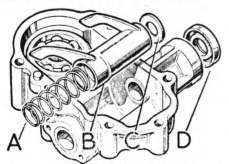

Fig. 5.18. Location of release fork assembly

A  Spring
B  Fork
C  Thrust washer
D  Oil seal

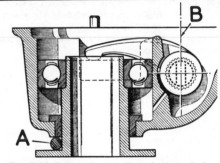

Fig. 5.19. Correct installation of release fork

A  Sleeve held out by 7/16 in (11 mm) diameter bar
B  Hole in cross-shaft must be in line with sleeve

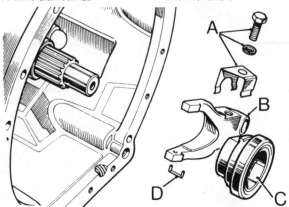

Fig. 5.20. Later type clutch release mechanism

A  Release fork retaining clip
B  Release fork
C  Thrust bearing and sleeve
D  Retaining clip

### 13 Clutch - fault finding

#### Clutch squeal

1   If, on taking up the drive, or when changing gear, the clutch squeals, this is a sure indication of a badly worn clutch release bearing. As well as regular wear due to normal use, wear of the clutch release bearing is accentuated if the clutch is ridden, or held down for long periods in gear, with the engine running. To minimise wear of this component the vehicle should always be taken out of gear at traffic lights and for similar hold ups.

2   The clutch release bearing is not an expensive item.

#### Clutch slip

1   Clutch slip is a self evident condition which occurs when the clutch disc is badly worn; the release arm free travel is insufficient; oil or grease have got onto the flywheel or pressure plate faces; or the press pressure plate itself is faulty.

2   The reason for clutch slip is that, due to one of the faults listed above, there is either insufficient pressure from the pressure plate, or insufficient friction from the clutch disc to ensure solid drive.

3   If small amounts of oil get onto the clutch disc, they will be burnt off under the heat of clutch engagement, in the process gradually darkening the linings. Excessive oil on the clutch will burn off leaving a carbon deposit which can cause quite bad slip, or fierceness, spin and judder.

4   If clutch slip is suspected, and confirmation of this condition is required, there are several tests which can be made:

a) *With the engine in second or third gear and pulling lightly up a moderate incline, sudden depression of the accelerator pedal may cause the engine to increase its speed without any increase in road speed. Easing off on the accelerator will then give a definite drop in engine speed without the car slowing.*

b) *Drive the car at a steady speed in top gear, and braking with the left leg, try and maintain the same speed by pressing down on the accelerator. Providing the same speed is maintained, a change in the speed of the engine confirms that slip is taking place.*

c) *In extreme cases of clutch slip the engine will race under normal acceleration conditions.*

5   If slip is due to oil or grease on the linings a temporary cure can sometimes be effected by squirting carbon tetrachloride into the clutch. The permanent cure, of course, is to renew the clutch disc, and trace and rectify the oil leak.

#### Clutch spin

1   Clutch spin is a condition which occurs when there is a leak in the clutch hydraulic actuating mechanism; the release arm free travel is excessive; there is an obstruction in the clutch either on the primary gear splines, or in the operating lever itself; or the oil may have partially burnt off the clutch linings and have left a resinous deposit which is causing the clutch disc to stick to the pressure plate or flywheel.

2   The reason for clutch spin is that due to any, or a combination of, the faults just listed, the clutch pressure plate is not completely freeing from the centre plate even with the clutch pedal fully depressed.

3   If clutch spin is suspected, the condition can be confirmed by extreme difficulty in engaging first gear from rest, difficulty in changing gear, and very sudden take-up of the clutch drive at the fully depressed end of the clutch pedal travel as the clutch is released.

4   Check the clutch master and slave cylinders and the connecting hydraulic pipe for leaks. Fluid in one of the rubber boots fitted over the end of either the master or slave cylinders is a sure sign of a leaking piston seal.

5   If these points are checked and found to be in order then the fault lies internally in the clutch, and it will be necessary to remove it for examination .

#### Clutch judder

1   Clutch judder is a self evident condition which occurs when the power unit mountings are loose or too flexible; when there is oil on the faces of the clutch disc; or when the clutch has been assembled incorrectly.

2   The reason for clutch judder is that due to one of the faults just listed, the clutch pressure plate is not freeing smoothly from the clutch disc, and is snatching.

3   Clutch judder normally occurs when the clutch pedal is released in first or reverse gear, and the whole vehicle shudders, as it moves backwards or forwards.

# Chapter 6 Gearbox

*For modifications, and information applicable to later models, see Supplement at end of manual*

## Contents

## Specifications

### Main gearbox

| | |
|---|---|
| Type: | |
|     Series II and IIA ... ... ... ... ... ... ... ... | Four speed and reverse with synchromesh on 3rd and 4th gears only |
|     Series III ... ... ... ... ... ... ... ... | Four speed and reverse with synchromesh on all forward gears |
| Oil capacity ... ... ... ... ... ... ... ... | 2½ pints (1.5 litres) |
| Oil level plug ... ... ... ... ... ... ... ... | Left-hand side of casing |

Gear ratios:

| | Up to gearbox suffix 'B' | From gearbox suffix 'C' onwards |
|---|---|---|
| Top ... ... ... ... ... ... ... ... ... ... | 1 : 1 | 1 : 1 |
| Third ... ... ... ... ... ... ... ... ... | 1.377 : 1 | 1.50 : 1 |
| Second ... ... ... ... ... ... ... ... ... | 2.043 : 1 | 2.22 : 1 |
| First ... ... ... ... ... ... ... ... ... | 2.996 : 1 | 3.60 : 1 |
| Reverse ... ... ... ... ... ... ... ... ... | 2.547 : 1 | 3.02 : 1 |

### Transfer gearbox

| | |
|---|---|
| Type ... ... ... ... ... ... ... ... ... | Two speed (high or low ratio) |
| Oil capacity ... ... ... ... ... ... ... ... | 4½ pints (2.5 litres) |

Gear ratios:

| | Up to gearbox suffix 'B' | From gearbox suffix 'C' onwards |
|---|---|---|
| High ... ... ... ... ... ... ... ... ... | 1.148 : 1 | 1.148 : 1 |
| Low ... ... ... ... ... ... ... ... ... | 2.888 : 1 | 2.350 : 1 |

### Overall gear ratios

| | Main gearbox | Transfer box | |
|---|---|---|---|
| | | High ratio | Low ratio |
| **Up to gearbox suffix 'B'** | | | |
| | Top | 5.396 | 13.578 |
| | Third | 7.435 | 18.707 |
| | Second | 11.026 | 27.742 |
| | First | 16.171 | 40.688 |
| | Reverse | 13.745 | 34.585 |
| **From gearbox suffix 'C' onwards** | | | |
| | Top | 5.40 : 1 | 11.28 : 1 |
| | Third | 8.15 : 1 | 17.06 : 1 |
| | Second | 11.98 : 1 | 25.04 : 1 |
| | First | 19.42 : 1 | 40.61 : 1 |
| | Reverse | 16.30 : 1 | 34.07 : 1 |
| **Optional helical gear transfer box** | | | |
| | Top | 7.19 : 1 | 15.4 : 1 |
| | Third | 10.8 : 1 | 23.1 : 1 |
| | Second | 15.96 : 1 | 34.1 : 1 |
| | First | 25.9 : 1 | 55.3 : 1 |
| | Reverse | 21.7 : 1 | 46.4 : 1 |

### Speedometer drive

| | |
|---|---|
| Ratio ... ... ... ... ... ... ... ... ... ... | 2.2 : 1 |
| Location ... ... ... ... ... ... ... ... ... | Rear of transfer box |

## Transmission brake

Type ... ... ... ... ... ... ... ... ...                Drum, on transfer box output shaft

## Main gearbox dimensions

Reverse gear bush
Reamed bore ... ... ... ... ... ... ... ...          0.8125 in + 0.001 in (20.637 mm + 0.0254 mm)
Mainshaft bush
    Fit in gears ... ... ... ... ... ... ... ...       0.0025 in to 0.0035 in (0.0635 mm to 0.0889 mm)
    Fit on shaft ... ... ... ... ... ... ... ...       Zero to 0.001 in (zero to 0.0254 mm)
    Endfloat ... ... ... ... ... ... ... ...       0.001 in to 0.008 in (0.0254 mm to 0.20 mm)
2nd and 3rd speed gears
    Endfloat on distance sleeve ... ... ... ... ... ...   0.004 in to 0.007 in (0.10 mm to 0.18 mm)
Synchronising clutch load ... ... ... ... ... ... ...   15 lb to 20 lb (6.5 kg to 9 kg)
2nd gear stop
    Adjustment ... ... ... ... ... ... ... .... ...   0.002 in (0.05 mm) clearance
Reverse gear stop
    Adjustment ... ... ... ... ... ... ... ... ...   0.002 in (0.05 mm) clearance

## Transfer gearbox dimensions

Dog clutch selector shaft bush
    Reamed bore ... ... ... ... ... ... ... ...    1.148 in − 0.001 in (29.17 mm − 0.025 mm)
Output shaft front and rear bearings
    Endfloat ... ... ... ... ... ... ... ... ...   Zero
    Preload ... ... ... ... ... ... ... ... ...   2 lb to 4 lb (0.28 kg to 0.55 kg)
High speed gear
    Endfloat ... ... ... ... ... ... ... ...   0.004 in to 0.008 in (0.10 mm to 0.20 mm) (after adjusting
        output shaft endfloat)

Intermediate gear
    Endfloat ... ... ... ... ... ... ... ...   0.004 in to 0.008 in (0.10 mm to 0.20 mm)

**Note:** *The dimensions of the optional helical gear transfer box are as above with the following exceptions:*

Low speed gear
    Endfloat ... ... ... ... ... ... ... ...   0.002 in to 0.009 in (0.05 mm to 0.23 mm)
High speed gear
    Endfloat ... ... ... ... ... ... ... ...   0.005 in to 0.022 in (0.12 mm to 0.57 mm)

## Front output shaft housing dimensions

Transfer selector shaft, spring
    Free length ... ... ... ... ... ... ... ...   7.156 in (181.76 mm)
    Length in position ... ... ... ... ... ... ...   3.875 in (98.43 mm)
    Load in position ... ... ... ... ... ... ...   24 lb (10.89 kg)
Dog clutch selector springs
    Free length ... ... ... ... ... ... ... ...   2.75 in (69.8 mm)
    Solid length ... ... ... ... ... ... ... ...   0.64 in (16.2 mm)
    Maximum load ... ... ... ... ... ... ...   13 lb (5.9 kg)

## Torque wrench settings

|                                  | lb f ft | kg fm |
|----------------------------------|---------|-------|
| Output drive flange nut ... ... ... ... ... ... ... | 85 | 11.75 |
| Layshaft bolt (Series III) ... ... ... ... ... ... ... | 65 | 8.5 |
| Layshaft nut (Series II and IIA) ... ... ... ... ... ... | 75 | 10.0 |

## 1  General description

The transmission unit on the Land Rover provides four forward
speeds and one reverse in either high or low ratio gearing, thus giving
a total selection of eight forward and two reverse speeds. When the
low ratio gearing is selected, four wheel drive is automatically engaged
while the high ratio can be used in either two or four wheel drive as
required.

Basically the transmission assembly is comprised of three units.
First there is the main four speed gearbox with synchromesh on third
and fourth gears (Series III models have synchromesh on all four gears).
Attached to the rear of the main gearbox is the two speed (high or low)
transfer box. On earlier models the high ratio gear wheels have helical
cut teeth, while the low ratio gears have straight-cut teeth. On the
later models all the gear wheels in the transfer box are of the helical
type. The third part of the transmission is the four wheel drive
selector unit attached to the front of the transfer box. This comprises
the front wheel driveshaft and housing and a dog clutch and selector
mechanism.

When viewed as a complete assembly, the transmission may appear
to be a rather complex mechanism. However, providing the three basic
units are dealt with separately as described, the DIY mechanic with a

well equipped workshop, and a reasonable engineering knowledge,
should not experience any major problems in overhauling part, or all
of the transmission assembly.

## 2  Transmission - removal and refitting

1  Because the gearbox can only be removed from inside the vehicle
through the passenger doorway it is essential that a wheeled hoist with
an extended lifting arm is available. This will enable the transmission
assembly to be lifted from its mountings and then manoeuvred through
the doorway.
2  Begin by removing the front floor panels and transmission cover
panels as described in Chapter 1.
3  It is necessary to remove the complete seat base. Commence by
lifting out the seat cushions and then release the seat squab retaining
straps from the support rail.
4  Working underneath the vehicle, undo the two nuts securing the
handbrake lever assembly to the chassis. **Note:** On early models fitted
with the short horizontal brake lever this operation is not necessary
as it is possible to lift the seat base over the lever.
5  Undo and remove all the bolts securing the seat base to the floor
structure (see Fig. 6.4).

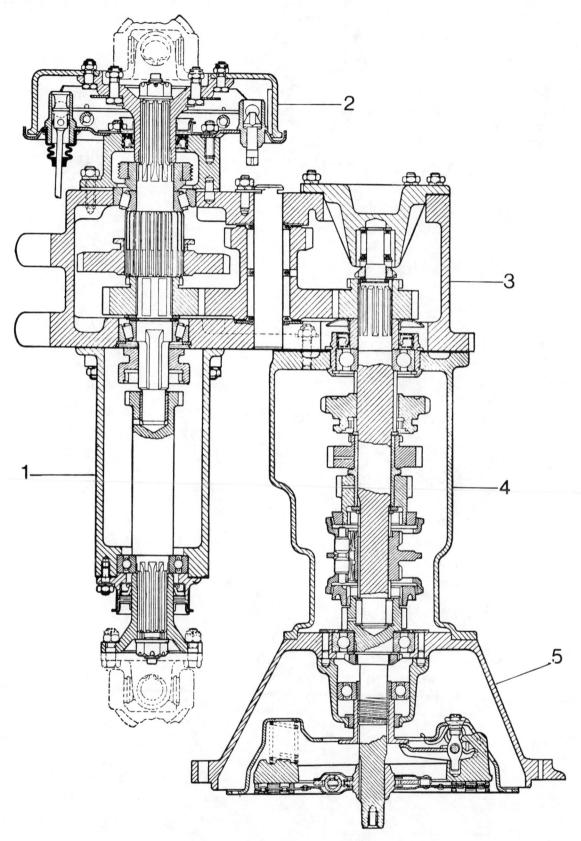

Fig. 6.1. Cross-section view of transmission assembly

| 1 Output shaft housing | 3 Transfer box | 4 Main gearbox | 5 Bellhousing |
| 2 Transmission brake | | | |

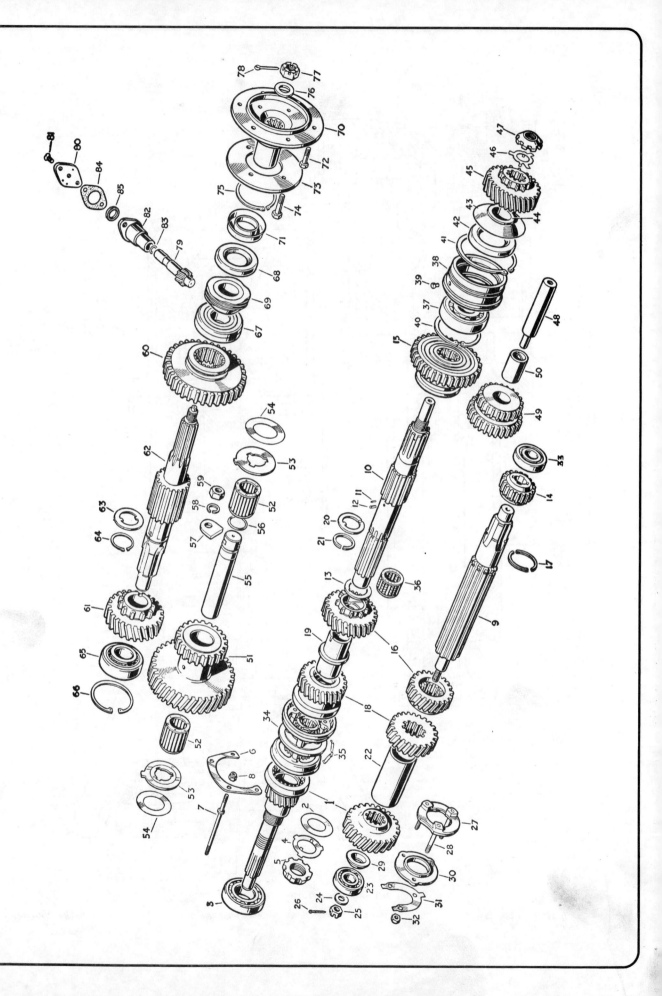

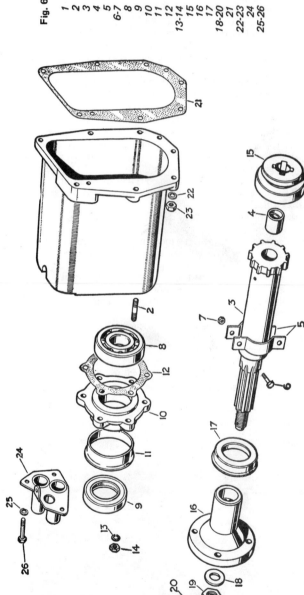

Fig. 6.2. Exploded view of gearbox and transfer box internal components

1 Primary pinion and constant gear
2 Shield for primary pinion
3 Ball bearing for primary pinion
4-5 Nut and washer for bearing
6-8 Fixings for bearing
9 Layshaft
10 Mainshaft
11 Peg for 2nd gear thrust washer
12 Peg for mainshaft distance sleeve
13 Thrust washer for 2nd speed gear
14 1st speed layshaft gear
15 1st speed mainshaft gear
16 2nd speed layshaft and mainshaft gear
17 Split ring for 2nd speed layshaft gear (early gearboxes)
18 3rd speed layshaft and mainshaft gear
19 Distance sleeve for mainshaft
20 Thrust washer for 3rd speed mainshaft gear
21 Spring ring fixing 2nd and 3rd mainshaft gears

22 Sleeve for layshaft
23 Bearing for layshaft, front
24-26 Fixings for bearing to layshaft
27 Bearing plate assembly for layshaft
28 Stud for bearing cap
29 Distance piece for layshaft
30 Retaining plate for layshaft front bearing
31-32 Fixings for cap and bearing
33 Bearing for layshaft rear
34 Synchronising clutch
35 Detent spring for clutch
36 1st speed mainshaft gear
37 Ball bearing for mainshaft
38 Roller bearing for mainshaft
39 Housing for mainshaft bearing, rear
40 Peg, housing to casing
41 Circlip, bearing to housing
42 Oil seal for rear of mainshaft
43 Oil thrower for mainshaft

44 Distance piece, rear of mainshaft
45 Mainshaft gear for transfer box
46-47 Nut and washer for gear
48 Shaft for reverse gear
49 Reverse wheel assembly
50 Bush for reverse wheel
51 Gear, intermediate
52 Roller bearing for intermediate gear
53 Thrust washer for intermediate gear
54 Shim for intermediate gear
55 Shaft for intermediate gear
56 Sealing ring for intermediate gear
57 Retaining plate for shaft
58-59 Nut and washer for plate
60 Low gear wheel
61 High gear wheel
62 Output shaft, rear drive
63 Thrust washer for high gear wheel
64 Circlip fixing washer to shaft

65 Bearing for output shaft, front
66 Circlip fixing bearing to case
67 Bearing for output shaft, rear
68 Oil seal fro output shaft
69 Speedometer worm complete
70 Flange for output shaft, rear drive
71 Mudshield for flange
72 Fitting bolt for brake drum
73 Retaining flange for brake drum bolts
74 Fitting bolt for propeller shaft
75 Circlip retaining bolts and flange
76-78 Fixings for flange
79 Speedometer pinion
80 Retaining plate for pinion
81 Sleeve for pinion
82 Sealing ring for sleeve
83 Sealing ring for sleeve
84 Joint washer for sleeve
85 Oil seal for pinion

Fig. 6.3. Output shaft and housing assembly

1 Output shaft housing assembly
2 Stud for oil seal retainer
3 Front output shaft assembly
4 Bush for shaft
5 Oil thrower for output shaft
6-7 Nut and bolt for oil thrower
8 Bearing for front output shaft
9 Oil seal for shaft
10 Retainer for oil seal
11 Mudshield for retainer
12 Joint washer for retainer
13-14 Nut and washer for retainer
15 Locking dog, four wheel drive
16 Flange for transfer shaft
17 Mudshield for flange
18-20 Nut for flange
21 Joint washer for transfer housing
22-23 Nuts for housing
24 Dust cover plate for selector shafts
25-26 Bolt for dust cover

6 With an assistant, lift the complete seat base out of the vehicle. If the earlier type handbrake lever is fitted, move the seat assembly forward first to enable the lever to pass through the aperture in the front of the seat base.

7 Drain the transfer box and gearbox oil into a suitable container (refer to the Maintenance Section at the front of this manual for the location of the two drain plugs).

8 Disconnect the rear propeller shaft from the transmission brake drum studs and the front propeller shaft from the output flange (refer to Chapter 7 if necessary). If a winch is fitted, the driveshaft for this must also be removed.

9 Remove the split pin and unscrew the threaded clevis pin and spring from the transmission brake operating lever (see Fig. 6.5).

10 Undo the securing nut, unhook the return spring and lift away the transmission brake operating lever assembly (see Fig. 6.5). **Note:** On left-hand drive models it is necessary to remove the brake lever cross-shaft.

11 Undo the two retaining screws and withdraw the speedometer cable from the rear of the transfer box (see Fig. 6.6).

12 Remove the two bolts from each of the transmission assembly mountings (see Fig. 6.7). On some models it may be necessary to remove the front exhaust pipe which passes over the left-hand mounting.

13 If a tie-rod is fitted between the chassis and the gearbox, remove the two front bracket securing bolts and push the tie-rod clear of the chassis (see Fig. 6.8).

14 On earlier models, remove the clevis pin from the clutch operating shaft, undo the three nuts securing the clutch slave cylinder bracket to the bellhousing and lift away the slave cylinder bracket and cross-shaft assembly. Tie the assembly out of the way taking care not to strain the flexible hydraulic pipe.

15 On later models undo the two retaining bolts and withdraw the slave cylinder from the side of the bellhousing. Avoid any excessive bending of the hydraulic inlet pipe.

16 Remove the earthing strap between the gearbox and chassis, if fitted.

17 Jack up the rear of the engine just enough to fit a 1 in (25 mm) wooden block between the flywheel housing and the chassis cross-member and then lower the jack.

18 Place a suitable sling around the transmission assembly and raise the hoist sufficiently to support the weight.

19 Undo and remove the remaining nine nuts and washers securing the bellhousing to the rear of the engine.

20 Withdraw the transmission rearwards until the input shaft is clear of the clutch assembly and then carefully lift the complete transmission assembly out of the vehicle (photos).

21 Refitting is basically the reverse of the removal procedure. However, if the clutch cover has been removed, ensure the driven plate is centralised as described in Chapter 5, before attempting to refit the transmission.

22 After refitting, check and top-up the gearbox and transfer box oil levels and check the clutch adjustment as described in Chapter 5.

2.20a Withdrawing the transmission from the engine

2.20b Complete transmission assembly removed from vehicle

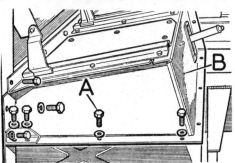

Fig. 6.4. Seat base attachment bolts

A  Securing bolts                    B  Seat base

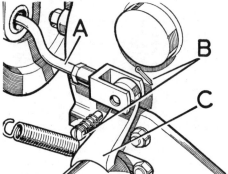

Fig. 6.5. Transmission brake operating lever

A  Brake rod                         C  Operating lever
B  Split pin and clevis pin

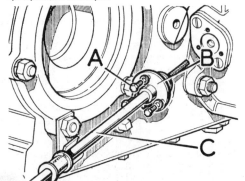

Fig. 6.6. Speedometer cable

A  Securing bolts                    C  Cable assembly
B  Retaining plate

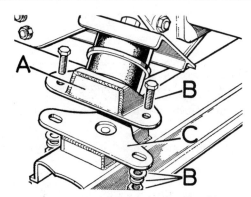

**Fig. 6.7. Transmission mounting assembly**

A  Upper mounting plate          C  Chassis plate
B  Securing bolt and nut

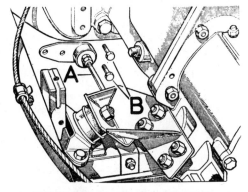

**Fig. 6.8. Transmission tie-rod (if fitted)**

A  Tie-rod assembly              B  Securing bolts

### 3  Transmission - separation into major assemblies

1   Before the four speed gearbox or transfer box assembly can be dismantled for inspection and repair, it is necessary to separate the three major transmission units from each other, ie; the transfer box must first be removed from the gearbox and then the front output shaft (four wheel drive) housing from the transfer box.
2   Before commencing work, clean off all dirt and grease from the transmission casing using paraffin or a water soluble grease solvent.
3   To separate the transfer box from the gearbox, first undo the bolts securing the transfer gearlever bracket to the bellhousing and remove the complete lever and bracket assembly. Take care not to lose the spacers or the small spring on the lever ball (see Fig. 6.9).
4   Undo the ten screws and remove the inspection plate from the bottom of the transfer box.
5   Remove the nuts and prise off the mainshaft rear bearing housing (see Fig. 6.10).
**Note:** If the optional power take-off drive unit is fitted it must be removed.
6   Remove the nut and retaining plate that secures the grooved end of the intermediate shaft to the transfer box casing.
7   Support the intermediate gear cluster with one hand and extract the intermediate shaft using a sprocket puller. If a puller is not available, the shaft can be extracted using a tyre lever and a suitable piece of bar as a fulcrum.
8   Remove the intermediate gear cluster and any associated shims and thrust washers.
9   Referring to Fig. 6.11, remove the nuts and washers securing the transfer box to the gearbox and separate the two components.
10  To remove the output shaft housing from the transfer box, first remove the large split-pinned nut securing the brake drum and output flange and remove the drum and flange assembly from the splined shaft.
11  Undo the four nuts and washers and remove the complete brake

anchor plate and shoe assembly (see Fig. 6.12).
12  Undo the plug from the top of the transfer box and remove the selector shaft spring and plunger.
13  Remove the cover plate from the top of the transfer box and unscrew the pinch bolt from the transfer selector fork (see Fig. 6.13).
14  Undo the nuts securing the output shaft housing to the transfer box and remove the housing complete with output shaft and selector mechanism. Retrieve the four wheel drive locking dog which is now released.
15  Lift out the selector fork from inside the transfer box.
16  The transmission assembly is now separated into its three major component parts. To dismantle each unit, refer to the following Sections.

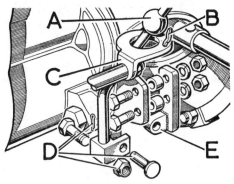

**Fig. 6.9. Transfer gear lever bracket**

A  Transfer gear lever          D  Alternative fixings,
B  Spring, lever ball to gearbox link     lever to bellhousing
C  Link, for lever              E  Bracket, lever to bellhousing

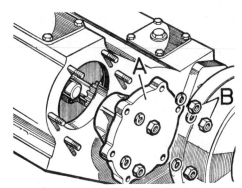

**Fig. 6.10. Mainshaft rear bearing housing**

A  Bearing housing              B  Securing nuts

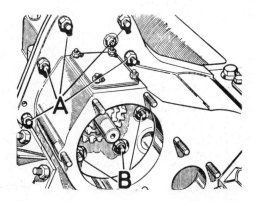

**Fig. 6.11. Location of transfer box attachment bolts**

A  External securing nut        B  Internal securing nuts

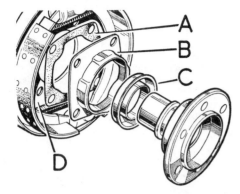

**Fig. 6.12. Transmission brake components**

A  Joint washer for oil catcher      C  Mud shield for flange
B  Oil catcher                        D  Brake anchor plate

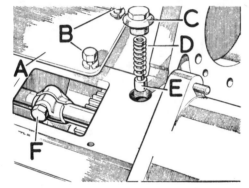

**Fig. 6.13. Location of transfer gear selector and detent spring**

A  Top cover, transfer box           D  Spring for plunger
B  Bolts, top cover                   E  Plunger, transfer selector shaft
C  Plug for plunger                   F  Pinch bolt securing sleetor fork

---

#### 4  Main gearbox - dismantling

1  First remove the transfer box from the rear end of the gearbox as described in the previous Section.

2  Remove the clutch release assembly from inside the bellhousing as described in Chapter 5.

3  Undo the two rear nuts and two front bolts and remove the gearchange lever and bracket from the gearbox.

4  From inside the bellhousing, remove the split pin and undo the large nut from the end of the layshaft (Fig. 6.14). On later models nut is replaced by a bolt and large washer which must be removed. To prevent the layshaft rotating while the nut (or bolt) is removed, select top gear and grip the main output shaft at the rear of the gearbox.

5  Unscrew the four retaining nuts and carefully remove the bellhousing, complete with primary shaft from the gearbox casing.

6  Referring to Fig. 6.15, remove the two retaining plates and the centre plug from the rear of the top cover and lift out the three selector springs.

7  Unscrew the securing nuts and remove the top cover. Retrieve the three selector balls from the top cover.

8  The type of selector forks and the method of removal is different on the earlier gearbox, fitted with synchromesh on third and fourth gears only, compared with the later all-synchromesh unit.

9  On the earlier type, select first gear and remove the reverse gear selector shaft and fork by lifting it up and turning it approximately a quarter of a turn to the left (see Fig. 6.16). Lift out the interlocking plunger.

10  Next, push the first/second selector shaft fully forward (second gear position) and lift it out. Remove the second interlocking plunger.

11  Push the third/fourth selector shaft fully rearward (third gear position) and lift it out.

12  If working on the later all-synchromesh gearbox, first select third gear and lift out the third/fourth gear selector, turning it as necessary to clear the casing. Remove the interlocking plunger.

13  Withdraw the first/second selector shaft followed by the reverse selector shaft, and lift out the second interlocking plunger.

14  The next task is to remove the layshaft. First slide off the large constant speed gear from the front of the layshaft and withdraw the synchromesh clutch unit from the mainshaft.

15  Manoeuvre the layshaft forward and downwards to clear the mainshaft and withdraw it from the gearbox.

16  Turning to the rear end of the mainshaft, bend up the lock tab and remove the large castle nut using special tool No. 600300. If this tool is not available, use an alloy drift and a light hammer, but take care not to burr over the edges of the nut.

17  Withdraw the lockwasher, shim, mainshaft gear and oil thrower from the end of the mainshaft (see Fig. 6.17).

18  Using a soft-faced mallet drive the mainshaft out from the rear of the gearbox.

19  To remove the reverse gear assembly, gently warm the gear casing with a gas blowtorch and drive out the reverse gear shaft from inside the casing.

20  The mainshaft rear oil seal can be prised out of the rear bearing housing.

21  Check the mainshaft rear bearing for wear. If it is decided to renew it, remove the circlip retaining the bearing housing to the casing, and, using a suitable drift, drive the housing and bearing assembly forward into the casing until it is free (see Fig. 6.18).

22  Remove the inner circlip from the bearing housing and press out the bearing.

23  The gearbox is now stripped out and the individual gears and synchromesh components can be dismantled and examined for wear as described in the following Sections.

---

#### 5  Mainshaft - servicing

1  Examine the gear teeth for excessive wear or chipping. If, even with the clutch correctly adjusted, the gears 'crashed' when changing gear, the synchromesh units will require attention. Do not forget that the Series II and IIA models only have synchromesh on third and fourth gears.

2  The mainshaft fitted to the Series III models has synchromesh on all four gears and is different from the earlier type, so the servicing procedures are described under separate headings.

*Series II and IIA mainshaft*

3  First withdraw the first speed gear from the rear end of the mainshaft (see Fig. 6.19).

4  Prise out the spring ring located in front of the third speed gear and withdraw the thrust washer, third speed gear, distance sleeve and second speed gear (see Fig. 6.20).

5  To remove the second speed thrust washer, it is necessary to remove the locating peg which is a press fit in the mainshaft (see Fig. 6.21).

6  Examine the shaft and gears for wear and renew if necessary. Check the synchromesh unit and if worn, a complete new assembly must be obtained. If the mainshaft sleeve has worn it should be replaced by the new type which has a groove cut in the centre flange.

7  During reassembly of the mainshaft, smear all components with gear oil.

8  If the inner thrust washer was removed, slide it onto the shaft ensuring it is correctly located on the peg (photo).

9  Before fitting the larger sleeve locating peg, temporarily refit the sleeve onto the shaft and refit the outer spacer and spring ring.

10  Now check the endfloat of the sleeve, which should be between 0.001 to 0.008 in (0.03 to 0.20 mm). Adjustment can be made by fitting different thrust washers which are available in a range of thicknesses.

11  If the endfloat is correct, remove the sleeve and fit the second gear onto the end of the sleeve with the larger slot. Fit a new locating peg in the shaft and slide on the sleeve and gear with the dog coupling facing towards the rear end of the shaft (photo).

12  Holding the sleeve hard against the inner thrust washer, check that the endfloat of the second speed gear is within 0.004 to 0.007 in (0.10 to 0.18 mm). (See Fig. 6.22).

13  Slide the third speed gear onto the sleeve followed by the thrust washer and, holding the thrust washer hard against the sleeve, check

that the third gear endfloat is within the same tolerance given for the second gear. **Note:** If the clearance is insufficient, a new sleeve must be fitted. Excessive clearance can be reduced by carefully rubbing down the appropriate end face of the sleeve using a sheet of emery cloth on a facing plate or thick piece of glass.

14 When the clearances are correct, fit a new spring ring in front of the third gear thrust washer.

15 Fit the first speed gear onto the rear end of the shaft ensuring it engages with the second gear dog.

16 The mainshaft is now ready to be refitted into the gearbox casing (see Section 9).

*Series III mainshaft*

17 From the rear end of the mainshaft, lift off the thrust washer and withdraw the first speed gear and bush (see Fig. 6.23).

18 Withdraw the rear synchro cone and lift off the complete first/second speed synchro unit followed by the front synchro cone.

19 Remove the second and third speed gears from the front of the mainshaft using the procedure described in paragraphs 4 and 5 in this Section.

20 Examine the shaft and gears for wear and renew if necessary. Check the third/fourth gear synchromesh clutch unit and if worn, a complete new assembly must be obtained.

21 The first/second gear synchromesh is a fairly complex unit containing a number of balls and springs that tend to fly out when the inner hub is removed, therefore, unless it is obviously badly worn it should be left well alone.

22 If it must be dismantled, ensure the workbench is clear and spread some clean paper over it.

23 Cover the synchro unit with a piece of clean cloth and push out the inner hub; remove the cloth and retrieve the three springs, balls and sliding blocks.

24 Check the components for wear and renew where necessary. The springs should be renewed as a matter of course.

25 To reassemble the synchro unit, first refit the inner hub into the

outer gear unit with the detent spring holes aligned with the ball retaining grooves in the outer gear unit. Note that the longer splines on the inner hub must be entered into the outer unit from the gear teeth side (see Fig. 6.24).

26 If the inner hub is a tight fit, withdraw it and rotate it 120° in either direction until an easy sliding fit is obtained.

27 Position the sliding blocks on the inner hub with the radiused face outwards and fit the springs through the blocks and into the holes in the inner hub.

28 Position the balls on the ends of the springs and push them down as far as possible by hand. At this stage the help of a friend will be advantageous.

29 With the balls held down, push the inner hub fully home into the outer gear unit until the balls are correctly located in the retaining grooves.

30 To reassemble the mainshaft, first refit the second and third speed gears to the front end of the mainshaft as described in paragraphs 8 to 14 in this Section.

31 Hold the mainshaft in a soft-jawed vice with the rear end uppermost and slide a synchro cone down the shaft onto the second speed gear.

32 Fit the first/second gear synchromesh unit to the shaft with the gear uppermost and position the second synchro cone on the inner synchro hub (Fig. 6.25).

33 Refit the first gear bush with the oil groove facing towards the rear of the shaft. Temporarily refit the thrust washer and check that the clearance between the end of the bush and the thrust washer is within 0.002 to 0.007 in (0.05 to 0.18 mm). Adjustment is made by grinding down or renewing the bush.

34 When the clearance is correct, remove the thrust washer and fit the first speed gear followed by the thrust washer with the stepped side facing to the rear end of the shaft.

35 The mainshaft assembly is now ready to be installed into the gearbox casing. Note that the third/fourth synchromesh clutch unit is assembled on the mainshaft after it is refitted in the casing.

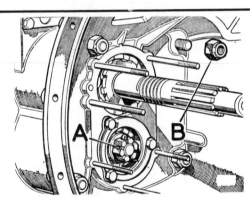

Fig. 6.14 Bellhousing attachment points

A  Layshaft securing nut          B  Bellhousing securing nuts
   (earlier type)

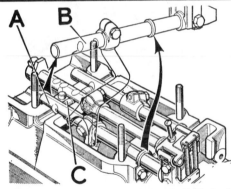

Fig. 6.16. Removing the reverse gear selector shaft (Series II and IIA)

A  Reverse gear selector shaft     B  Method of removal
   in position                     C  Interlocking plunger

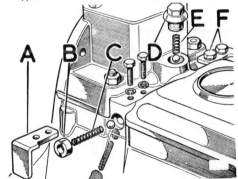

Fig. 6.15. Location of top cover detent balls and springs

A  Retainer plate            D  Plug
B  Rubber sealing grommet     E  Spring, 1st-2nd selector shaft
C  Spring reverse selector shaft   F  Bolts, 3rd-4th selector spring

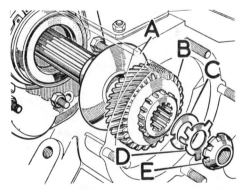

Fig. 6.17. Transfer gear on rear end of mainshaft

A  Oil thrower        D  Lockwasher
B  Mainshaft gear     E  Special nut
C  Shim washer

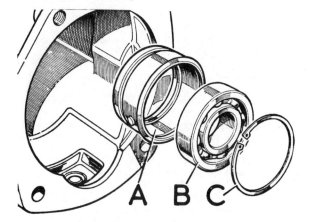

**Fig. 6.18. Removing the mainshaft rear bearing**

A   Bearing housing          C   Circlip
B   Bearing

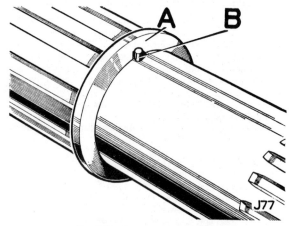

**Fig. 6.21. 2nd gear thrust washer**

A   Thrust washer          B   Peg for sleeve

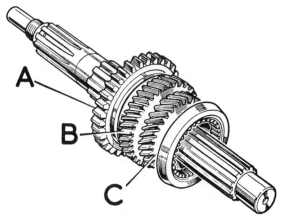

**Fig. 6.19. Mainshaft assembly (Series II and IIA)**

A   1st speed gear          C   3rd speed gear
B   2nd speed gear

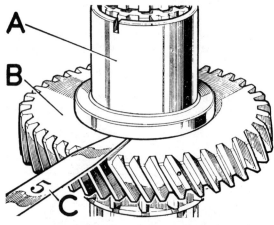

**Fig. 6.22. Checking the 2nd gear end-float**

A   Sleeve                  C   Feeler gauge
B   2nd gear

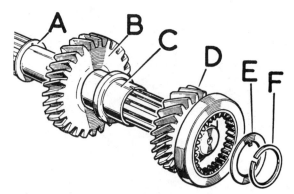

**Fig. 6.20. Removing the mainshaft gears (front end)**

A   Thrust washer, 2nd speed gear    D   3rd speed gear
B   2nd speed gear                   E   Thrust washer, 3rd speed gear
C   Distance sleeve                  F   Spring ring

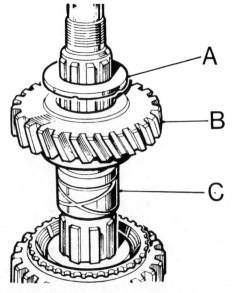

**Fig. 6.23. Mainshaft rear end assembly (Series III)**

A   Thrust washer          C   Bush
B   1st gear

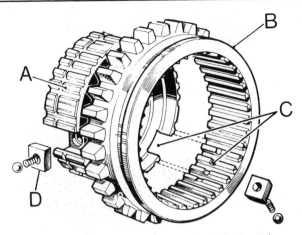

**Fig. 6.24. 1st/2nd gear synchromesh unit (Series III)**

A  Inner hub
B  Outer gear assembly

C  Locating grooves
D  Sliding blocks (3 off)

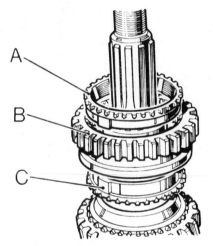

**Fig. 6.25. Assembling the 1st/2nd gear synchromesh unit onto the mainshaft (Series III)**

A  Rear Synchro cone
B  1st/2nd gear synchromesh unit

C  Front synchro cone

5.8 Fitting the inner mainshaft thrust washer

5.11 Fitting the 2nd gear and sleeve onto the mainshaft, (note the sleeve locating peg)

### 6  Input shaft - servicing

*Series II and IIA*

1  Remove the four nuts securing the input shaft bearing retaining plate to the gearbox side of the bellhousing. Carefully warm the bellhousing using a gas blowlamp and then drive out the input shaft and bearing using a soft-faced mallet (see Fig. 6.26).
2  Grip the input shaft in a soft-jawed vice using an old clutch plate as shown in Fig. 6.27 and remove the **left-hand** threaded nut from the input shaft using an alloy drift.
3  Press the bearing and shield from the shaft.
4  Examine the bearing for wear and renew it if necessary. If the input shaft pinion gear is chipped or worn a complete new input shaft assembly must be obtained.
5  To reassemble, first fit the shield onto the shaft with the dished side towards the pinion gear.
6  Press the bearing onto the shaft and refit the lockwasher and special **left-hand** threaded nut. Tighten the nut using an alloy drift and bend over the lockwasher.
7  Drive the shaft and bearing back into the bellhousing and refit the bearing retaining plate (photo).

*Series III*

8  The input shaft servicing procedure for the Series III models is the same as that described for the Series II and IIA with an exception, the special nut and lockwasher are replaced by a circlip and distance washer which must be removed before the bearing can be pressed off the input shaft (see Fig. 6.28).

### 7  Gearbox layshaft and bearings - servicing

1  With the exception of the large constant speed gear on the front of the layshaft, the gears on the Series III models are integral with the shaft and if they are worn or chipped the complete layshaft assembly must be renewed.
2  On the Series II and IIA models the gears are renewable and the third and fourth gears can be withdrawn from the shaft together with the sleeve.
3  Using a suitable puller, withdraw the bearing and first gear from the rear end of the shaft.
4  On both types of gearbox, examine the front and rear bearings for wear and renew if necessary. The front bearing can be pressed out from the bellhousing after first removing the bearing retainer plates (photo).
5  The rear bearing outer race can be removed by first warming the gearbox casing around the race, then driving it out through the two access holes provided. Alternatively, allow the heated race to shrink onto a close-fitting mandrel and withdraw it.
6  To reassemble the earlier type layshaft, first refit the first gear onto the shaft with the chamfered side of the teeth facing towards the front of the shaft.

7  Press the rear bearing onto the shaft until it fits tightly against the first gear.

8  On earlier Series II models, fit the spring ring into the groove on the rear end of the shaft (photo). Note that on later models the ring is replaced by a shoulder (see Fig. 6.29).

9  Fit the second gear with the recessed side facing towards the rear end of the shaft.

10  Fit the third gear onto the shaft with the thicker shoulder facing towards the front of the shaft. Refit the sleeve.

11  Temporarily refit the conical distance piece and constant gear and insert the shaft into the bellhousing bearing, ensuring that the constant speed gear is correctly meshed with the input pinion (see Fig. 6.30).

12  Secure the shaft with the washer and castle nut and check the gears do not have any endfloat on the shaft. If endfloat is present a new sleeve should be fitted and the shaft re-checked.

13  When the tolerances are correct, remove the layshaft assembly from the bellhousing.

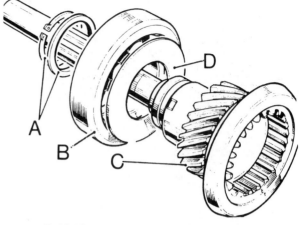

**Fig. 6.28. Input shaft and bearing (Series III)**

A  Circlip and washer      C  Pinion gear
B  Bearing      D  Oil shield

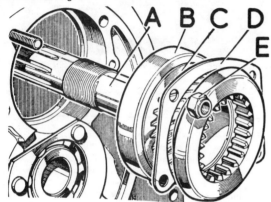

**Fig. 6.26. Removing the input shaft (Series II and IIA)**

A  Primary pinion      D  Retaining plate for pinion
B  Bearing for pinion      E  Nuts retaining plate
C  Shield for pinion

**Fig. 6.29. Rear end of layshaft (Series II and IIA)**

A  Bearing      C  Integral shoulder (or split ring
B  Chamfered teeth on 1st speed      on early shafts) for 2nd speed
    gear      gear location

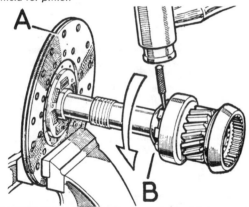

**Fig. 6.27. Method of gripping input shaft while removing nut**

A  Old clutch plate      B  Drifting off the nut

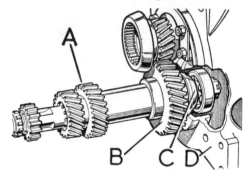

**Fig. 6.30. Checking the layshaft endfloat**

A  Layshaft      C  Conical distance piece
B  Constant gear      D  Bellhousing

6.7  Input shaft bearing retaining plate

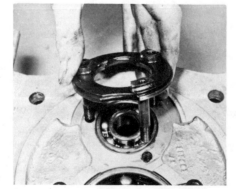

7.4  Layshaft bearing retaining plate

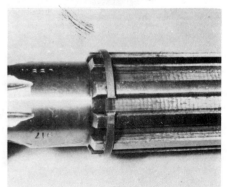

7.8  Layshaft spring ring (earlier models)

## 8 Reverse pinion and gear casing - servicing

1 To remove the reverse idler gear, gently warm the gearbox casing and then drive out the reverse gear shaft from inside the casing.
2 Lift out the reverse gear assembly.
3 Examine the gear teeth for excessive wear or chipping and renew the gear assembly if necessary. If the bush in the gear assembly is worn it can be pressed out and a new one fitted. However, the bush must be reamed to .8125 in + or − .001 in (20.637 mm + or − .25 mm) diameter and this task is best left to an engineering firm.
4 When refitting the reverse gear into the casing, make sure the smaller (or boss, Series III) gear is to the rear of the gearbox (photo).
5 Holding the reverse gear in position carefully drive in the shaft. Note that on later models the spring pin in the end of the shaft must align with the slot in the rear face of the gearbox casing.

## 9 Gearbox - reassembly

1 To avoid damaging the rear mainshaft oil seal, fit the oil thrower in the seal.
2 Make sure the rear thrust washer (if fitted) is positioned on the mainshaft and then insert the shaft through the front of the gearbox. Carefully drive it through the rear bearing using a soft-faced mallet.
3 Refit the transfer gear, shim washer, lockwasher and special nut. Tighten the nut and secure with the lockwasher (photo).
4 Lubricate the rear bearing of the layshaft and install the layshaft through the front of the gearbox, ensuring the rear bearing is correctly located in the outer race.
5 Now fit the first/second gear synchromesh clutch assembly, ensuring that the recessed end of the inner hub faces towards the rear of the mainshaft (photo).
6 Fit the roller bearing onto the front end of the mainshaft (photo).
7 Install the constant speed gear onto the front end of the layshaft, followed by the conical distance piece (chamfered side towards the front of the shaft).
8 Fit a new gasket to the front face of the gearbox, lubricate the front mainshaft roller bearing and carefully lower the bellhousing into position ensuring the input shaft pinion fits correctly over the mainshaft roller bearing and that the layshaft enters the front bearing. Gently tap the bellhousing with a soft-faced mallet until it is flush with the gearbox front face (photo).
9 Tighten the four bellhousing securing nuts. Refit the layshaft washer and castle nut and tighten to the specified torque before fitting a new split pin. On later models the castle nut is replaced by a bolt and this must be tightened to the specified torque.
10 Check that the mainshaft and layshaft rotate freely with minimum endfloat.
11 Refit the clutch release bearing assembly referring to Chapter 5 if necessary.
12 The basic gearbox components are now installed and the selector

rods and forks can be refitted using the procedures described in the following Section.

## 10 Gearbox selector forks - reassembly

1 The methods of reassembling the Series II and IIA and Series III selector forks are different and are therefore described under the following separate headings.

### Series II and IIA

2 Using a long blunt screwdriver, push the inner hub of the synchromesh unit fully rearward into the third gear position.
3 Carefully fit the third/fourth gear selector shaft and fork making sure that the seal on the shaft is correctly located in the front gearbox casing groove.
4 Push the synchromesh inner hub forward to the neutral position and then move the second gear fully rearwards. Fit the first/second gear selector shaft and fork ensuring that the seal is correctly seated.
5 Move the first/second gear selector shaft fully rearward and push the reverse idler gear fully forward. Fit the reverse gear selector shaft by inserting the fork into the gearbox with the shaft turned approximately 90° to the left and then manoeuvre the shaft and fork down to the correct position.
6 Push all the selector shafts into the neutral position and fit the interlocking plungers (photos).
7 Check that all the selector forks are correctly engaged and then fit the top cover (photo).
8 Refit the balls and springs into each hole in either side of the top cover noting that the reverse selector spring is slightly thicker. Fit the seals and spring retaining plates (photos).
9 Refit the top cover spring and ball and retaining plug (photo).
10 Check the operation of the three selector shafts and, rotating the input shaft by hand, ensure that all gears (including reverse) are obtainable.
11 Select second gear and, using a feeler gauge through the inspection cover, adjust the second gear stop bolt to obtain a .002 in (0.05 mm) clearance between the bolt head and the stop on the selector shaft (photo). Tighten the locknut.
12 After the transfer box has been refitted to the main gearbox the reverse gear stop bolt must be adjusted, as described in Section 12.
13 Refit the gearchange lever and bracket assembly (photo) and adjust the reverse hinge stop screw so that the hinge prevents accidental selection of the reverse gear, but when the lever is pushed firmly over to the reverse position the hinge rides smoothly up the lever.

### Series III

14 If new seals are fitted to the selector shaft ensure that the larger diameter seal is fitted on the reverse selector shaft and all seals are positioned with the larger inside diameter facing towards the front of the shaft.
15 First fit the reverse selector shaft and fork ensuring that the seal is correctly located in the gearbox casing groove.
16 Next fit the first/second selector shaft and fork.
17 Push the third/fourth gear synchro hub unit fully rearward, into the third gear position and fit the third/fourth gear selector shaft by inserting the fork into the gearbox with the shaft turned approximately 90° to the left and then turning and lowering the shaft and fork to its correct position.
18 Push all the selector shafts to the neutral position and fit the interlocking plungers.
19 Refit the top cover and check the operation of the gears and carry out the reverse gear adjustments as described in paragraphs 7 to 10 and 12 and 13 in this Section. Note that there is no second gear stop bolt on the Series III gearbox.
20 The gearbox and selector mechanism are now completely reassembled.

## 11 Transfer box - dismantling and inspection

1 Remove the transfer box from the gearbox and the output shaft and housing from the transfer box as described in Section 3.
2 The main task on the transfer box is the removal of the output shaft assembly. Begin by removing the securing nuts and washers and withdrawing the speedometer drive housing. Retrieve the shims and worm gear (see Fig. 6.33).

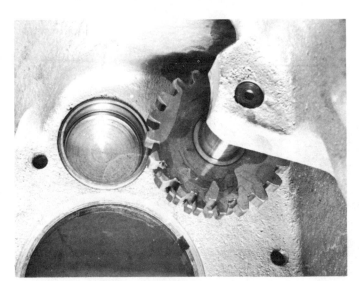

8.4 Correct installation of reverse idler gear

9.3 Transfer gear installed on rear end of mainshaft

9.5 Installing the 3rd/4th gear synchro unit

9.6 Refitting the front mainshaft bearing

9.8 Reassembling the bellhousing to the gearbox

10.6a Correct installation of selector shafts and forks (Series II and IIA)

10.6b Interlocking plungers installed

10.7 Refitting the top gearbox cover

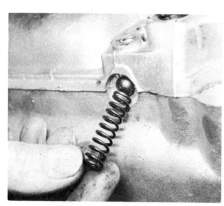

10.8a Fitting a detent ball and spring into the side of the top cover ...

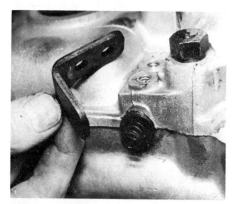

10.8b ... followed by a seal and retaining plate

10.9 Installing the detent ball and spring in the top of the cover

10.11 Checking the second gear stop bolt clearance (Series II and IIA only)

10.13 Gearlever and bracket assembly

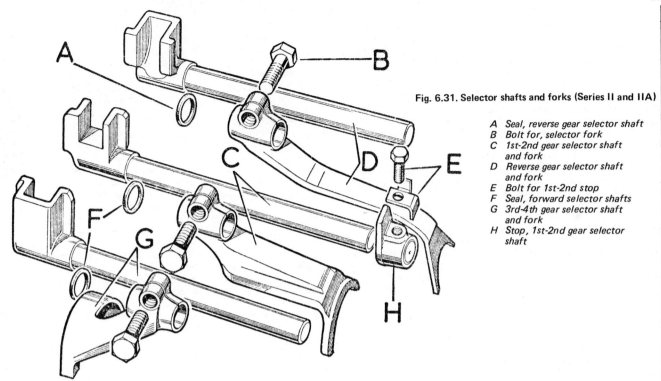

Fig. 6.31. Selector shafts and forks (Series II and IIA)

A  Seal, reverse gear selector shaft
B  Bolt for, selector fork
C  1st-2nd gear selector shaft
   and fork
D  Reverse gear selector shaft
   and fork
E  Bolt for 1st-2nd stop
F  Seal, forward selector shafts
G  3rd-4th gear selector shaft
   and fork
H  Stop, 1st-2nd gear selector
   shaft

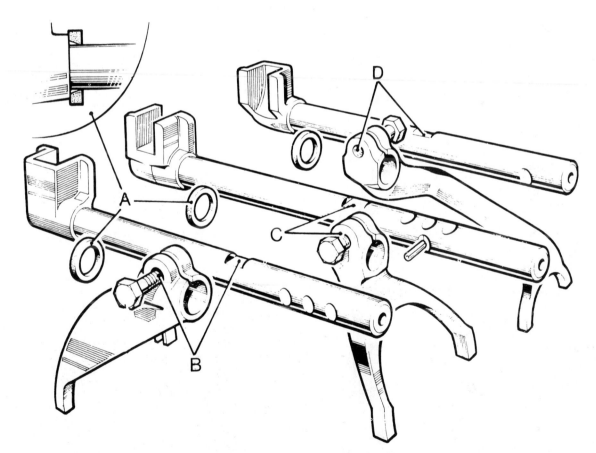

Fig. 6.32. Selector shafts and forks (Series III)

A  Seals and fitting detail

B  3rd/4th gear selector shaft
   and fork

C  1st/2nd gear selector shaft
   and fork

D  Reverse gear selector shaft
   and fork

3   There are two types of transfer box used on the Land Rover, the earlier type is fitted with a combination of helical and spur gears, while the later type has all helical gearing. As the method of dismantling and reassembling differ, the instructions are given under separate headings.

### Helical and spur gear type

4   To remove the output shaft, first remove the circlip retaining the front bearing in the transfer box casing.

5   Using a soft-faced mallet, drive the output shaft rearwards to free the rear bearing outer race from the casing.

6   Refit the flange nut onto the threaded end of the output shaft to avoid damage and then drive the shaft forward as far as possible. To free the front bearing completely from the casing, the output shaft must now be slid back to the rear and a suitable sized tubular packing piece inserted between the outer race and the shaft (see Fig. 6.34).

7   With the packing piece in position continue to drive the shaft forward until the front bearing outer race is freed from the casing.

8   Using a mild steel wedge or chisel inserted between the helical gear and the front bearing inner race, drive the bearing off the output shaft.

9   Remove the circlip and thrust washer from the front of the output shaft. Withdraw the shaft and remove the gears through the bottom of the casing.

10   The rear bearing inner race can now be pressed off the output shaft, or driven off using a mild steel chisel.

11   The transfer box is now completely dismantled and all components should be examined for wear and the gear teeth for chipping. Renew where necessary. Note that the larger low speed gear wheel is meant to be a loose fit on the shaft, allowing it to tilt in operation and grip the splines.

12   Earlier transfer boxes are fitted with a bush for the selector shaft which is a press fit in the casing. If the bush is renewed it must be reamed out to 1.148 in (29.17 mm).

### All-helical gear type

**Note:** This type of box can be identified by a selector shaft adjusting bolt on the front of the output shaft housing (see Fig. 6.35).

13   To remove the output shaft assembly, first remove the circlip retaining the front bearing outer race.

14   Place two pieces of 0.625 in (16 mm) mild steel bar between the rear face of the larger (low speed) gear wheel and the inside of the transfer box.

15   Hold the bars in position and using a soft-faced mallet, drive the output shaft rearwards until the low speed gear wheel just touches the bars.

16   Insert a mild steel chisel between the smaller (high speed) gear bush and the front bearing and lever the bearing outward through the casing approximately 0.25 in (6 mm) (see Fig. 6.36).

17   Separate the change speed inner hub from the high speed gear wheel and rotate the output shaft until the peg is visible on the shaft.

18   Locate the slot in the thrust washer and using a thin bladed knife or feeler gauge, move the thrust washer rearwards over the peg (see Fig. 6.37).

19   Again position the steel bars between the low speed gear wheel and the casing and, using a soft-faced mallet, drive the output shaft rearwards until it can be withdrawn, complete with the thrust washer and roller bearing, from the casing.

20   Remove the gear assembly and front bearing from the casing.

21   Press the rear bearing from the shaft and retrieve the thrust washer. If it requires renewal, carefully drift the front bearing outer race from the casing.

22   Examine all the components for wear, especially the roller bearing and splined sections of the output shaft. Renew all components that show signs of excessive wear. Check that the locating pegs in the shaft are not burred over.

23   If the selector shaft bush is renewed it must be reamed out to 1.148 in (29.17 mm) after refitting.

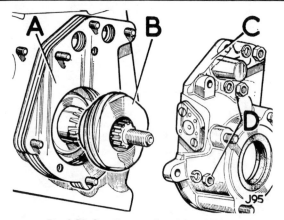

**Fig. 6.33. Speedometer housing and shims**

A   Shims                    C   Housing
B   Worm gear                D   Securing nuts

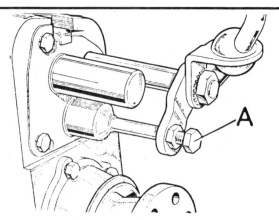

**Fig. 6.35. Identification of all-helical transfer box**
A   Adjustable selector shaft stop bolt

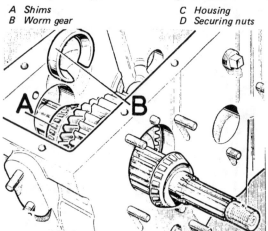

**Fig. 6.34. Removing the front bearing outer race**

A   Front inner bearing          B   Tubular packing piece

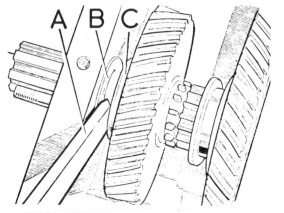

**Fig. 6.36. Levering out the front bearing**

A   Mild steel chisel          C   Bush
B   Front bearing

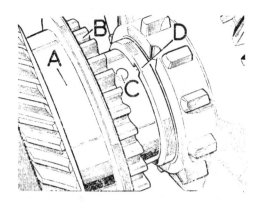

**Fig. 6.37. Location of output shaft peg**

A *Outer member for transfer change speed*
B *Inner member for transfer gear wheel*
C *Peg for output shaft*
D *Thrust washer for high gear wheel*

**Note:** The space shown between the change speed outer member and the high gear wheel has been exaggerated for clarity.

---

### 12 Transfer box - reassembly

*Helical and spur gear type*

1 Before refitting the output shaft in the transfer casing, temporarily assemble the high speed gear wheel onto the shaft, followed by the thrust washer and circlip. Using a set of feeler gauges, check that the clearance between the gear and the shaft is within .006 to .008 in (0.15 to 0.20 mm). If the clearance is excessive, fit a new thrust washer and circlip (see Fig. 6.38).
2 When the correct clearance has been obtained remove the circlip, thrust washer and gear wheel and press the inner roller bearing onto the rear end of the shaft.
3 Hold the gear assembly in the transfer casing and insert the shaft through the rear aperture and guide it through the gears (photo).
4 Fit the thrust washer and circlip onto the output shaft (photo).
5 Refit the front bearing outer race into the casing and secure with the circlip (photos).
6 Carefully drift the rear inner roller bearing onto the shaft and then refit the outer race (photo) and tap it lightly in until all the output shaft endfloat is removed but it still rotates freely (photo).
7 The output shaft bearing pre-load should be checked using the following method:
    a) *Refit the speedometer housing without the shims and tighten the nuts finger tight.*
    b) *Wind a piece of nylon cord or a similar type of cord around the selector groove in the low gear wheel and attach a spring balance to the end.*
    c) *The bearing pre-load is correct when a pull of 2 to 4 lb (0.9 to 1.8 kg) is required to rotate the shaft. To achieve this figure tighten the speedometer housing nuts progressively and evenly.*
    d) *When the pre-load is correct, measure the gap between the speedometer housing and the transfer box using feeler gauges, ensuring the gap is even all the way round. The measurement obtained is equal to the total thickness of shims required.*
8 Remove the cord and spring balance.
9 Fit the pre-determined number of shims over the speedometer housing studs and slide on the speedometer worm drive (photo).
10 Before refitting the speedometer housing, examine the oil seal and, if necessary, drive it out and fit a new one (photo).
11 Before installing the intermediate gears and shaft the transfer box must be reassembled onto the rear end of the gearbox. If the output shaft housing has been removed for overhaul it should be refitted on the transfer box as described in Section 14.
12 Fit a new gasket to the rear face of the gearbox and offer up the transfer box, locating it on the studs and dowel (photo).
13 Screw on the outer retaining nuts and the nuts located inside the transfer box. Tighten them using a ring spanner (photo).
14 Apply a thin film of grease on the two intermediate shaft thrust washers and stick them in place inside the transfer casing (photo).

15 Carefully examine the roller bearings for pitting or scoring before fitting them into the intermediate gear assembly (photo). Renew if necessary.
16 Examine the intermediate shaft for areas of excessive wear (see photo) and renew if necessary.
17 Hold the intermediate gear assembly inside the transfer casing and slide the shaft through the casing, bearings and thrust washers (photos).
18 Using a set of feeler gauges, check that the intermediate gear endfloat is within 0.004 to 0.008 in (0.10 to 0.20 mm). If the endfloat is excessive (see Fig. 6.39) fit a thicker thrust washer which is available in steps of 0.010 in (0.25 mm). **Note:** When fitting the thrust washers, ensure that the bronze faces are towards the intermediate gear assembly.
19 When the endfloat is correct, fit the retaining plate in the slot in the end of the intermediate shaft and over the adjacent stud and secure with a washer and nut.
20 Examine the gearbox mainshaft rear bearing for wear before installing it in the rear bearing housing and retaining it with the circlip (photo). Renew if necessary.
21 Fit a new gasket over the studs around the rear bearing aperture on the transfer box and then refit the bearing housing, ensuring the gearbox mainshaft is correctly located in the bearing before tightening the securing nuts (photo).
22 Fit the speedometer drive pinion assembly into the side of the speedometer drive housing (photo), ensuring that the oil seals are in good condition.
23 Remove the inspection cover from the top at the rear of the gearbox and select reverse gear. Slacken the locknut on the reverse gear stop bolt and adjust it to obtain a clearance of 0.002 in (0.05 mm) between the end of the reverse gear selector shaft and the stop bolt (photos). Tighten the locknut.
24 Refit the transmission brake anchor plate and shoe assembly, followed by the drum and output shaft flange. For further details of the transmission brake refer to Chapter 9.
25 Refit the transfer box bottom cover plate and tighten the securing screws.
26 Before refitting the transmission assembly into the vehicle make sure that the transfer box and gearbox drain plugs are fully tightened. The transmission oil levels can be filled prior to refitting, but must be re-checked after the transmission is installed in the vehicle.

*All-helical gear type*

27 Before refitting the output shaft in the transfer casing, temporarily fit the steel thrust washer and rear bearing onto the rear end of the shaft.
28 Now slide the low gear wheel and bush onto the shaft and holding it firmly against the thrust washer, check that the low gear wheel endfloat is within 0.002 to 0.009 in (0.05 to 0.22 mm) (see Fig. 6.40).
29 Remove the low gear wheel from the shaft and refit the centre bush. Fit the change speed inner member, the thrust washer and the high speed gear wheel complete with bush.
30 Holding the high speed gear wheel bush in firm contact with the thrust washer, check that the high speed gear wheel endfloat is within 0.005 and 0.022 in (0.12 to 0.55 mm) (see Fig. 6.41).
31 Insufficient endfloat on either gear wheel should be rectified by fitting a new bush. If the endfloat is excessive reduce the respective bush should be reduced in length by carefully rubbing down the end on a piece of fine emery cloth stretched across a face plate.
32 When the endfloat clearances are correct, remove all the components from the output shaft with the exception of the steel thrust washer and the rear, inner roller bearing.
33 Referring to Fig. 6.42, fit the bush in the low speed gear with the flange on the internal teeth side of the gear, followed by the change speed inner and outer hubs. Note that the recessed side of the inner hub must be facing the bush.
34 Place the high gear wheel minus its bush against the low gear assembly with the dog teeth abutting the change speed hub, and hold the complete gear assembly in position inside the transfer casing
35 Insert the output shaft through the rear of the casing and on through the gear assembly ensuring the low speed gear wheel bush is correctly located on the peg in the shaft.
36 Slide the thrust washer over the front of the shaft and through the centre of the high speed gear, ensuring that the washer passes over the peg and is correctly located in the change speed hub recess. Fit the bush through the high speed gear wheel ensuring that it is also located on the peg (see Fig. 6.43).

37 Fit the flange nut onto the threaded end of the output shaft to protect the thread and turn the casing on its side so that the threaded end is resting on the bench. Carefully drift the front inner roller bearing onto the shaft, taking care not to separate the gears and hub assembly (Fig. 6.44).

38 Now tap the front outer race into the casing and retain with a circlip. Gently drive the output shaft forward until the bearing is hard against the circlip.

39 Fit the rear bearing into the casing and lightly tap it in until all the output shaft endfloat is just taken up.

40 For instructions on setting the output shaft pre-load and the remaining transfer box reassembly procedures, refer back to paragraphs 7 to 26 in this Section. Note that on the all-helical transfer boxes the intermediate gear assembly comprises a cluster of three gears.

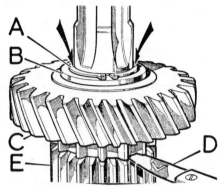

**Fig. 6.38. Checking the high gear wheel endfloat**

A  Circlip                         D  Feeler gauges
B  Thrust washer                   E  Output shaft
C  High gear wheel

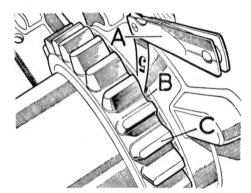

**Fig. 6.39. Checking the intermediate gear endfloat**

A  Feeler gauge                    C  Intermediate gear
B  Thrust washer

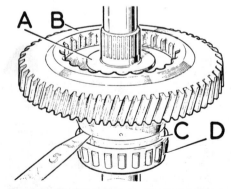

**Fig. 6.40. Checking the low gear wheel endfloat**

A  Bush                            C  Thrust washer
B  Low gear wheel                  D  Rear bearing

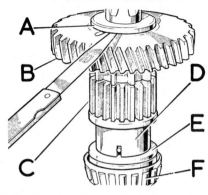

**Fig. 6.41. Checking the high gear wheel endfloat, (all helical type)**

A  Bush for high gear wheel        D  Bush for low gear wheel
B  High gear wheel                 E  Steel thrust washer
C  Change speed inner member       F  Rear bearing for output shaft

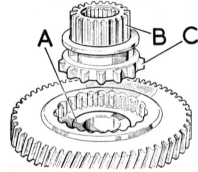

**Fig. 6.42. Assembling the inner hub to the low gear**

A  Bush                            C  Outer hub
B  Inner hub

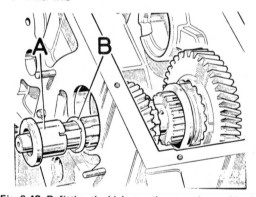

**Fig. 6.43. Refitting the high gear thrust washer and bush**

A  Bush                            B  Thrust washer

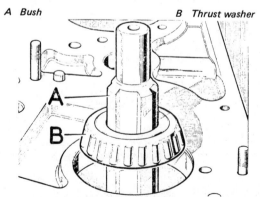

**Fig. 6.44. Refitting the front inner bearing**

A  Shaft                           B  Roller bearing

12.3 Installing the input shaft into the transfer box

12.4 Fitting the thrust washer and circlip to the input shaft

12.5a Refit the front bearing outer race ...

12.5b ... and secure with the circlip

12.6a The rear bearing outer race prior to tapping home

12.6b After installation check that the input shaft rotates freely

12.9 Speedometer worm gear in position

12.10 Speedometer housing oil seal removed

12.12 Refitting the transfer box to the gearbox

12.13 Tightening the internal transfer box securing nuts

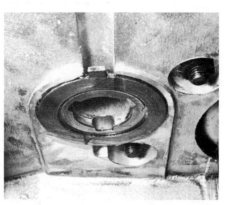

12.14 Intermediate gear thrust washer

12.15 Installing the intermediate gear roller bearings

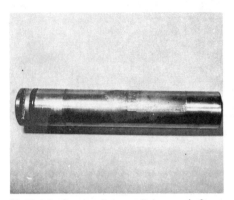

12.16 A badly worn intermediate gear shaft

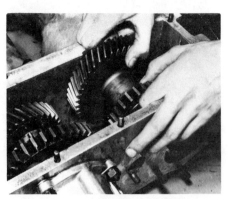

12.7a Hold the intermediate gear in position ...

12.7b ... and slide the shaft in

12.20 Mainshaft rear bearing assembly

12.21 Refitting the rear bearing housing

12.22 Refitting the speedometer drive pinion

12.23a Location of reverse gear stop bolt

12.23b Checking the reverse stop clearance

### 13 Front output shaft housing - dismantling and inspection

1   First remove the complete output shaft housing from the transfer box as described in Section 3.

2   Remove the nut and washer and withdraw the transfer gear lever support bracket from the end of the selector shaft.

3   Undo the pivot bolt and remove the four wheel drive control lever and locking pin.

4   Undo the three securing bolts and withdraw the metal dust cover from the ends of the selector shafts (Fig. 6.45).

5   Carefully withdraw the complete selector shaft assemblies and locking dog from the housing. **Note:** It is highly unlikely that any wear will have occurred to the selector shaft assemblies and unless any of the components are broken it is strongly recommended that no attempt be made to dismantle the selector shafts.

6   If the shafts are dismantled, carefully lay out the components on a clean sheet of paper in the order of removal and refer to Figs. 6.46 and 6.47 for correct reassembly.

7   To remove the front output shaft from the housing, undo the castle nut and withdraw the flange from the end of the shaft.

8   Undo the securing nuts and remove the oil seal housing and gasket from the front of the output shaft housing.

9   Withdraw the output shaft from the housing and, if worn and requiring renewal, drive out the front bearing.

10   Examine all the components for wear and renew where necessary. If the bush located inside the rear end of the front output shaft is renewed it must be reamed after installation to .8755 + or − .0005 in (22.2 mm + or − 0.013 mm) diameter.

11   If the dog teeth on the output shaft are worn, the complete shaft assembly must be renewed. Refer to Fig. 6.48 for the correct location of the oil thrower.

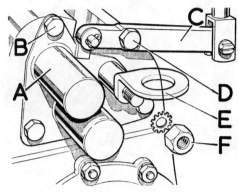

Fig. 6.45. Front view of output shaft housing

A  Dust cover, selector shafts       D  Lever fixings
B  Cover fixings                     E  Link, transfer gear lever
C  Selector lever, four wheel drive  F  Link fixings

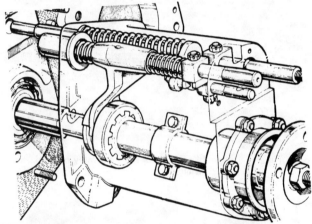

Fig. 6.46. Inside view of output shaft and selector shafts

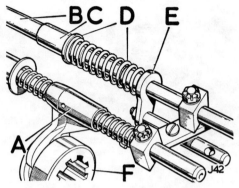

Fig. 6.47. Selector shaft assemblies

A  Selector shaft, four wheel   D  Locating bush and spring for
   drive                            selector fork
B  Selector shaft, transfer gear  E  Gearchange pivot shaft assembly
C  Distance tube                 F  Locking dog, four wheel drive

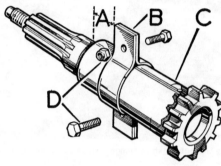

Fig. 6.48. Four-wheel drive output shaft

A  1 in ± 1/32 in (25.4 mm ± 0.75 mm)
B  Oil thrower
C  Front output shaft
D  Securing nut and bolt

## 14  Front output shaft housing - reassembly

1  Commence by refitting the front bearing into the output shaft housing (photo).
2  Insert the output shaft into the housing and carefully drive it through the front bearing until it is fully home (photo).
3  Fit a new gasket to the front end of the housing and install the seal retainer assembly (photo). **Note:** If the seal is renewed it must be fitted with the lipped side facing the output shaft housing.
4  Refit the output shaft flange and tighten the nut to the specified torque. Secure the nut with a new split pin (photo).
5  Check that the selector shaft and locking pin 'O' ring seal are correctly located in the end of the housing (photo).
6  With the selector shafts correctly assembled, fit the four wheel drive locking dog into the selector fork and carefully insert the complete assembly into the housing, ensuring that the ends of the shafts slide through the holes in the front of the housing and that the locking dog is correctly engaged on the output shaft gear (photos).
7  Fit the four wheel drive locking pin through the hole in the front face of the housing making sure it passes through the hole in the pivot shaft inside the housing (photo).
8  Fit a new gasket to the front face of the transfer box.
9  Position the transfer gear selector fork in the transfer box and install the output shaft housing onto the transfer box making sure the selector shaft passes through the fork (photo). Refit and tighten the housing nuts.
10  Refit the pinch bolt through the selector fork and the groove in the shaft and tighten.
11  Install the plunger and spring in the top of the transfer box and retain it with the threaded plug (photo).
12  Check that the selector fork is correctly located on the transfer gear hub and then refit the transfer box inspection cover.
13  Refit the four wheel drive selector lever and arm to the front of the housing and secure the locking pin to the arm using a new split pin.

14  Refit the selector shaft dust cover.
15  Refit the transfer gear lever bracket to the end of the selector shaft (photo).
16  On later models fitted with a transfer stop bolt, engage four wheel drive low ratio and adjust the stop bolt so that the locking pin is an easy sliding fit through the housing and pivot shaft (see Fig. 6.49). Tighten the locknut.
17  When the transfer box and output shaft housing have been installed on the main gearbox, refit the transfer gear lever bottom bracket to the bellhousing.
18  Rotate the gearbox input shaft by hand and check the operation of the four wheel drive and high and low gear selection before refitting the complete transmission into the vehicle as described in Section 2.

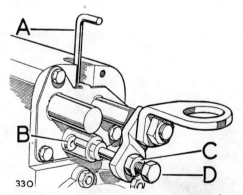

Fig. 6.49. Adjusting the transfer selector shaft stop bolt (later models only)

A  Four wheel drive locking pin   C  Locknut
B  Pivot shaft                    D  Adjuster bolt

14.1 Refitting the bearing into the front of the output shaft housing

14.2 Ouput shaft installed in housing

14.3 Installing the seal retainer onto the front of the housing

14.4 Refitting the output shaft flange

14.5 Location of oil seals in output shaft housing

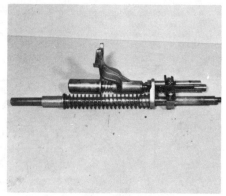

14.6a Selector shaft assembly prior to installation

14.6b Installing the selector shafts into the housing

14.6c Correct location of output shaft locking dog

14.7 Installation of four-wheel drive locking pin

14.9a Refitting the output shaft housing to the transfer box

14.9b Refitting the detent spring and plug

14.15 Transfer gear lever and top bracket

## 15 Fault diagnosis - transmission

| Symptom | Reason/s |
|---|---|
| Ineffective synchromesh | Worn baulk rings or synchro hubs. |
| Jumps out of one or more gears (on drive or over-run) | Weak detent spring, worn selector forks, worn gears or worn synchro sleeves. |
| Noisy, rough, whining and vibration | Worn bearings and/or thrust washers (initially) resulting in extended wear generally due to play and backlash. |
| Noisy and difficult engagement of gears | Clutch fault. |
| Jumps out of high transfer gear | Rubber boot on transfer gear lever fitted incorrectly. Weak or broken selector detent spring. |
| Jumps out of low transfer gear | Either of the above reasons, or excessive endfloat of the intermediate gear in transfer box. |
| Transfer box is excessively noisy | Insufficient oil in box. Excessive endfloat of intermediate gear, or worn bearings. |
| Difficulty in engaging four-wheel drive | Locking pin seized in casing, broken selector shaft spring or selector shafts sticking in the casing. |
| Difficulty in disengaging four-wheel drive | Spring on selector lever, (yellow knob) broken or missing. Selector shafts sticking in casing or broken selector shaft spring. Different type tyres fitted on the front and rear wheels or excessively worn tyres. |

**Note:** *It is sometimes difficult to decide whether it is worthwhile removing and dismantling the gearbox for a fault which may be nothing more than a minor irritant. Gearboxes which howl, or where the synchromesh can be 'beaten' by a quick gear change, may continue to perform for a long time in this stage. A worn gearbox usually needs a complete rebuild to eliminate noise because the various gears, if re-aligned on new bearings will continue to howl when different wearing surfaces are presented to each other.*

*The decision to overhaul therefore, must be considered with regard to time and money available, relative to the degree of noise or malfunction that the driver can tolerate.*

# Chapter 7 Propeller shaft

*For modifications, and information applicable to later models, see Supplement at end of manual*

## Contents

## Specifications

| | |
|---|---|
| **Type** ... ... ... ... ... ... ... ... ... ... | Tubular shaft with Hardy Spicer joint at each end |
| **Shaft diameter** ... ... ... ... ... ... ... ... | 2 in (50.8 mm) |

**Shaft length**

| | |
|---|---|
| 88 in model (front) ... ... ... ... ... ... ... ... | 23.812 in (604.8 mm) |
| 88 in model (rear) ... ... ... ... ... ... ... ... | 21.812 in (554 mm) |
| 109 in model (front) ... ... ... ... ... ... ... ... | 23.812 in (604.8 mm) |
| 109 in model (rear) ... ... ... ... ... ... ... ... | 42.812 in (1,087 mm) |

## 1 General description

The drive from the transmission assembly to the front and rear axles is transmitted by two tubular propeller shafts fitted with a universal joint at each end. The universal joints cater for the varying angle between the axle and transmission, caused by road spring deflection, while any fore-or-aft variation is taken care of by means of a splined sleeve in each shaft.

Although of different lengths, the front and rear propeller shafts are virtually identical in construction with the exception of the position of the spline sleeve which is on the transmission end of the rear shaft and the axle end of the front shaft.

## 2 Propeller shaft - removal and refitting

1 The method of removing either the front or rear propeller shaft is the same. Any differences in procedure will be mentioned where

necessary.

2 Depending on the shaft to be removed, jack-up the appropriate end of the vehicle until the wheels are just clear of the ground. Place heavy duty axle stands beneath the chassis.

3 Scribe a line across the side of the axle coupling flange and the propeller shaft flange, remove the four nuts and bolts and lower the end of the shaft to the ground (see Fig. 7.2).

4 If the rear propeller shaft is being removed, undo the four nuts securing the shaft flange to the brake drum. Pull the shaft rearwards to clear the studs and remove the complete shaft assembly from beneath the vehicle (see Fig. 7.3).

5 In the case of the front propeller shaft, remove the four nuts and bolts securing the rear end of the shaft to the front output shaft flange on the transfer box and remove the shaft assembly from the vehicle.

6 Refitting the propeller shafts is the reverse sequence to removal. Note that the splined sleeve on the front shaft must be towards the front axle while the sleeve on the rear shaft must be adjacent to the transmission brake (see Fig. 7.4).

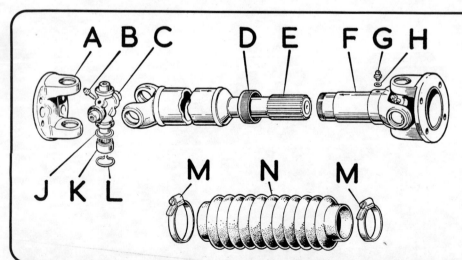

**Fig. 7.1. Exploded view of a propeller shaft**

A Flanged yoke
B Grease nipple for universal joint
C Journal for bearings
D Dust cap
E Splined shaft
F Splined sleeve
G Grease nipple for splined joint
H Washer for nipple
J Seal for journal bearing
K Needle roller bearing assembly
L Circlip retaining bearing
M Clips fixing rubber grommet
N Rubber grommet for sliding joint

### 3 Universal joints - inspection and repair

1 Wear in the needle roller bearings is characterised by vibration in the transmission, 'clonks' on taking up the drive and in extreme cases of lack of lubrication, metallic squeaking, and ultimately grating and shrieking sounds as the bearings break up.

2 To test the universal joints for wear prior to removing the propeller shaft(s) from the vehicle, apply the handbrake and engage four-wheel drive in the low ratio. Working under the vehicle, grip the shaft to be tested and try and rotate it. Wear is indicated by movement between the shaft yoke and the coupling flange. Check both universal joints using this method.

3 To check the splined sleeve on the front of both shafts, attempt to push the shaft from side-to-side and note any excessive movement between the sleeve and the shaft.

4 If the universal joint is worn, a repair kit comprised of a new spider, bearings and seals should be purchased prior to removing the affected shaft.

### 4 Universal joints and sleeve - dismantling and inpsection

1 If a protective rubber boot is fitted over the sleeve section, slacken the hose clips and slide the boot rearwards.

2 Check that the alignment marks are visible on the sleeve and shaft, (see Fig. 7.5). If no marks can be found, scribe a line along the sleeve and shaft to ensure the splined shaft and sleeve are reassembled in the original position to maintain the balanced setting.

3 Unscrew the dust cap and withdraw the front universal joint and sleeve assembly from the splined end of the shaft (Fig. 7.6).

4 Clean away all traces of dirt and grease from the circlips located on the ends of the spiders, and remove the circlips by pressing their open ends together with a pair of circlip pliers and lever them out with a screwdriver. **Note:** If they are difficult to remove, tap the bearing face resting on top of the spider with a mallet which will ease the press pressure on the circlip.

5 Hold the joint housing in one hand and remove the bearing caps and needle rollers by tapping the yoke at each bearing with a soft-faced mallet (see Fig. 7.7). As soon as the bearings start to emerge they can be drawn out with the fingers. If the bearing cup refuses to move then place a thin bar against the inside of the bearing and tap it gently until the cup starts to emerge.

6 With the bearings removed it is relatively easy to extract the spiders from their yokes. If the bearings and spider journals are thought to be badly worn this can easily be ascertained visually with the universal joints dismantled.

7 Temporarily fit the splined end of the shaft into the sleeve, and then grip the sleeve in a soft-jawed vice and ascertain the amount of spline wear by turning the shaft in either direction. The maximum permissible movement is 0.004 in (0.10 mm) and this can be checked using a dial test indicator as shown in Fig. 7.8.

### 5 Universal joints - reassembly

1 Clean out the yokes and trunnions and fit new oil seals to the spider journals.

2 Place the spider on the propeller shaft yoke and assemble the needle rollers into the bearing cups retaining them with some thick grease.

3 Fill each bearing cup about ½ full with Castrol LM Grease. Also fill the grease holes on the spider with grease taking care that all air bubbles are eliminated.

4 Refit the bearing cups on the spider and tap the bearings home so that they lie squarely in position.

5 Lock the cups in position with new circlips. Check the spider movement and if it is tight try tapping the yokes with a mallet. If this does not do the trick then something is amiss requiring investigation.

6 If the grease nipple was removed, screw it back into the spider.

7 Smear the splines on the end of the shaft with grease. Carefully match up the alignment mark and slide the shaft into the sleeve. Tighten the dust cap.

**Note:** Do not pack grease into the sleeve prior to fitting the shaft as it may prevent the shaft being pushed fully home.

8 If the front propeller shaft is being serviced, pull the rubber boot

over the sleeve and tighten the hose clips.

9 Refit the shaft to the vehicle as described in Section 2 and lubricate the bearings using a grease gun applied to the universal joint and sleeve nipples.

**Note:** If the sleeve is fitted with a plug instead of a grease nipple, replace it with a nipple to enable lubrication of the sleeve splines.

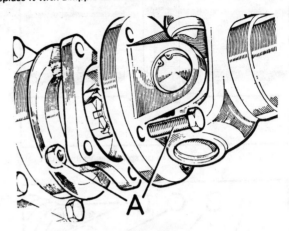

**Fig. 7.2. Propeller shaft and axle coupling flanges**
*A Securing nut and bolt - 4off*

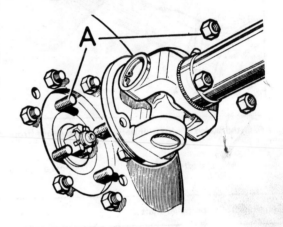

**Fig. 7.3. Rear propeller shaft and transmission brake coupling flanges**
*A Studs and securing nuts*

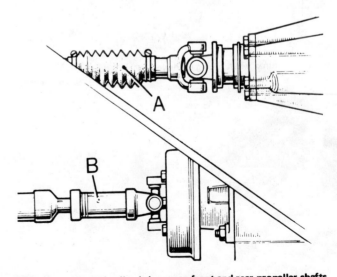

**Fig. 7.4. Location of splined sleeves on front and rear propeller shafts**

*A Front propeller shaft sleeve*      *B Rear propeller shaft sleeve*

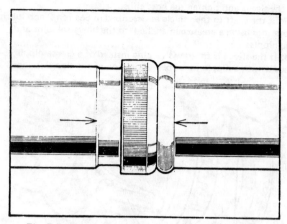

Fig. 7.5. Alignment marks on spline sleeve and shaft

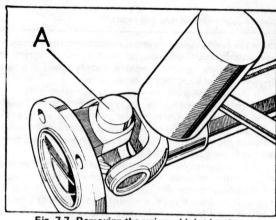

Fig. 7.7. Removing the universal joint bearings

A    Bearing cup

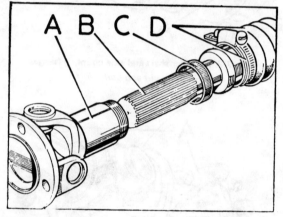

Fig. 7.6. Withdrawing the front universal joint and sleeve (front shaft)

A  Sleeve              C  Dust cap
B  Splined shaft       D  Hose and clips

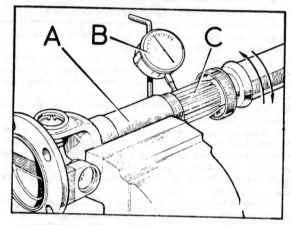

Fig. 7.8. Check the sleeve splines for wear

A  Sleeve          C  Splined end of shaft
B  Dial test indicator

## 6  Fault diagnosis - propeller shaft

| Symptom | Reason/s |
|---|---|
| Vibration | Wear in sliding sleeve splines. |
| | Worn universal joint bearings. |
| | Propeller shaft out of balance. |
| | Distorted propeller shaft. |
| Knock or 'clunk' when taking up drive | Worn universal joint bearings. |
| | Worn rear axle drive pinion splines. |
| | Loose rear drive flange bolts. |
| | Excessive backlash in rear axle gears. |

# Chapter 8 Front and rear axles

*For modifications, and information applicable to later models, see Supplement at end of manual*

## Contents

## Specifications

### Axle type

| | |
|---|---|
| Front ... ... ... ... ... ... ... ... ... ... | Rover (spiral bevel) |
| Rear: | |
|    Series II and IIA ... ... ... ... ... ... ... | Rover or ENV (spiral bevel) |
|    Series III ... ... ... ... ... ... ... ... | Rover (spiral bevel) or Salisbury (hypoid) |

### Ratio ... ... ... ... ... ... ... ... ... ...
4.7:1

### Oil capacities

| | |
|---|---|
| Rover ... ... ... ... ... ... ... ... ... ... | 3 Imp. pints (3.5 US pints, 1.75 litres) |
| ENV ... ... ... ... ... ... ... ... ... ... | 2.6 Imp. pints (3.1 US pints, 1.4 litres) |
| Salisbury ... ... ... ... ... ... ... ... ... | 4.5 Imp. pints (5.5 US pints, 2.5 litres) |

### Front and rear hub lubrication

| | |
|---|---|
| Earlier models ... ... ... ... ... ... ... ... | Oil - 1/3 Imp pint (0.4 US pints - 0.2 litres) |
| Later models ... ... ... ... ... ... ... ... | Grease packed |

### Hub endfloat

| | |
|---|---|
| ENV and early Rover ... ... ... ... ... ... | 0.004 to 0.006 in (0.10 to 0.15 mm) |
| Salisbury and later Rover ... ... ... ... ... ... | 0.002 to 0.004 in (0.05 to 0.10 mm) |

### Swivel pin housing oil capacity ... ... ... ... ... ...
1 Imp. pint (1.2 US pints - 1.4 litres)

### Swivel pin settings

| | |
|---|---|
| Coil spring type ... ... ... ... ... ... ... ... | Resistance of 14 lb to 16 lb (6.3 kg to 7.3 kg) at steering lever eye |
| Railko bush type ... ... ... ... ... ... ... ... | Resistance of 12 lb to 14 lb (5.4 kg to 6.3 kg) at steering lever eye |
| Clearance between stub and halfshaft yoke lugs and swivel pin end faces ... ... ... ... ... ... ... ... ... ... | 0.050 in (1.27 mm) |
| Cone spring: | |
|    Number of working coils ... ... ... ... ... | 3 |
|    Free length ... ... ... ... ... ... ... | 1.150 $\pm$ 0.010 in (29.2 $\pm$ 0.25 mm) |
|    Length in position ... ... ... ... ... ... | 0.687 in (17.4 mm) |
|    Rate ... ... ... ... ... ... ... ... | 660 lb/in$^2$ (7.5 kg/m$^2$) |
|    Fit of retaining collar on shaft ... ... ... ... | 0.001 in (0.025 mm) interference (selective assembly) |

### Torque wrench settings

| | lb f ft | kg f m |
|---|---|---|
| Hub flange bolts: | | |
|   ENV and early Rover ... ... ... ... ... ... | 28 | 3.9 |
|   Salisbury and later Rover ... ... ... ... ... | 30 to 38 | 4.2 to 5.2 |
| Hub securing nut (front): | | |
|   Early Rover ... ... ... ... ... ... ... | 10 to 15 | 1.4 to 2.0 |
|   Later Rover ... ... ... ... ... ... ... | 15 to 20 | 2.0 to 2.7 |
| Hub securing nut (rear)* ... ... ... ... ... ... | 10 to 15 | 1.4 to 2.0 |
| Pinion flange nut (for oil seal renewal): | | |
|   Rover ... ... ... ... ... ... ... ... | 85 | 11.7 |
|   ENV ... ... ... ... ... ... ... ... | 100 to 120 | 14.0 to 16.0 |
|   Salisbury ... ... ... ... ... ... ... | see text | |
| Steering balljoint nuts ... ... ... ... ... ... | 30 | 4.0 |

*\* Rover type axle only*

## 1 General description

Both the front and rear axles on the Land Rover are of a similar design, comprising a one-piece steel casing housing the differential assembly and two driveshafts, (halfshafts). The rear shafts are solid steel bars, the inner end of which is splined into the differential assembly, while the outer end drives the rear wheel hub via a flange.

To enable the front wheels to turn from lock-to-lock while being driven, the front halfshafts incorporate a universal coupling on the outer end.

The universal couplings run inside oil-filled swivel pin housings, the bottom swivel pin is located in a tapered roller bearing while the top pin turns in a plain bush.

Both the front and rear axle assemblies are attached to the chassis via semi-elliptical leaf springs and telescopic shock absorbers.

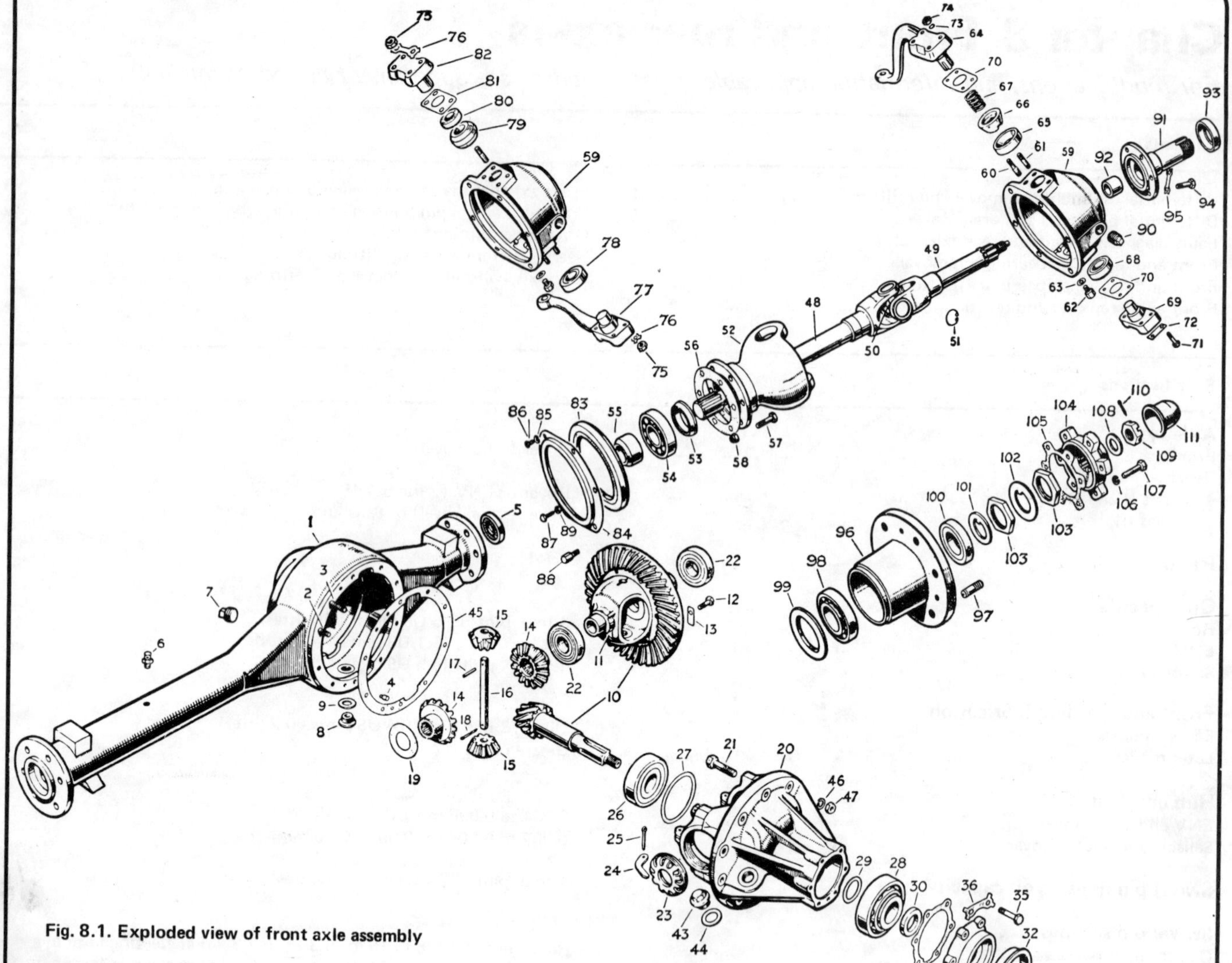

Fig. 8.1. Exploded view of front axle assembly

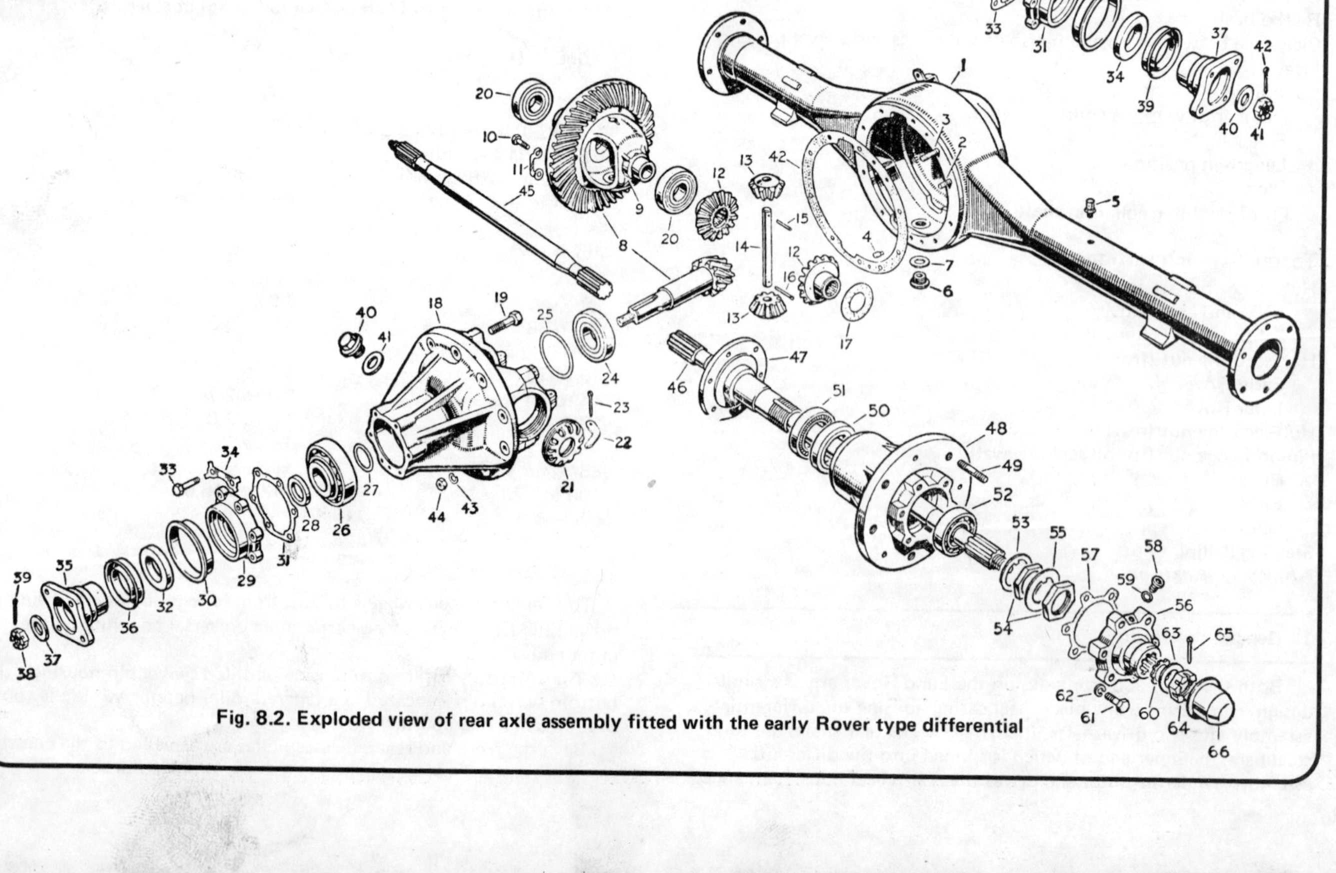

Fig. 8.2. Exploded view of rear axle assembly fitted with the early Rover type differential

## Fig. 8.1. Exploded view of front axle assembly

| | |
|---|---|
| 1 | Axle casing complete |
| 2-3 | Fixings, bevel pinion housing to axle casing |
| 4 | Dowel, locating housing |
| 5 | Oil seal, in casing |
| 6 | Breather |
| 7 | Oil filler plug |
| 8-9 | Drain plug and joint washer |
| 10 | Crownwheel and bevel pinion |
| 11 | Differential casing |
| 12 | Set bolt |
| 13 | Locker (double type) |
| 14 | Differential wheel |
| 15 | Differential pinion |
| 16 | Spindle for pinion |
| 17 | Plain pin ⎫ For spindle |
| 18 | Split pin ⎭ |
| 19 | Thrust washer |
| 20 | Bevel pinion housing |
| 21 | Special bolt, fixing bearing cap |
| 22 | Taper roller bearing for differential |
| 23-24 | Bearing adjustment |
| 25 | Split pin, fixing lock tab |
| 26 | Bearing for bevel pinion, pinion end |
| 27 | Shim, bearing adjustment, pinion end |
| 28 | Bearing for bevel pinion, flange end |
| 29 | Shim, bearing adjustment, flange end |
| 30 | Washer for pinion bearing |
| 31 | Retainer for oil seal |
| 32 | Mudshield for retainer |
| 33 | Joint washer for oil seal retainer |
| 34 | Oil seal for pinion |
| 35-36 | Fixings, oil seal retainer |
| 37 | Driving flange |
| 39 | Mudshield for driving flange |
| 40-42 | Fixings for flange |
| 43-44 | Oil filler plug and joint washer |
| 45 | Joint washer, differential to axle casing |
| 46-47 | Fixings, differential to axle casing |
| 48 | Halfshaft |
| 49 | Stub shaft |
| 50 | Journal assembly |
| 51 | Circlip for journal |
| 52 | Housing for swivel pin bearing |
| 53 | Distance piece for bearing |
| 54 | Bearing for halfshaft |
| 55 | Retaining collar for bearing |
| 56 | Joint washer for housing |

| | |
|---|---|
| 57-58 | Fixings, housing to front axle casing |
| 59 | Housing assembly for swivel pin |
| 60 | Special stud for steering lever and bracket |
| 61 | Stud for steering lever |
| 62-63 | Drain plug and joint washer |
| 64 | Swivel pin and steering lever |
| 65 | Cone seat for swivel pin, top |
| 66 | Cone bearing for swivel pin, top |
| 67 | Spring for cone bearing |
| 68 | Bearing for swivel pin, bottom |
| 69 | Swivel pin and bracket |
| 70 | Shim, for swivel pin bearing |
| 71-74 | Fixings, swivel pin to swivel pin housings |
| 75-76 | Fixings, swivel pins to swivel pin housings |
| 77 | Swivel pin and steering lever |
| 78 | Bearing for bottom swivel pin |
| 79 | Bush for top swivel pin |
| 80 | Thrust washer for bush |
| 81 | Shim for top swivel pin |
| 82 | Swivel pin and bracket |
| 83 | Oil seal for swivel pin bearing housing |
| 84 | Retainer for oil seal |
| 85-89 | Fixings, retainer and lock stop plate to swivel pin housing |
| 90 | Oil filler plug for swivel pin housing |
| 91 | Stub axle assembly |
| 92 | Bush for driving shaft, early models only |
| 93 | Distance piece for inner bearing |
| 94-95 | Fixings, stub axle to swivel pin housing |
| 96 | Front hub assembly |
| 97 | Stud for roadwheel |
| 98 | Bearing for front hub, inner |
| 99 | Oil seal for inner bearing |
| 100 | Bearing for front hub |
| 101 | Keywasher ⎫ Fixing front hub bearing |
| 102 | Locker ⎭ |
| 103 | Special nut |
| 104 | Driving member for front hub |
| 105 | Joint washer for driving member |
| 106-107 | Fixings, driving member to front hub |
| 108 | Plain washer ⎫ Fixing driving member |
| 109 | Slotted nut ⎬ to driving shaft |
| 110 | Split pin ⎭ |
| 111 | Hub cap, front |

Early type: items 60–74

Latest type: items 75–82

## Fig. 8.2. Exploded view of rear axle assembly fitted with the early Rover type differential

| | |
|---|---|
| 1 | Rear axle casing |
| 2-3 | Bolts securing differential |
| 4 | Dowel locating differential |
| 5 | Breather |
| 6-7 | Oil drain plug |
| 8 | Crownwheel and bevel pinion |
| 9 | Differential casing |
| 10-11 | Bolt and locking tab for crownwheel |
| 12 | Differential wheel |
| 13 | Differential pinion |
| 14 | Spindle for pinions |
| 15-16 | Pins for spindles |
| 17 | Thrust washer for differential |
| 18 | Bevel pinion housing |
| 19 | Bolt securing bearing cap |
| 20 | Roller bearings for differential |
| 21 | Serrated nut ⎫ |
| 22 | Lock tab ⎬ For bearing adjustment |
| 23 | Split pin ⎭ |

| | |
|---|---|
| 24 | Bearing for bevel pinion, pinion end |
| 25 | Shims for bearing adjustment, pinion end |
| 26 | Bearing for bevel pinion, flange end |
| 27 | Shims for bearing adjustment, flange end |
| 28 | Washer for bearing |
| 29 | Retainer for oil seal |
| 30 | Mudshield for retainer |
| 31 | Joint washer for retainer |
| 32 | Oil seal for pinion |
| 33-34 | Bolt and locking tab for retainer |
| 35 | Driving flange |
| 36 | Dust shield for driving flange |
| 37-39 | Washer, nut and split pin for driving flange |
| 40-41 | Oil filler plug and washer |
| 42 | Joint washer for differential |
| 43-44 | Nut and washer for differential |
| 45 | Axle shaft, right-hand |

| | |
|---|---|
| 46 | Axle shaft, left-hand |
| 47 | Rear hub bearing sleeve |
| 48 | Rear hub assembly |
| 49 | Stud for roadwheel |
| 50 | Hub bearing, inner |
| 51 | Oil seal for inner bearing |
| 52 | Hub bearing, outer |
| 53-55 | Nuts and lockwasher - for hub bearing |
| 56 | Driving member for rear hub |
| 57 | Joint washer for driving member |
| 58 | Filler plug for hub driving member |
| 59 | Joint washer for filler plug |
| 60 | Oil seal for rear axle shaft |
| 61-62 | Bolt and washer - driving member to rear hub |
| 63-65 | Washer, nut and split pin - axle shaft to driving member |
| 66 | Hub cap, rear |

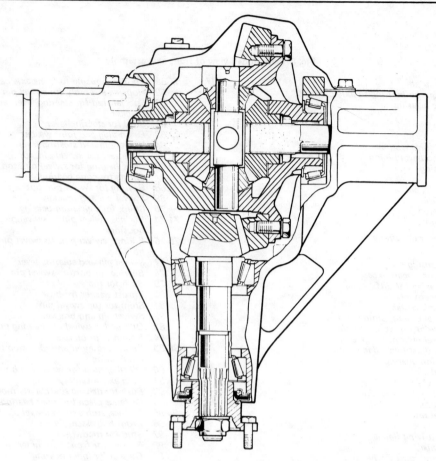

**Fig. 8.3. Sectional view of Salisbury type differential**

## 2  Rear axle halfshafts - removal and refitting

### Rover and Salisbury axles

1    The rear halfshafts are exceptionally easy to remove from the Land Rover as it is not necessary to jack the vehicle up or remove the brake drums.

2    If possible, park the vehicle on flat and level ground. Chock the front wheels to prevent the vehicle from moving. Remove the six bolts securing the halfshaft to the wheel hub. Carefully prise the flange away from the brake drum and withdraw the halfshaft from the axle (see Fig. 8.4).

3    The flange can be withdrawn from the shaft by prising off the hub cap and removing the castle nut, washer and seal (Fig. 8.5) (Rover) or circlip (Salisbury).

### ENV axle

4    Jack up the rear of the vehicle, chock the front wheels, then remove the rear wheel and brake drum, referring to Chapter 9 if necessary.

5    Disconnect the brake pipe at the brake anchor plate, remove the bolts securing the plate to the axle casing, then remove the plate assembly and bearing sleeve. Finally, withdraw the hub and halfshaft assembly.

6    The drive flange can be separated from the hub by removing the securing bolts, and from the halfshaft by prising off the hub cap and removing the circlip (Fig. 8.6).

### All models

7    Refitting is a reverse of the removal procedure. In the case of the ENV axle, bleed the brakes upon completion.

## 3  Front and rear wheelbearings - removal

1    Jack-up the appropriate end of the vehicle and remove the

relevant roadwheel and brake drum (refer to Chapter 9 if necessary).

2    If working on a rear wheel, for Rover and Salisbury axles, remove the halfshaft as described in the previous Section. For ENV axles, prise off the hub cap, remove the circlip from the halfshaft (Fig. 8.6), and unbolt the drive flange. Withdraw the flange from the hub. In the case of a front wheel, prise off the hub cap and remove the castle nut and washer. Undo the six securing bolts and prise the drive flange off the stub axle and hub (see Fig. 8.7 and photo).

3    From inside the hub, tap back the lockwasher using a hammer and screwdriver and remove the two large nuts and washers that secure the hub and bearings to the stub axle (see Fig. 8.8).

4    Hold one hand over the end of the hub to prevent the outer bearing from falling out and withdraw the hub and bearings from the stub axle.

5    Withdraw the outer roller bearing from the hub. Carefully prise out the oil seal from the rear of the hub and remove the inner roller bearing (see Fig. 8.9).

6    Examine the bearings for wear. If the outer races require renewal, support the hub on wooden blocks and drive the races out using a suitable drift.

## 4  Front and rear wheelbearings - refitting

1    Carefully drive the outer bearing races into the hub ensuring the smaller inside diameter of each race faces in toward the centre of the hub.

2    Refit the inner wheel bearing. Smear some sealing compound around the outside of the oil seal. Place it in the hub with the lipped side facing towards the centre of the hub and carefully tap it home, using a flat block of wood until it is flush with the rear face of the hub.

3    Pack the inside of the hub with the correct grade of grease. Pack the outer roller bearing with the same grease and fit it in the outer race.

4    Holding the outer roller bearing in position slide the hub assembly onto the stub axle.

5   Fit the inner washer and nut and tighten the nut just enough to take up the hub endfloat. Spin the hub several times to settle the bearings and check that it turns easily with no harshness. The endfloat should be as specified, but this can only be accurately checked using a dial gauge indicator.

6   When the hub is adjusted correctly, fit the lockwasher and outer nut; tighten the outer nut and recheck that the hub rotates freely before securing it with the lockwasher.

7   Refit the hub driving flange (and halfshaft if working on the rear axle) and tighten the securing bolts to the specified torque.

8   In the case of the front axle hubs, refit the washer and castle nut onto the end of the driveshaft. Tighten the nut to the specified torque and secure with a new split pin.

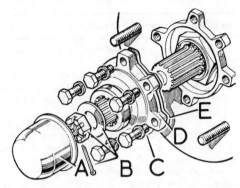

**Fig. 8.7. Removing the front halfshaft driving flange**

| | | |
|---|---|---|
| A | Hub cap | D | Flange |
| B | Securing nut and washer | E | Gasket |
| C | Flange bolts | | |

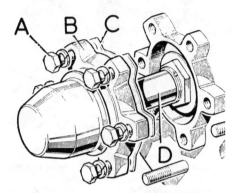

**Fig. 8.4. Removing a rear halfshaft (Rover)**

| | | |
|---|---|---|
| A | Securing bolts | C | Gasket |
| B | Driving flange | D | Halfshaft |

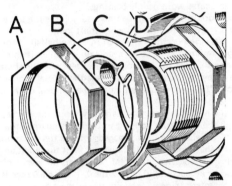

**Fig. 8.8. Wheel bearing hub securing nuts**

| | | |
|---|---|---|
| A | Locknut | C | Nut for bearing adjustment |
| B | Lockwasher | D | Hub |

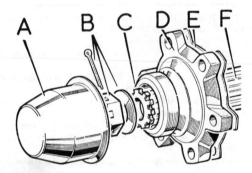

**Fig. 8.5. Halfshaft flange assembly (Rover)**

| | | |
|---|---|---|
| A | Hub cap | D | Flange |
| B | Retaining nut and washer | E | Gasket |
| C | Seal | F | Halfshaft |

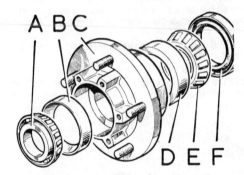

**Fig. 8.9. Hub and bearings assembly**

| | | |
|---|---|---|
| A | Outer roller bearing | D | Outer race for inner bearing |
| B | Outer race for outer bearing | E | Inner roller bearing |
| C | Hub | F | Oil seal |

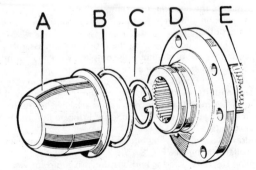

**Fig. 8.6. ENV type rear halfshaft flange assembly**

| | | |
|---|---|---|
| A | Hub cap | D | Driving member |
| B | Oil seal 'O' ring | E | Axle halfshaft |
| C | Circlip | | |

3.2 Front hub driving flange removed

## 5   Front axle halfshafts - removal and refitting

1   Jack-up the front of the vehicle and place heavy duty axle stands beneath the chassis.

2   Remove the roadwheel and brake drum and drain the oil from the swivel pin housing and the differential casing into a suitable container.

3   Remove the front hub and bearings as described in the previous Section.

4   Remove the brake anchor plate assembly as described in Chapter 9. Note that it is not necessary to disconnect the brake pipes and flexible hose, but the anchor plate should be tied out of the way to avoid straining the hose.

5   The stub axle can now be drawn off the halfshaft. Remove the gasket from the swivel pin housing.

6   Carefully withdraw the complete halfshaft assembly from the axle casing (see Fig. 8.10).

7   Examine the halfshaft universal joint for wear by gripping each end of the shaft and turning them in opposite directions. Any movement in the joint indicates worn needle bearings.

8   The procedure for renewing the universal joint is the same as that described in Chapter 7 for the propeller shaft joints.

9   Check the bearing on the inner section of the halfshaft for wear. The bearing is retained in place by a steel collar which is an extremely tight fit on the shaft. If the bearing requires renewal  the shaft should be taken to a Leyland dealer who will have the special tool and adaptor kit (Part No. 275870) that is essential for the removal of the collar and bearing.

10  To refit the halfshaft assembly, carefully insert the long end of the shaft through the swivel pin housing and axle casing until the splines on the end of the shaft are fully engaged in the differential unit.

11  Rotate the shaft and, with the universal joint turned at an angle, check the clearance between the joint yokes and the swivel pin face which should be at least 0.050 in (1.2 mm). If the clearance is insufficient, the chamfered side of the joint yokes must be carefully filed down (see Fig. 8.11)

CAUTION: *Great care must be taken not to remove too much metal from the yokes.*

12  Refit the stub axle to the swivel pin housing using a new gasket.

13  Refit the brake anchor plate assembly referring to Chapter 9 if necessary.

14  Refit the hub and adjust the wheel bearing pre-load as described in Section 4.

15  Refill the swivel pin housing and axle with Castrol Hypoy EP 90 oil to the top of the filler/level plugs. Refit the plugs and tighten.

16  Refit the roadwheel, remove the axle stands and lower the vehicle to the ground.

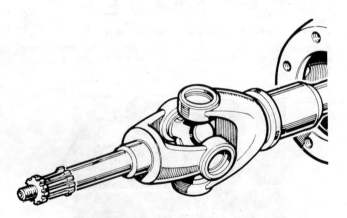

**Fig. 8.10. Withdrawing the front halfshaft**

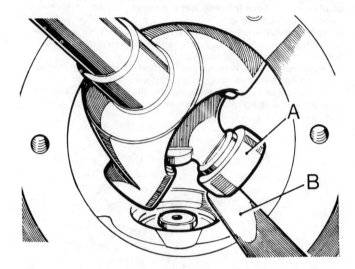

**Fig. 8.11. Measuring the clearance of the front halfshaft coupling**

A   *Coupling yoke*                          B   *Feeler gauges*

## 6   Front axle swivel pin housing - removal, servicing and refitting

1   Jack-up the front of the vehicle and support it on axle stands.

2   Remove the roadwheel and drain the oil from the swivel pin housing and front axle into a suitable container.

3   Remove the brake drum and the wheel bearing hub as described in Section 3.

4   Remove the brake anchor plate, stub axle and halfshaft assembly as described in the previous Section.

5   Disconnect the trackrod balljoint from the swivel pin housing steering lever using the method described in Chapter 11.

6   Remove the nuts and bolts securing the swivel pin housing assembly to the axle casing flange. Note the positions of the steering lock stop and jack stop (see Fig. 8.12).

7   Withdraw the complete swivel pin housing assembly and remove the gasket.

8   Before dismantling the swivel pin housing it should be noted that the earlier type of spring-loaded bush fitted to the top swivel pin has been replaced by a Railko type bush which considerably improves steering damping and reduces any tendency to wheel wobble. A Railko bush conversion kit is available from Leylands under Part No. 532268, and if the top swivel pin assembly requires renewal, it is recommended that this kit is obtained before commencing work.

9   To dismantle the housing, first remove the six bolts from the inner side of the housing, remove the retaining ring and prise out the oil seal from the housing (see Fig. 8.13).

10  Remove the four bolts securing the top swivel pin assembly to the housing and lift it out of the housing complete with any shims and, in the case of the earlier type, the cone spring.

11  Remove the four bolts securing the bottom swivel pin assembly to the housing and lift it out of the housing complete with any shims.

Note: On earlier models the steering arm is attached to the top of the swivel pin housing while on later models it is located on the bottom of the housing (see Fig. 8.14).

12  Withdraw the inner bearing housing assembly and remove the bottom roller bearing (see Fig. 8.15).

13  Examine the roller bearing and bottom swivel pin for wear and renew if necessary. The outer bearing race can be driven from the bearing housing using a suitably sized drift.

14  Check the upper swivel pin and bush (or cone) for excessive wear and renew if necessary. In the case of the earlier spring-loaded cone, this should be replaced with the Railko bush conversion kit mentioned earlier in this Section.

15 Inspect the roller bearing inside the bearing housing for wear and if it requires renewal drive it out from the inside of the housing using a suitably sized drift (see Fig. 8.16).

16 Remove the oil seal located in the end of the axle casing. Smear jointing compound around the outside of the new seal and fit it into the casing with the lipped side inwards (Fig. 8.17). Carefully tap it home until it is flush with the recessed end of the axle casing.

17 Begin reassembly by fitting the tapered roller bearing into the bearing housing. Note that if the bearing outer race was removed it must be refitted with the narrower inside diameter facing upwards.

18 Lubricate the top swivel pin bush with gear oil and press it into the top of the bearing housing followed by the thrust washer, if fitted (see Fig. 8.18).

19 If the earlier type cone bearing is being renewed, ensure it is refitted in the bearing housing with the oil hole in the position shown in Fig. 8.19.

20 Holding the bottom swivel pin roller bearing in position, insert the bearing housing assembly into the main housing.

21 Smear some sealing compound on the face of the bottom swivel pin assembly, refit any shims that were removed and insert the pin through the housing and into the taper roller bearing. Secure the swivel pin plate with the four nuts but do not bend over the locking tabs at this stage.

22 Note that on later models with the steering arm fitted to the bottom swivel pin plate, there is an 'O' ring type oil seal on the pin and there are no shims (see Fig. 8.20).

23 If the cone type bearing for the top swivel pin is being used fit the thrust spring into the bearing.

24 Insert the top swivel pin assembly through the housing and into the top bush (or cone). Secure with the four nuts, but do not bend over the locking tabs at this stage.
**Note:** On later models, any shims that were beneath the top swivel pin plate must be refitted prior to the pin.

25 Check that the outer housing turns smoothly on the inner bearing assembly. If it feels excessively tight, add another shim between the swivel pin plate and the housing, tighten the nuts and recheck it.

26 Should the outer housing turn far too easily and feels slack, remove one of the shims.

27 As a final check, hold the flange of the inner bearing housing in a soft-jawed vice, attach a spring balance to the end of the steering arm and check that a pull of 14 to 16 lb (6.3 to 7.3 kg) is required to turn the outer swivel pin housing. Add or remove shims as necessary to obtain the correct amount of resistance (see Fig. 8.21).

28 When the swivel pins are correctly adjusted bend the locking tabs over the securing nuts.

29 Pack a new swivel pin housing oil seal with grease, fit it to the rear of the housing and secure it in place with the retainer and six bolts and washers. Note that the steering lock stop bolt must be fitted on the forward edge of the housing flange (see Fig. 8.22).

30 Check that the seal is a tight fit across the complete face of the inner bearing housing when the outer housing is turned from lock-to-lock. Slacken the retainer bolts and reset the seal if necessary.

31 Smear both sides of a new gasket with grease and position on the axle casing flange.

32 Offer up the swivel pin housing assembly to the axle flange, fit the bolts and secure with the locknuts. Ensure the jack stop and steering stop plates are correctly positioned (see Fig. 8.12).

33 Refit the trackrod balljoint(s) to the steering arm, tighten the nuts to a torque wrench setting of 30 lb f ft (4 kg f m) and secure with a split pin.

34 Turn the housing onto full lock and adjust the steering lock stop bolt to obtain a clearance of ½ in (12.5 mm) between the bolt head and the stop plate (see Fig. 8.23). Tighten the locknut.

35 Refit the halfshaft, stub axle and brake anchor plate as described in Section 5.

36 Refit the hub and bearings as described in Section 3.

37 Refill the swivel pin housing and axle with Castrol Hypoy gear oil (photos).

38 Refit the roadwheel and lower the vehicle to the ground. Before road testing, check the steering at full lock to ensure the front wheels do not touch the chassis. If necessary re-adjust the steering lock stop bolt.

---

**7 Differential pinion oil seal - renewal**

1 Failure of the front or rear pinion oil seal will be indicated by oil

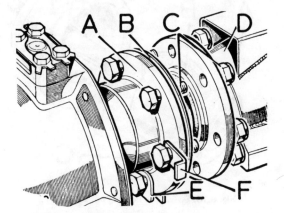

**Fig. 8.12. Removing the swivel pin housing**

A Swivel pin housing  
B Joint washer  
C Bolts, swivel pin housing to axle case  
D Axle case  
E Location stop for jack (RH side only)  
F Lock stop plate

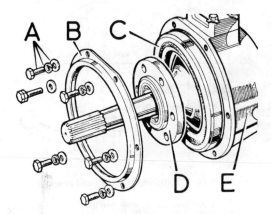

**Fig. 8.13. Swivel pin housing oil seal assembly**

A Bolts (6 off), oil seal retainer to swivel pin housing  
B Oil seal retainer  
C Oil seal  
D Swivel pin bearing housing  
E Swivel pin housing

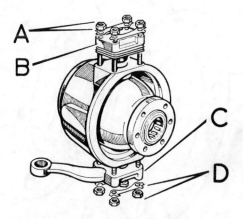

**Fig. 8.14. Later type swivel pin housing**

A Securing nuts (top)  
B Top swivel pin assembly  
C Bottom steering arm and pin assembly  
D Securing nuts (bottom)

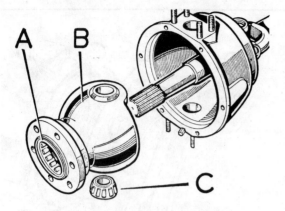

**Fig. 8.15. Swivel pin bearing housing**

A  Roller bearing for axle halfshaft
B  Bearing housing
C  Taper roller bearings for bottom swivel pin

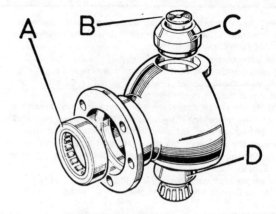

**Fig. 8.18. Refitting the bearings into the housing**

A  Roller bearing for axle halfshaft
B  Thrust washer for top swivel pin (early models)
C  Railko bush for top swivel pin
D  Outer race for bottom swivel pin bearing

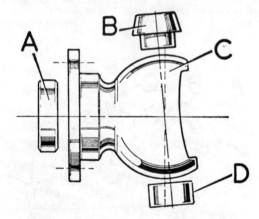

**Fig. 8.16. Location of the bush and bearings**

A  Roller bearing for axle halfshaft
B  Railko bush
C  Top of housing
D  Outer race for taper roller bearing

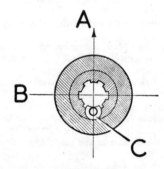

**Fig. 8.19. Correct location of earlier cone type bush**

A  Front of vehicle          C  Oil hole
B  Front axle centre line

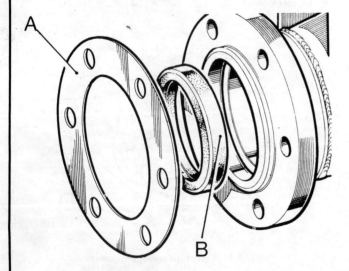

**Fig. 8.17. Axle flange oil seal**

A  Gasket      B  Oil seal

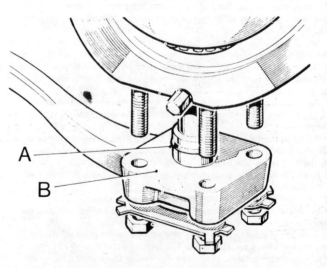

**Fig. 8.20. Lower swivel pin and steering arm (later models)**

A  'O' ring          B  Steering arm

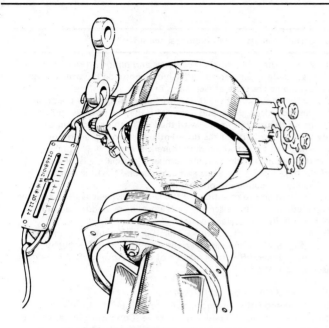

Fig. 8.21. Checking the bearing resistance

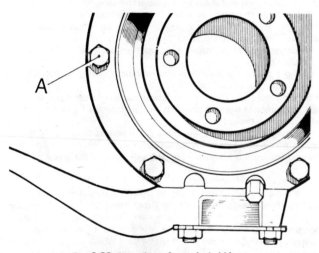

Fig. 8.22. Location of stop bolt 'A'

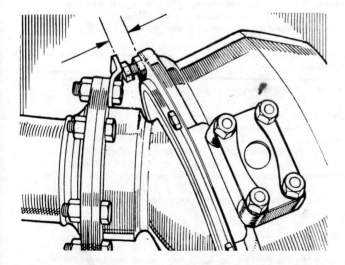

Fig. 8.23. Setting the steering lock stop bolt (dimension between arrows must be ½ in (12.5 mm)

6.37a Filling the swivel pin housing with lubricating oil

6.37b Front axle filler plug

thrown around the differential casing and in extreme cases, oil dripping out of the pinion housing.

2   The procedure for renewing both front and rear differential pinion oil seals is the same on the Rover type axles. The Salisbury and ENV type rear axles differ slightly and details are given where necessary.

3   Disconnect the front or rear propeller shaft as appropriate from the axle flange as described in Chapter 7.

4   Get an assistant to apply the footbrake to lock the rear wheels. On Salisbury axles, carefully mark the relationship between the pinion shaft, pinion flange and flange nut. (It is important that the nut is eventually refitted the same number of turns to its precise previous position.) Where applicable, remove the split pin from the flange castle nut; undo the nut using a socket wrench.

CAUTION: If the vehicle has been jacked up, take great care not to dislodge it from the axle stands when applying the foot brake.

5   Remove the flange from the pinion shaft.

6   Except on early Rover axles, the seal can now be prised out of the end of the pinion housing (see Fig. 8.25).

7   In the case of early Rover axles, remove the bolts securing the oil seal retainer to the pinion housing and remove the oil seal retainer and gasket (Fig. 8.24).

8   Drive the oil seal out of the retainer, (see Fig. 8.26).

9   Except on early Rover axles, smear the outside diameter of the seal with jointing compound and carefully tap the seal into the pinion housing with the lipped side facing in towards the axle.

10 On ENV and later Rover axles, refit the pinion flange and securing nut and, with the footbrake firmly applied, tighten the nut to the specified torque. On Salisbury axles, refit the pinion flange, nut and

washer, making sure that the marks made on dismantling are correctly aligned. On no account must the nut be excessively tightened.

11 If working on the early Rover type axle, gently warm the seal retainer, smear the outside of the seal with jointing compound, and fit it into the retainer with the lipped side facing the bolt holes.

12 Smear both sides of a new gasket with jointing compound and refit the seal retainer to the end of the pinion housing ensuring that the oilways in the housing gasket and retainer are aligned.

13 Tighten the retainer securing bolts and bend over the locking tabs.

14 Refit the pinion flange, washer and, with the rear wheels locked by means of the foot brake, tighten the nut to the specified torque wrench setting. Secure the nut with a split pin.

15 Finally, refit the propeller shaft, check the axle oil level and lower the vehicle to the ground.

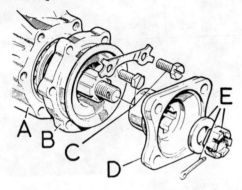

Fig. 8.24. Remove the pinion flange (early Rover type axle)

A   Bevel pinion housing
B   Oil seal retainer
C   Fixings, oil seal retainer
D   Driving flange for bevel pinion
E   Nut and washer for bevel pinion driving flange

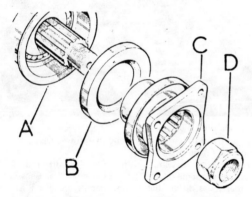

Fig. 8.25. Pinion flange and seal (ENV type axle)

A   Pinion housing
B   Seal
C   Flange
D   Securing nut

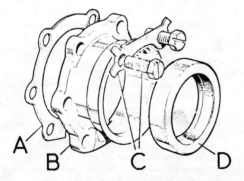

Fig. 8.26. Pinion oil seal and retainer (early Rover type axle)

A   Gasket
B   Retainer
C   Bolts and locking tabs
D   Oil seal

## 8   Differential assemblies - removal and refitting

1   Wear in the differential crownwheel and pinion on the front or rear axle is usually accompanied by a whining noise on the overrun and, depending on the state of wear, also in drive.

2   As the condition of the differential gears deteriorate the noise will increase to a deep growl, and although it may be possible to carry on for many thousands of miles with the axle in this condition, there is always the possibility of the differential breaking up at any time.

3   The task of overhauling the differential assembly is a highly skilled job that requires a considerable number of special tools, and because of the high cost of new gears and bearings and the time involved, it is not really an economical proposition.

4   The best course of action for the D-I-Y mechanic is to replace the complete differential assembly with a new or reconditioned unit obtainable from a Leyland dealer.

5   All models are fitted with Rover type differentials to the front axle (Fig. 8.27), although early and late versions differ slightly in design. The rear differential may be of ENV, Rover or Salisbury design (see Specifications).

### Rover and ENV type differential

6   The method of removing and refitting either the front or rear differential assembly is basically the same. Commence by jacking up the front or rear of the vehicle as appropriate, place axle stands beneath the chassis and drain the oil from the axle.

7   Withdraw both halfshafts until the inner splines are clear of the differential. Refer to Section 2 for instructions on removing the rear shafts and Section 5 for the front shafts.

8   Disconnect the relevant propeller shaft from the axle as described in Chapter 7.

9   Remove the nuts and washers securing the pinion shaft housing to the axle casing (see Fig. 8.30).

10 Support the pinion housing with both hands and carefully withdraw the complete housing and differential assembly from the axle casing. Remove the gasket.

11 Refitting the differential assembly is the reverse sequence of the removal procedure. Use a new gasket between the pinion housing and axle case and do not forget to refill the axle with EP 90 gear oil.

### Salisbury type differential

12 The Salisbury differential fitted to the rear axle of some Series III models differs considerably from the Rover and ENV types. To remove the differential assembly, the complete axle casing must be removed from the vehicle and then, after the rear cover and bearing caps are removed, a special spreader tool must be used which literally stretches the casing apart to enable the differential assembly to be levered out.

13 Due to the damage that could be caused by incorrect use of the spreader tool, (presuming one could be obtained) it is strongly recommended that the vehicle is taken to a Land Rover dealer or transmission specialist should the differential require attention.

## 9   Front axle - removal and refitting

1   Slacken the front wheel nuts, jack-up the front of the vehicle and support it on stands.

2   Remove both front wheels.

3   Disconnect the front propeller shaft from the front axle as described in Chapter 7.

4   Remove the front flexible brake hoses from the pipe unions and securing brackets on each side of the chassis (refer to Chapter 9 if necessary). Plug the ends of the brake pipes to avoid losing all the fluid.

5   Refer to Chapter 11 and disconnect the steering drag-link balljoint from the relay lever.

6   Disconnect the lower ends of the shock absorbers from the road spring bottom plates.

7   Undo the nuts and remove the four 'U' bolts securing the axle casing to the front spring (see Fig. 8.31). Note which way round the bottom plates are fitted.

8   Support the weight of the axle on a trolley jack, remove the front shackle pins from both road springs (Chapter 11) and lower them to the ground.

9 Lower the jack and withdraw the complete axle assembly from beneath the vehicle.

10 Installation is the reversal of the removal procedure, but before refitting the axle, check that the axle case breather valve is clear, (see Fig. 8.32).

11 Before the spring shackle pins and locknuts are fully tightened, lower the vehicle to the ground and move it backwards and forwards to settle the springs and then tighten the shackle pins.

12 Refill the axle to the correct level with gear oil and bleed the brakes as described in Chapter 9.

## 10 Rear axle - removal and refitting

1 Slacken the rear wheel nuts, jack-up the rear of the vehicle and support it on stands. Remove both rear wheels.

2 Disconnect the propeller shaft from the rear axle as described in Chapter 7.

3 Disconnect the rear flexible brake hose from the pipe union and the chassis bracket, (refer to Chapter 9 if necessary). Plug the end of the flexible pipe to prevent all the fluid escaping.

4 Support the axle assembly on a trolley jack and remove the nuts and bolts securing one end of each check strap (see Fig. 8.33).

5 Remove the two rear shock absorbers as described in Chapter 11.

6 Undo the nuts and remove the four 'U' bolts securing the rear axle casing to the road springs.

7 Make sure the axle is supported by the trolley jack and then remove the rear shackle pins from both road springs (Chapter 11) and lower them to the ground.

8 Lower the jack and withdraw the complete axle assembly from beneath the vehicle.

9 Refitting is the reversal of the removal procedure, but before the rear shackle pins are fully tightened, the vehicle should be lowered to the ground and pushed backwards and forwards to settle the springs before finally tightening the shackle pins.

10 Refill the axle with the correct grade of gear oil, and bleed the brakes as described in Chapter 9.

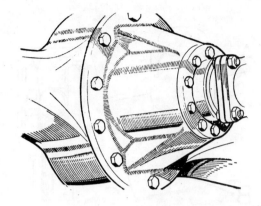

Fig. 8.29. ENV type differential

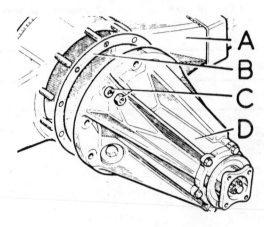

Fig. 8.30. Removing the pinion housing and differential assembly (Rover)

| | |
|---|---|
| A Axle casing | C Securing nuts and washers |
| B Gasket | D Pinion housing |

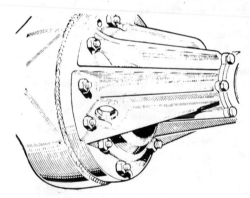

Fig. 8.27. Rover type differential

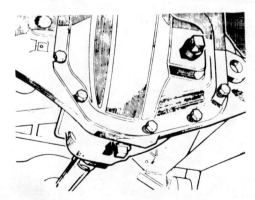

Fig. 8.28. Salisbury type differential

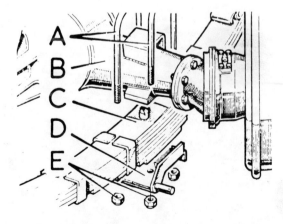

Fig. 8.31. Axle 'U' bolts and clamp

| | |
|---|---|
| A 'U' bolts | D Bottom clamp |
| B Axle casing | E Securing nuts |
| C Road spring | |

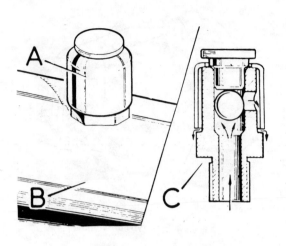

Fig. 8.32. Axle case breather valve

A  Breather          B  Axle case          C  Flow through breather

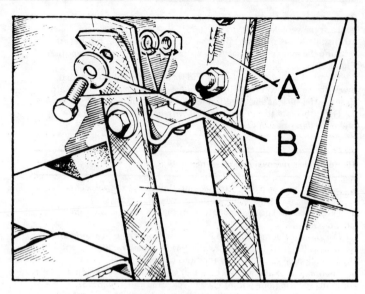

Fig. 8.33. Axle check strap

A  Chassis          B  Securing bolts          C  Check strap

## 11 Fault diagnosis - front and rear axles

| Symptom | Reason/s |
| --- | --- |
| Vibration | Worn halfshaft bearings. |
| | Loose drive flange bolts. |
| | Out of balance propeller shaft. |
| | Wheels require balancing. |
| | Worn swivel pins/bearings. |
| | Universal joints on front halfshafts worn. |
| Noise | Insufficient lubricant. |
| | Worn gears and differential components generally. |
| 'Clunk' on acceleration or deceleration | Incorrect crownwheel and pinion mesh. |
| | Excessive backlash due to wear in crownwheel and pinion teeth. |
| | Worn halfshaft or differential side gear splines. |
| | Lose drive flange bolts. |
| | Worn drive pinion flange splines. |
| Oil leakage | Faulty pinion or halfshaft oil seals. |
| | May be caused by blocked axle housing breather. |

# Chapter 9 Braking system

*For modifications, and information applicable to later models, see Supplement at end of manual*

## Contents

## Specifications

**Type** ... ... ... ... ... ... ... ... ...    Hydraulically operated drum brakes. Mechanically operated transmission brake

### 10 in diameter type (SWB models)
Lining.
| | |
|---|---|
| Length ... ... ... ... ... ... ... ... ... | 8½ in (215 mm) |
| Width ... ... ... ... ... ... ... ... ... | 1½ in (38 mm) |
| Thickness ... ... ... ... ... ... ... ... | 3/16 in (4.75 mm) |
| Drum regrinding limit ... ... ... ... ... ... | + 0.030 in (+ 0.75 mm) oversize |

### 11 in diameter type (LWB models)
Lining (front)
| | |
|---|---|
| Length ... ... ... ... ... ... ... ... ... | 10.45 in (265 mm) |
| Width ... ... ... ... ... ... ... ... ... | 2¼ in (57 mm) |
| Thickness ... ... ... ... ... ... ... ... | 3/16 in (4.75 mm) |

Lining (rear)
| | |
|---|---|
| Length ... ... ... ... ... ... ... ... ... | 8.6 in (218 mm) |
| Width ... ... ... ... ... ... ... ... ... | 2¼ in (57 mm) |
| Thickness ... ... ... ... ... ... ... ... | 3/16 in (4.75 mm) |
| Drum regrinding limit ... ... ... ... ... ... | As for 10 in drums |

### Transmission brake
Lining
| | |
|---|---|
| Length ... ... ... ... ... ... ... ... ... | 8.64 in (219 mm) |
| Width ... ... ... ... ... ... ... ... ... | 1¾ in (44.5 mm) |
| Thickness ... ... ... ... ... ... ... ... | 3/16 in (4.75 mm) |
| Drum diameter ... ... ... ... ... ... ... | 9 in (228.6 mm) |
| Drum regrinding limit ... ... ... ... ... ... | As for 10 in drums |

### Master cylinder
| | |
|---|---|
| Type (SWB models) ... ... ... ... ... ... ... | Girling CV |
| Bore ... ... ... ... ... ... ... ... ... | ¾ in (19 mm) |
| Stroke ... ... ... ... ... ... ... ... ... | 1½ in (38 mm) |
| Type (LWB models) ... ... ... ... ... ... ... | Girling CV or CB |
| Bore ... ... ... ... ... ... ... ... ... | 1 in (25 mm) |
| Stroke ... ... ... ... ... ... ... ... ... | 1½ in (38 mm) |
| Pushrod free movement ... ... ... ... ... ... | 1/16 in (1.5 mm) |

## 1 General description

The braking system on the 2¼ litre Land Rovers is comprised of drum brakes on the front and rear wheels operated by an hydraulic master cylinder connected to the brake pedal. The handbrake lever is mechanically linked to a drum brake mounted on the rear of the gearbox. Application of the lever locks the rear propeller shaft and if four-wheel drive is selected, also the front propeller shaft.

The short wheel based (SWB) models are fitted with 10 in (254 mm) diameter drums on the front and rear wheels, while the long wheel based (LWB) models are equipped with 11 in (279 mm) diameter drums.

The Series IIA and III models have the option of a dual braking system with servo assistance.

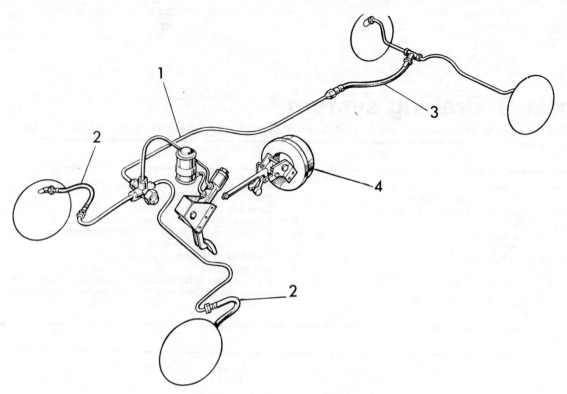

**Fig. 9.1. Layout of earlier type braking system**

| | | | |
|---|---|---|---|
| 1 *Brake fluid reservoir* | 2 *Front flexible brake pipes* | 3 *Rear flexible brake pipe* | 4 *Transmission brake* |

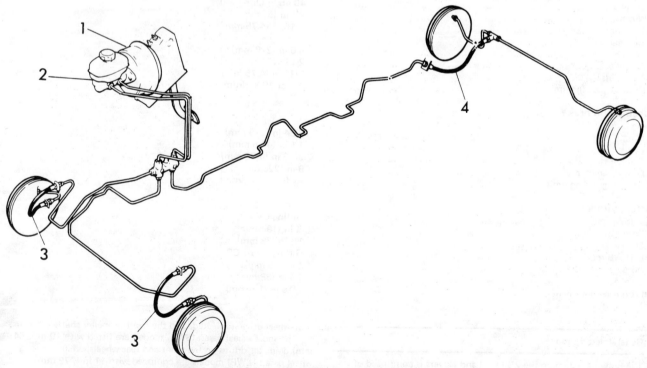

**Fig. 9.2. Dual braking system with servo unit**

| | | | |
|---|---|---|---|
| 1 *Servo unit* | 2 *Master cylinder* | 3 *Front flexible brake pipes* | 4 *Rear flexible brake pipes* |

## 2  Front and rear brakes - adjustment

1   At the service intervals detailed in the Routine Maintenance
Section at the beginning of the Manual, it will be necessary to adjust
the brakes to compensate for lining wear.
2   The SWB models are fitted with a single hexagon adjustment bolt
at the back of each brake anchor plate (see photo), while the LWB
models are equipped with two hexagon adjusters on each anchor plate.
**Note:** On some earlier LWB models a single square-headed adjuster is
fitted on the rear brakes.
3   The method of adjusting the brakes on all models is basically the
same. Jack-up each wheel in turn until the tyre is just clear of the
ground and support the vehicle on axle stands. It is not necessary to
remove the wheels.
4   From the rear of the anchor plate, check that the wheel turns
freely (slacken the adjuster(s) if necessary) and then turn the
adjuster(s) clockwise until the brake shoes are in firm contact with
the drum.
5   Slacken the adjuster(s) anti-clockwise just enough to enable the
wheel to rotate freely.
6   Lower the vehicle to the ground and repeat the operation on the
other three wheels.
7   For handbrake adjustment refer to Section 4.

## 3  Brake drums and shoes - removal, inspection and refitting

1   If, after adjusting the brakes they are still inefficient and there are
no signs of hydraulic leaks, the drums should be removed and the
linings checked for wear.
2   The procedure for removing the brake drums and shoes is basically
the same for all models. Commence by jacking-up the front of the
vehicle, place axle stands under the chassis and remove the road-
wheels.
3   Slacken off the brake adjuster(s) as described in Section 2, remove
the screws securing the drum to the hub and draw it off. If the drum
tends to stick, tap the periphery with a soft-faced mallet to loosen it.
4   Examine the friction surface on the interior of the drum. Normally
this should be completely smooth and bright. Remove any dust with a
dry cloth and examine the surface for any score marks or blemishes.
Very light hairline scores running around the surface are not serious
but indicate that the shoes may be wearing out, or heavy grit and dirt
have got into the drum at some time. If there are signs of deep scoring
the drum needs reconditioning or renewal.
5   The brake linings should be renewed if they are so worn that the
rivet heads are flush with the surface of the lining. If bonded linings
are fitted they must be renewed when the material has worn down to
1/32 inch at its thinnest point. If the shoes are being removed to give
access to the wheel cylinders, then cover the linings with masking tape
to prevent any possibility of their becoming contaminated with grease.
6   Using a screwdriver, scratch a mark alongside the holes in each
shoe through which the return springs are hooked. This will avoid any
confusion when the springs are refitted.
7   Slacken the adjuster(s) right back.
8   On the SWB models, remove the anchor plate securing the trailing
shoe to the pivot post (see Fig. 9.3).
9   Using a screwdriver or a pair of grips, carefully lever the bottom
ends of the shoes away from the anchor post. If working on the LWB
model, lever the trailing end of each shoe from the plain end of each
wheel cylinder (see Fig. 9.4).
10   Release the other end of each shoe and remove them complete with
springs.
11   Place a rubber band round each wheel cylinder piston to prevent
their coming out causing loss of brake fluid and the necessity of
bleeding the braking system.
12   Thoroughly clean all traces of dust from the shoes, backplates and
brake drums with a dry paint brush and compressed air if available. Do
not breathe in any dust as it will be of asbestos nature. Brake dust can
cause squeal and judder and it is therefore important to clean out the
brakes thoroughly.
13   Check that the pistons are free in their cylinders and that the
rubber dust covers are undamaged and in position and that there are
no hydraulic fluid leaks.
14   Prior to reassembly smear a trace of white brake grease to all
sliding surfaces. It is vital that no grease or oil comes into contact with

the brake drums or the brake linings.
15   Refitting is a straight forward reversal of the removal procedure
but note the following points:

> a) Ensure that the return springs are located in the correct holes
>    in the shoes.
> b) Check that the snail type adjusting cam(s) are correctly
>    located against the post on the shoe.
> c) After refitting the drums, adjust the brakes as described in
>    Section 2.
> d) If brake shoe steady posts are fitted and have been
>    disturbed, these should be adjusted to the position shown
>    in Fig. 9.7.

16   After reassembling the front brakes, carry out the same procedure
on the rear brakes. It will be noticed that there are differences in
design between the slave cylinders fitted to the SWB and LWB models,
but providing reference is made to the exploded diagrams in this
Chapter no major problems should be encountered.

## 4  Transmission brake - adjustment

1   The transmission brake, located at the rear of the transfer box, has
a single adjuster which protrudes from the front of the backplate (see
Fig. 9.8).
2   Access can be gained to the brake adjuster either by removing the
centre seat box panel, or from beneath the vehicle. If working beneath
the vehicle place chocks on either side of two wheels as the handbrake
must be in the off position while adjusting the brake.
3   Rotate the adjuster clockwise until the brake shoes are in firm
contact with the drum.
**Note:** The adjuster is not very accessible and a proper square-jawed
brake adjusting spanner should be used to avoid burring over the head
of the adjuster.
4   Unscrew the adjuster just enough to release the brake (approximately two clicks) and then apply and release the handbrake lever to
centralise the shoes.
5   Adjust the two locknuts on the handbrake lever vertical adjuster
rod so that the lever has two clicks free movement on the ratchet
before the brake is applied, (photo).

2.2 Front wheel brake adjuster (SWB models)

4.5 Handbrake lever vertical adjuster rod

**Fig. 9.3. Exploded view of the 10 in diameter brakes fitted to all SWB models (front and rear)**

1  Brake anchor plate assembly
2  Shoe, steady post
3  Locknut for steady post
4  Set bolt (3/8 x 1 in long, securing front anchor plate to axle case
5  Locker, securing front anchor plate to axle case
6  Brake shoe assembly, front and rear
7  Linings complete with rivets, for brake shoe
8  Spring post for brake shoe
9  Anchor for brake shoe
10  Special set screw, securing anchor
11  Locking plate for bolt

12  Pull-off spring for brake shoe
13  Pull-off spring for leading shoe
14  Wheel cylinder assembly
15  Spring for piston, front
16  Washer for spring, front
17  Bleed screw
18  Special nut, securing wheel cylinder
19  Spring washer, securing wheel cylinder
20  Brake drum
21  Set screw, securing brake drum

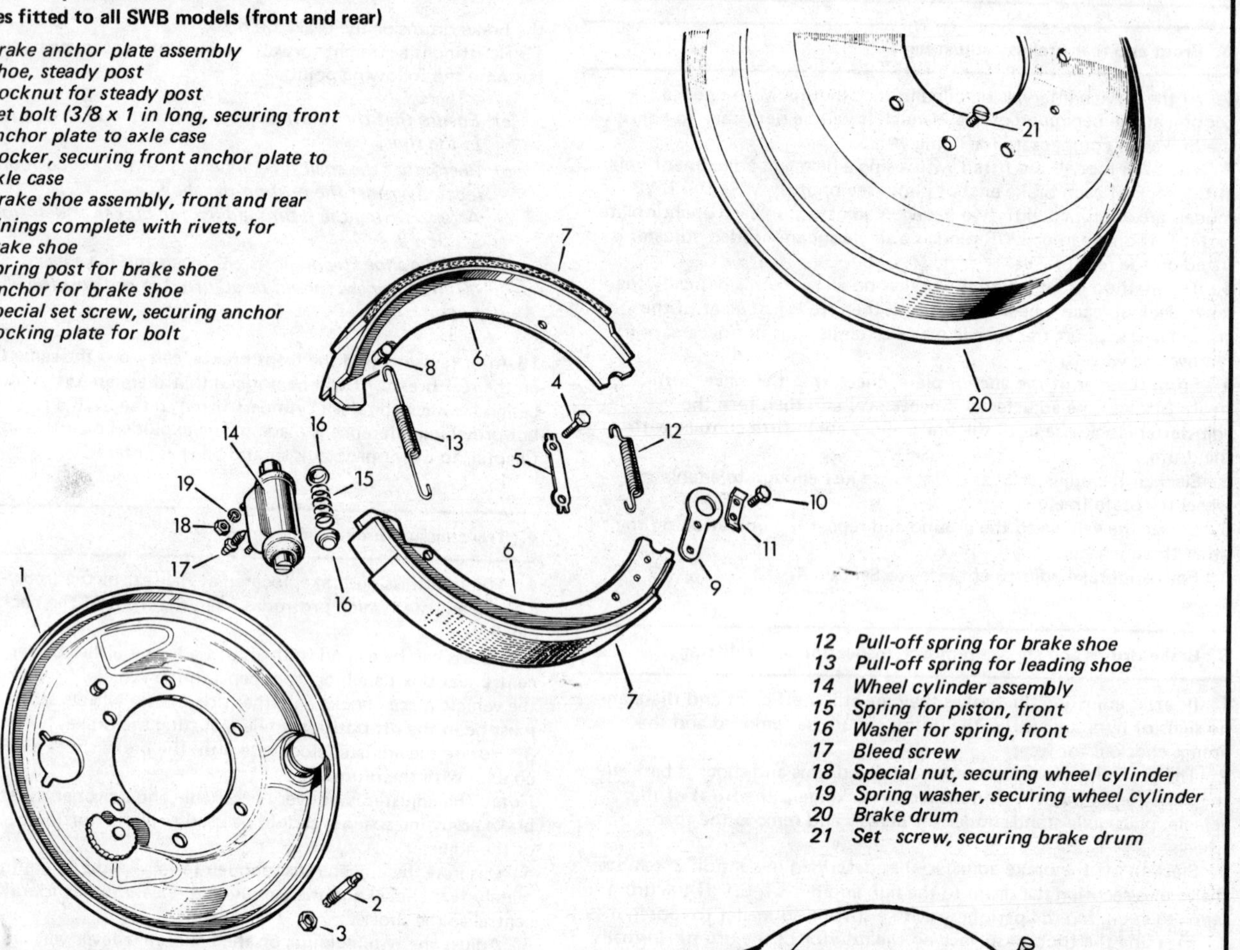

**Fig. 9.4. Exploded view of the front brake fitted to all LWB models**

1  Brake anchor plate
2  Steady post for brake shoe
3  Bush for steady post
4  Special nut, securing steady post
5  Brake shoe assembly
6  Lining complete with rivets, for brake shoe

7  Pull-off spring for brake shoe
8  Wheel cylinder assembly - 2 off
9  Spring (5/8 in diameter), for piston
10  Air excluder, for piston
11  Sealing ring for cylinder
12  Bleed screw
13  Spring washer, securing wheel cylinder
14  Special nut, securing wheel cylinder
15  Connecting pipe for wheel cylinder
16  Brake drum
17  Set screw, securing brake drum

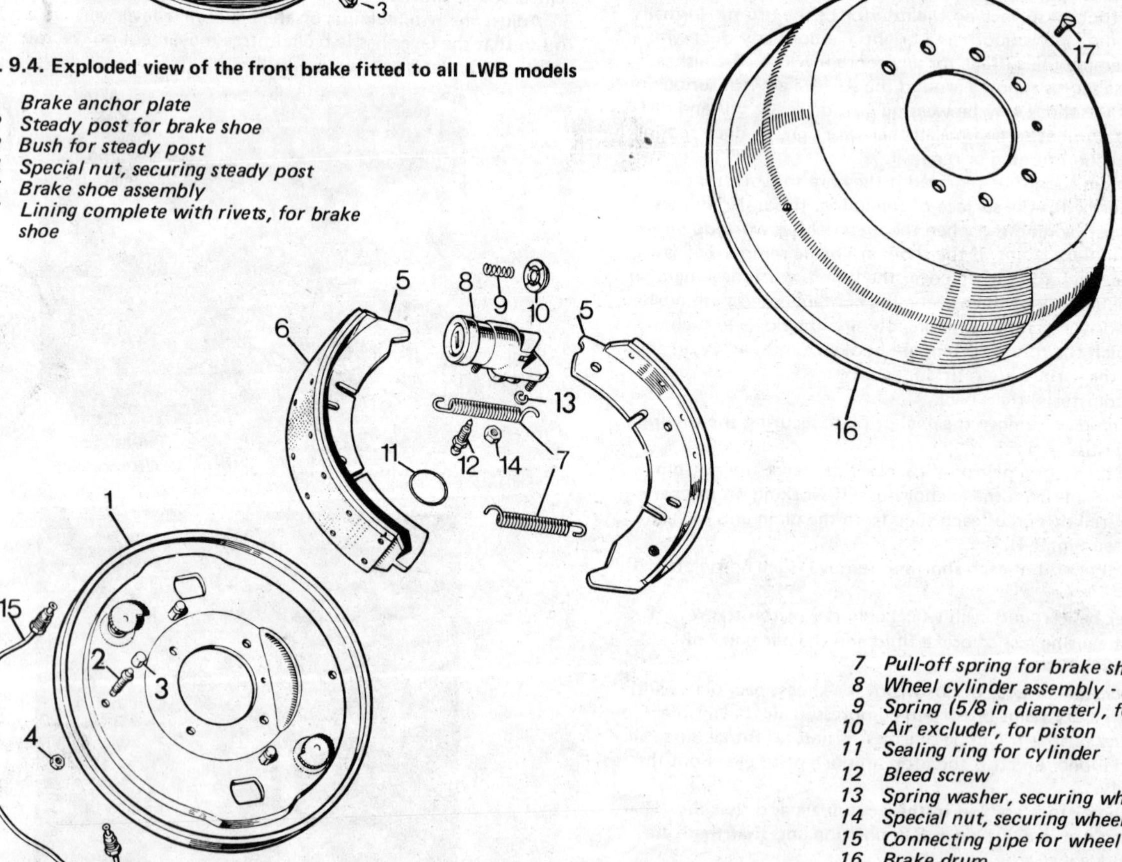

**Fig. 9.5. Exploded view of the rear brake fitted to Series II, LWB models**

1 Brake anchor plate
2 Steady post for brake shoe
3 Bush for steady post
4 Special nut for steady post
5 Brake shoe assembly
6 Lining complete with rivets, for
  brake shoe
7 Spring, adjuster end, for brake shoe
8 Spring, wheel cylinder end, for brake shoe
9 Adjuster housing

10 Spring washer, securing adjuster housing
11 Special set bolt, securing adjuster housing
12 Plunger, LH
13 Plunger, RH
14 Cone for adjuster

15 Wheel cylinder assembly
16 Spring
17 Air excluder
18 Bleed screw
19 Brake shoe abutment plate
20 Retainer for brake shoe abutment plate
21 Screw, securing retainer and abutment
   plate
22 Shakeproof washer, securing retainer and
   abutment plate
23 Dust cover plate for brake wheel cylinder
24 Spring washer, securing wheel cylinder
25 Self-locking nut, securing wheel cylinder
26 Brake drum
27 Set screw, securing brake drum

**Fig. 9.6. Exploded view of the rear
brake fitted to Series IIA and III, LWB models**

1 Brake anchor plate
2 Brake shoe assembly
3 Lining complete with rivets, for
  brake shoe
4 Spring, abutment end, for brake shoe
5 Spring, wheel cylinder end, for
  brake shoe
6 Wheel cylinder assembly
7 Spring for piston

8 Washer for spring
9 Screw
10 Special nut, securing wheel cylinder
11 Spring washer, securing wheel cylinder
12 Brake drum
13 Set screw, securing brake drum

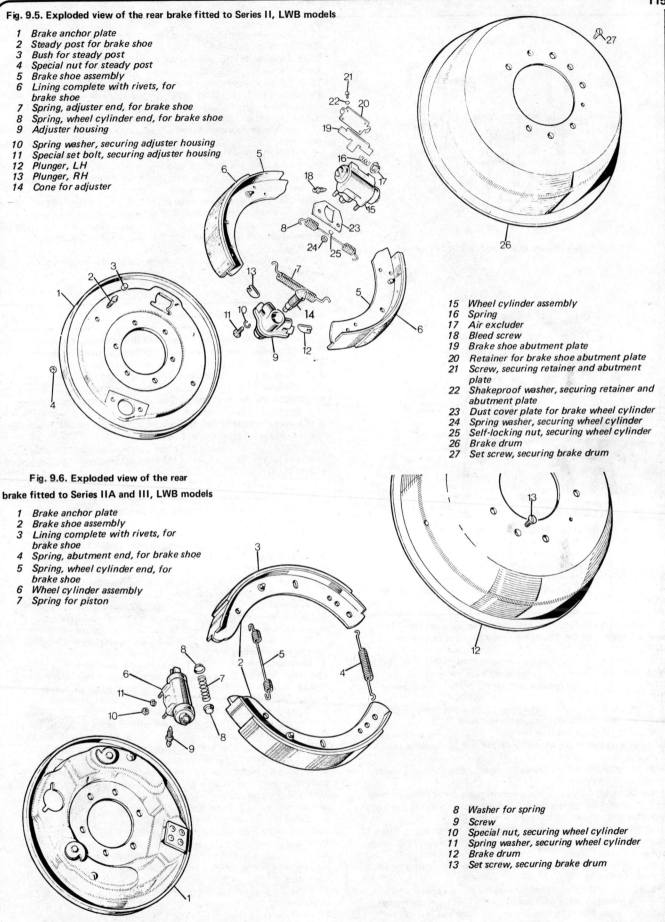

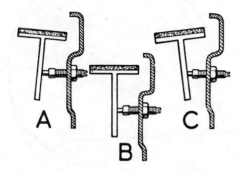

**Fig. 9.7. Adjustment of brake shoe steady post**

A  Incorrect                        B  Correct
                                    C  Incorrect

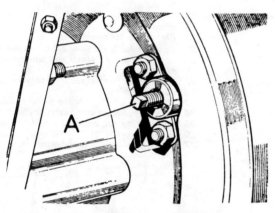

**Fig. 9.8. Transmission brake adjuster 'A'**

### 5  Transmission brake drum and shoes - removal, inspection and refitting

1   Access to the transmission brake is gained from beneath the vehicle. Ensure that the wheels are firmly chocked before commencing work.
2   Remove the six nuts securing the brake drum to the output shaft flange and withdraw the drum rearwards over the propeller shaft. If the drum is difficult to remove, slacken the brake adjuster several turns.
3   Using a screwdriver mark the holes in the shoes through which the return spring are hooked to ensure correct reassembly.
4   Lever the end of each shoe out of the adjuster unit and then slide the other ends out of the expander unit (Fig. 9.9). Remove the shoes and return springs.
5   Examine the drum and linings for wear as described in Section 3 and renew if necessary.
6   Check that the plungers in the adjuster unit move freely. If they are stiff or seized, unscrew the two securing nuts from the front of the backplate and remove the complete unit (see Fig. 9.10).
7   Unscrew the adjuster cone and tap out the two plungers. Clean all the components in petrol and allow to dry before reassembly using grease.
8   Do not forget to bend the locking tabs over the adjuster retaining nuts when refitting.
9   Check the brake shoe expander unit for correct operation.
10 If it is necessary to remove the expander unit from the backplate, first remove the clevis pin securing the expander rod fork to the handbrake linkage.

11 Unhook the return spring and remove the rubber dust cover from the front of the backplate.
12 On later models, remove the spring clip securing the expander unit to the backplate (see 9.12).
13 Withdraw the complete expander unit from the backplate.
14 Remove the spring clip and tap out the plungers and rollers from the expander unit. Note that on earlier models steel balls are used in place of rollers and the plungers are retained by split pins.
15 Clean the components in petrol and grease them before reassembling.
16 Reassembling of the brake adjuster unit, expander unit and brake shoes is basically the reverse procedure to removal. Refer to Figs. 9.13 and 9.14) for the correct reassembly of the expander unit and, (on later models) the securing clips.
**Note:** If difficulty is experienced in removing or refitting any of the transmission brake components it may be necessary to remove the propeller shaft as described in Chapter 7. Then undo the large castle nut and withdraw the output shaft flange complete with drum (see Fig. 9.15).
17 After reassembly, adjust the transmission brake as described in Section 4.

### 6  Handbrake lever - removal and refitting

1   The handbrake lever can be removed from beneath the vehicle. Ensure the wheels are firmly chocked before commencing work.
2   Remove the clevis pin securing the operating rod to the relay lever.
3   Remove the nut securing the relay lever to the chassis and withdraw the lever (Fig. 9.16). Disconnect the return spring.
4   Remove the two nuts and washers securing the handbrake lever assembly to the chassis bracket.
5   Carefully withdraw the complete handbrake assembly through the aperture in the front of the seat box.
6   Refit the handbrake using the reversal of the removal procedure. If necessary adjust the locknuts on the vertical operating rod as described in Section 4.

### 7  Wheel cylinders (SWB models) - removal, inspection and refitting

1   The procedure for overhauling either the front or rear wheel cylinders on the SWB models is basically the same.
2   Jack-up the vehicle, support it on stands and remove the road-wheel.
3   Remove the brake drum and shoes as described in Section 3.
4   Before continuing, examine the rubber boots on each end of the wheel cylinder for fluid leakage then get someone to gently press the footbrake, and check that the pistons push the shoes outwards and return fully. Do not push the pedal too far down as the piston may be ejected from the cylinder and it will become necessary to bleed the system after refitting it.
5   Disconnect the brake pipe from the rear side of the wheel cylinder. Note that the front brakes are fitted with a flexible pipe and this must first be disconnected from the pipe union on the side of the chassis member (see Fig. 9.17).
6   Plug the ends of the hydraulic pipes to reduce fluid loss.
7   Remove the two retaining nuts and withdraw the complete wheel cylinder from the backplate.
8   Withdraw the rubber boots, pistons, seals and spring from the wheel cylinder making a careful note of the assembly order (Fig. 9.18).
9   Inspect the surfaces of the pistons and cylinder bores. If any scoring or 'bright' wear areas are evident, renew the complete assembly.
10 If the components are in good condition, discard the rubber seals and obtain new ones in the form of a repair kit.
11 Install the new seals using the fingers only to manipulate them into position. Dip the pistons into clean hydraulic fluid before installing them and then fit the dust excluders.
12 Installation is a reversal of removal but make sure that the locating boss on the cylinder body is engaged correctly in the hole in the backplate.
13 Refit the brake shoes and drum and bleed the system as described in Section 18.
14 Refit the roadwheel, adjust the brakes and lower the vehicle to the ground.

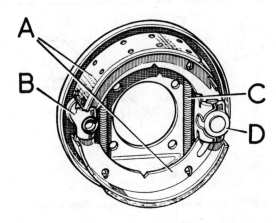

**Fig. 9.9. Transmission brake assembly**

A  Brake shoes
B  Adjuster unit
C  Brake shoe return springs
D  Expander unit

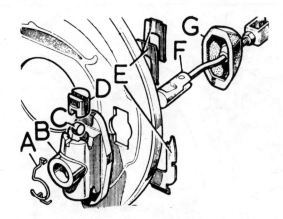

**Fig. 9.12. Transmission brake expander assembly**

A  Spring clip
B  Housing
C  Roller
D  Plunger
E  Fixings for expander unit
F  Operating rod
G  Rubber dust excluder

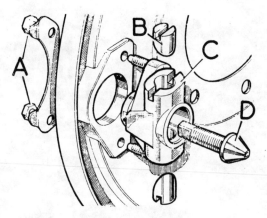

**Fig. 9.10. Transmission brake adjuster assembly**

A  Securing nuts
B  Plungers
C  Housing
D  Adjuster cone

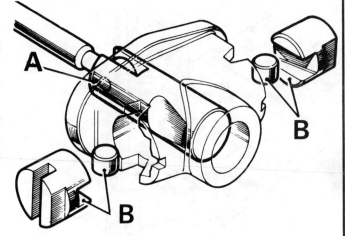

**Fig. 9.13. Correct assembly of expander rod and plungers**

A  Expander rod
B  Plunger and rollers

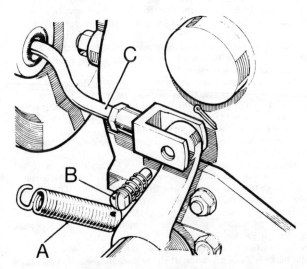

**Fig. 9.11. Transmission brake operating rod**

A  Return spring
B  Clevis pin
C  Operating rod

**Fig. 9.14. Expander unit retaining plates (later models)**

A  Expander housing
B  Packing piece
C  Locking plate
D  Retaining spring

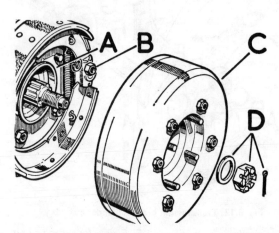

**Fig. 9.15. Transmission brake drum and output drive flange removed**

A  Brake anchor plate        C  Brake drum and flange
B  Anchor plate securing nuts  D  Securing nut

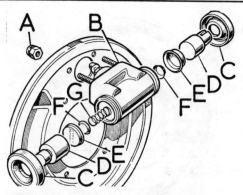

**Fig. 9.18. Wheel cylinder components (SWB models)**

A  Fixings for wheel cylinder     E  Seal
B  Wheel cylinder                 F  Support for seal
C  Dust cover                     G  Spring
D  Piston

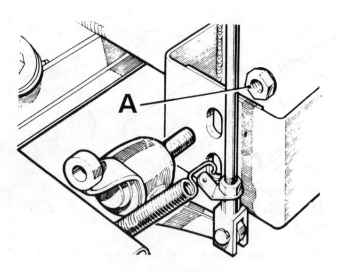

**Fig. 9.16. Handbrake relay lever**

*A  Securing nut*

7.3 Brake shoes and wheel cylinder (SWB models)

**8  Wheel cylinders (LWB models) - removal, inspection and refitting**

1    The front brakes of the LWB model are fitted with two single piston wheel cylinders while the rear brakes have a single, twin piston wheel cylinder. The overhaul procedure for both types of cylinder is basically the same, but any differences will be detailed where necessary.
2    Remove the brake drum and shoes as described in Section 3.
3    Check the wheel cylinder(s) for leaks or faulty operation as described in Section 7, paragraph 4.
4    Disconnect the brake pipe from the rear wheel cylinder. In the case of the front wheels, remove the crossfeed pipe from each wheel cylinder and then disconnect the flexible hose from the chassis union first before unscrewing the other end from the wheel cylinder.
5    Plug the ends of the hydraulic pipes to reduce fluid loss.
6    Remove the securing nuts and withdraw the wheel cylinder(s) from the backplate.
7    Referring to Fig. 9.19 (front cylinder) or Fig. 9.20 (rear cylinder) as appropriate, remove the pistons, seals and spring from the wheel cylinder. Note that the rear cylinder fitted to the Series IIA model is exactly the same as that fitted to the SWB model (see Section 7, Fig. 9.18).
8    Examine the pistons and cylinders for wear and then fit new seals as described in Section 7, paragraphs 9 to 11 inclusive.
9    Refit the wheel cylinder(s) using the reversal of the removal procedure. Check the operation of the brake adjuster and if necessary, remove, clean and lubricate the plungers and threaded adjuster cone (see Fig. 9.21).
10 Refit the brake shoes and drum, and bleed the system as described in Section 18.
11 Refit the roadwheel, adjust the brakes and lower the vehicle to the ground.

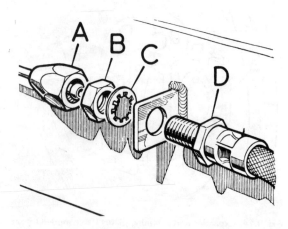

**Fig. 9.17. Flexible brake hose connection**

A  Pipe from master cylinder     C  Shakeproof washer
B  Locknut                       D  Flexible brake pipe

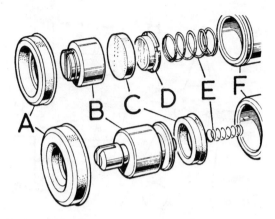

**Fig. 9.19. The two types of piston and seals fitted in the front wheel cylinders of the LWB models**

A  Dust cover
B  Piston
C  Seal for piston

D  Support for seal
E  Spring
F  Wheel cylinder

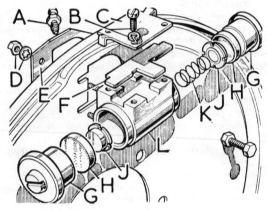

**Fig. 9.20. Wheel cylinder assembly fitted to the rear brakes of LWB models**

A  Bleed nipple
B  Screws for retainer
C  Retainer for abutment plate
D  Nuts for dust cover
E  Dust cover
F  Abutment plate for shoes

G  Piston
H  Seal for piston
J  Support for seal
K  Spring
L  Wheel cylinder

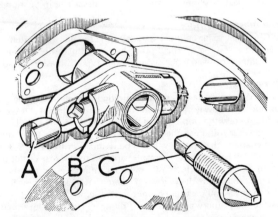

**Fig. 9.21. Rear wheel brake adjuster (Series II, LWB)**

A  Plunger
B  Adjuster housing

C  Adjuster cone

## 9 Master cylinder - removal and refitting

1  Three different types of master cylinder have been fitted to the Land Rover. The Series II and IIA models are equipped with either the centre valve (CV) type or the compression barrel (CB) type (see Fig. 9.22).
2  Series III models are fitted with either the CV type or, on later models the dual system type (see Fig. 9.23). The latter type is fitted in conjunction with a servo unit.

### CB type master cylinder
3  With a suitable container in readiness, remove the brake and clutch pipe unions from the combined fluid reservoir and allow the fluid to drain into the container.
4  Remove the single securing nut and lift the reservoir off the bracket.
5  Disconnect the two hydraulic pipes from the master cylinder.
6  From inside the vehicle, remove the brake pedal return spring and unscrew the bolts securing the pedal bracket to the bulkhead (see Fig. 9.24).
7  Withdraw the bracket and master cylinder from the engine compartment manoeuvring it as necessary to enable the pedal to pass through the bulkhead aperture.
8  Remove the top cover and gasket from the bracket.
9  Remove the nut and washer securing the master cylinder pushrod to the brake pedal trunnion. Remove the two nuts and bolts securing the cylinder to the bracket and withdraw the complete cylinder (see Fig. 9.25).
10  Refit the master cylinder and bracket using the reversal of the removal procedure. Adjust the pushrod nuts to obtain 1/16 in (1.5 mm) free-play on the pushrod (see Fig. 9.26).
11  Refit the fluid reservoir and bleed the brakes as described in Section 18.

### CV type master cylinder (without servo unit)
12  Drain and remove the fluid reservoir as described in paragraph 3 of this Section.
13  Disconnect the two hydraulic pipes from the master cylinder.
14  Remove the top cover and gasket from the brake pedal bracket.
15  Undo the master cylinder pushrod nut and the two flange nuts and withdraw the cylinder rearwards from the bracket.
16  Refit the master cylinder using the reverse procedure. Adjust the pushrod nuts as shown in Fig. 9.26.
17  Refit the fluid reservoir and bleed the brakes.

### CV type and dual master cylinder (with servo unit)
18  Disconnect the hydraulic pipe(s) from the master cylinder.
19  Remove the two securing nuts and washers and withdraw the complete master cylinder and reservoir assembly from the servo unit.
20  Refit using the reverse procedure and bleed the brakes as described in Section 18.

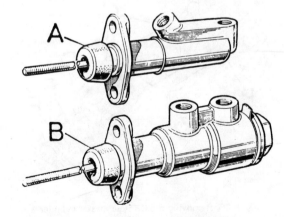

**Fig. 9.22. Two types of master cylinder fitted to earlier models**

A  'CV' type

B  'CB' type

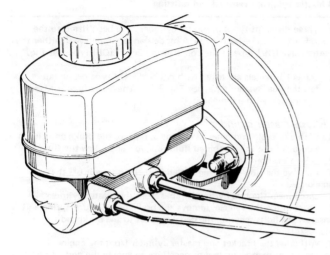

Fig. 9.23. Later type of dual master cylinder

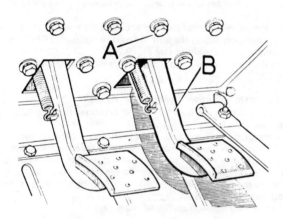

Fig. 9.24. Brake pedal attachment bolts

A   Securing bolts              B   Brake pedal

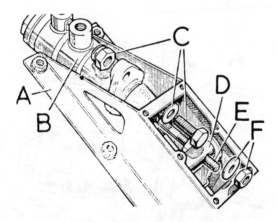

Fig. 9.25. Removing the CB type master cylinder

A   Brake pedal bracket         D   Brake pedal trunnion
B   Master cylinder             E   Pushrod
C   Securing nuts               F   Pushrod securing nuts

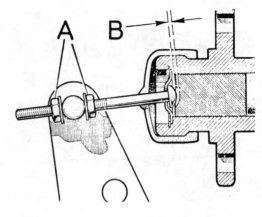

Fig. 9.26. Master cylinder pushrod adjustment

A   Adjusting nuts              B   Free-play - 1/16 in (1.5 mm)

---

### 10 Master cylinder - overhaul

*CB type master cylinder*
1   With the master cylinder on the bench, remove the nut from the pushrod and prise off the rubber cover from the end of the cylinder.
2   Remove the circlip from inside the end of the cylinder and withdraw the pushrod and retaining washer.
3   Gently tap the cylinder on a wooden block until the piston emerges from the cylinder. Withdraw the piston and spring (Fig. 9.28).
4   Turning to the other end of the cylinder unscrew the end cap and remove the recuperating seal assembly (Fig. 9.29).
5   Examine the piston and cylinder bore surfaces for scoring or 'bright' wear areas. Where these are evident, renew the complete master cylinder.
6   If the components are in good order, discard the seals and obtain new ones, preferably in the form of a repair kit.
7   Lubricate the new seals and the cylinder barrel with brake fluid and fit the seal into the piston groove with the larger outside diameter of the seal facing away from the pushrod end of the piston (see Fig. 9.30).
8   Insert the piston into the cylinder taking care not to pinch the seal. Refit the pushrod, retaining washer and circlip.
9   Fit the washer and seal into the other end of the cylinder making sure that the flat face of the seal faces the piston (see Fig. 9.31).
10 Insert the spring into the centre bore of the piston and refit the seal support, gasket and end cap and tighten the cap.
11 Smear some rubber grease inside the rubber cover and fit it over the pushrod and cylinder.
12 Refit the master cylinder to the vehicle as described in Section 9.

*CV type master cylinder*
13 The CV type master cylinder is exactly the same as the clutch master cylinder and the overhaul procedure and illustrations given in Chapter 5 should be used when servicing this type of master cylinder.

*Dual type master cylinder*
14 Undo and remove the two screws holding the reservoir to the cylinder body. Lift away the reservoir. Using a suitable sized Allen key or wrench unscrew the tipping valve nut and lift away the seal. Using a suitable diameter rod, push the primary plunger down the bore, this operation enabling the tipping valve to be withdrawn (see Fig. 9.32).
15 Using a compressed air jet, carefully applied to the rear outlet pipe connection, blow out all the master cylinder internal components. Alternatively, shake out the parts. Take care that adequate precautions are taken to ensure all parts are caught as they emerge.
16 Separate the primary and secondary plungers from the intermediate spring. Use the fingers to remove the gland seal from the primary plunger.
17 The secondary plunger assembly should be separated by lifting the thimble leaf over the shouldered end of the plunger. Using the fingers, remove the seal from the secondary plunger.

18 Depress the secondary spring, allowing the valve stem to slide through the keyhole in the thimble, thus releasing the tension in the spring.

19 Detach the valve spacer, taking care of the spring washer which will be found located under the valve head.

20 Examine the bore of the cylinder carefully for scores, ridges or excessive wear. If the bore is found to be completely smooth, with only negligible wear, new seals can be fitted. If, however, there is any doubt about the condition of the bore, fit a new cylinder.

21 Thoroughly clean all parts in either fresh hydraulic fluid or methylated spirits. Ensure that the bypass ports are clear.

22 All components should be assembled wet by dipping in clean brake fluid. Using fingers only, fit new seals to the primary and secondary plungers, ensuring that they are the correct way round. Place the dished washer with the dome against the underside of the valve seat. Hold it in position with the valve spacers ensuring that the legs face towards the valve seal.

23 Refit the plunger return spring centrally on the spacer, insert the thimble into the spring and depress until the valve stem engages in the keyhole of the thimble.

24 Insert the reduced end of the plunger into the thimble, until the thimble engages under the shoulder of the plunger, and press home the thimble leaf. Refit the intermediate spring between the primary and secondary plungers.

25 Check that the master cylinder bore is clean and smear with clean brake fluid. With the complete assembly suitably lubricated with brake fluid, carefully insert the assembly into the bore. Ease the lips of the plunger seals carefully into the bore. Push the assembly fully home.

26 Refit the tipping valve assembly and seal into the cylinder and tighten the securing nut. Refit the fluid reservoir and tighten the two retaining screws.

27 The master cylinder can now be refitted to the vehicle as described in Section 9.

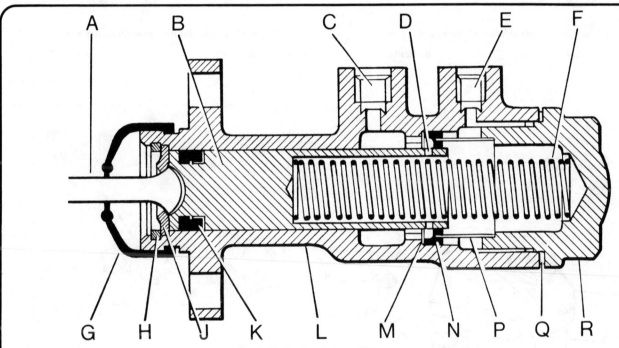

Fig. 9.27. Sectional view of CB type master cylinder

| | | | |
|---|---|---|---|
| A Pushrod | E Outlet to wheel cylinders | J Retaining washer | N Recuperating seal |
| B Piston | F Piston spring | K End seal | P Seal support |
| C Inlet from reservoir | G Dust cover | L Cylinder | Q Gasket |
| D Inlet ports | H Circlip | M Shim | R End cap |

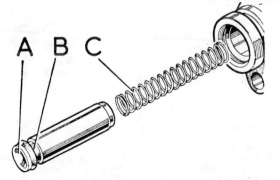

Fig. 9.28. Removing the piston and spring from master cylinder (CB type)

| | |
|---|---|
| A Seal | C Spring |
| B Piston | |

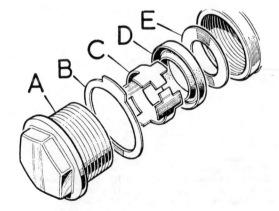

Fig. 9.29. End cap assembly (CB type)

| | |
|---|---|
| A End cap | D Recuperating seal |
| B Gasket for end cap | E Shim |
| C Support for seal | |

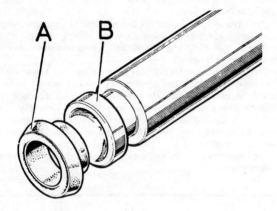

**Fig. 9.30. Correct location of piston seal**

A Seal                                    B Piston

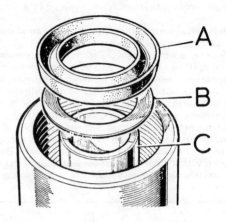

**Fig. 9.31. Correct location of recuperating seal**

A Seal                                    C Piston
B Shim

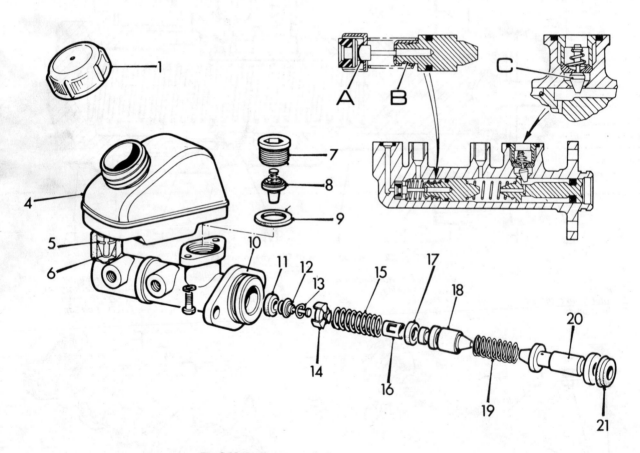

**Fig. 9.32. Dual master cylinder components**

| | | | |
|---|---|---|---|
| 1 Filler cap | 8 Tipping valve | 13 Spring washer - curved | 18 Secondary plunger |
| 4 Reservoir - dual | 9 Face seal | 14 Valve spacer | 19 Intermediate spring (black) |
| 5 Circlip - internal | 10 Cylinder body | 15 Secondary spring | 20 Primary plunger |
| 6 Seal | 11 Valve seal | 16 Spring retainer | 21 Gland seal |
| 7 Securing nut | 12 Valve stem | 17 Seal | |

A   Correct assembly of spring washer in centre valve

B   Leaf of spring retainer

C   As the brakes are applied the primary plunger moves down the cylinder and al-lows the tipping valve (C) to close the primary sup-ply port. The assembly shows the unit in the off position

## 11 Servo unit - description

The vacuum servo unit is fitted into the brake hydraulic circuit in series with the master cylinder to provide assistance to the driver when the brake pedal is depressed. This reduces the effort required by the driver to operate the brakes under all braking conditions.

The unit operates by vacuum obtained from the induction manifold and comprises, basically, a booster diaphragm, control rod, slave cylinder and non-return valve.

The servo unit and hydraulic master cylinder are connected together so that the servo unit piston rod acts as the master cylinder pushrod. The driver's braking effort is transmitted through another pushrod to the servo unit piston and its built-in control system. The servo unit piston does not fit tightly into the cylinder, but has a strong diaphragm to keep its edges in contact with the cylinder wall, so assuring an air-tight seal between the two parts. The forward chamber is held under vacuum conditions created in the inlet manifold of the engine, and during periods when the brake pedal is not in use, the controls open a passage to the rear chamber so placing it under vacuum conditions as well. When the brake pedal is depressed, the vacuum passage to the rear chamber is cut off and the chamber opened to atmospheric pressure. The consequent rush of air pushes the servo piston forward in the vacuum chamber and operates the main pushrod to the master cylinder.

The controls are designed so that assistance is given under all conditions and, when the brakes are not required, vacuum in the rear chamber is established when the brake pedal is released. All air from the atmosphere entering the rear chamber is passed through a small air filter.

Under normal operation conditions the vacuum servo unit is very reliable and does not require overhaul except at very high mileage. In this case it is necessary to obtain a service exchange unit, rather than attempt to repair the orginal unit.

## 12 Servo unit - removal and refitting

1   Refer to Section 9 and remove the master cylinder from the servo unit.

2   Slacken the clip and disconnect the vacuum hose from the servo unit non-return valve.
3   Remove the screws securing the switch plate to the top of the pedal box and lift off the switch and plate (see Fig. 9.34).
4   Prise out the rubber plugs either side of the pedal box. Remove the split pin and withdraw the clevis pin securing the servo rod to the brake pedal.
5   Remove the four nuts and washers securing the servo unit to the pedal box and lift away the complete servo unit.
6   Refitting the servo unit is the reverse sequence to removal. It will be necessary to bleed the brakes as described in Section 18.

## 13 Servo unit non-return valve - removal and refitting

1   The servo unit should not be completely dismantled so if it develops an internal fault it should be renewed. Even if the unit is dismantled there would probably be extreme difficulty in obtaining spare parts. The only two service operations that may be carried out are renewing the non-return valve (this Section) and the air filter (Section 14).
2   To renew the non-return valve first detach the vacuum hose from the valve union.
3   Note the angle of the valve union and then insert a wide blade screwdriver between the valve and grommet. Pull on the valve whilst twisting the screwdriver to release it from the body.
4   Recover the grommet.
5   Refitting the grommet and valve is the reverse sequence to removal. Lubricate the ribs of the valve with a little rubber grease.

## 14 Servo unit filter - removal and refitting

1   Carefully pull back the dust cover and then ease the filter retainer from the servo neck.
2   Using a small screwdriver ease out the filter. Cut it in half and lift away.
3   Cut a new filter diagonally to the centre hole, fit it over the pushrod and carefully ease it into the housing.
4   Refit the filter retainer and dust cover.

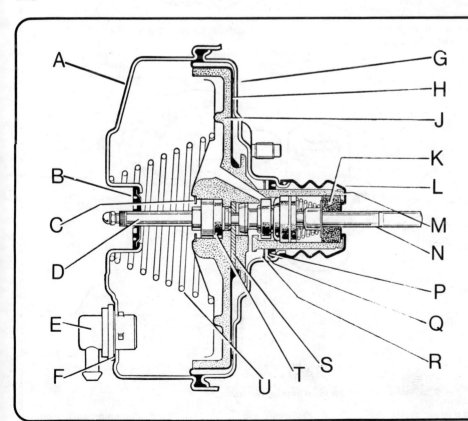

**Fig. 9.33. Sectional view of servo unit**

A  Front shell
B  Seal and plate assembly
C  Retainer sprag washer
D  Hydraulic pushrod
E  Non-return valve
F  'O' ring
G  Rear shell
H  Diaphragm
J  Diaphragm plate
K  Filter

L  Dust cover
M  End cap
N  Valve operating rod assembly
P  Seal
Q  Bearing

R  Retainer
S  Valve retaining plate
T  Reaction disc
U  Diaphragm return spring

### 15 Brake failure valve (dual braking system only) - removal, inspection and refitting

1   On vehicles fitted with the dual braking system (Series III models) a brake failure valve and switch is located inside the engine compartment on the RH side chassis member. The unit is basically a two-way shuttle valve through which the front and rear brake lines pass.

2   In the event of a leakage in either the front or rear braking system, the faulty system is cut off but hydraulic braking pressure is maintained in the remaining system. At the same time, the switch on the valve is actuated by the movement of the piston and the brake warning light on the instrument panel will illuminate.

3   To test the valve switch, remove the wire from the switch terminal and earth it against the valve body, with the ignition switched on. The brake warning lamp will illuminate.

4   To remove the valve unit, disconnect the five hydraulic pipe unions, detach the switch wire and remove the single retaining bolt. Lift the unit away from the chassis member.

5   Referring to Fig. 9.36, remove the switch and ball, and the two end plugs.
    Using a soft drift, carefully push out the two-part piston.

6   Examine the piston and valve bore for signs of scoring and if evident, renew the affected component.

7   Dip some new seals in brake fluid and fit them to the piston using the fingers only.

8   Fit the pistons back into the valve bore ensuring they are the correct way round.

9   Refit the ball and switch ensuring the ball is located in the piston groove.

10 Screw on the end cap and union and tighten them. Refit the valve unit to the vehicle using the reverse procedure to removal.

11 Bleed the brake system as described in Section 18.

12 The valve must now be reset. First apply the brake pedal hard and the warning light should go out, and stay out, even when the brake pedal is released.

13 Should the light not go out, the pressure in the system is unbalanced and the valve or the switch should be checked for correct operation.

14 If the brake failure warning light is off, check that the bulb is in order. Press the test-push and the light should glow.

15 Apply pressure to the brake pedal. The warning light will remain off if the hydraulic system is functioning satisfactorily and will come on to indicate hydraulic failure in one side of the system.

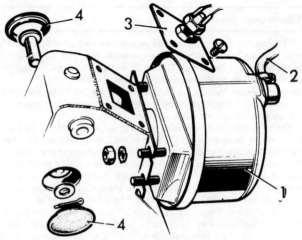

**Fig. 9.34. Removing the servo unit**

| | | | |
|---|---|---|---|
| 1 | Servo unit | 3 | Brake switch |
| 2 | Vacuum pipe | 4 | Rubber plugs |

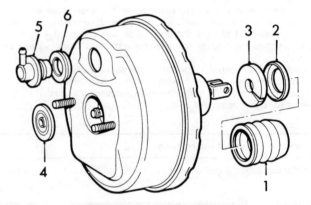

**Fig. 9.35. Servo unit components**

| | | | |
|---|---|---|---|
| 1 | Rubber dust cover | 4 | Grommet |
| 2 | Retainer | 5 | Non-return valve |
| 3 | Filter | 6 | Grommet |

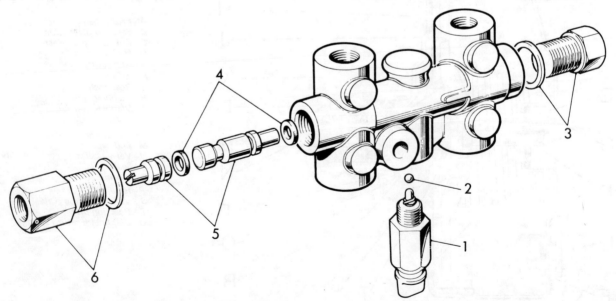

**Fig. 9.36. Brake failure valve (dual braking system)**

| | | | | | | | |
|---|---|---|---|---|---|---|---|
| 1 | Switch | 3 | End plug and gasket | 5 | Pistons | 6 | End union and gasket |
| 2 | Switch ball | 4 | Seals | | | | |

## 16 Brake pedal - removal and refitting

1   Referring to Section 9, paragraphs 3 to 9 inclusive, remove the complete brake pedal and bracket.
2   Using a suitable punch, drive out the pin securing the pedal shaft to the bracket. Remove the shaft and withdraw the pedal complete with bushes and trunnion (see Fig. 9.37).
3   Examine the bushes and shaft for wear and renew if necessary. Note that new bushes must be reamed to 0.750 in (15.875 mm) before fitting.
4   Grease the pedal shaft and bushes and refit using the reverse procedure to removal.
5   Bleed the brake system and adjust the pedal height and pushrod free-play to the dimensions shown in Fig. 9.38.

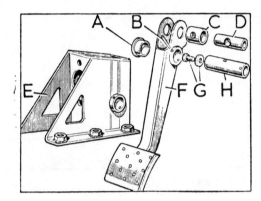

**Fig. 9.37. Brake pedal assembly**

| | |
|---|---|
| A   *Bush for pedal* | E   *Bracket for brake pedal* |
| B   *Pin for pedal shaft* | F   *Brake pedal* |
| C   *Distance piece* | G   *Oil plug and washer* |
| D   *Trunnion for pedal* | H   *Shaft for pedal* |

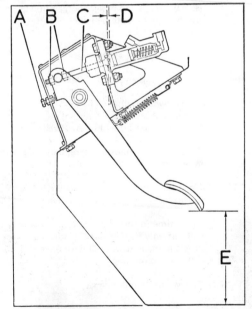

**Fig. 9.38. Setting the brake pedal height**

| | |
|---|---|
| A   *Pedal stop* | D   *1/16 in (1.5 mm)* |
| B   *Locknuts for master cylinder pushrod* | E   *Pedal height 6¼ in (158 mm)* |
| C   *Master cylinder pushrod* | |

## 17 Hydraulic pipes and hoses - general

1   Carefully examine all brake pipes/hoses, pipe hose connections and unions, periodically.

2   First examine for signs of leakage where the pipe unions occur. Then examine the flexible hoses for signs of chafing and fraying and, of course, leakage. This is only a preliminary part of the flexible hose inspection, as exterior condition does not necessarily indicate the interior condition, which will be considered later.
3   The steel pipes must be examined carefully and methodically. They must be cleaned off and examined for any signs of dents, corrosion or other damage and corrosion should be scraped off and, if the depth of pitting is significant, the pipes will need renewal. This is particularly likely in those areas underneath the vehicle body where the pipes are exposed and unprotected.
4   If any section of pipe is to be taken off, first wipe and then remove the fluid reservoir cap and place a piece of polythene over the reservoir neck. Refit the cap, this will stop syphoning during subsequent operations.
5   Rigid pipe removal is usually quite straightforward. The unions at each end are undone, the pipe and union pulled out, and the centre sections of the pipe removed from the body clips. Where the pipes are exposed to the full force of road and weather they can sometimes be very tight. As one can only use an open ended spanner and the unions are not large, burring of the flats is not uncommon when attempting to undo them. For this reason a self-locking grip wrench (mole) is often the only way to remove a stubborn union.
6   To remove a flexible hose, wipe the unions and bracket free from dust and undo the union nut from the metal pipe end.
7   Detach the hose from the bracket, be it either a clip or locknut.
8   The flexible hose may now be unscrewed from its attachment.
9   With the flexible hose removed, examine the internal bore. If it is blown through first, it should be possible to see through it. Any specks of rubber which come out, or signs of restriction in the bore, mean that the rubber lining is breaking up and the pipe must be renewed.
10  Rigid pipes which need renewing can usually be purchased at any garage where they have the pipe, unions and special tools to make them up. All they need to know is the total length of the pipe, the type of flare at each end with the union, and the length and thread of the union.
11  Refitment of the pipe is a straightforward reversal of the removal procedure. If the rigid pipes have been made up it is best to get all the 'sets' (bends) in them before trying to install them. Also, if there are any acute bends, ask your supplier to put these in for you on a special tube bender, otherwise you may kink the pipe and thereby decrease the bore area and fluid flow.
12  With the pipes refitted, remove the polythene from the reservoir cap and bleed the system as described in Section 18.

## 18 Bleeding the hydraulic system

Whenever the brake hydraulic system has been overhauled, partially renewed, or the level in the reservoir becomes too low, air will have entered the system necessitating bleeding. During the operation, the level of hydraulic fluid in the reservoir should not be allowed to fall below half full, otherwise air will be drawn into the system again.
1   Obtain a clean and dry glass jar, plastic tubing at least 15 inches (40 cm) long and of suitable diameter to fit tightly over the bleed screw, and a supply of hydraulic fluid.
2   Fill the master cylinder reservoir and the bottom inch of the jar with hydraulic fluid. Take extreme care that no fluid is allowed to come into contact with the paintwork as it acts as a solvent and will damage the finish.
3   **Single master cylinder type system:** Start bleeding at the front bleed screw which is furthest from the master cylinder and finish at the rear brake nearest to the master cylinder. The correct sequence is as follows: Front left, front right, rear left and rear right.
4   **Tandem master cylinder type system:** Bleed the system supplied by the secondary master cylinder chamber first. Commence bleeding at the front bleed screw and then bleed the diagonally opposite rear brake. The correct sequence is as follows: Front right, rear left, front left and rear right.
5   **All models:** Having decided the procedure open the first bleed screw about three quarters of a turn. Place one end of the bleed tube over the bleed nipple and submerge the other end of the tube in the fluid in the jar. **Note:** The end of the tube must remain submerged, throughout the bleeding operation.
6   An assistant should now pump the brake pedal by first depressing it one full stroke followed by three short but rapid strokes and

allowing the pedal to return of its own accord. Check the fluid level in the reservoir. Carefully watch the flow of fluid into the glass jar and, when air bubbles cease to emerge with the fluid during the next down stroke, tighten the bleed screw. Remove the plastic bleed tube and tighten the bleed screw. Do not overtighten. Refit the rubber dust cap supplied. Top up the fluid in the reservoir.

7   Continue bleeding the hydraulic system until all four units have been bled.

8   Sometimes it may be found that the bleed operation for one or more cylinders is taking a considerable time. The cause is probably air being drawn past the bleed screw threads when the screw is loose. To counteract this condition, it is recommended that at the end of each downward stroke the bleed screw be tightened to stop air being drawn past the threads.

9   If, after the bleed operation has been completed, the brake pedal operation still feels spongy, this is an indication that there is still air in the system, or that the master cylinder is faulty.

10  **Brake failure valve (dual line systems only).** Should it be noticed that during the bleed operation and with the ignition switched on the warning light glows, the bleed operation must be continued until all traces of air are removed. Ascertain which wheel caused the light to glow and then attach a tube to the bleed screw at the opposite end of the vehicle and open the bleed screw. Slowly depress the brake pedal and, when the light goes out, release the pedal and tighten the bleed screw.

11  Check and top up the reservoir fluid level with fresh hydraulic fluid. Never re-use old brake fluid. Finally, check the drum brake adjustment.

### 19  Fault finding - braking system

Before diagnosing faults from the following chart, check that any braking irregularities are not caused by:

1   Uneven and incorrect tyre pressures.
2   Incorrect 'mix' of radial and cross-ply tyres.
3   Wear in the steering mechanism.
4   Defects in the suspension and dampers.
5   Misalignment of the body frame.

| Symptoms | Reason/s | Remedy |
| --- | --- | --- |
| Pedal travels a long way before the brakes operate | Brake shoes set too far from the drums | Adjust the brake. |
| Stopping ability poor, even though pedal pressure is firm | Linings and/or drums badly worn or scored | Dismantle, inspect and renew as required. |
| | Failure of one circuit, dual hydraulic system | Check both circuits for hydraulic leaks and repair. |
| | One or more wheel hydraulic cylinders seized, resulting in some brake shoes not pressing against the drums | Dismantle and inspect wheel cylinders. Renew as necessary. |
| | Brake linings contaminated with oil | Renew linings and repair source of oil contamination. |
| | Wrong type of linings fitted (too hard) | Verify type of material which is correct for the vehicle, and fit it. |
| | Brake shoes wrongly assembled | Check for correct assembly. |
| | Servo unit not functioning (if fitted) | Check and repair as necessary. |
| Vehicle veers to one side when the brakes are applied | Brake linings on one side are contaminated with oil | Renew linings and stop oil leak. |
| | Hydraulic wheel cylinder(s) on one side partially or fully seized | Inspect wheel cylinders for correct operation and renew as necessary. |
| | A mixture of lining materials fitted between sides | Standardise on type of lining fitted. |
| | Unequal wear between sides caused by partially seized wheel cylinders | Check wheel cylinders and renew linings and drums as required. |
| Pedal feels spongy when the brakes are applied | Air is present in the hydraulic system | Bleed the hydraulic system and check for any signs of leakage. |
| Pedal feels springy when the brakes are applied | Brake linings not bedded into the drums (after fitting new ones) | Allow time for new linings to bed in after which it will certainly be necessary to adjust the shoes to the drums as pedal travel will have increased. |
| | Master cylinder or brake backplate mounting bolts loose | Retighten mounting bolts. |
| | Severe wear in brake drums causing distortion when brakes are applied | Renew drums and linings. |
| Pedal travels right down with little or no resistance and brakes are virtually non-operative. (With dual braking systems this would be extraordinary as both systems would have to fail at the same time). | Leak in hydraulic systems resulting in lack of pressure for operating wheel cylinders | Examine the whole of the hydraulic system and locate and repair source of leaks. Test after repairing each and every leak source. |
| | If no signs of leakage are apparent all the master cylinder internal seals are failing to sustain pressure | Overhaul master cylinder. If indications are that seals have failed for reasons other than wear all the wheel cylinder seals should be checked also and the system completely replenished with the correct fluid. |
| Binding, juddering, overheating | One or a combination of causes given in the foregoing sections | Complete and systematic inspection of the whole braking system. |

# Chapter 10 Electrical system

*For modifications, and information applicable to later models, see Supplement at end of manual*

## Contents

## Specifications

| | | |
|---|---|---|
| **System type** ... ... ... ... ... ... ... ... ... | 12v, positive earth, (negative earth on vehicles from suffix D onwards) | |
| | | |
| **Battery rating** ... ... ... ... ... ... ... ... | 58 amp/hour | |

| **Dynamo** | *Series II* | *Series IIA* |
|---|---|---|
| Type ... ... ... ... ... ... ... ... ... ... | Lucas C39 | Lucas C40/1 |
| Output ... ... ... ... ... ... ... ... ... ... | 19 amps | 22 amps |
| Cut-in speed ... ... ... ... ... ... ... ... ... | 1450 rpm | 1350 rpm |
| Field resistance ... ... ... ... ... ... ... ... | 6 ohms | 5.9 ohms |
| Number of brushes ... ... ... ... ... ... ... | 2 | 2 |
| Brush length (new) ... ... ... ... ... ... ... | 0.718 inch (18.24 mm) | 0.718 inch (18.24 mm) |
| Minimum brush length ... ... ... ... ... ... ... | 0.28 inch (7.11 mm) | 0.28 inch (7.11 mm) |
| Brush spring pressure (new) ... ... ... ... ... ... | 30 oz (850 g) | 30 oz (850 g) |

| **Alternator** | | |
|---|---|---|
| Type ... ... ... ... ... ... ... ... ... ... | Lucas 11AC | Lucas 16ACR |
| Output ... ... ... ... ... ... ... ... ... ... | 45 amps | 34 amps |
| Voltage ... ... ... ... ... ... ... ... ... ... | 12v | 12v |
| Field resistance ... ... ... ... ... ... ... ... | 3.8 ohms | 4.33 ohms |
| Minimum brush length ... ... ... ... ... ... ... | 0.2 in (5 mm) | 0.2 in (5 mm) |
| Maximum continuous speed ... ... ... ... ... ... | 12,500 rpm | 12,500 rpm |

| **Starter motor** | |
|---|---|
| Make/type ... ... ... ... ... ... ... ... ... | Lucas M418G |
| Brush spring tension ... ... ... ... ... ... ... | 850 to 1134 g (30 to 40 oz) |
| Brush minimum length ... ... ... ... ... ... ... | 0.312 in (8.0 mm) |
| Shaft endfloat ... ... ... ... ... ... ... ... | Zero |

## Fuses

| | |
|---|---|
| Quantity ... ... ... ... ... ... ... ... ... ... | Two |
| Amperage ... ... ... ... ... ... ... ... ... | 35 |
| Protecting: | |
|     A1—A2 ... ... ... ... ... ... ... ... ... | Interior lamps, fog lamps, etc, as applicable |
|     A3—A4 ... ... ... ... ... ... ... ... ... | Windscreen wiper, fuel tank level unit and stop lights |

## Bulbs and units

| | |
|---|---|
| Headlamps with bulbs: | |
|   LHStg Italy ... ... ... ... ... ... ... ... ... | Lucas 410, 12v, 45/40w, Duplo clear |
|   LHStg France ... ... ... ... ... ... ... ... | Lucas 411, 12v, 45/40w, Duplo yellow |
| Headlamps with sealed beam units: | |
|   RHStg ... ... ... ... ... ... ... ... ... | Lucas 54521872 60/45w |
|   LHStg Europe except France and Italy ... ... ... ... | Lucas 54523079 60/50w |
|   LHStg except Europe ... ... ... ... ... ... | Lucas 54522231 50/40w |
| Sidelamps ... ... ... ... ... ... ... ... ... | Lucas 207, 12v, 6w |
| Stop, tail lamps ... ... ... ... ... ... ... ... | Lucas 380, 12v, 21/6w |
| Flasher lamps ... ... ... ... ... ... ... ... | Lucas 382, 12v, 21w |
| Rear number plate lamp ... ... ... ... ... ... ... | Lucas 989, 12v, 6w |
| Instrument panel lights ... ... ... ... ... ... ... | Lucas 987, 12v, 2.2w MES |
| Warning lights ... ... ... ... ... ... ... ... | Lucas 987, 12v, 2.2w MES |
| Warning light, brakes ... ... ... ... ... ... ... | Lucas 281, 12v, 2w |
| Warning light, flashers ... ... ... ... ... ... | Magnatex GBP 12v, 2.2w |
| Interior light ... ... ... ... ... ... ... ... | Lucas 382, 12v, 21w |

## Torque wrench setting

| | lb f in | kg f m |
|---|---|---|
| Alternator through bolts ... ... ... ... ... ... ... | 45 - 50 | 0.518 - 0.576 |

## 1 General description

The electrical system on all Land Rovers is 12 volt. Generally speaking the Series II and IIA models have a positive earth system, while the later Series III models have a negative earth system. However, before fitting a radio or tape player or wiring up a similar device, a careful check must be made to check which battery terminal is connected to earth.

The basic units of the electrical system comprise a lead-acid type battery, a dynamo or alternator belt driven from the crankshaft pulley, a starter motor of the inertia engaged drive type and the necessary voltage regulating and cut-out equipment.

Although repair procedures and methods are fully described in this Chapter, in view of the long life of the major electrical components, it is recommended that when a fault does develop, consideration should be given to exchanging the unit for a factory reconditioned assembly rather than renew individual components of a well worn unit.

## 2 Battery - removal and refitting

1 The battery is located at the front, right-hand side of the engine compartment.
2 Disconnect the live lead from the battery terminal post and then the earth lead similarly. The leads are held by either a clamp, which necessitates slackening the clamp bolt and nut, or by a screw driven through an all enclosing shroud.
3 Remove the battery clamp and carefully lift the battery out of its compartment. Hold the battery vertical to ensure that none of the electrolyte is spilled.
4 Refit the battery using the reverse procedure to that of removal. Before refitting the terminals clean off any corrosion and smear them with petroleum jelly (vaseline).

## 3 Battery - maintenance and inspection

1 Normal weekly battery maintenance consists of checking the electrolyte level of each cell to ensure that the separators are covered by ¼ inch of electrolyte. If the level has fallen, top up the battery using distilled water only. Do not overfill. If a battery is over-filled or any electrolyte spilled, immediately wipe away the excess

as electrolyte attacks and corrodes any metal it comes into contact with very rapidly.
2 As well as keeping the terminals clean and covered with petroleum jelly, the top of the battery, and especially the top of the cells, should be kept clean and dry. This helps prevent corrosion and ensures that the battery does not become partially discharged by leakage through dampness and dirt.
3 Once every three months, remove the battery and inspect the battery securing bolts, the battery clamp plate, tray and battery leads for corrosion (white fluffy deposits on the metal which are brittle to touch). If any corrosion is found, clean off the deposits with ammonia and paint over the clean metal with an anti-rust/anti-acid paint.
4 At the same time inspect the battery case for cracks. If a crack is found, clean and plug it with one of the proprietary compounds marketed by firms, such as Holts, for this purpose. If leakage through the crack has been excessive, then it will be necessary to refill the appropriate cell with fresh electrolyte as detailed later. Cracks are frequently caused to the top of battery cases by pouring in distilled water in the middle of winter AFTER instead of BEFORE a run. This gives the water no chance to mix with the electrolyte and so the former freezes and splits the battery case.
5 If topping up the battery becomes excessive and the case has been inspected for cracks that could cause leakage, but none are found, the battery is being overcharged and the voltage regulator will have to be checked and reset.
6 With the battery on the bench at the three monthly interval check, measure its specific gravity with a hydrometer to determine the state of charge and condition of the electrolyte. There should be very little variation between the different cells and if a variation in excess of .025 is present it will be due to either:
a) Loss of electrolyte from the battery at some time caused by spillage or a leak, resulting in a drop in the specific gravity of the electrolyte when the deficiency was replaced with distilled water instead of fresh electrolyte.
b) An internal short circuit caused by buckling of the plates or a similar malady pointing to the likelihood of total battery failure in the near future.
7 The specific gravity of the electrolyte for fully charged conditions at various electrolyte temperatures, is listed in Table A. The specific gravity of a fully discharged battery at different temperatures of the electrolyte is given in Table B.

**TABLE A**

Specific gravity - battery fully charged

1.268 at 100°F or  38°C electrolyte temperature
1.272 at  90°F or  32°C electrolyte temperature
1.276 at  80°F or  27°C electrolyte temperature
1.280 at  70°F or  21°C electrolyte temperature
1.284 at  60°F or  16°C electrolyte temperature
1.288 at  50°F or  10°C electrolyte temperature
1.292 at  40°F or   4°C electrolyte temperature
1.296 at  30°F or -1.5°C electrolyte temperature

**TABLE B**

Specific gravity - battery fully discharged

1.098 at 100°F or  38°C electrolyte temperature
1.102 at  90°F or  32°C electrolyte temperature
1.106 at  80°F or  27°C electrolyte temperature
1.110 at  70°F or  21°C electrolyte temperature
1.114 at  60°F or  16°C electrolyte temperature
1.118 at  50°F or  10°C electrolyte temperature
1.122 at  40°F or   4°C electrolyte temperature
1.126 at  30°F or -1.5°C electrolyte temperature

### 4  Battery electrolyte replenishment

1  If the battery is in a fully charged state and one of the cells maintains a specific gravity reading which is .025 or more lower than the others, and a check of each cell has been made with a voltage meter to check for short circuits (a four to seven second test should give a steady reading of between 1.2 to 1.8 volts), then it is likely that electrolyte has been lost from the cell with the low reading at some time.
2  Top the cell up with a solution of 1 part sulphuric acid to 2.5 parts water. If the cell is already fully topped up draw some electrolyte out of it with an hydrometer.
3  When mixing the sulphuric acid and water **NEVER ADD WATER TO SULPHURIC ACID** - always pour the acid slowly onto the water in a glass container. **IF WATER IS ADDED TO SULPHURIC ACID IT WILL EXPLODE.**
4  Continue to top up the cell with the freshly made electrolyte and then recharge the battery and check the hydrometer readings.

### 5  Battery charging

1  In winter time when heavy demand is placed upon the battery, such as when starting from cold, and much of the electrical equipment is continually in use, it is a good idea occasionally to have the battery fully charged from an external source at the rate of 3.5 to 4 amps.
2  Continue to charge the battery at this rate until no further rise in specific gravity is noted over a four hour period.
3  Alternatively, a trickle charger, charging at the rate of 1.5 amps can be safely used overnight.
4  Specially rapid 'boost' charges which are claimed to restore the power of the battery in 1 to 2 hours are not recommended as they can cause serious damage to the battery plates through overheating.
5  While charging the battery note that the temperature of the electrolyte should never exceed 100°F.

### 6  Alternator - general description and maintenance

1  The Series II and IIA Land Rovers were usually fitted with a dynamo as standard equipment, but had the option of the Lucas 11AC alternator. The Series III models are equipped with the Lucas 16ACR alternator as a standard fitment.
2  The type 16ACR alternator incorporates its own built-in regulator and is shown in exploded form in Fig. 10.1.

3  Maintenance consists of occasionally wiping away any dirt or oil which may have collected around the apertures in the slip ring end bracket and moulded cover.
4  Check the fan belt tension every 5,000 miles (8,000 km) and adjust as described in Chapter 2 by loosening the mounting bolts. Pull the alternator body away from the engine block, do not use a lever as it will distort the alternator casing.
5  No lubrication is required as the bearings are grease sealed for life.
6  Take extreme care when making circuit connections to a vehicle fitted with an alternator and observe the following:
   *When making connections to the alternator from a battery always match correct polarity.*
   *Before using electric-arc welding equipment to repair any part of the vehicle, disconnect the connector from the alternator and disconnect the positive battery terminal.*
   *Never start the car with a battery charger connected.*
   *Always disconnect both battery leads before using a mains charger.*
   *If boosting from another battery, always connect in parallel using heavy cable.*
   It is not recommended that testing of an alternator should be undertaken at home due to the testing equipment required and the possibility of damage occurring during testing. It is best left to automotive electrical specialists.

### 7  Alternator - removal and refitting

1  Loosen the alternator mounting bracket bolts and strap, push the unit towards the engine block sufficiently to enable the fan belt to be slipped off the alternator pulley.
2  Remove the cable connectors from the alternator and withdraw the mounting bracket bolts. Lift away the alternator.
3  Refitting is a reversal of removal procedure but ensure that the connections are correctly made and that the fan belt is adjusted as described in Chapter 2.

### 8  Alternator - servicing (type 16ACR)

1  Servicing other than renewal of the brushes is not recommended. The major components should normally last the life of the unit and in the event of failure a factory exchange replacement should be obtained.
2  To renew the brushes, refer to Fig. 10.1, remove the two cover screws and withdraw the moulded cover.
3  Unsolder the three stator connections to the rectifier assembly noting carefully the order of connection.
4  Withdraw the two brush moulding securing screws, slacken the nut on the rectifier assembly bolt.
5  Remove the regulator securing screw and (if fitted) the suppressor cable at the rectifier.
6  Withdraw the brush moulding and rectifier assembly complete with short linking cable.
7  Inspect the brushes which should protrude 2 inch (5 mm) beyond the box moulding when in a free position. Renew if worn to, or below this amount, and do not lose the leaf spring fitted at the side of the inner brush.
8  Should a brush stick, then clean it with petrol or lightly rub with a smooth file.
9  The surfaces of the slip rings should be clean and smooth. If necessary, clean with a petrol moistened cloth. If there is evidence of burning, use very fine glass paper to clean (not emery).

### 9  Alternator - servicing (type 11AC)

1  As in the case of the type 16 ACR alternator servicing should be restricted to the inspection or renewal of the brushes.
2  After removing the fan and pulley nut, the through bolts may be removed. Mark the position of the end covers relative to the stator and withdraw the drive end cover and rotor together. The brushes may be checked for length and the slip rings cleaned up with fine glass paper.

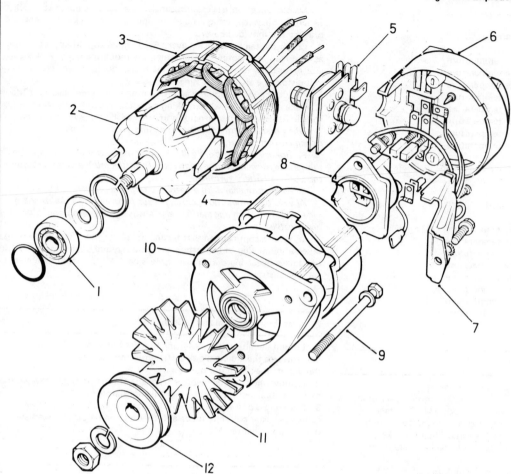

**Fig. 10.1. Exploded view of type 16ACR alternator**

1   Drive end bearing
2   Rotor and slip-ring
3   Stator
4   Slip-ring bracket
5   Rectifier
6   End cover
7   Regulator unit
8   Brush box
9   Through bolt
10  Drive end bracket
11  Fan
12  Pulley

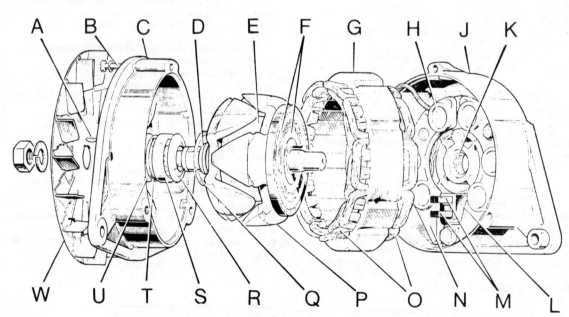

**Fig. 10.2 . Exploded view of type 11 AC alternator**

| | | | |
|---|---|---|---|
| A   Woodruff key | G   Stator lamination | M   Brushes (2) | R   Bearing retaining plate |
| B   Through bolt (3) | H   Silicon diodes (6) | N   Diode heat sink (2) | S   Ball bearing, drive end |
| C   Drive end bracket | J   Slip-ring end bracket | O   Stator winding | T   'O' ring |
| D   Jump ring shroud | K   Needle roller bearing | P   Rotor | U   'O' ring retaining washer |
| E   Rotor (field) winding | L   Brush box | Q   Circlip | W   Fan |
| F   Slip rings | | | |

## 10 Dynamo - routine maintenance

1    Routine maintenance consists of checking the tension of the fan belt, and lubricating the dynamo rear bearing once every 5,000 miles.
2    The fan belt should be tight enough to ensure no slip between the belt and the dynamo pulley. If a shrieking noise comes from the engine when the unit is accelerated rapidly, it is likely that it is the fan belt slipping. On the other hand, the belt must not be too taut or the bearings will wear rapidly and cause dynamo failure or bearing seizure. Ideally ½ inch of total free movement should be available at the fan belt, midway between the fan and the dynamo pulley.
3    To adjust the fan belt tension, slightly slacken the three dynamo retaining bolts, and swing the dynamo on the lower two bolts outwards to increase the tension, and inwards to lower it.
4    It is best to leave the bolts fairly tight so that considerable effort has to be used to move the dynamo, otherwise it is difficult to get the correct setting. If the dynamo is being moved outwards to increase the tension and the bolts have only been slackened a little, a long spanner acting as a lever placed behind the dynamo with the lower end resting against the block, works very well in moving the dynamo outwards. Retighten the dynamo bolts and check that the dynamo pulley is correctly aligned with the fan belt.
5    Lubrication on the dynamo consists of inserting three drops of SAE 30 engine oil in the small oil hole in the centre of the commutator end bracket. This lubricates the rear bearing. The front bearing is pre-packed with grease and requires no attention. See Fig. 10.3.

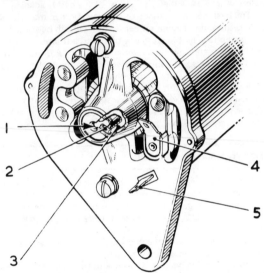

**Fig. 10.3. End view of dynamo**

1    Lubrication hole
2    Felt ring
3    Bearing bush
4    Terminal connector
5    Terminal connector

## 11 Dynamo - testing in position

1    If, with the engine running, no charge comes from the dynamo or the charge is very low, first check that the fan belt is in place and is not slipping. Then check that the leads from the control box to the dynamo are firmly attached and that one has not come loose from its terminal.
2    The lead from the D terminal on the dynamo should be connected to the D terminal on the control box, and similarly the F terminals on the dynamo and control box should also be connected together. Check that this is so and that the leads have not been incorrectly fitted.
3    Make sure none of the electrical equipment (such as the lights or radio) is on, and then pull the leads off the dynamo terminals marked D and F. Join the dynamo terminals together with a short length of wire.
4    Attach to the centre of this length of wire the negative clips of a 0 - 20 volts voltmeter and run the other clip to earth on the dynamo yoke. Start the engine and allow it to idle at approximately 750 rpm. At this speed the dynamo should give a reading of about 15 volts on the voltmeter. There is no point in raising the engine speed above a fast idle as the reading will then be inaccurate.
5    If no reading is recorded, then check the brushes and brush connections. If a very low reading of approximately 1 volt is observed, then the field winding may be suspect.
6    If a reading of between 4 to 6 volts is recorded, it is likely that the armature winding is at fault.
7    If the voltmeter shows a good reading, then with the temporary link still in position, connect both leads from the control box to D and F on the dynamo (D to D and F to F). Release the lead from the D terminal at the control box end and clip one lead from the voltmeter to the end of the cable, and the other lead to a good earth. With the engine running at the same speed as previously, an identical voltage to that recorded at the dynamo should be noted on the voltmeter. If no voltage is recorded, then there is a break in the wire. If the voltage is the same as recorded at the dynamo, then check the F lead in similar fashion. If both readings are the same as at the dynamo, then it will be necessary to test the control box.
8    Fig. 10.4 shows the system circuit in diagrammatic form.

## 12 Dyanmo - removal and refitting

1    Slacken the two dynamo retaining bolts, and the nut on the sliding link and move the dynamo in towards the engine so that the fan belt can be removed (photo).
2    Disconnect the two leads from the dynamo terminals.
3    Remove the nut from the sliding link bolt and remove the two upper bolts. The dynamo is then free to be lifted away from the engine.
4    Refitting is a reversal of the above procedure. Do not finally tighten the retaining bolts and the nut of the sliding link until the fan belt has been tensioned.

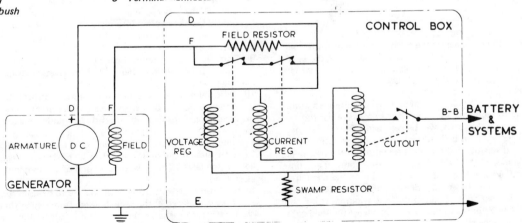

**Fig. 10.4. Wiring diagram for dynamo charging system**

12.1 Dynamo top securing bracket

## 13 Dynamo - dismantling and inspection

1   Mount the dynamo in a vice and unscrew and remove the two
through bolts from the commutator end bracket (1) (Fig. 10.5).
2   Mark the commutator end bracket and the dynamo casing so the
end bracket can be refitted in its original position. Pull the end bracket
off the armature shaft. Note: Some versions of the dynamo may have
a raised pip on the end bracket which locates in a recess on the edge
of the casing. If so, marking the end bracket and casing is not necessary.
A pip may also be found on the drive end bracket at the opposite end
of the casing.
3   Lift the two brush springs and draw the brushes out of the brush
holders.
4   Measure the brushes and, if worn down to 0.28 in (7.1 mm) or less,
undo the screws holding the brush leads to the end bracket. Take off
the brushes complete with leads.
5   If no locating pip can be found, mark the drive end bracket and the
dynamo casing so that the drive end bracket can be replaced in its
original position. Then pull the drive end bracket complete with
armature out of the casing.
6   Check the condition of the ball bearing in the drive end plate by
firmly holding the plate and noting if there is visible side movement of
the armature shaft in relation to the end plate. If play is present, the
armature assembly must be separated from the end plate. If the bearing
is sound there is no need to carry out the work described in the
following two paragraphs.
7   Hold the armature in one hand (mount it carefully in a vice if
preferred) and undo the nut holding the pulley and fan in place. Pull off
the pulley and fan.
8   Next remove the Woodruff key from its slot in the armature shaft
and also the bearing locating ring.
9   Place the drive end bracket across the open jaws of a vice with the
armature downwards and gently tap the armature shaft from the bearing in the end plate with the aid of a suitable drift. Support the armature
so that it does not fall to the ground.
10 Carefully inspect the armature and check it for open or short
circuited windings. It a good indication of an open circuited armature
when the commutator segments are burnt. If the armature has short
circuited the commutator segments will be very badly burnt, and the
over-heated armature windings badly discoloured. If open or short
circuits are suspected substitute the suspect armature with a new one.
11 Check the resistance of the field coils. To do this, connect an ohmmeter between the field terminal and the yoke and note the reading on
the ohmmeter which should be about 6 ohms. If the ohmmeter reading
is infinity this indicates an open circuit in the field winding. If the ohmmeter reading is below 5 ohms this indicates that one of the field coils
is faulty and must be renewed.
12 Field coil renewal involves the use of a wheel operated screwdriver,
a soldering iron, caulking and rivetting and this operation is considered

to be beyond the scope of most owners. Therefore, if the field coils
are at fault either purchase a rebuilt dynamo, or take the casing to a
Leyland dealer or electrical engineering works for new field coils to be
fitted.
13 Next check the condition of the commutator (arrowed). If it is dirty
and blackened, as shown, clean it with a petrol dampened rag. If the
commutator is in good condition the surface will be smooth and quite
free from pits or burnt areas, and the insulated segments clearly defined.
14 If, after the commutator has been cleaned, pits and burnt spots are
still present, wrap a strip of glass paper round the commutator taking
great care to move the commutator ¼ of a turn every ten rubs till it is
thoroughly clean.
15 In extreme cases of wear the commutator can be mounted in a lathe
and with the lathe turning at high speed, a very fine cut may be taken
off the commutator. Then polish the commutator with glass paper. If
the commutator has worn so that the insulators between the segments
are level with the top of the segments, then undercut the insulators to
a depth of 1/32 in (0.8 mm). This applies to fabricated commutators
only. Do NOT undercut moulded commutators. (See Fig. 10.6). The
best tool to use for this purpose is half a hacksaw blade ground to the
thickness of the insulator, and with the handle end of the blade covered
in insulating tape to make it comfortable to hold.
16 Check the bush bearing in the commutator end bracket for wear,
by noting if the armature spindle rocks when placed in it. If worn, it
must be renewed.
17 The bush bearing can be removed by a suitable extractor or by
screwing a 5/8 in (15.87 mm) tap four or five times into the bush. The
tap complete with bush is then pulled out of the end bracket.
18 Note: The bush bearing is made of a porous bronze material which
needs to be saturated in engine oil before use. Oil can be forced through
it, before installation, by blocking one end with a thumb, filling it with
oil and squeezing it through the material by forcing a finger in at the
other end. Otherwise, soak it in oil for several hours. If the oil is hot
it will saturate the material more quickly.
19 Carefully fit the new bush into the end plate, pressing it in until the
end of the bearing is flush with the inner side of the end plate. If
available, press the bush in with a smooth shouldered mandrel the same
diameter as the armature shaft.

## 14 Dynamo - repair and reassembly

1   To renew the ball bearing fitted to the drive end bracket, drill out
the rivets which hold the bearing retainer plate to the end bracket and
lift off the plate (see Fig. 10.10.7). On later models the bearing is held
by a circlip which is quite simply removed to release the bearing from
the end plate.
2   Press out the bearing from the end bracket and remove the corrugated
and felt washers from the bearing housing.
3   Thoroughly clean the bearing housing and the new bearing, and pack
with high melting point grease.
4   Place the felt washer and corrugated washer, in that order, in the
end bracket bearing housing. On later models when the bearing is retained by a circlip there is a felt ring, retaining washer and pressure
ring to be fitted in the housing before the bearing.
5   Then fit the new bearing.
6   Gently tap the bearing into place with the aid of a suitable drift.
7   Refit the bearing plate and fit three new rivets (or fit the collar and
circlip).
8   Open up the rivets with the aid of a suitable punch.
9   Finally peen over the open end of the rivets with the aid of a ball
pein hammer.
10 Refit the drive end bracket to the armature shaft. Do not try and
force the bracket on but, with the aid of a suitable socket abutting
the bearing, tap the bearing on gently, so pulling the end bracket
down with it.
11 Slide the spacer up the shaft and refit the Woodruff key.
12 Refit the fan and pulley and then fit the spring washer and nut and
tighten the latter. The drive bracket end of the dynamo is now fully
assembled.
13 If the brushes are a little worn and are to be used again then ensure
that they are placed in the same holders from which they were removed.
When refitting brushes, either new or old, check that they move freely
in their holders. If either brush sticks, clean with a petrol moistened
rag and if still stiff, lightly polish the sides of the brush with a very fine
file until the brush moves quite freely in its holder.

14 Tighten the two retaining screws and washers which hold the wire leads to the brushes in place.

15 It is far easier to slip the end piece with brushes over the commutator if the brushes are raised in their holders, and held in this position by the pressure of the springs resting against their flanks.

16 Refit the armature to the casing and then the commutator end plate, and screw up the two through bolts.

17 Finally, hook the ends of the two springs off the flanks of the brushes and onto their heads so that the brushes are forced down into contact with the armature.

## 15 Starter motor - general description

The starter motor is mounted on the right-hand lower side of the engine backplate and is held in position by two bolts which also clamp the bellhousing flange. The motor is of the four field coil, four pole piece type and utilizes four spring loaded commutator brushes. Two of these brushes are earthed, and the other two are insulated and attached to the field coil ends.

### Starter motor - testing in engine

1 If the starter motor fails to operate then check the condition of the battery by turning on the headlamps. If they glow brightly for several seconds and then gradually dim, the battery is in an uncharged condition.

2 If the headlamps glow brightly and it is obvious that the battery is in good condition then check the tightness of the battery wiring connections (and in particular the earth lead from the battery terminal to its connection on the body frame). Check the tightness of the connections at the relay switch and at the starter motor. Check the wiring with a voltmeter for breaks or shorts.

3 If the wiring is in order then check that the starter motor switch is operating. To do this press the rubber button in the centre of the relay switch under the bonnet (later models only). If it is working the starter motor will be heard to 'click' as it tries to rotate. Alternatively check it with a voltmeter.

4 If the battery is fully charged, the wiring in order, and the switch working and the starter motor fails to operate then it will have to be removed from the vehicle for examination. Before this is done, however, ensure that the starter pinion has not jammed in mesh with the flywheel. Check this by turning the square end of the armature shaft with a spanner. This will free the pinion if it is stuck in engagement with the flywheel teeth.

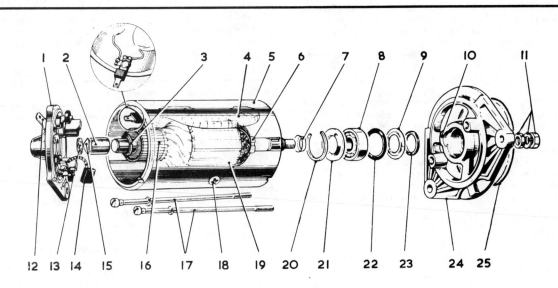

Fig. 10.5. Exploded view of dynamo

| | | | |
|---|---|---|---|
| 1 Commutator end bracket | 7 Retaining cup | 13 Felt ring | 19 Armature |
| 2 Bearing bush | 8 Drive end bearing | 14 Carbon brush | 20 Circlip |
| 3 Fibre washer | 9 Pressure ring plate | 15 Felt ring retainer | 21 Bearing retaining plate |
| 4 Field winding | 10 Extractor notch | 16 Commutator | 22 Pressure ring |
| 5 Yoke | 11 Nut and washers | 17 Through bolts | 23 Felt ring |
| 6 Armature shaft | 12 Terminal D | 18 Pole shoe screw | 24 Drive end bracket |
| | | | 25 Pulley |

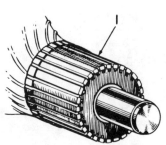

Fig. 10.6. Different types of dynamo commutators

1 Moulded type          2 Fabricated type

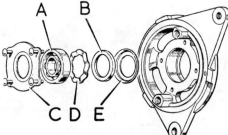

Fig. 10.7. Early type of dynamo bearing retainer

A Bearing
B Felt washer
C Bearing retaining plate

D Corrugated washer
E Retaining washer

## 16 Starter motor - removal and refitting

1   First remove the bonnet as described in Chapter 1 and disconnect both battery terminals.
2   Unscrew the securing bolts and remove the heat shield from the exhaust/inlet manifold.
3   Remove the three nuts retaining the front exhaust pipe to the manifold and carefully move the pipe to one side. If necessary remove the clamp securing the lower end of the pipe.
4   Disconnect the electrical lead from the starter motor.
5   Unscrew and remove the two nuts that hold the starter motor to the engine backplate and the flywheel housing flange.
6   Lift the starter motor out of the engine compartment.
7   Refitting is a straightforward reversal of the removal procedure.

## 17 Starter motor - dismantling and reassembly

1   With the starter motor on the bench, loosen the screw on the cover band and slip the cover band off. With a piece of wire bent into the shape of a hook, lift back each of the brush springs in turn and check the movement of the brushes in their holders by pulling on the flexible connectors. If the brushes are so worn that their faces do not rest against the commutator, or if the ends of the brush leads are exposed on their working face, they must be renewed.
2   If any of the brushes tend to stick in their holders then wash them with a petrol moistened cloth and, if necessary, lightly polish the sides of the brush with a very fine file, until the brushes move quite freely in their holders.
3   If the surface of the commutator is dirty or blackened, clean it with a petrol dampened rag. Secure the starter motor in a vice and check it by connecting a heavy gauge cable between the starter motor terminal and and a 12 volt battery.
4   Connect the cable from the other battery terminal to earth in the starter motor body. If the motor turns at high speed it is in good order.
5   If the starter motor still fails to function or if it is wished to renew the brushes, then it is necessary to further dismantle the motor.
6   Lift the brush springs with the wire hook and lift all four brushes out of their holders one at a time.
7   Remove the terminal nuts and washers from the terminal post on the commutator end bracket.
8   Unscrew the two through bolts which hold the end plates together and pull off the commutator end bracket. Also remove the driving end bracket which will come away complete with the armature.
9   At this stage if the brushes are to be renewed, their flexible connectors must be unsoldered and the connectors of new brushes soldered in their place. Check that the new brushes move freely in their holders as detailed above. If cleaning the commutator with petrol fails

to remove all the burnt areas and spots, then wrap a piece of glass paper round the commutator and rotate the armature.
10 If the commutator is very badly worn, remove the drive gear as detailed in the following Section. Then mount the armature in a lathe and, with the lathe turning at high speed, take a very fine cut out of the commutator and finish the surface by polishing with glass paper. **Do not undercut the mica insulators between the commutator segments.**
11 With the starter motor dismantled, test the four field coils for an open circuit. Connect a 12-volt battery with a 12 volt bulb in one of the leads between the field terminal post and the tapping point of the field coils to which the brushes are connected. An open circuit is proved by the bulb not lighting.
12 If the bulb lights, it does not necessarily mean that the field coils are in order, as there is a possibility that one of the coils will be earthing to the starter yoke or pole shoes. To check this, remove the lead from the brush connector and place it against a clean portion of the starter yoke. If the bulb lights, the field coils are earthing. Renewal of the field coils calls for the use of a wheel operated screwdriver, a soldering iron, caulking and riveting operations and is beyond the scope of the majority of owners. The starter yoke should be taken to a reputable electrical engineering works for new field coils to be fitted. Alternatively, purchase an exchange Lucas starter motor.
13 If the armature is damaged this will be evident after visual inspection. Look for signs of burning, discolouration, and for conductors that have lifted away from the commutator. Reassembly is a straightforward reversal of the dismantling procedure.

## 18 Starter motor drive - servicing

1   On earlier models the starter motor drive gear is secured on the shaft by a special nut and split pin.
2   Using a pair of pliers, remove the split pin and undo the nut.
3   Slide off the spring, thrust washer, screwed sleeve and pinion, second thrust washer, and smaller spring and sleeve (see Fig. 10.8).
4   On later types of starter motor the drive gear is retained on the shaft by a spring clip.
5   To remove the clip it is necessary to compress the spring using a special spring compressor obtainable either from a Leyland dealer or Accessory shop. If a spring compressor is not available it is possible to do the job using a vice and a piece of tubing.
6   After removing the spring clip, withdraw the drive gear components and lay them out in the correct order of removal.
7   Clean the components in petrol and examine them for wear. If there are any doubts regarding their condition it is best to renew the complete drive assembly.
8   Refit the drive assembly to the starter shaft using the reversal of the removal procedure.

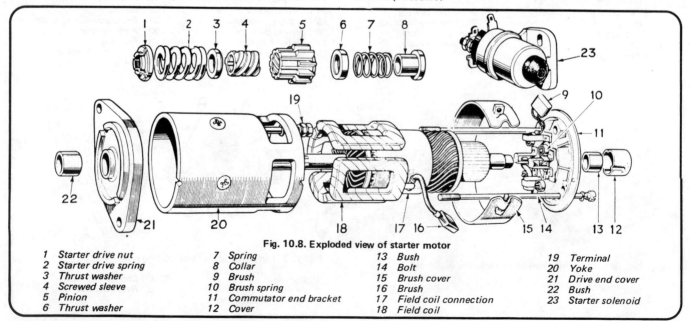

Fig. 10.8. Exploded view of starter motor

| | | | | | |
|---|---|---|---|---|---|
| 1 | Starter drive nut | 7 | Spring | 13 | Bush | 19 | Terminal |
| 2 | Starter drive spring | 8 | Collar | 14 | Bolt | 20 | Yoke |
| 3 | Thrust washer | 9 | Brush | 15 | Brush cover | 21 | Drive end cover |
| 4 | Screwed sleeve | 10 | Brush spring | 16 | Brush | 22 | Bush |
| 5 | Pinion | 11 | Commutator end bracket | 17 | Field coil connection | 23 | Starter solenoid |
| 6 | Thrust washer | 12 | Cover | 18 | Field coil | | |

### 19 Starter motor solenoid - description

1    Earlier Land Rovers were not fitted with a starter solenoid, the starting circuit being closed by the contacts of the push-type starter switch.
2    Later models have a solenoid in the starter circuit located in the engine compartment. Operation of the solenoid can be checked by pressing the rubber cover on the end of the solenoid thus manually over-riding the starter switch circuit.
3    If it is suspected that the solenoid is faulty, the best method is to substitute it for a new one. It is not possible to repair the solenoid.

### 20 Voltage control box (dynamo only) - general description

The control box is positioned on the engine compartment bulkhead and is comprised of three units; two separate vibrating armature-type single contact regulators and a cut-out relay. One of the regulators is sensitive to changes in current and the other to changes in voltage.

Adjustment can only be made with a special tool which resembles a screwdriver, with a multi-toothed blade. This can be obtained through Lucas agents.

The regulators control the output from the dynamo depending on the state of the battery and the demands of the electrical equipment, and ensures that the battery is not overcharged. The cut-out is really an automatic switch and connects the dynamo to the battery when the dynamo is turning fast enough to produce a charge. Similarly, it disconnects the battery from the dynamo when the engine is idling or stationary so that the battery does not discharge through the dynamo.

### 21 Cut-out and regulator contacts - maintenance

1    Every 12,000 miles check the cut-out and regulator contacts. If they are dirty, rough or burnt place a piece of fine glass paper **(do not use emery paper or carborundum paper)** between the cut-out contacts, close them manually and draw the glass paper through several times.
2    Clean the regulator contacts in exactly the same way, but use emery or carborundum paper and not glass paper. Carefully clean both sets of contacts from all traces of dust with a rag moistened in methylated spirits.

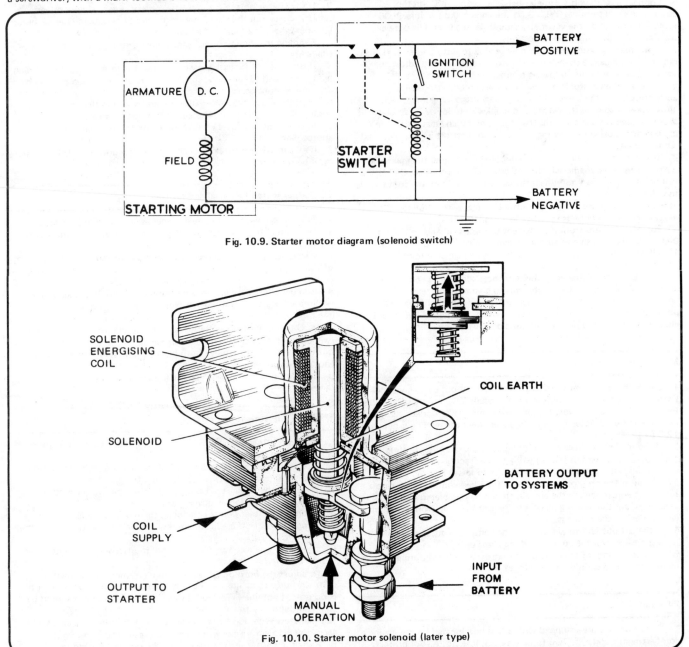

Fig. 10.9. Starter motor diagram (solenoid switch)

Fig. 10.10. Starter motor solenoid (later type)

## 22 Current regulator - adjustment

1  The regulator requires very little attention during its service life, and should there be any reason to suspect its correct functioning, tests of all circuits should be made to ensure that they are not the reason for the trouble.

2  These checks include the tension of the fan belt, to make sure that it is not slipping and so providing only a very low charge rate. The battery should be carefully checked for possible low charge rate due to a faulty cell, or corroded battery connections.

3  The leads from the generator may have been crossed during refitting, and if this is the case then the regulator points will have stuck together as soon as the dynamo starts to charge. Check for loose or broken leads from the dynamo to the regulator.

4  If, after a thorough check, it is considered advisable to test the regulator, this should only be carried out by an electrician who is well acquainted with the correct method, proceed by reference to Fig. 10.11.

5  Pull off the Lucar connections from the two adjacent control box terminals 'B'. To start the engine it will now be necessary to join together the ignition and battery leads with a suitable wire.

6  Connect a 0.-30 volt voltmeter between terminal 'D' on the control box and terminal 'WL'. Start the engine and run it at 2000 rpm. The reading on the voltmeter should be steady and lie between the limits detailed in the Specifications.

7  If the reading is unsteady this may be due to dirty contacts. If the reading is outside the specified limits stop the engine and adjust the voltage regulator in the following manner.

8  Take off the control box cover and start and run the engine at 2000 rpm. Using the correct tool turn the voltage adjustment cam anticlockwise to raise the setting and clockwise to lower it. To check that the setting is correct, stop the engine, and then start it and run it at 2000 rpm noting the reading. Refit the connections to the 'WL' and 'D' terminals.

9  The output from the current regulator should equal the maximum output from the dynamo which is 19 amps (22 amps model C40-I). To test this it is necessary to bypass the cut-out by holding the contacts together.

10 Remove the cover from the control box and with a bulldog clip hold the cut-out contacts together (see Fig. 10.12).

11 Pull off the wires from the adjacent terminals 'B' and connect a 0-40 moving coil ammeter to one of the terminals and to the leads.

12 All the other load connections including the ignition must be made to the battery.

13 Turn on all the lights and other electrical accessories and run the engine at 2000 rpm. The ammeter should give a steady reading between 19 and 25 amps. If the needle flickers it is likely that the points are dirty. If the reading is too low turn the special Lucas tool clockwise to raise the setting and anticlockwise to lower it.

## 23 Cut-out - adjustment

1  Check the voltage required to operate the cut-out by connecting a voltmeter between the control box terminals 'D' and 'WL'. Remove the control box cover, start the engine and gradually increase its speed until the cut-outs close. This should occur when the reading is between 12.6 to 13.4 volts.

2  If the reading is outside these limits turn the cut-out adjusting cam, (Fig. 10.12) by means of the adjusting tool a fraction at a time clockwise to raise the voltage and anticlockwise to lower it.

3  To adjust the drop off voltage bend the fixed contact blade carefully. The adjustment to the cut-out should be completed within 30 seconds of starting the engine otherwise heat build-up from the shunt coil will affect the readings.

4  If the cut-out fails to work, clean the contacts, and, if there is still no response, renew the cut-out and regulator unit.

5  Air gap settings of the control box are accurately set during manufacture and should not be altered.

## 24 Fuses

1  Earlier models are equipped with a fuse box located on the engine compartment bulkhead. Two fuses are used; fuse no. A3-A4 protects the wiper, fuel tank unit and stop light circuits while fuse no. A1-A2 protects the interior and auxiliary lighting circuits.

2  Two spare fuses are carried in the fuse box and only 35 amp cartridge fuses should be used when renewing.

3  The fuse box on later models is attached on the underside of the steering column nacelle and contains four fuses (see Fig. 10.14).

4  Fuse no. 7-8 protects the fuel guage, water gauge and stop light circuits, fuse no. 5-6 protects the direction indicator and wiper circuits while fuse no. 1-2 protects the lighting circuits (fuse no. 3-4 is a spare circuit).

5  If a fuse blows always replace it with a 35 amp fuse. If the trouble persists, refer to the appropriate wiring diagram and check the affected circuit for earthing faults.

## 25 Flasher circuit - fault tracing and rectification

1  The flasher unit is located behind the instrument panel. To gain access to it, withdraw the instrument panel as described in Section 37. Pull off the electrical leads, undo the securing screw (earlier models) and remove the flasher unit.

   The flasher unit is a sealed component and cannot be repaired.

2  If the flasher unit fails to operate, or works very slowly or very rapidly, check out the flasher indicator circuit as detailed below, before assuming there is a fault in the unit itself.

3  Examine the direction indicator bulbs front and rear for broken filaments.

4  If the external flashers are working but the internal flasher warning light has ceased to function, check the filament of the warning bulb and renew if necessary.

5  With the aid of the wiring diagram check all the flasher circuit connections if a flasher bulb is sound but does not work.

6  In the event of total direction indicator failure, check the appropriate fuse.

7  If all other items check out then the flasher unit itself is faulty and must be renewed.

## 26 Flasher switch - removal and refitting

1  First withdraw the instrument panel as described in Section 37.

2  Disconnect the lead from the flasher unit and the main harness at the rear of the instrument panel.

3  Withdraw the flasher switch leads through the grommet in the side of the instrument box and release the retaining clips on the steering column.

4  Remove the securing bolt from the flasher switch bracket and withdraw the switch and bracket from the steering column (see Fig. 10.17).

**Note:** On later models the flasher switch also operates the horn and headlight dip facility. The removal procedure is basically the same but it is necessary to remove both halves of the switch shroud from the steering column.

5  The flasher switch cannot be repaired and if faulty must be renewed.

## 27 Horn - adjustment

1  The horn is located behind the radiator grille. Remove the grille as described in Chapter 2.

2  Disconnect the electrical leads from the snap connectors (or horn terminals), remove the securing bolts and lift out the horn.

3  To adjust the earlier type Lucas horn, first remove the securing clip and lift off the domed cover.

4  Clean the contact points and adjust them until they are almost touching, then turn the adjusting screw one-half a turn to increase the gap (see Fig. 10.18).

5  Check the operation of the horn and, if unsatisfactory, a new one should be fitted.

6  To adjust the horn on Series IIA models remove the domed cover and turn the adjustment screw a small amount either way until a good note is obtained. To avoid blowing the fuse the horn should be connected directly to the battery.

7  The latest type horns have no adjustment and the only check necessary is to ensure the wiring connectors are clean and tight.

8  Refit the horn using the reversal of the removal procedure.

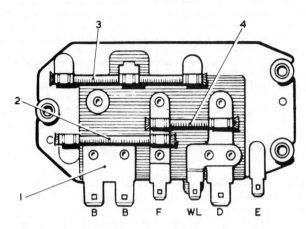

Fig. 10.11. Underside of electrical control box

1 Terminal plate B-B
2 Field parallel resistor
   (when fitted)
3 Swamp resistor
4 Field series resistor

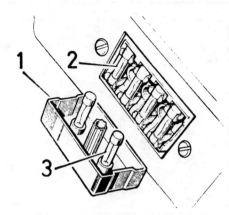

Fig. 10.14. Fuse box (later type)

1 Cover
2 Fuses
3 Spare fuses

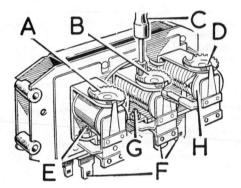

Fig. 10.12. Current voltage regulator

A Adjustment cam of voltage regulator
B Adjustment cam of current regulator
C Special setting tool
D Adjustment cam of cut-out relay
E Adjustable contact of voltage regulator
F 'Lucar' connection terminals
G Adjustable contact of current regulator
H Core face of cut-out relay

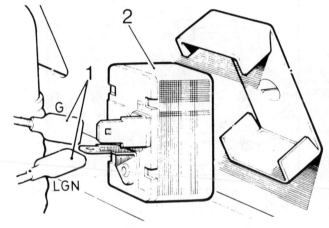

Fig. 10.15. Flasher unit (later type)

1 Wiring connectors
2 Flasher unit

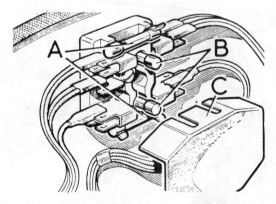

Fig. 10.13. Fuse box (earlier models)

A Fuses
B Spare fuses
C Cover

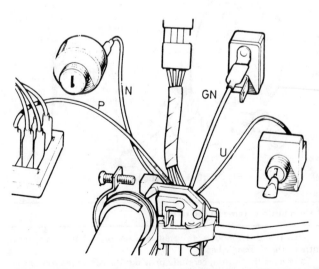

Fig. 10.16. Wiring connections on the later type flasher/dipswitch

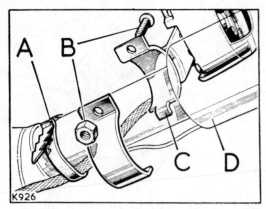

**Fig. 10.17. Flasher switch attachment clamp (earlier type shown)**

A  *Wiring clip*              C  *Flasher switch*
B  *Clamp bolt*              D  *Steering column*

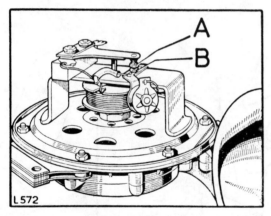

**Fig. 10.18. Earlier type horn**

A  *Adjustable contact*              B  *Locknut*

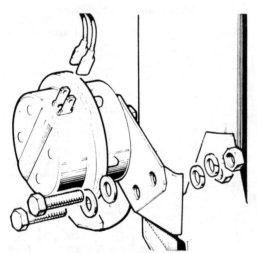

**Fig. 10.19. Later type horn**

### 28 Horn button - removal and refitting

1  Series II and IIA models are fitted with a horn push button in the centre of the steering wheel.
2  To remove the button, carefully prise out the centre section of the steering wheel using a thin-bladed screwdriver (photo).
3  Check the button for correct operation and clean the contacts.
4  Refit the horn assembly using the reverse procedure to removal.

### 29 Headlamps mounted in grille panel - removal and refitting

1  Remove the screw from the bottom of the headlamp rim and carefully prise off the rim and rubber dust cover (photo).
2  Press the headlamp unit inwards and rotate it anticlockwise to release it from the spring-loaded adjustment screws.
3  Turn the bulb holder anticlockwise to release it and remove the bulb.
4  If the headlamp is the sealed beam type, remove the three screws securing the rim to the headlamp shell, support the light unit and pull off the electrical plug from the rear of the unit (see photos).
5  Refit the headlamp assembly using the reverse procedure to removal.

### 30 Headlamps (wing mounted) - removal and refitting

1  Referring to Fig. 10.22, remove the four screws securing the headlamp bezel to the wing.
2  Slacken the three screws securing the chrome rim, turn it enough to clear the screw heads and lift off.
3  Withdraw the light unit and disconnect the electrical plug (or bulb holder).
4  Renew the bulb or light unit as applicable and refit the headlamp assembly using the reversal of the removal procedure.

### 31 Headlamp beam - adjustment

1  The headlights may be adjusted for both vertical and horizontal beam position by the screws located as shown in Fig. 10.23 and photo.
2  They should be set so that on full or high beam, the beams are set slightly below parallel with a level road surface. Do not forget that the beam position is affected by how the vehicle is normally loaded for night driving and set the beams loaded to this condition. Before adjustment is commenced check that the tyre pressures are correct.
3  Although this adjustment can be approximately set at home using a vertical wall it is recommended that this be left to the local garage who will have the necessary optical equipment to do the job more accurately.

### 32 Front and rear sidelights - removal and refitting

1  The method of removing the front and rear side, flasher and stop lamps is the same on all vehicles.
2  Remove the two retaining screws and ease the lens out of the rubber moulding (photo).
3  Renew the bulb if necessary and refit the lens into the moulding ensuring the beaded lip fits snugly around the base of the lens.
4  Refit the two retaining screws taking care not to overtighten them.

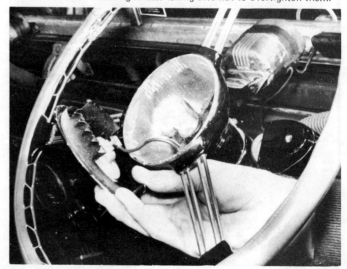

28.2 Removing the horn button

29.1 Headlamp with rim removed

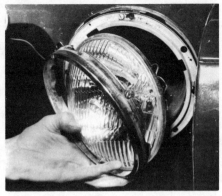

29.4a Removing headlamp assembly

29.4b Electrical plug at rear of sealed beam unit

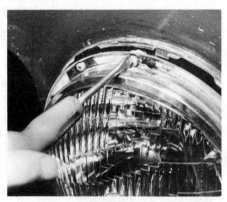

31.1 Headlamp vertical adjusting screw (earlier models)

32.2 Removing a rear light lens

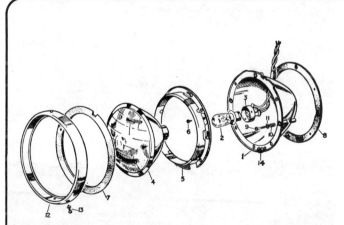

Fig. 10.20. Headlamp assembly (earlier models)

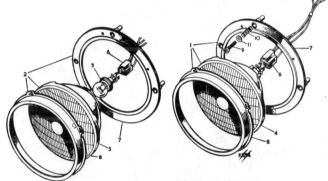

Fig. 10.21. Headlamp assemblies fitted to later models

| | | |
|---|---|---|
| 1 | Body for headlamp | |
| 2 | Bulb | |
| 3 | Adaptor for bulb | |
| 4 | Light unit | |
| 5 | Rim complete for light unit | |
| 6 | Special screw for light unit rim | |
| 7 | Rubber gasket for headlamp rim | |
| 8 | Gasket | |
| 9 | Special screw. Light unit adjustment | |
| 10 | Spring. Light unit adjustment | |
| 11 | Cup washer. Light unit adjustment | |
| 12 | Rim for headlamp | |
| 13 | Screw. Retaining rim | |
| 14 | Spire nut. Retaining rim | |

1   Headlamp complete, sealed beam
2   Headlamp complete
3   Bulb
4   Light unit, sealed beam
5   Light unit
6   Adaptor and leads for headlamp
7   Rim for light unit
8   Rim for headlamp
9   Screw. For light unit adjustment and fitting headlamp to front grille
10   Spring. For light unit adjustment and fitting headlamp to front grille
11   Fibre washer. For light unit adjustment and fitting headlamp to front grille

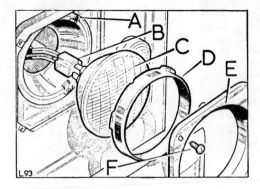

**Fig. 10.22. Removing the sealed beam unit**

A   *Screws for rim*
B   *Connector, electrical leads*
C   *Light unit*
D   *Rim for headlamp*
E   *Bezel*
F   *Screws for bezel*

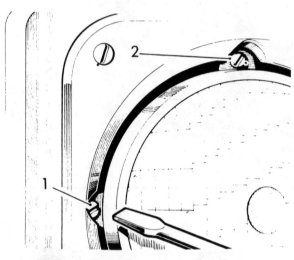

**Fig. 10.23. Headlamp adjustment screws (later models)**

1   *Horizontal adjustment screw*      2   *Vertical adjustment screw*

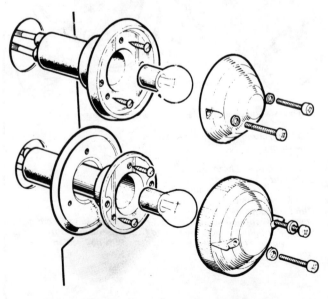

**Fig. 10.24. Side and indicator light assemblies**

### 33 Windscreen wiper motor (early type) - removal and refitting

1   The Series II Land Rovers were fitted with a single wiper arm driven directly from a motor located below the windscreen (photo).
2   To remove the motor, slacken the nut on the wiper arm spindle, give it a sharp tap to release the collets and withdraw the complete arm and blade (photo).
3   Undo the securing nuts and remove the wiper arm stop and rubber mounting block from the front of the windscreen.
4   Withdraw the motor from inside the cab and retrieve the brass spindle bushes.
5   Refit the motor using the reversal of the removal procedure. Before refitting the wiper arm and blade set the motor to the parked position and refit the arm accordingly.

### 34 Windscreen wiper motor (early type) - servicing

1   If the movement of the wiper arm is erratic or stops altogether, remove the motor as described previously and lubricate the spindle bushes with thin oil.
2   With the motor withdrawn from the screen but the wires still connected, switch on the ignition and motor, and check that the spindle moves backwards and forwards quite freely.

If, on refitting the motor, arm and blade, the performance is still unsatisfactory, the fault probably lies in the armature windings and it is best to obtain a replacement motor.

33.1 Location of earlier type wiper motor

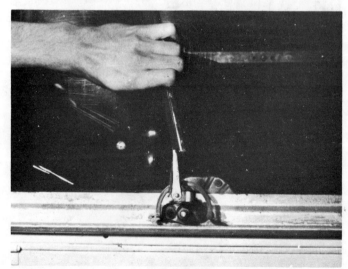

33.2 Removing the wiper blade and arm (earlier models)

### 35 Windscreen wiper motor and linkage (twin wipers) - removal and refitting

1   Later versions of the Land Rover are fitted with a wiper motor located in the glove compartment behind a cover plate which drives the two wiper arms via a cable and two wheel boxes (see Fig. 10.25)
2   To remove the motor, first disconnect the battery earth terminal and remove the dash cover plate, secured by four screws (Fig. 10.26).
3   Unscrew the nut securing the drive cable outer tube to the motor.
4   On earlier versions remove the four bolts securing the motor mounting plate to the side of the glove box.
5   Prise off each wiper arm from the drive spindles and then withdraw the motor complete with the inner drive cable.
6   On later models the motor is secured by two bolts in the glove box and a nut plate on the engine compartment bulkhead. After removing these, withdraw the motor and inner cable as described previously.
7   The two wiper arm drive boxes can be removed by first unscrewing the six screws securing the windscreen lower panel and lifting off the panel.
8   Remove the wiper arms and then slacken the lockscrew and pull

off the splined adaptors from the spindles (see Fig. 10.27).
9   Remove the rubber grommet (or escutcheon plate) from the spindles and undo the spindle locknuts.
10   Remove the motor and inner cable as described previously.
11   The drive boxes can now be withdrawn from inside the cab complete with the cable tubes.
12   Undo the two securing screws and remove the cover plate from each drive box. Check the gears and cable for wear and renew if necessary.
13   Lubricate the spindles, gears and the inside of the cable tubes with grease.
14   Reassemble the tubes onto the drive boxes and secure with the cover plate. Make sure the flared ends of the tubes are correctly positioned as shown in Fig. 10.28.
15   Refit the drive boxes and motor using the reverse procedure to that of removal. Grease the inner drive cable before sliding it through the outer tubes.
16   After reconnecting the battery terminal and motor electrical leads, switch the motor on and then off so that the spindles stop in the parked position and then refit the wiper arms and blades in the parked position.

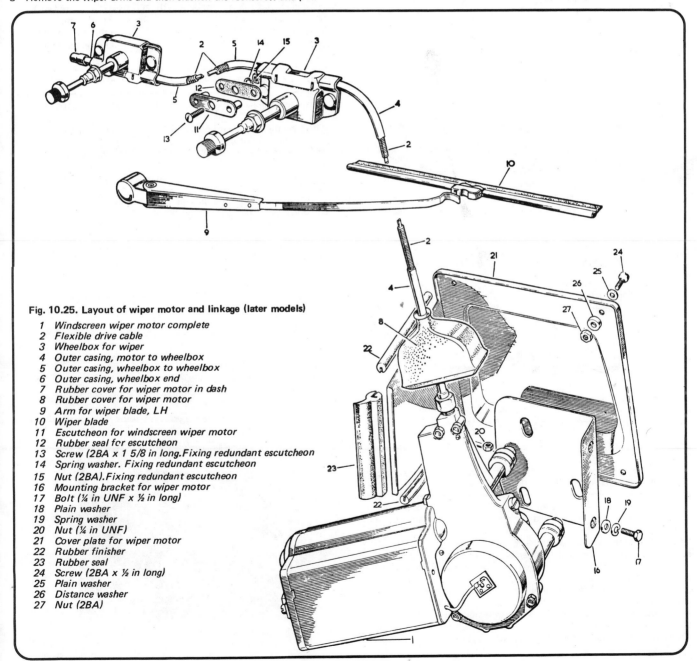

**Fig. 10.25. Layout of wiper motor and linkage (later models)**

 1   Windscreen wiper motor complete
 2   Flexible drive cable
 3   Wheelbox for wiper
 4   Outer casing, motor to wheelbox
 5   Outer casing, wheelbox to wheelbox
 6   Outer casing, wheelbox end
 7   Rubber cover for wiper motor in dash
 8   Rubber cover for wiper motor
 9   Arm for wiper blade, LH
10   Wiper blade
11   Escutcheon for windscreen wiper motor
12   Rubber seal for escutcheon
13   Screw (2BA x 1 5/8 in long.Fixing redundant escutcheon
14   Spring washer. Fixing redundant escutcheon
15   Nut (2BA).Fixing redundant escutcheon
16   Mounting bracket for wiper motor
17   Bolt (¼ in UNF x ½ in long)
18   Plain washer
19   Spring washer
20   Nut (¼ in UNF)
21   Cover plate for wiper motor
22   Rubber finisher
23   Rubber seal
24   Screw (2BA x ½ in long)
25   Plain washer
26   Distance washer
27   Nut (2BA)

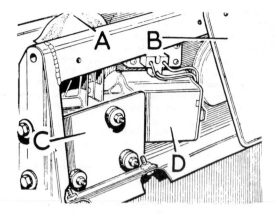

**Fig. 10.26. Location of wiper motor (later models)**

A  Rubber cover for wiper          C  Mounting bracket for wiper
B  Cover for glove box aperture    D  Wiper motor

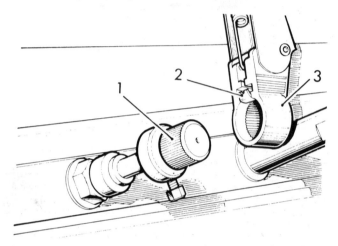

**Fig. 10.27. Wiper arm attachment point (later models)**

1  Splined adaptor                3  Wiper arm
2  Spring clip

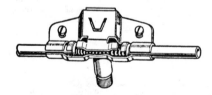

**Fig. 10.28. Correct assembly of wiper drive box**

### 36 Windscreen wiper motor (later type) - overhaul

1  Mark the domed cover in relation to the flat gearbox lid, undo the
four screws holding the gearbox lid in place and lift off the lid and
domed cover.
2  Pull off the small circlip and remove the limit switch wiper. The
connecting rod and cable rack (18) can now be lifted off. Take particular note of the spacer located between the final drive wheel and the
connecting rod.
3  Undo and remove the two through bolts from the commutator end
cover. Pull off the end cover.
4  Lift out the brush gear retainer and then remove the brush gear.
Clean the commutator and brush gear and, if worn, fit new brushes.
The resistance between adjacent commutator segments should be 0.34
to 0.41 ohm.

5  Carefully examine the internal wiring for signs of chafing, breaks
or chafing which would lead to a short circuit. Insulate or renew
any damaged wiring.
6  Measure the value of the field resistance which should be between
12.8 and 14 ohms. If a lower reading than this is obtained it is likely
that there is a short circuit and a new field coil should be fitted.
7  Renew the gearbox gear if the teeth are damaged, chipped or
worn.
8  Reassembly is a straightforward reversal of the dismantling
sequence, but ensure the following items are lubricated:-

a)  Immerse the self-aligning armature bearing in
engine oil for 24 hours before assembly.
b)  Oil the armature bearings with engine oil.
c)  Soak the felt lubricator in the gearbox with
engine oil.
d)  Grease generously the wormwheel bearings,
crosshead, guide channel, connecting rod, crankpin,
worm, cable rack and wheelboxes and the final
gear shaft.

**Note:** Some Series IIA, and all Series III Land Rovers are fitted with
a later type wiper motor. The method of overhauling this motor is
virtually identical to the one described in this Section, and providing
reference is made to Fig. 10.30, no problems should be encountered.

### 37 Instrument panel - removal and refitting

1  Disconnect the battery earth terminal and remove the instrument
panel retaining screws.
2  Withdraw the instrument panel far enough to gain access to the
rear of the panel (photo).
**Note:** On Series III models it may be necessary to remove the steering
wheel to provide sufficient clearance.
3  Disconnect the drive cable from the rear of the speedometer.
4  Prise out all the illumination and warning light bulb holders from
the rear of the panel and the speedometer housing.
5  Disconnect the inspection lamp socket leads.
6  Disconnect the wiring leads from the lighting switch and the fuel
mixture warning light (if fitted).
7  Disconnect all the wires from the dynamo warning light (earlier
models) and the instrument panel gauges. Make a careful note
of the location of each wire and if necessary identify it with paint or
coloured tape as it is removed.
8  On later models, disconnect the Lucar connectors from the rear of
the panel as necessary and slacken the knurled nut securing the earth
leads.
9  Disconnect the wires from the wiper switch, ignition switch and
voltage stabiliser where fitted.
10  Make a careful check that all the leads have been disconnected and
then lift the panel away complete with instruments.
11  The instruments can be removed from the panel by releasing the
retaining clips or brackets. The switches and warning lights are secured
either by circlips or threaded bezels.
12  Refit the instruments and panel assembly using the reverse procedure to that of removal.

37.1 Withdrawing the instrument panel

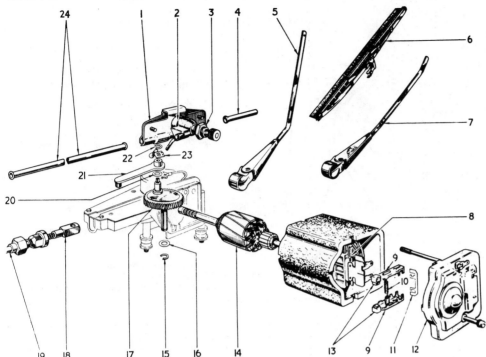

**Fig. 10.29. Exploded view of wiper motor**

1 Drive box
2 Jet and bush assembly
3 Nut
4 Rigid tubing - right-hand side
5 Wiper arm
6 Blade
7 Wiper arm
8 Field coil assembly
9 Brush gear
10 Tension spring & retainers
11 Brush gear retainer
12 End cover
13 Brushes
14 Armature
15 Circlip
16 Washer
17 Final drive wheel
18 Cable rack
19 Rigid tubing- left-hand side
20 Spacer
21 Connecting rod
22 Circlip
23 Parking switch contact
24 Rigid tubing - centre section

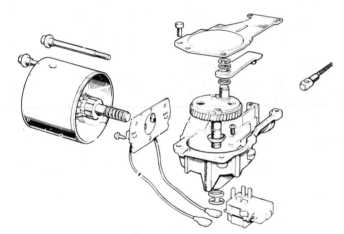

Fig. 10.30. Exploded view of latest type wiper motor

### 38 Fuel gauge sender unit - removal and refitting

1 The fuel gauge sender unit is located on the top of the fuel tank and is basically a float operated variable resistor that controls the amount of current to the fuel gauge. If the fuel gauge appears to give a faulty reading it is probably due to the float arm sticking or the resistor coil breaking down.

2 To remove the unit, first disconnect the battery earth terminal and lift off the right-hand seat cushion and remove the tank cover panel.
**Note:** In the case of a rear mounted tank remove the inspection cover from the rear floor section.

3 Mark the position of the sender unit in relation to the top of the tank and disconnect the electrical lead and earth lead.

4 Remove the retaining screws and lift out the sender unit complete with float.

5 Check that the float moves freely without sticking. If the resistor coil is suspect the complete unit must be renewed as it cannot be repaired.

6 Refit the unit in the tank using a new gasket smeared with a fuel resistant jointing compound such as 'Osotite'.

### 39 Temperature gauge sender unit - removal and refitting

1 The temperature gauge sender unit is located on the front left-hand side of the engine adjacent to the thermostat housing (photo). It is basically a bi-metal resistor that increases the current to the gauge as it is progressively heated by the coolant.

2 Drain the coolant as described in Chapter 2, slacken the domed nut and remove the feed wire.

3 Remove the three securing bolts and lift out the sender unit.

4 The unit cannot be repaired and if faulty must be renewed.
When refitting the sender unit always use a new gasket.
**Note:** On some later models the sender unit is the plug type that screws into an adaptor plug beneath the thermostat housing.

5 Do not forget to refill the radiator after refitting the sender unit. Run the engine and check for coolant leaks.

39.1 Location of temperature gauge sender unit

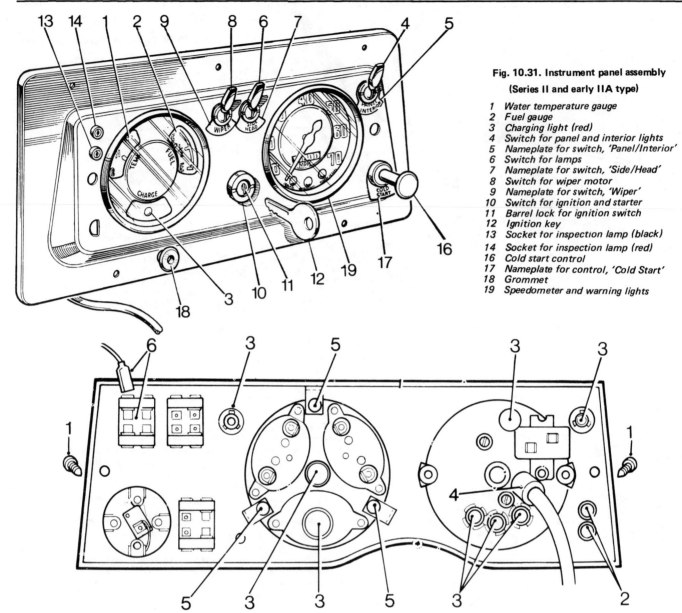

Fig. 10.31. Instrument panel assembly

(Series II and early IIA type)

1   Water temperature gauge
2   Fuel gauge
3   Charging light (red)
4   Switch for panel and interior lights
5   Nameplate for switch, 'Panel/Interior'
6   Switch for lamps
7   Nameplate for switch, 'Side/Head'
8   Switch for wiper motor
9   Nameplate for switch, 'Wiper'
10  Switch for ignition and starter
11  Barrel lock for ignition switch
12  Ignition key
13  Socket for inspection lamp (black)
14  Socket for inspection lamp (red)
16  Cold start control
17  Nameplate for control, 'Cold Start'
18  Grommet
19  Speedometer and warning lights

Fig. 10.32. Rear views of instrument panel (Series III models)

1   Panel securing screws        3   Illumination and warning lamps   5   Earth terminal nuts          6   'Lucar' connectors
2   Inspection lamp socket       4   Speedometer cable

## 40 Fault diagnosis - electrical system

| Symptom | Reason |
| --- | --- |
| **Starter motor fails to turn engine** | |
| No electricity at starter motor | Battery discharged. |
| | Battery defective internally. |
| | Battery terminal leads loose or earth lead not securely attached to body. |
| | Loose or broken connections in starter motor circuit. |
| | Starter motor switch or solenoid faulty. |
| Electricity at starter motor: faulty motor | Starter motor pinion jammed in mesh with flywheel gear ring. |
| | Starter brushes badly worn, sticking, or brush wire loose. |
| | Commutator dirty, worn or burnt. |
| | Starter motor armature faulty. |
| | Field coils earthed. |
| **Starter motor turns engine very slowly** | |
| Electrical defects | Battery in discharged condition. |
| | Starter brushes badly worn, sticking, or brush wires loose. |
| | Loose wires in starter motor circuit. |

| Symptom | Reason |
|---|---|
| **Starter motor operates without turning engine** | |
| Dirt or oil on drive gear | Starter motor pinion sticking on the screwed sleeve. |
| | Pinion or flywheel gear teeth broken or worn. |
| | |
| Electrical defect | Battery almost completely discharged. |
| | |
| **Starter motor noisy or excessively rough engagement** | |
| Lack of attention or mechanical damage | Pinion or flywheel gear teeth broken or worn. |
| | Starter drive main spring broken. |
| | Starter motor retaining bolts loose. |
| | |
| **Battery will not hold charge for more than a few days** | |
| Wear or damage | Battery defective internally. |
| | Electrolyte level too low or electrolyte too weak due to leakage. |
| | Plate separators no longer fully effective. |
| | Battery plates severely sulphated. |
| | |
| Insufficient current flow to keep battery charge | Battery plates severely sulphated. |
| | Fan belt slipping. |
| | Battery terminal connections loose or corroded. |
| | Alternator (or dynamo) regulator unit not working correctly. |
| | Short in lighting circuit causing continual battery drain. |
| | Generator regulator unit not working correctly. |
| | |
| **Ignition light fails to go out, battery runs flat in a few days** | |
| Generator not charging | Fan belt loose and slipping or broken. |
| | Brushes worn, sticking, broken or dirty. |
| | Brush springs weak or broken. |
| | Slip rings dirty, greasy, worn or burnt. |
| | Alternator stator coils burnt, open, or shorted. |
| | |
| **Horn** | |
| Horn operates all the time | Horn push either earthed or stuck down. |
| | Horn cable to horn push earthed. |
| | |
| Horn fails to operate | Blown fuse. |
| | Cable or cable connection loose, broken or disconnected. |
| | Horn has an internal fault. |
| | |
| Horn emits intermittent or unsatisfactory noise | Cable connections loose or horn needs adjusting. |
| | |
| **Lights** | |
| Lights do not come on | If engine not running, battery discharged. |
| | Light bulb filament burnt out or bulbs broken. |
| | Wire connections loose, disconnected or broken. |
| | Light switch shorting or otherwise faulty. |
| | |
| Lights come on but fade out | If engine not running battery discharged. |
| | Light bulb filament burnt out or bulbs or sealed beam units broken. |
| | Wire connections loose, disconnected or broken. |
| | Light switch shorting or otherwise faulty. |
| | |
| Lights give very poor illumination | Lamp glasses dirty. |
| | Lamps badly out of adjustment. |
| | |
| Lights work erratically - flashing on and off, especially over bumps | Battery terminal or earth connection loose. |
| | Lights not earthing properly. |
| | Contacts in light switch faulty. |
| | |
| **Wipers** | |
| Wiper motor fails to work | Blown fuse. |
| | Wire connections loose, disconnected or broken. |
| | Brushes badly worn. |
| | Armature worn or faulty. |
| | Field coils faulty. |
| | |
| Wiper motor works very slowly and takes excessive current | Commutator dirty, greasy or burnt. |
| | Armature bearings dirty or unaligned. |
| | Armature badly worn or faulty. |
| | |
| Wiper motor works slowly and takes little current | Brushes badly worn. |
| | Commutator dirty, greasy or burnt. |
| | Armature badly worn or faulty. |
| | |
| Wiper motor works but wiper blades remain static | Wiper motor gearbox parts badly worn. |

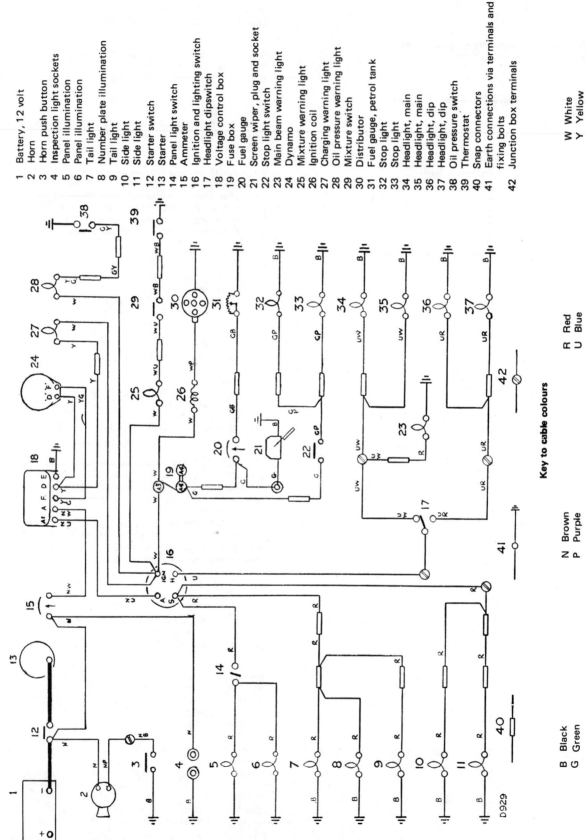

**Fig. 10.33. Series II models, positive earth**

1  Battery, 12 volt
2  Horn
3  Horn push button
4  Inspection light sockets
5  Panel illumination
6  Panel illumination
7  Tail light
8  Number plate illumination
9  Tail light
10  Side light
11  Side light
12  Starter switch
13  Starter
14  Panel light switch
15  Ammeter
16  Ignition and lighting switch
17  Headlight dipswitch
18  Voltage control box
19  Fuse box
20  Fuel gauge
21  Screen wiper, plug and socket
22  Stop light switch
23  Main beam warning light
24  Dynamo
25  Mixture warning light
26  Ignition coil
27  Charging warning light
28  Oil pressure warning light
29  Mixture switch
30  Distributor
31  Fuel gauge, petrol tank
32  Stop light
33  Stop light
34  Headlight, main
35  Headlight, main
36  Headlight, dip
37  Headlight, dip
38  Oil pressure switch
39  Thermostat
40  Snap connectors
41  Earth connections via terminals and fixing bolts
42  Junction box terminals

**Key to cable colours**

B  Black
G  Green
N  Brown
P  Purple
R  Red
U  Blue
W  White
Y  Yellow
RN  Red with Brown, etc.

D929

147

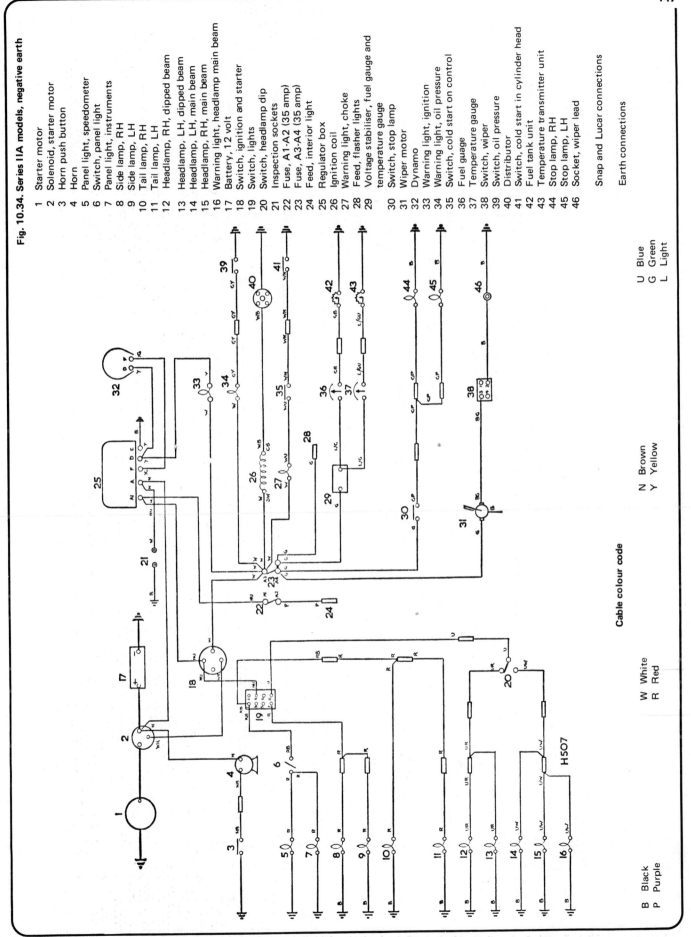

**Fig. 10.34. Series IIA models, negative earth**

1 Starter motor
2 Solenoid, starter motor
3 Horn push button
4 Horn
5 Panel light, speedometer
6 Switch, panel light
7 Panel light, instruments
8 Side lamp, RH
9 Side lamp, LH
10 Tail lamp, RH
11 Tail lamp, LH
12 Headlamp, RH, dipped beam
13 Headlamp, LH, dipped beam
14 Headlamp, LH, main beam
15 Headlamp, RH, main beam
16 Warning light, headlamp main beam
17 Battery, 12 volt
18 Switch, ignition and starter
19 Switch, lights
20 Switch, headlamp dip
21 Inspection sockets
22 Fuse, A1-A2 (35 amp)
23 Fuse, A3-A4 (35 amp)
24 Feed, interior light
25 Regulator box
26 Ignition coil
27 Warning light, choke
28 Feed, flasher lights
29 Voltage stabiliser, fuel gauge and temperature gauge
30 Switch, stop lamp
31 Wiper motor
32 Dynamo
33 Warning light, ignition
34 Warning light, oil pressure
35 Switch, cold start on control
36 Fuel guage
37 Temperature gauge
38 Switch, wiper
39 Switch, oil pressure
40 Distributor
41 Switch, cold start in cylinder head
42 Fuel tank unit
43 Temperature transmitter unit
44 Stop lamp, RH
45 Stop lamp, LH
46 Socket, wiper lead

Snap and Lucar connections

Earth connections

**Cable colour code**

| | | |
|---|---|---|
| N Brown | U Blue | |
| Y Yellow | G Green | |
| W White | L Light | |
| R Red | | |
| B Black | | |
| P Purple | | |

H5O7

148

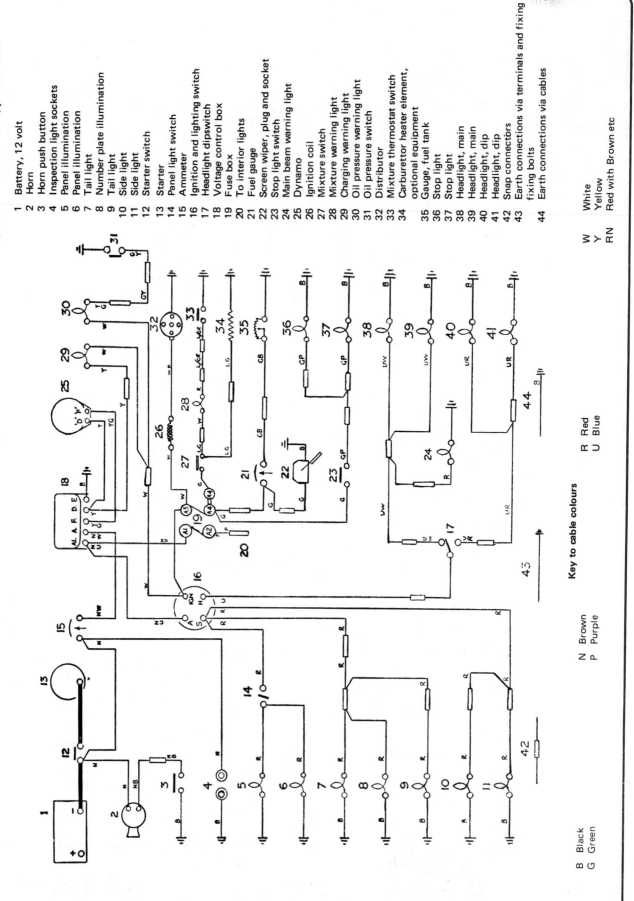

Fig. 10.35. Series IIA models, positive earth

1 Battery, 12 volt
2 Horn
3 Horn push button
4 Inspection light sockets
5 Panel illumination
6 Panel illumination
7 Tail light
8 Number plate illumination
9 Tail light
10 Side light
11 Side light
12 Starter switch
13 Starter
14 Panel light switch
15 Ammeter
16 Ignition and lighting switch
17 Headlight dipswitch
18 Voltage control box
19 Fuse box
20 To interior lights
21 Fuel gauge
22 Screen wiper, plug and socket
23 Stop light switch
24 Main beam warning light
25 Dynamo
26 Ignition coil
27 Mixture switch
28 Mixture warning light
29 Charging warning light
30 Oil pressure warning light
31 Oil pressure switch
32 Distributor
33 Mixture thermostat switch
34 Carburettor heater element, optional equipment
35 Gauge, fuel tank
36 Stop light
37 Stop light
38 Headlight, main
39 Headlight, main
40 Headlight, dip
41 Headlight, dip
42 Snap connectors
43 Earth connections via terminals and fixing bolts
44 Earth connections via cables

W   White
Y   Yellow
RN  Red with Brown etc

**Key to cable colours**

R   Red
U   Blue

N   Brown
P   Purple

B   Black
G   Green

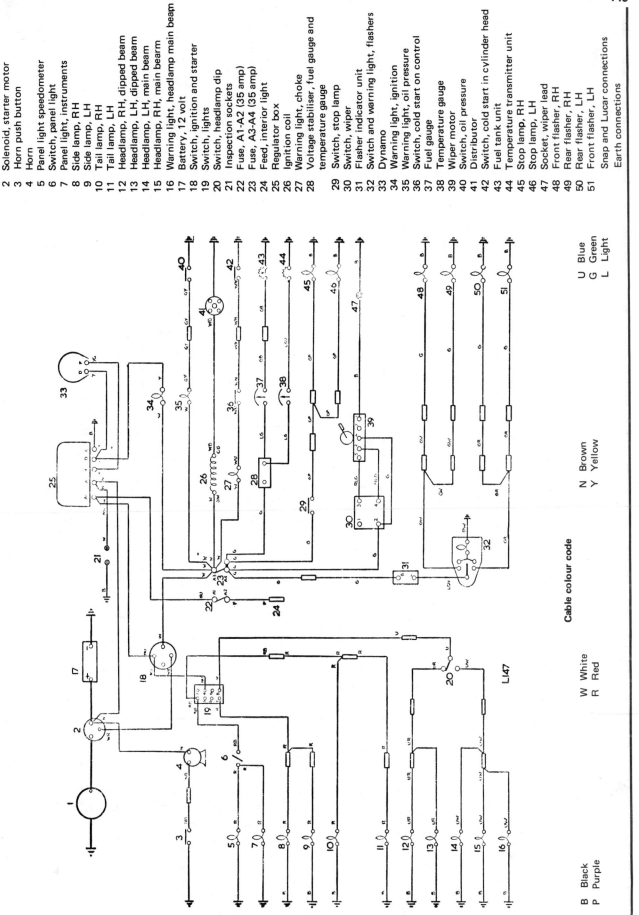

**Fig. 10.36. Series IIA models with headlamps in the front wings (negative earth)**

1  Starter motor
2  Solenoid, starter motor
3  Horn push button
4  Horn
5  Panel light speedometer
6  Switch, panel light
7  Panel light, instruments
8  Side lamp, RH
9  Side lamp, LH
10 Tail lamp, RH
11 Tail lamp, LH
12 Headlamp, RH, dipped beam
13 Headlamp, LH, dipped beam
14 Headlamp, LH, main beam
15 Headlamp, RH, main bearm
16 Warning light, headlamp main beam
17 Battery, 12 volt
18 Switch, ignition and starter
19 Switch, lights
20 Switch, headlamp dip
21 Inspection sockets
22 Fuse, A1-A2 (35 amp)
23 Fuse, A3-A4 (35 amp)
24 Feed, interior light
25 Regulator box
26 Ignition coil
27 Warning light, choke
28 Voltage stabiliser, fuel gauge and temperature gauge
29 Switch, stop lamp
30 Switch, wiper
31 Flasher indicator unit
32 Switch and warning light, flashers
33 Dynamo
34 Warning light, ignition
35 Warning light, oil pressure
36 Switch, cold start on control
37 Fuel gauge
38 Temperature gauge
39 Wiper motor
40 Switch, oil pressure
41 Distributor
42 Switch, cold start in cylinder head
43 Fuel tank unit
44 Temperature transmitter unit
45 Stop lamp, RH
46 Stop lamp, LH
47 Socket, wiper lead
48 Front flasher, RH
49 Rear flasher, RH
50 Rear flasher, LH
51 Front flasher, LH
   Snap and Lucar connections
   Earth connections

**Cable colour code**

B  Black
P  Purple

W  White
R  Red

N  Brown
Y  Yellow

U  Blue
G  Green
L  Light

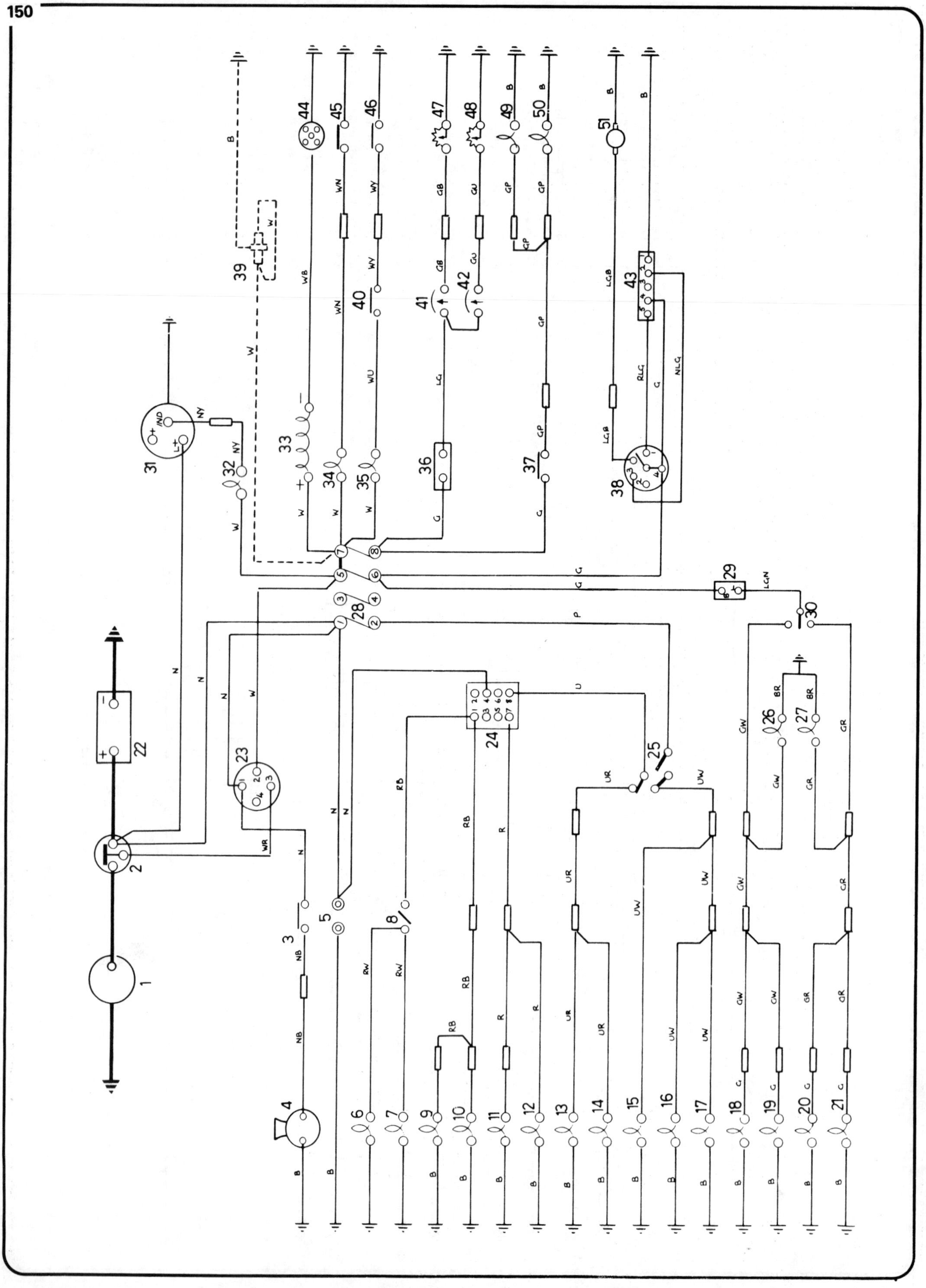
1
2
3
4
5
6
7
8
9
10
11
12
13
14
15
16
17
18
19
20
21
22
23
24
25
26
27
28
29
30
31
32
33
34
35
36
37
38
39
40
41
42
43
44
45
46
47
48
49
50
51

**Fig. 10.37. Series III models, negative earth**

1 Starter motor
2 Solenoid, starter motor
3 Switch for horns
4 Horn
5 Inspection sockets
6 Instrument panel illumination
7 Instrument panel illumination
8 Switch, panel lights
9 Tail lamp, LH
10 Tail lamp, RH
11 Side lamp, LH
12 Side lamp, RH
13 Headlamp, LH dipped beam
14 Headlamp, RH dipped beam
15 Warning light, headlamp main beam
16 Headlamp, LH main beam

17 Headlamp, RH main beam
18 Direction indicator lamp, rear RH
19 Direction indicator lamp, front RH
20 Direction indicator lamp, front LH
21 Direction indicator lamp, rear LH
22 Battery
23 Switch, ignition and starter
24 Switch, lights
25 Switch, headlamp flash and dip
26 Warning light, indicator RH
27 Warning light, indicator LH
28 Fuses, 1 to 8, 35 amp
29 Indicator unit, flasher
30 Swtich, direction indicators
31 Alternator, Lucas 16 ACR
32 Warning light, ignition

33 Ignition coil
34 Warning light, oil pressure
35 Warning light, choke
36 Voltage stabiliser, fuel guage and water temperature gauge
37 Switch, stop lamp
38 Switch, windscreen wiper
39 Dual fuel pump, 6 cylinder models only
40 Switch, cold start warning light
41 Fuel gauge
42 Water temperature gauge
43 Screenwiper motor
44 Distributor
45 Switch, oil pressure

46 Switch, cold start termostat
47 Fuel tank unit
48 Water temperature transmitter unit
49 Stop lamp, LH
50 Stop lamp, RH
51 Screenwasher motor (when fitted)

‑ Snap connections and/or plugs and sockets

‑ Earth connections via cables

‑ Earth connections via terminals or fixing bolts

6-cylinder models only

**Key to cable colours**

B Black
G Green
L Light
N Brown
P Purple
R Red
U Blue
W White
Y Yellow

The last letter of a colour code denotes the tracer colour

# Chapter 11 Suspension and steering

*For modifications, and information applicable to later models, see Supplement at end of manual*

## Contents

## Specifications

### Steering
| | |
|---|---|
| Type ... ... ... ... ... ... ... ... ... ... | Re-circulating ball |
| Ratio: | |
| Straight ahead ... ... ... ... ... ... ... | 15.6 : 1 |
| Full lock ... ... ... ... ... ... ... ... | 23.8 : 1 |
| Number of steering wheel turns lock-to-lock ... ... ... ... | 3.3 |

### Front wheel alignment
| | |
|---|---|
| Wheel camber ... .. ... ... ... ... ... ... ... | 1½° |
| Wheel castor ... ... ... ... ... ... ... ... | 3° |
| Swivel pin inclination ... ... ... ... ... ... ... | 7° |
| Toe-in ... ... ... ... ... ... ... ... ... | 1.2 to 2.4 mm |

### Front spring dimensions
| | |
|---|---|
| Length ... ... ... ... ... ... ... ... ... | 36.25 in (920.7 mm) |
| Width ... ... ... ... ... ... ... ... ... | 2.5 in (63.5 mm) |
| Number of leaves: | |
| SWB models ... ... ... ... ... .. ... ... ... | 9 |
| LWB models ... ... ... ... ... ... ... ... | 11 |

### Rear spring dimensions
| | |
|---|---|
| Length ... ... ... ... ... .. ... ... ... ... | 48 in (1219 mm) |
| Width ... ... ... ... ... ... ... ... ... | 2.5 in (63.5 mm) |
| Number of leaves: | |
| SWB models ... ... ... ... ... ... ... ... | 11 |
| LWB models ... ... ... ... ... ... ... ... | 10 |

### Shock absorber
| | |
|---|---|
| Shock absorber ... ... ... ... ... ... ... ... | Telescopic type, front and rear |

### Tyre sizes
| | |
|---|---|
| SWB models ... ... ... ... ... ... ... ... ... | 6.00 x 16, 6.50 x 16, 7.00 x 16, 7.10 x 16 and 7.50 x 16 |
| LWB models ... ... .. ... ... ... ... ... ... | 7.50 x 16 |

### Tyre pressures (front and rear)
| | |
|---|---|
| Tyre pressures (front and rear) ... ... .. ... ... | 25 lb/in$^2$ (1.8 kg/cm$^2$) |

**Note:** If the load is over 550 lb (250 kg) the rear tyre pressures should be increased to 30 lb/in$^2$ (2.1 kg/cm$^2$)

### Torque wrench settings
| | lb f ft | kg f m |
|---|---|---|
| Steering wheel nut ... ... ... ... ... ... ... | 40 | 5.4 |
| Balljoint nuts ... ... ... ... ... ... ... ... | 30 | 4 |
| Brackets to steering box bolts ... ... ... ... ... | 30 | 4 |
| Steering box brackets to chassis bolts ... ... ... ... | 15 | 2 |
| Drop arm securing nut ... ... ... ... ... ... ... | 60 - 80 | 8.5 - 11 |
| Relay lever pinchbolt ... . ... ... ... ... ... | 55 | 7.6 |

## 1 General description

The suspension on the Land Rover is ruggedly simple and comprises semi-elliptical leaf springs fitted to the front and rear axle. The ends of each spring are attached to the chassis brackets via metal-clad rubber bushes. Shackle plates on each spring allow it to flex under load. Spring rebound is controlled by telescopic shock absorbers fitted between the axles and chassis. The ends of the shock absorbers are located in

from a Leyland dealer as separate items, however, if any of the other leaves have broken a complete new spring must be obtained.

4 To remove either a front or rear spring, first jack-up the appropriate end of the vehicle and place heavy duty axle stands beneath the chassis.

5 Remove both wheels and support the weight of the axle on a jack.

6 Undo the nuts from the four axle 'U' bolts and remove the bottom spring retaining plate.

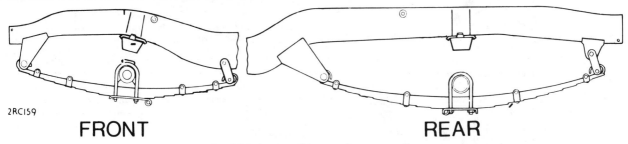

2RC159

## FRONT          REAR

Fig. 11.1. Layout of front and rear suspension

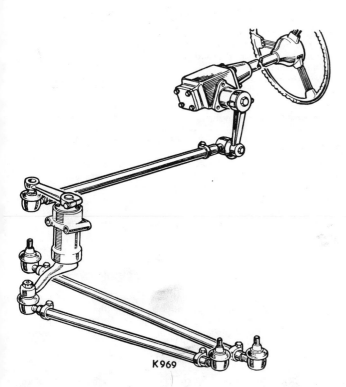

K969

Fig. 11.2. Layout of steering gear

rubber bushes.

The steering gear is the recirculating ball type and the steering shaft lower end rotates in two ball races within the gear housing and a bush (or bearing) at the steering column end. Steering movement is transmitted from the gear housing drop arm to the trackrod via a spring-loaded relay unit and drag link.

All the steering balljoints are packed with grease during manufacture and sealed by means of a rubber boot secured with spring clips.

## 2 Front and rear springs - removal and refitting

1 The procedure for removing either the front or rear springs is basically the same and any differences will be detailed where necessary. It should be noted that the front and rear springs on the driver's side are not interchangeable with those on the passenger side, the driver's side springs having a greater free camber.

2 The process of ordering a new spring will be easier if the part number on the underside of the spring can be quoted (see Fig. 11.3).

3 If only the main or second leaf has broken, these can be obtained

**Note:** On some models the shockabsorber is attached to the bottom plate but there is no need to disconnect it, simply extend the shock absorber until the plate is free, (see Fig. 11.4).

7 Make sure the axle is firmly supported and then remove the self-locking nuts from the shackle pins at each end of the spring.

8 Remove both shackle pins noting that the rear pin is threaded into the inner shackle plate (photo).

9 Withdraw the road spring from beneath the vehicle.

10 To dismantle the springs, remove the bolts from the spring retaining clip and remove the clips. Remove the centre securing bolt and separate the spring leaves.

11 Examine the spring leaves for cracks and the bushes for wear and renew where necessary. The bushes can be driven out of the spring eyes using a suitably sized drift or piece of tubing. Remove the shackle plates from the rear spring hanger and check the top shackle bush for wear. Renew the bush if worn.

12 If while driving the bush out it breaks up leaving the outer casing jammed in the chassis bracket, it can be removed by carefully sawing through it with a hacksaw (Fig. 11.5). Take great care not to cut into the chassis bracket. If any of the shackle bolts are worn they should be renewed.

13 Smear the spring leaves and bushes with graphite grease before reassembly. Refit the shackle plates and spring to the vehicle using the reverse procedure to removal, but do not tighten any of the shackle pin nuts at this stage.

14 After the springs are correctly installed, refit the wheels and lower the vehicle to the ground. Rock the vehicle from side-to-side to settle the springs and then fully tighten all the shackle pin lock nuts.

2.8 Rear spring shackle assembly

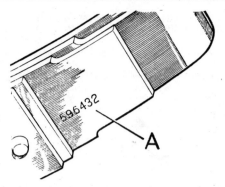

**Fig. 11.3. Part No. on underside of roadspring "A"**

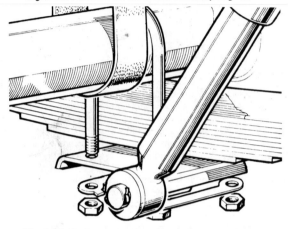

**Fig. 11.4. Removing the bottom spring clamping plate**

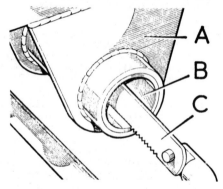

**Fig. 11.5. Cutting through the outer casing of a spring shackle bush**

A  Chassis bracket          C  Hacksaw
B  Bush

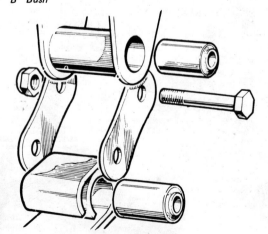

**Fig. 11.6. Spring shackle plates and bushes**

## 3  Shock absorbers - removal and refitting

1    The front and rear shock absorbers are identical and the method of attachment is also similar, although there are minor differences on certain models which will be described where necessary.
2    Jack-up the appropriate end of the vehicle and support it on axle stands. Remove the roadwheel (photo).
3    Remove the nut and bolt securing the top of the shock absorber to the chassis (Fig. 11.7).
4    Referring to Fig. 11.8 remove the split pin and washer securing the bottom end of the shock absorber to the spring plate. Note that on some models the end of the shock absorber terminates in a threaded stud which passes through a bracket welded to the axle. If working on the latter type, remove the securing nut and retrieve the steel and rubber washers.
5    Withdraw the ends of the shock absorber from the mounting brackets and retrieve the washers and rubber bushes.
6    Inspect the shock absorber for signs of hydraulic fluid leakage which, if evident, indicates that the unit must be renewed.
7    Clean the exterior and wipe dry with a non-fluffy rag.
8    Inspect the shaft for signs of corrosion or distortion and the body for damage.
9    Check the action by expanding and contracting to ascertain if equal resistance is felt on both strokes. If the resistance is very uneven the unit should be fully expanded and contracted at least eight times. If this does not cure the problem the unit must be renewed.
10  Check the rubber bushes and washers for signs of deterioration and obtain new if evident.
11  Refit the shock absorber using the reverse procedure to removal.

## 4  Steering wheel - removal and refitting

### Earlier type
1    Set the front wheels in the straight ahead position and mark the position of the steering wheel in relation to the column.
2    Disconnect the battery earth terminal, prise out the horn button from the centre of the wheel and disconnect the horn lead from the snap connector at the dash panel.
3    Remove the nut and bolt securing the wheel to the column and withdraw the wheel from the splined shaft (See Fig. 11.9).
4    Refit the steering wheel using the reversal of the removal procedure ensuring the alignment marks are matched up.

### Later type
5    Set the front wheels in the straight ahead position and mark the position of the steering wheel in relation to the column.
6    Prise out the cover from the centre of the steering. If the horn push is located in the centre cover, disconnect the battery and remove the horn leads (see Fig. 11.10).
7    Bend back the locking washer tab and remove the centre retaining nut. Withdraw the wheel from the splined shaft (Fig. 11.11).
8    Refit the steering wheel using the reversal of the removal procedure. Ensure the alignment marks are matched up and then tighten the retaining nut to the specified torque and bend over the locking tab.

3.2 Front shock absorber assembly

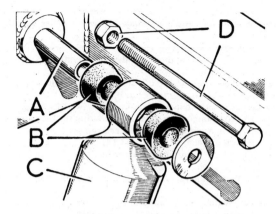

**Fig. 11.7. Shock absorber top attachment point**

A  Chassis          C  Shock absorber
B  Rubber bushes      D  Securing bolt

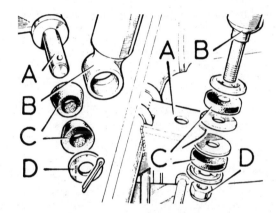

**Fig. 11.8. Shock absorber lower attachment points (showing alternative method)**

A  Chassis           C  Rubber bushes
B  Shock absorber     D  Securing nut (or washer)

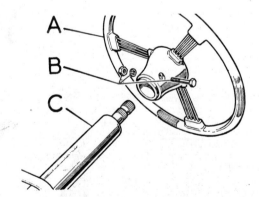

**Fig. 11.9. Removing the steering wheel (earlier models)**

A  Wheel             C  Steering column
B  Securing bolt

---

## 5  Steering trackrod and drag link balljoints - removal and refitting

1  Excessive play in the steering usually indicates that one or more of the balljoints have worn. To check them, get an assistant to turn the steering wheel from side-to-side. From beneath the vehicle visually

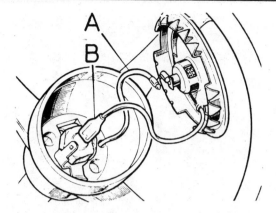

**Fig. 11.10. Disconnecting the horn leads (later models)**

A  Connection to horn button      B  Connection to steering column

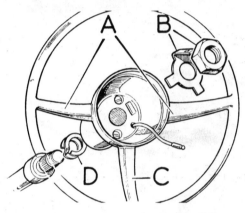

**Fig. 11.11. Removing the later type steering wheel**

A  Spokes facing sideways        C  Spoke facing rearward
B  Nut and washer for steering    D  Special spring washer
    wheel

check for movement between the balljoints and the steering arms and relay lever. If wear is evident the balljoints should be renewed as soon as possible.

2  Place chocks behind the rear wheels, jack up the front of the vehicle, support it on axle stands and remove the appropriate road wheel (photo).

3  Remove the split pin and undo the castle nut securing the balljoint to the steering arm. Using an universal balljoint separator or Leyland tool No. 600590, extract the tapered shaft of the balljoint from the steering arm or relay lever (see Fig. 11.12).

4  Carefully note how much of the threaded portion of the balljoint is protruding from the trackrod (or drag link) and mark it with some paint. Slacken the clamp and unscrew the balljoint. Note that the balljoints on one end of the trackrod and drag link have left-hand threads.

5  If the balljoint is worn it must be renewed. However, if it is in good condition, it can be lubricated by removing the rubber boot, pressing the ball down into the housing against the spring and forcing grease into the housing. Fill a new boot with grease and refit it using new spring retaining rings (see Fig. 11.13).

6  Screw the balljoint into the end of the trackrod (or drag link) up to the paint mark made previously on the threads. If fitting a new balljoint use the mark on the old one as a guide. Check that the distance between the balljoint centres is 30.812 to 30.937 in (782.62 to 785.79 mm) on the drag link and 45.56 to 45.68 in (1157 to 1160 mm) on the trackrod. Screw the balljoint in or out as appropriate until this figure is achieved.

7  Before tightening the clamp, refit the balljoint to the steering arm, tighten the nut to the specified torque and secure with a new split pin. Then tighten the clamps.

8  Refit the wheels and lower the vehicle to the ground. As a final check take the vehicle to a Leyland dealer who will have the necessary optical alignment equipment to check that the front wheel toe-in is set correctly.

5.2 Front steering arm ball joints

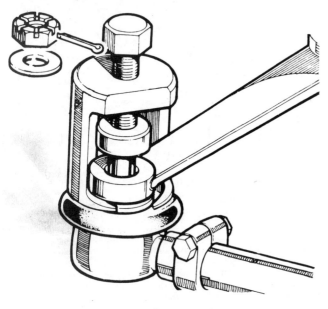

**Fig. 11.12. Removing a balljoint**

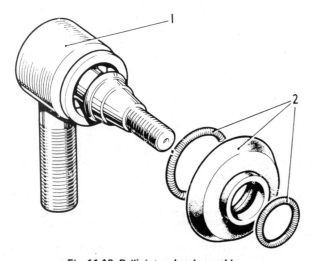

**Fig. 11.13. Balljoint and seal assembly**

1  *Balljoint*                              2  *Seal and retaining springs*

### 6  Steering column lock and ignition/starter switch (series III models) - removal and refitting

1  Disconnect the battery and remove the choke control cable from the carburettor (refer to Chapter 3 if necessary).
2  Undo the securing screws and lift off the steering column top shroud followed by the bottom shroud. If necessary remove the steering wheel as described in Section 4.
3  Carefully centre punch each shear bolt securing the lock assembly to the column. Drill a suitable sized hole and remove both shear bolts using an 'easy-out' extractor, (see Fig. 11.14).
4  Make a note of the positions of the wiring connection on the ignition switch and then remove them.
5  Withdraw the steering lock/ignition switch assembly complete with the choke control.
6  The ignition switch can be removed by undoing the two small retaining screws and withdrawing it from the housing. It is not a repairable item and if faulty must be renewed.
7  Refit the lock and switch assembly using the reversal of the removal procedure. New shear bolts must obviously be used and these have to be tightened until the heads shear off.
8  After refitting, check that the steering column is unlocked when the ignition key is set to the 'services' position and locked when the key is withdrawn.

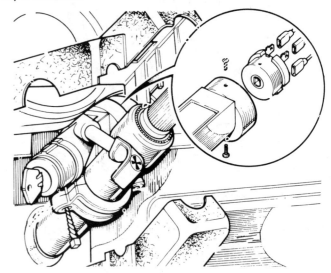

**Fig. 11.14. Steering lock and ignition/starter switch (Series III models only)**

### 7  Steering gear assembly - removal and refitting

1  Remove the complete bonnet assembly and disconnect the battery earth terminal.
2  Refer to Chapter 3 and remove the air cleaner assembly.
3  Remove the steering wheel as described in Section 4 of this Chapter and the flasher/combination switch as described in Chapter 10.
4  On Series III models, remove the ignition switch/steering column lock as described in the previous Section.
**Note:** On Series III models without a steering column lock, remove the ignition switch assembly by unscrewing the lock ring.
5  Referring to Fig. 11.16, remove the complete lower column support bracket assembly from the engine compartment bulkhead.
6  Remove the drop arm securing nut and washer and using Leyland special tool No. 600000, pull the arm from the steering box and move the arm and longitudinal steering tube out of the way (Fig. 11.17).
7  If working on a vehicle with left-hand steering, disconnect the throttle linkage from the steering box support bracket.
8  Slacken the nuts of the front roadwheel on the steering box side of the vehicle.
9  Chock the rear wheels, jack-up the front of the vehicle and support it on axle stands. Remove the roadwheel.
10  Remove the nuts and bolts securing the steering gear cover box and lift away the box (see Fig. 11.18).

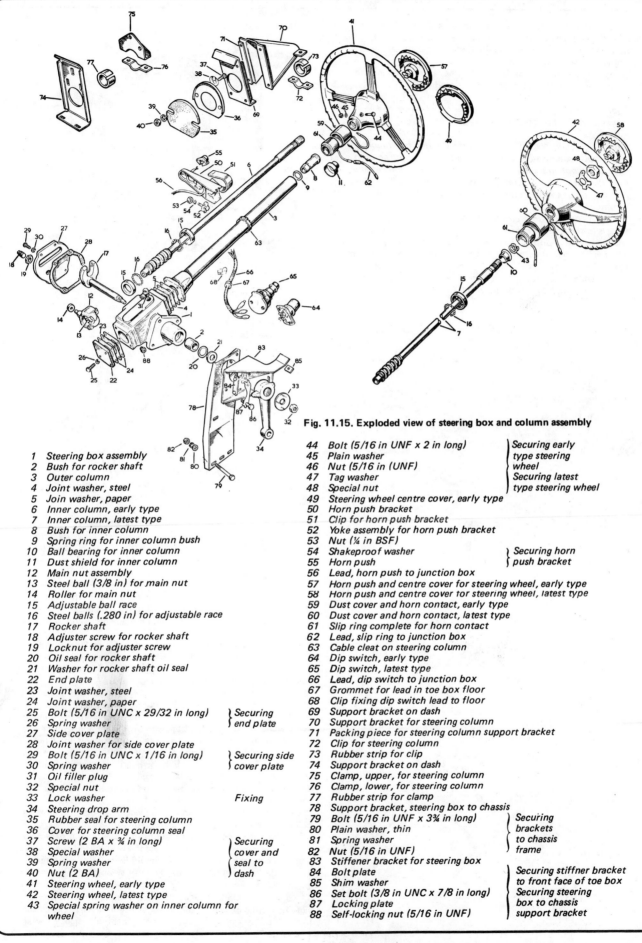

**Fig. 11.15. Exploded view of steering box and column assembly**

| | | |
|---|---|---|
| 1 | Steering box assembly | |
| 2 | Bush for rocker shaft | |
| 3 | Outer column | |
| 4 | Joint washer, steel | |
| 5 | Join washer, paper | |
| 6 | Inner column, early type | |
| 7 | Inner column, latest type | |
| 8 | Bush for inner column | |
| 9 | Spring ring for inner column bush | |
| 10 | Ball bearing for inner column | |
| 11 | Dust shield for inner column | |
| 12 | Main nut assembly | |
| 13 | Steel ball (3/8 in) for main nut | |
| 14 | Roller for main nut | |
| 15 | Adjustable ball race | |
| 16 | Steel balls (.280 in) for adjustable race | |
| 17 | Rocker shaft | |
| 18 | Adjuster screw for rocker shaft | |
| 19 | Locknut for adjuster screw | |
| 20 | Oil seal for rocker shaft | |
| 21 | Washer for rocker shaft oil seal | |
| 22 | End plate | |
| 23 | Joint washer, steel | |
| 24 | Joint washer, paper | |
| 25 | Bolt (5/16 in UNC x 29/32 in long) | } Securing |
| 26 | Spring washer | } end plate |
| 27 | Side cover plate | |
| 28 | Joint washer for side cover plate | |
| 29 | Bolt (5/16 in UNC x 1/16 in long) | } Securing side |
| 30 | Spring washer | } cover plate |
| 31 | Oil filler plug | |
| 32 | Special nut | |
| 33 | Lock washer | Fixing |
| 34 | Steering drop arm | |
| 35 | Rubber seal for steering column | |
| 36 | Cover for steering column seal | |
| 37 | Screw (2 BA x ¾ in long) | } Securing |
| 38 | Special washer | } cover and |
| 39 | Spring washer | } seal to |
| 40 | Nut (2 BA) | } dash |
| 41 | Steering wheel, early type | |
| 42 | Steering wheel, latest type | |
| 43 | Special spring washer on inner column for wheel | |

| | | |
|---|---|---|
| 44 | Bolt (5/16 in UNF x 2 in long) | } Securing early |
| 45 | Plain washer | } type steering |
| 46 | Nut (5/16 in (UNF) | } wheel |
| 47 | Tag washer | } Securing latest |
| 48 | Special nut | } type steering wheel |
| 49 | Steering wheel centre cover, early type | |
| 50 | Horn push bracket | |
| 51 | Clip for horn push bracket | |
| 52 | Yoke assembly for horn push bracket | |
| 53 | Nut (¼ in BSF) | |
| 54 | Shakeproof washer | } Securing horn |
| 55 | Horn push | } push bracket |
| 56 | Lead, horn push to junction box | |
| 57 | Horn push and centre cover for steering wheel, early type | |
| 58 | Horn push and centre cover for steering wheel, latest type | |
| 59 | Dust cover and horn contact, early type | |
| 60 | Dust cover and horn contact, latest type | |
| 61 | Slip ring complete for horn contact | |
| 62 | Lead, slip ring to junction box | |
| 63 | Cable cleat on steering column | |
| 64 | Dip switch, early type | |
| 65 | Dip switch, latest type | |
| 66 | Lead, dip switch to junction box | |
| 67 | Grommet for lead in toe box floor | |
| 68 | Clip fixing dip switch lead to floor | |
| 69 | Support bracket on dash | |
| 70 | Support bracket for steering column | |
| 71 | Packing piece for steering column support bracket | |
| 72 | Clip for steering column | |
| 73 | Rubber strip for clip | |
| 74 | Support bracket on dash | |
| 75 | Clamp, upper, for steering column | |
| 76 | Clamp, lower, for steering column | |
| 77 | Rubber strip for clamp | |
| 78 | Support bracket, steering box to chassis | |
| 79 | Bolt (5/16 in UNF x 3¾ in long) | } Securing |
| 80 | Plain washer, thin | } brackets |
| 81 | Spring washer | } to chassis |
| 82 | Nut (5/16 in UNF) | } frame |
| 83 | Stiffener bracket for steering box | |
| 84 | Bolt plate | } Securing stiffner bracket |
| 85 | Shim washer | } to front face of toe box |
| 86 | Set bolt (3/8 in UNC x 7/8 in long) | } Securing steering |
| 87 | Locking plate | } box to chassis |
| 88 | Self-locking nut (5/16 in UNF) | } support bracket |

11  Remove all the bolts securing the steering box support brackets to the bulkhead, wing valance and chassis member (see Fig. 11.19).

12  Withdraw the steering box and column assembly complete with support brackets from beneath the front wing.

13  Refitting the steering column is basically the reverse sequence to removal, but the following points should be noted:

a) *Prior to installing the steering box refit the stiffener and support brackets and tighten to the specified torque wrench setting.*

b) *Before tightening the bolts securing the steering box brackets to the bulkhead, wing and chassis, adjust the steering column position to obtain a snug fit in the upper support bracket and then tighten the column retaining clamp bolts. Finally, tighten the steering box bracket bolts to the specified torque wrench setting.*

c) *When refitting the drop arm to the steering box, set the front wheels in the straight ahead position and the steering wheel in the intermediate position and push the arm onto the splines. Tighten the securing nut to the specified torque wrench setting.* **Note:** *On later models the steering box shaft and drop arm have alignment marks, and the forward mark on the drop arm must line up with the mark cut in the end of the shaft.*

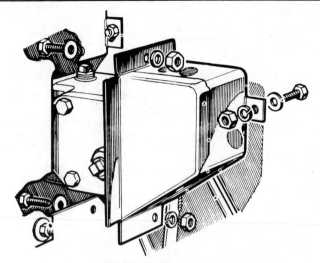

Fig. 11.18. Steering box cover

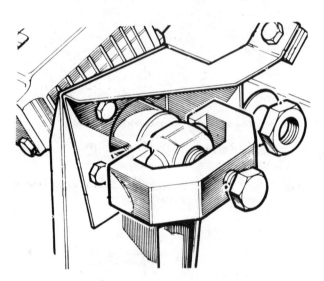

Fig. 11.16. Steering column clamp (earlier models may vary slightly)

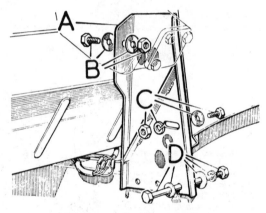

Fig. 11.19. Steering box bracket

A  Support bracket       C  Wing bolts
B  Bulkhead bolts       D  Chassis bolts

### 8  Steering column and gearbox - overhaul

1  With the steering box and column assembly on the bench, remove the side cover plate and drain the oil into a suitable container.

2  Lift out the roller from the main nut assembly and withdraw the rocker shaft (see Fig. 11.20).

3  Hold the outer steering column in a soft-jawed vice and remove the four bolts securing the end of the column to the steering box.

4  Using a soft-faced mallet, gently tap the inner column at the steering wheel end until the steering box is free of the column. Withdraw the box and inner column complete and retrieve the steel balls from the upper race if freed from the box (see Fig. 11.21).

5  Rotate the inner column until the main nut is midway along the worm shaft. Gently tap the box away from the inner column just enough to drive out the upper ball race, (presuming it has not already come out). Retrieve the steel balls.

6  Turn the worm shaft through the main nut assembly and remove the shaft, nut and any loose bearings.

7  Undo the four retaining bolts and remove the end cover, shims and lower bearing (see Fig. 11.22).

8  Tap the main nut assembly on a piece of wood until all the twelve ball bearings drop out of the recirculating tube.

9  Examine the rocker shaft and bush for wear and if necessary remove the washer and oil seal, press the bush out of the steering box and fit a new one. A new oil seal should be fitted as a matter of course.

10  Check the upper column ball race for wear (bush on earlier models) and renew if necessary (see Fig. 11.23).

11  Examine the inner track on the main nut and the worm shaft for signs of pitting or scaling and renew where necessary. Check the upper and lower ball bearings and races for similar signs of wear.

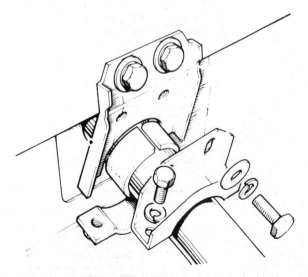

Fig. 11.17. Removing the steering box drop arm

12 If the worm shaft, main nut and bearings are all worn the most sensible solution is to obtain a replacement steering box assembly from a Leyland dealer.

13 Commence reassembly by retaining the ten steel balls in the upper race with grease and sliding the race over the steering wheel end of the inner column until it abuts the worm shaft.

14 Place a new gasket on the outer column flange and slide it over the inner column.

15 Locate the steel balls in the main nut with plenty of grease. Hold the nut in position inside the box and carefully wind the worm shaft through it. Ensure that none of the steel balls fall out of the main nut or upper bearing.

16 Secure the outer column to the box with the four washers and bolts.

17 Place the ten balls in the lower race using grease, and fit the race over the end of the inner column and into the box.

18 Fit a new gasket on each side of the shims and refit the shims and end cover. Tighten the four end cover securing bolts and check the inner column for freedom of rotation. It should rotate freely with no endfloat, and this condition can be achieved by removing or refitting the end cover shims as necessary (see Fig. 11.24).

19 Insert the rocker shaft into the box followed by the roller. Place a new gasket on the steering box aperture and refit the side cover ensuring the roller is correctly located in the groove on the underside of the cover. Tighten the retaining bolts.

20 Refit the steering box assembly to the vehicle as described in Section 7 and fill it with Castrol EP 90 gear oil.

21 Finally adjust the steering box as described in Section 11.

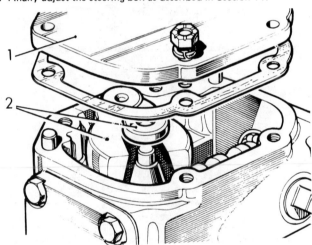

**Fig. 11.20. Removing the steering box cover plate**

1   Cover                     2   Roller and rocker shaft

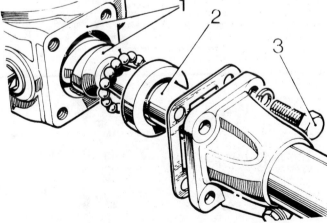

**Fig. 11.21. Withdrawing the outer column assembly**

1   Steering box and worm shaft        3   Securing bolt
2   Inner column

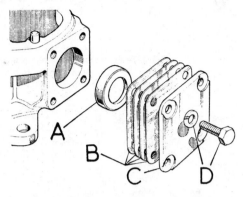

**Fig. 11.22. Removing the lower end plate**

A   Bearing                   C   Cover
B   Shims                     D   Securing bolt

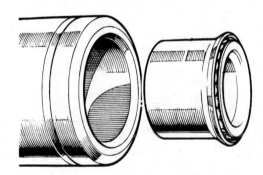

**Fig. 11.23. Steering column top bearing (bush on earlier models)**

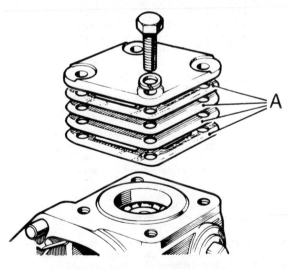

**Fig. 11.24. End cover and shims "A"**

**9   Steering relay unit - removal and refitting**

1   Remove the 'Land Rover' name plate and lift off the radiator grille.

2   Working through the grille panel aperture and from beneath the vehicle, remove the pinch-bolts and prise off the upper and lower relay lever (Fig. 11.25).

3   Remove the two bolts securing the top of the relay unit to the grille panel.

From beneath the vehicle, remove the four bolts securing the relay unit flange plate (Fig. 11.26).

5   Remove any equipment located directly above the relay unit, then, using a brass drift, drive the unit upwards to free it from the chassis. If the unit refuses to move, apply some penetrating oil between the base of the unit and the chassis.

6   Refit the relay unit using the reverse procedure to that of removal. Ensure that the upper and lower relay levers are refitted at an angle of 90° to each other as shown in Fig. 11.27. Note that the flat boss on the upper side of the unit must face away from the radiator.

### 10  Steering relay unit - overhaul

1   The relay unit contains a large spring under compression and before any attempt is made to dismantle the unit a Leyland spring compression tool (Part No. 600536) should be obtained. It may be possible to compress the spring using a made-up tool or with the help of an assistant but the task may prove to be rather difficult.

2   To dismantle the relay unit, first remove the oil filler and breather plugs from the top of the unit, (or bottom on later types) and drain out the oil.

3   Remove the four bolts from the bottom of the unit and lift off the retaining plate, oil seal and gasket (see Fig. 11.28).

CAUTION: As stated previously the relay unit contains a large spring under compression which will fly out when the shaft is driven out. To avoid injury or damage cover the bottom end of the unit with a heavy piece of cloth and tie it to the unit with string.

4   Mount the unit in a vice and with the cloth covering the bottom end, drive the shaft out from the top end of the unit.

5   Remove the piece of cloth and retrieve the spring, shaft, bushes and washers (see Fig. 11.29).

6   Remove the securing nuts and lift off the top retaining plate, oil seal and gasket.

7   The relay unit is now dismantled and the component can be examined for wear. Note that the free length of the spring should be 7.25 in (184 mm).

8   Examine the split bushes and shaft for signs of wear and renew if necessary.

9   Fit new oil seals into the top and bottom retaining plates, smearing a little jointing compound around the outside diameter of each seal.

10  To assemble, fit the two halves of a split bush on the top cone section of the shaft and insert the shaft and bush into the bottom end of the housing (Fig. 11.30).

11  Secure the housing and shaft in a vice with the bottom end upwards and a ¾ in (19 mm) block of wood under the end of the shaft.

12  Drop one of the washers down over the shaft and screw two of the retainer bolts into the housing diametrically opposite each other.

13  Slide the spring over the shaft and into the housing and place the second washer on top of the spring.

14  Using tool No. 600536 compress the spring until it is possible to turn the tool and lock the slots over the heads of the two bolts. Take care that the spring does not fly out (see Fig. 11.31).

15  Fit the other split bush onto the cone section of the protruding shaft and secure in place with a 2 in (50 mm) hose clip.

16  Turn the tool sufficiently to release it from the bolt heads and withdraw it from between the spring and split bush. Remove the two bolts.

17  Remove the housing from the vice and gently tap the shaft into the housing until the bush is half way in. Remove the hose clip and continue to tap the shaft in until the bushes are correctly located in the housing.

18  Fit the thrust washer, oil seal retainer and gasket to the bottom end of the housing and secure with the four bolts.

19  Fill the housing with EP 90 oil, injecting it through one of the bolt holes in the top of the housing or the plug on the side, if fitted.

20  Refit the top thrust washer, gasket and oil seal and retainer and tighten the four securing bolts.

21  Hold the housing in the vice and temporarily refit the upper relay lever. Using a spring balance attached to the end of the lever, check that the pull required to turn the lever is not less than 12 lb (5.4 kg) and not more than 16 lb (7.3 kg).

22  If the resistance to movement is less than specified a new spring should be fitted. If an excessive pull is required to move the lever the oil seal retainers should be removed and the bushes pushed inwards to enable oil to be injected directly onto the cone sections of the shaft.

23  Refit the relay to the vehicle using the procedure described in Section 9.

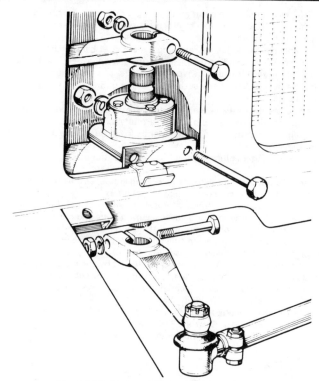

Fig. 11.25. Upper and lower steering relay levers

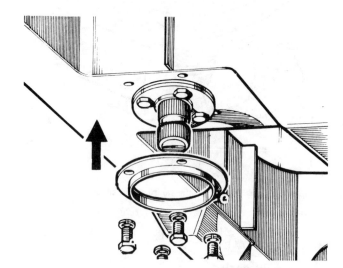

Fig. 11.26. Lower steering relay securing flange

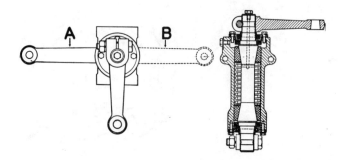

Fig. 11.27. Correct positioning of relay levers

A  Lower lever, LH steering          B  Lower lever RH steering

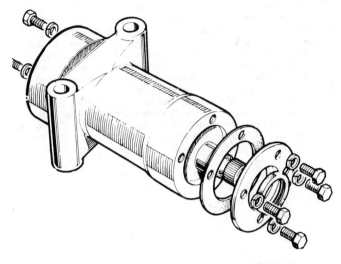

Fig. 11.28. Steering relay bottom retaining plate

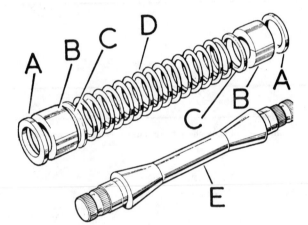

Fig. 11.29. Steering relay spring and shaft assembly

A   Thrust washer          D   Spring
B   Split bush             E   Relay shaft
C   Washer for spring

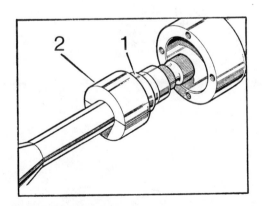

Fig. 11.30. Inserting the steering relay shaft

1   Shaft                          2   Split bush

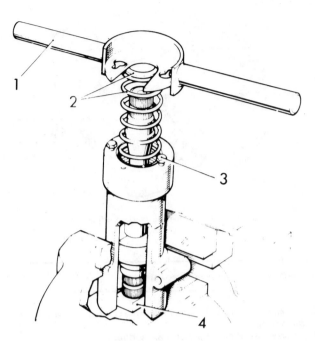

Fig. 11.31. Using the special tool to compress the spring into the housing

1   Special tool                   3   Retainer bolts in position
    (Leyland No. 600536)           4   Block of wood
2   Spring and washer

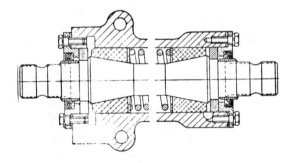

Fig. 11.32. Cross-sectional view of assembled steering relay unit

### 11 Steering gearbox - adjustment

1   Jack-up the vehicle until the front wheels are just clear of the ground and set the steering to the straight ahead position.

2   Slacken the adjuster screw and locknut located on the side of the steering gearbox and screw in the adjuster using the hand only until it stops.

3   Tighten the locknut ensuring the adjuster does not move, and then lower the vehicle to the ground.

4   If the steering is still excessively slack after adjustment, check the balljoints for wear as described in Section 5. If these appear in good condition, then it is possible that the steering gearbox requires overhauling (Section 8).

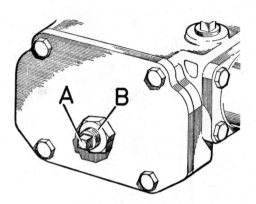

**Fig. 11.33. Steering gearbox adjuster**

A  Adjuster                                    B  Locknut

## 12 Steering geometry - checking and adjustment

1    Unless the front suspension has been damaged, the castor angle, camber angle and swivel pin inclination angles will not alter, provided of course, that the suspension balljoints are not worn excessively.
2    The toe-in of the front wheels is a setting which may be reset if new components are fitted - for example, after fitting new tie-rod balljoints it will be necessary to reset the toe-in.
3    Indications of incorrect wheel alignment (toe-in) are uneven tyre wear on the front wheels and erratic steering particularly when turning. To check toe-in accurately needs optical alignment equipment, so this is one job that must be left to the local Leyland garage. Ensure that they examine the linkage to ascertain the cause of any deviation from the original setting.

## 13 Fault diagnosis - suspension and steering

*Before diagnosing faults from the following chart check the irregularities are not caused by:*
*1   Binding brakes*
*2   Incorrect 'mix' of radial and crossply tyres*
*3   Incorrect tyre pressure*
*4   Misalignment of the chassis*

| Symptom | Reason/s | Remedy |
|---|---|---|
| Steering wheel can be moved considerably before any sign of movement is apparent at the roadwheels | Wear in steering linkage, gear and column bearings | Check all joints and gears. Renew as necessary. |
| Vehicle difficult to steer in a straight line - 'wanders' | As above<br>Wheel alignment incorrect (shown by uneven front tyre wear)<br>Front wheel bearings loose<br>Worn suspension unit swivel pins | As above.<br>Check wheel alignment.<br><br>Adjust or renew.<br>Renew as necessary. |
| Steering stiff and heavy | Incorrect wheel alignment (uneven or excessive tyre wear)<br>Wear or seizure in steering linkage joints<br>Wear or seizure in spring shackles<br>Excessive wear in steering gear unit | Check and adjust.<br><br>Grease or renew.<br>Grease or renew.<br>Adjust or renew. |
| Wheel wobble and vibration | Roadwheels out of balance<br>Roadwheels buckled<br>Wheel alignment incorrect<br>Wear in steering and suspension linkages<br>Broken front spring | Balance wheels.<br>Check for damage.<br>Check.<br>Check or renew.<br>Renew. |
| Excessive pitching and rolling on corners and during braking | Defective damper and/or broken spring | Renew. |

# Chapter 12 Chassis and bodywork

## Contents

## 1 General description

The backbone of the Land Rover is the box section chassis shown in Fig. 12.1. It is comprised of two longitudinal box section members joined by crossmembers to form a ladder type fabrication that is extremely strong and rigid.

The rear body and front sections are bolted directly onto the chassis and the extremities of the body are supported by outriggers welded to the two longitudinal sections.

The SWB model has an overall chassis length of 134.6 in (3420 mm) and a wheelbase length of 88 in (2235 mm). The LWB model has an overall chassis length of 166.9 in (4240 mm) and a wheelbase length of 109 in (2770 mm). It is for this reason that the two models are frequently referred to as '88' and the '109' model respectively.

With the exception of the radiator panel, dash panel, door frames and tail board frame which are steel, the body panels on the Land Rover are made of a magnesium-aluminium alloy known as 'Birmabright'.

This alloy is stronger than pure aluminium and will not rust or corrode under normal conditions. All the steel cappings and corner brackets are manufactured from galvanised steel.

## 2 Maintenance - body and chassis

1 Because most of the bodywork on the Land Rover is constructed from an aluminium alloy, rust is not a great problem. However, if the vehicle is being used in wet, muddy conditions the worst of the dirt should be washed off at least once a month using a hosepipe and brush. The hidden portions of the body, such as the wheel arches, the chassis and the engine compartment are equally important, though obviously not requiring such frequent attention as the immediately visible paintwork.

2 Once a year or every 12,000 miles it is sound advice to visit your local main agent and have the underside of the body steam cleaned. All traces of dirt and oil will be removed and the underside can then be inspected carefully for rust, damaged hydraulic pipes, frayed electrical wiring and other faults.

3 At the same time the engine compartment should be cleaned in the same manner. If steam cleaning facilities are not available then brush 'Gunk' or a similar cleanser over the whole engine and engine compartment with a stiff paintbrush, working it well in where there is an accumulation of oil and dirt. Do not paint the ignition system but protect it with oily rags when the 'Gunk' is washed off. As the 'Gunk' is washed away it will take with it all traces of oil and dirt, leaving the engine looking clean and bright.

## 3 Maintenance - upholstery and carpets

1 Mats and carpets should be brushed or vacuum cleaned regularly to keep them free of grit. If they are badly stained remove them from the car for scrubbing or sponging and make quite sure they are dry before replacement. Seats and interior trim panels can be kept clean by a wipe over with a damp cloth. If they do become stained (which can be more apparent on light coloured upholstery) use a little liquid detergent and a soft nail brush to scour the grime out of the grain of the material. Do not forget to keep the head lining clean in the same way as the upholstery. When using liquid cleaners inside the vehicle do not over-wet the surfaces being cleaned. Excessive damp could get into the seams and padded interior causing stains, offensive odours or even rot. If the inside of the vehicle gets wet accidently it is worthwhile taking some trouble to dry it out properly, particularly where carpets are involved. **Do not** leave oil or electrical heaters inside the car for this purpose.

## 4 Minor body repairs

*Repair of minor scratches in the vehicle's bodywork*

If the scratch is very superficial, and does not penetrate to the metal of the bodywork, repair is very simple. Lightly rub the area of the scratch with a paintwork renovator or a very fine cutting paste to remove loose paint from the scratch and to clear the surrounding bodywork of wax polish. Rinse the area with clean water.

Apply touch-up paint to the scratch using a thin paint brush, continue to apply thin layers of paint until the surface of the paint in the scratch is level with the surrounding paintwork. Allow the new paint at least two weeks to harden; then blend it into the surrounding paintwork by rubbing the paintwork in the scratch area with a paintwork renovator or a very fine cutting paste. Finally apply wax polish.

Where the scratch has penetrated right through to the metal of the bodywork, a different repair technique is required. Remove any loose paint, etc from the bottom of the scratch with a penknife. Using a rubber or nylon applicator, fill the scratch with bodystopper paste. If required, this paste can be mixed with cellulose thinners to provide a very thin paste which is ideal for filling narrow scratches. Before the stopper-paste in the scratch hardens, wrap a piece of smooth cotton rag around the top of a finger. Dip the finger in cellulose thinners and then quickly sweep it across the surface of the stopper-paste in the scratch; this will ensure that the surface of the stopper-paste is slightly hollowed. The scratch can now be painted over as described earlier in this section.

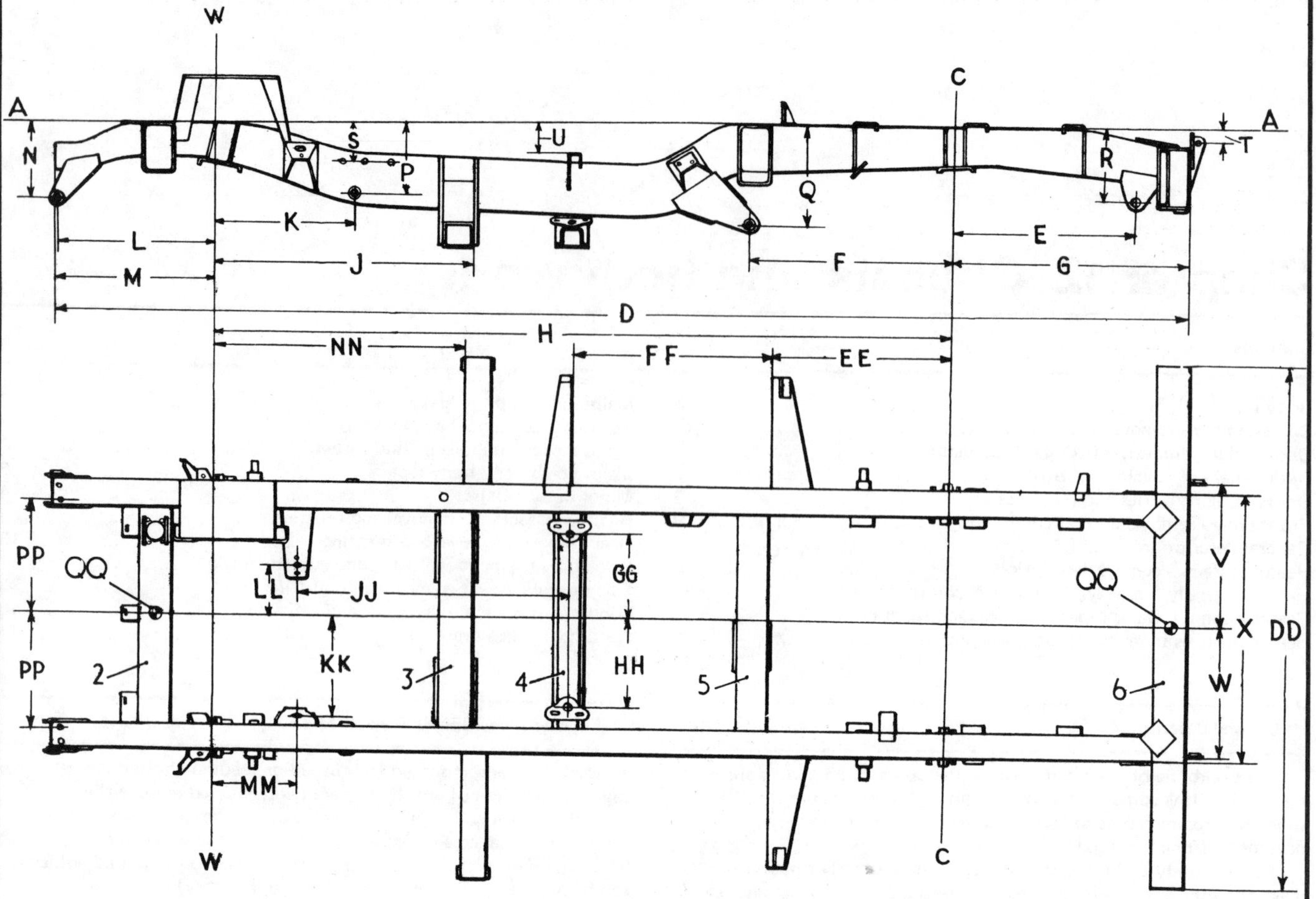

**Fig. 12.1. Chassis dimensions (SWB models)**

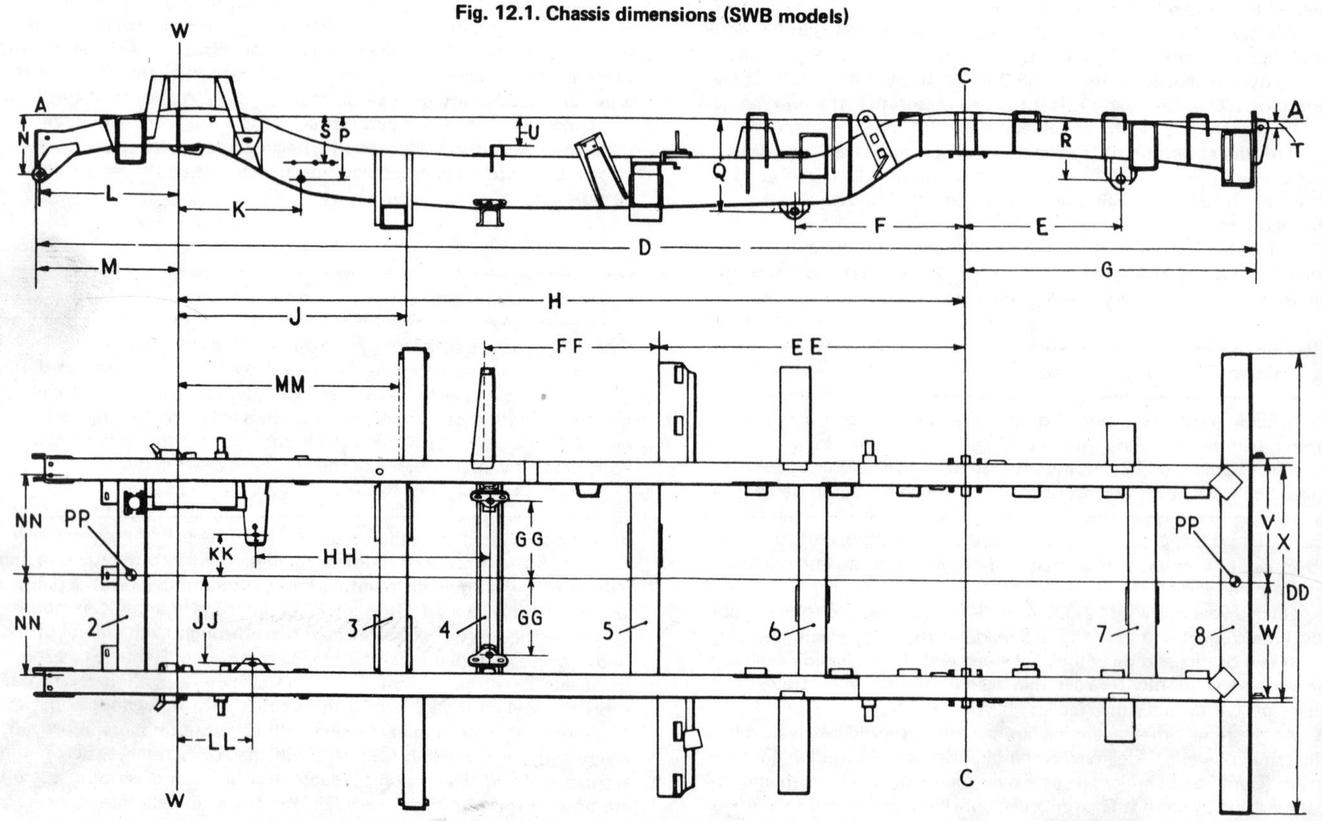

**Fig. 12.2. Chassis dimensions (LWB models)**

Fig. 12.1. Chassis dimensions (SWB models)

| AA | Datum line | N | 229 mm (9.0 in) | EE | 539.7 mm (21.25 in) |
|---|---|---|---|---|---|
| WW | Centre line of front axle | P | 212.7 mm (8.37 in) | FF | 610 mm (24.0 in) |
| CC | Centre line of rear axle | Q | 290.5 mm (11.44 in) | GG | 257 ± 0.8 mm (10.12 ± 0.030 in) |
| D | 3420 mm (134.6 in) | R | 198.4 mm (7.81 in) | HH | 254 ± 0.8 mm (10.00 ± 0.030 in) |
| E | 539.7 mm (21.25 in) | S | 120.6 mm (4.75 in) | JJ | 835 ± 0.8 mm (32.87 ± 0.030 in) |
| F | 610 mm (24.0 in) | T | 29.3 mm (1.15 in) | KK | 289.7 mm (11.40 in) |
| G | 713.2 mm (28.08 in) | U | 82.5 mm (3.25 in) | LL | 166.7 mm (6.56 in) |
| H | 2235 mm (88.0 in) | V | 432 mm (17.0 in) | MM | 250.8 ± 1.5 mm (9.875 ± 0.060 in) |
| J | 793.7 mm (31.25 in) | W | 387.3 mm (15.25 in) | NN | 768.3 mm (30.25 in) |
| K | 422.3 mm (16.625 in) | X | 787 mm (31.0 in) | PP | 331.78 ± 0.5 mm (13.062 ± 0.020 in) |
| L | 457 mm (18.0 in) | DD | 1536 mm (60.5 in) | QQ | 9.52 mm (0.375 in) diameter holes |
| M | 472.2 mm (18.58 in) | | | | |

Fig. 12.2 Chassis dimensions (LWB models)

| AA | Datum line | N | 229 mm (9.0 in) | EE | 1070 mm (42.12 in) |
|---|---|---|---|---|---|
| WW | Centre line of front axle | P | 212.7 mm (8.37 in) | FF | 641 mm (25.2 in) |
| CC | Centre line of rear axle | Q | 296.8 mm (11.68 in) | GG | 257 ± 0.8 mm (10.125 ± 0.030 in) |
| D | 4240 mm (166.9 in) | R | 204.7 mm (8.06 in) | HH | 835 ± 0.8 mm (32.87 ± 0.030 in) |
| E | 539.7 mm (21.25 in) | S | 120.6 mm (4.75 in) | JJ | 289.71 mm (11.406 in) 2¼ litre |
| F | 610 mm (24.0 in) | T | 29.3 mm (1.15 in) | | 290.51 mm (11.437 in) 2.6 litre |
| G | 1000 mm (39.375 in) | U | 82.5 mm (3.25 in) | KK | 166.7 mm (6.56 in) |
| H | 2770 mm (109 in) | V | 432 mm (17.0 in) | LL | 250.7 mm (9.87 in) 2¼ litre |
| J | 793.7 mm (31.25 in) | W | 387.3 mm (15.25 in) | MM | 763 mm (30 in) |
| K | 422.3 mm (16.625 in) | X | 787 mm (31.0 in) | NN | 331.8 ± 0.5 mm (13.06 ± 0.062 in) |
| L | 457 mm (18.0 in) | DD | 1536 mm (60.5 in) | PP | 9.52 mm (0.375 in) diameter holes |
| M | 472.2 mm (18.58 in) | | | | |

## 5 Body repairs

### Repair of dents in the vehicle's bodywork

The alloy body panels on the Land Rover are easier to work on than steel and minor dents or creases can be beaten out fairly easily. However, if the damaged area is quite large, prolonged hammering will cause the metal to harden and to avoid the possibility of cracking, it must be softened or 'annealed'. This can be done quite easily with a gas blowlamp but great care is required to avoid actually melting the metal. The blowlamp must always be kept moving in a circular pattern whilst being held a respectable distance from the metal.

One method of checking when the alloy is hot enough is to rub down the surface to be annealed and then apply a thin film of oil over it. The blowlamp should be played over the rear side of the oiled surface until the oil evaporates and the surface is dry. Turn off the blowlamp and allow the metal to cool naturally, the treated areas will now be soft and it will be possible to work it with a hammer or mallet. After panel beating, the damaged section should be rubbed down and painted as described later in this Section.

When deep denting of the vehicle's bodywork has taken place, the first task is to pull the dent out until the affected bodywork almost attains its original shape. There is little point in trying to restore the original shape completely, as the metal in the damaged area will have stretched on impact and cannot be reshaped to its original contour. It is better to bring the level of the dent up to a point which is about 1/8 in (3 mm) below the level of the surrounding bodywork. In cases where the dent is very shallow anyway, it is not worth trying to pull it out at all.

If the underside of the dent is accessible, it can be hammered out gently from behind using the method described earlier.

Should the dent be in a section of the bodywork which has a double skin or some other factor making it inaccessible from behind, a different technique is called for. Drill several small holes through the metal inside the dent area, particularly in the deeper sections. Then screw long self-tapping screws into the holes just sufficiently for them to gain a good purchase in the metal. Now the dent can be pulled out by pulling on the protruding heads of the screws with a pair of pliers.

The next stage of the repair is the removal of the paint from the damaged area and from an inch or so of the surrounding 'sound' bodywork.

**Note:** *On no account should coarse abrasives be used on aluminium panels in order to remove paint. The use of a wire brush or abrasive on a power drill for example, will cause deep scoring of the metal and in extreme cases, penetrate the thickness of the relatively soft aluminium alloy.*

Removal of paint is best achieved by applying paint remover to the area, allowing it to act on the paintwork for the specified time and then removing the softened paint with a wood or nylon scraper. This method may have to be repeated in order to remove all traces of paint. A good method of removing small stubborn traces of paint is to rub the area with a nylon scouring pad soaked in thinners or paint remover.

**Note:** *If it is necessary to use this method, always wear rubber gloves to protect the hands from burns from the paint remover. It is also advisable to wear protection over the eyes as any paint remover that gets into the eye will cause severe inflammation, or worse.*

Finally, remove all traces of paint and remover by washing the area down with plenty of clean fresh water.

To complete the preparations for filling, score the surface of the bare metal with a screwdriver or the tang of a file, or alternatively, drill small holes in the affected area. This will provide a really good 'key' for the filler paste.

To complete the repair, see the Section on filling and respraying.

## Repair of holes or gashes in the vehicle's bodywork

Remove all paint from the affected area and from an inch or so of the surrounding 'sound' bodywork, using the method described in the previous Section. With the paint removed you will be able to gauge the severity of the damage and therefore decide whether to replace the whole panel (if this is possible) or to repair the affected area. It is often quicker and more satisfactory to fit a new panel than to attempt to repair large areas of damage.

Remove all fittings from the affected area except those which will act as a guide to the original shape of the damaged bodywork (eg. headlamp shells etc). Then, using tin snips or a hacksaw blade, remove all loose metal and other metal badly affected by damage. Hammer the edges of the hole inwards in order to create a slight depression for the filler paste.

Before filling can take place it will be necessary to block the hole in some way. This can be achieved by the use of aluminium or plastic mesh, or aluminium tape.

Aluminium or plastic mesh is probably the best material to use for a large hole. Cut a piece to the approximate size and shape of the hole to be filled, then position it in the hole so that its edges are below the level of the surrounding bodywork. It can be retained in position by several blobs of filler paste around its periphery.

Aluminium tape should be used for small or very narrow holes. Pull a piece off the roll and trim it to the approximate size and shape required, then pull off the backing paper (if used) and stick the tape over the hole; it can be overlapped if the thickness of one piece is insufficient. Burnish down the edges of the tape with the handle of a screwdriver or similar, to ensure that the tape is securely attached to the metal underneath.

## Bodywork repairs — filling and respraying

Before using this Section, see the Section on dent, scratch, hole and gash repairs.

Many types of bodyfiller are available, but generally speaking those proprietary kits which contain a tin of filler paste and a tube of resin hardener are best for this type of repair. A wide, flexible plastic or nylon applicator will be found invaluable for imparting a smooth and well contoured finish to the surface of the filler.

Mix up a little filler on a clean piece of card or board. Use the hardener sparingly (follow the maker's instructions on the packet) otherwise the filler will set very rapidly.

Using the applicator, apply the filler paste to the prepared area; draw the applicator across the surface of the filler to achieve the correct contour and to level the filler surfaces. As soon as a contour that approximates the correct one is achieved, stop working the paste, if you carry on too long the paste will become sticky and begin to 'pick-up' on the applicator. Continue to add thin layers of filler paste at twenty-minute intervals until the level of the filler is just 'proud' of the surrounding bodywork.

Once the filler has hardened, excess can be removed using a metal plane or file. From then on, progressively finer grades of abrasive paper should be used, starting with a 40 grade production paper and finishing with 400 grade 'wet or dry' paper. Always wrap the abrasive paper around a flat rubber, cork, or wooden block, otherwise the surface of the filler will not be completely flat. During the smoothing of the filler surface, the 'wet-or-dry' paper should be periodically rinsed in water. This will ensure that a very smooth finish is imparted to the filler at the final stage.

At this stage, the 'dent' should be surrounded by a ring of bare metal, which in turn should be encircled by the finely 'feathered' edge of the good paintwork. Rinse the repair area with clean water, until all the dust produced by the rubbing-down operation is gone.

Spray the whole repair area with a light coat of grey primer, this will show up any imperfections in the surface of the filler. If at all possible, it is recommended that an etch-primer is used on untreated alloy surfaces, otherwise the primer may not be keyed sufficiently and may subsequently flake off. Repair imperfections with fresh filler paste or bodystopper and once more, smooth the surface with abrasive paper. If bodystopper is used, it can be mixed with cellulose thinners to form a really thin paste which is ideal for filling small holes. Repeat the spray and repair procedure until you are satisfied that the surface of the filler, and the feathered edge of the paintwork are perfect. Clean the repair area with clean water and allow it to dry fully.

The repair area is now ready for spraying. Paint spraying must be carried out in a warm, dry, windless and dust free atmosphere. This condition can be created artificially if you have access to a large indoor working area, but if you are forced to work in the open, you will have to pick your day very carefully. If you are working indoors, dousing the floor in the work area with water will 'lay' the dust which would otherwise be in the atmosphere. If the repair is confined to one body panel, mask off the surrounding panels; this will help to minimise the effects of a slight mis-match in paint colours. Bodywork fittings will also need to be masked off. Use genuine masking tape and several thicknesses of newspaper for the masking operation.

Before commencing to spray, agitate the aerosol can thoroughly, then spray a test area (an old tin, or similar) until the technique is mastered. Cover the repair area with a thick coat of primer; the thickness should be built up using several thin layers of paint rather one thick one. Using 400 grade 'wet or dry' paper, rub down the surface of the primer until it is really smooth. Whilst doing this the work area should be thoroughly doused with water, and the 'wet-or-dry' paper periodically rinsed in water. Allow to dry before spraying on more paint.

Spray on the top coat, again building up the thickness by using several thin layers of paint. Start spraying in the centre of the repair area and then, using a circular motion, work outwards until the whole repair area and about 2 in of the surrounding original paintwork is covered. Remove all masking material 10 to 15 minutes after spraying on the final coat of paint.

Allow the new paint at least 2 weeks to harden fully; then, using a paintwork renovator or a very fine cutting paste, blend the edges of the new paint into the existing paintwork. Finally, apply wax polish.

## 6  Major chassis and body repairs

1  Major chassis and body repair work cannot successfully be undertaken by the average owner. Work of this nature should be entrusted to a competent body repair specialist who should have the necessary jigs, welding and hydraulic straightening equipment as well as skilled panel beaters to ensure that a proper job is done.
2  If the damage is severe it is vital that on completion of repair the chassis is in correct alignment. Less severe damage may also have twisted or distorted the chassis although this may not be visible immediately. It is therefore always best on completion of repair to check for twist and squareness to ensure that all is correct.
3  If distortion of the chassis is suspected the chassis dimensions can be checked by reference to Fig. 12.1 or 12.2 as appropriate.

## 7  Maintenance - hinges and locks

1  Oil the hinges of the bonnet, tailgate and doors with a drop or two of light oil periodically. A good time is after the car has been washed.
2  Oil the bonnet release catch pivot pin and the safety catch pivot pin periodically.
3  Do not over lubricate door latches and strikers. Normally a little oil on the catch alone is sufficient.

## 8  Doors - tracing rattles and their rectification

1  Check first that the door is not loose at the hinges and that the latch is holding the door firmly in position. Check also that the door lines up with the aperture in the body.
2  If the hinges are loose or the door is out of alignment it will be necessary to rest the hinge positions as described in Section 12.
3  If the latch is holding the door properly it should hold the door tightly when fully latched and the door should line up with the body. If it is out of alignment it needs adjustment as described in Section 14. If loose, some part of the lock mechanism must be worn out and requiring renewal.

## 9  Front wing - removal and refitting

1  Remove the bonnet as described in Chapter 1.

2  Disconnect the battery earth terminal and then disconnect the sidelight and headlamp harness at the snap connectors in the engine compartment.

3  Remove the securing bolts and lift out the mudshield from under the wing. If working on the driver's side wing, remove the steering box mudshield (see Fig. 12.3).

4  Using a socket wrench, remove the bolts securing the wing to the scuttle pillar.

5  Remove the bolts securing the wing and stay to the sill panel.

6  Remove the bolts securing the rear end of the wing to the upper mounting bracket.

7  Remove the bolt securing the wing to the steering column support plate (refer to Chapter 11, if necessary).

8  Finally, remove the bolts securing the wing to the grille panel.

9  With an assistant, lift the complete wing assembly away from the vehicle.

10  Refit the wing using the reversal of the removal procedure.

**Fig. 12.3. Front wings, bonnet and seat base assemblies**

1   Seat base and floor assembly
2   Tool locker lid
3   Fuel tank cover panel
4   Lid hinge
5   Locker lid hasp
6   Locker lid turnbuckle
7   Centre cover panel
8   Extension panel, at seat base ends
9   Handbrake rubber cover
10  Retainer for rubber cover
11  Handbrake slot cover plate
12  Sill channel LH front
13  Sill channel securing bracket
14  Sill channel mounting bracket, to rear body
15  Front sill panel
16  Rear sill panel
17  Fixing plate for sill panels
18  Front floor complete
19  Inspection cover, for front floor
20  Stud plate for inspection cover wing nut
21  Wing nut, securing inspection cover
22  Transfer gear lever seal
23  Transfer lever seal retainer
24  Gear lever rubber seal
25  Operating rod cover plate
26  Gearbox cover complete
27  Seat squab
28  Squab spring case

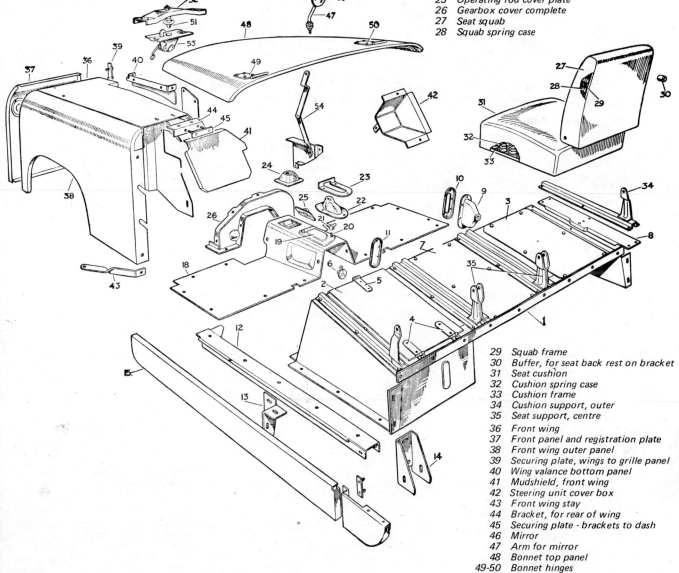

29  Squab frame
30  Buffer, for seat back rest on bracket
31  Seat cushion
32  Cushion spring case
33  Cushion frame
34  Cushion support, outer
35  Seat support, centre

36  Front wing
37  Front panel and registration plate
38  Front wing outer panel
39  Securing plate, wings to grille panel
40  Wing valance bottom panel
41  Mudshield, front wing
42  Steering unit cover box
43  Front wing stay
44  Bracket, for rear of wing
45  Securing plate - brackets to dash
46  Mirror
47  Arm for mirror
48  Bonnet top panel
49-50  Bonnet hinges
51  Bonnet catch striker pin
52  Bonnet striker bracket
53  Bonnet control
54  Bonnet prop rod

## 10 Windscreen assembly - removal and refitting

1   Remove the cab or hardtop as described in Section 17. If a hood is
fitted, release the front support stays and disconnect the drain
channels from the top of the windscreen.
2   On earlier models, disconnect the wiper lead plug from the socket
on the dash panel.
3   Slacken the nuts at each bottom corner of the windscreen.
4   Remove the windscreen pivot bolts and with the help of an assistant
lift away the complete windscreen assembly.
5   Refit the windscreen using the reverse procedure to that of
removal.

**Fig. 12.4. Dash panel and windscreen assemblies**

1   Dash complete
2   Panel for controls
3   Cover panel for steering cut-out
4   Cover plate for accelerator pedal hole
5   Cover panel for governor cut-out in
dash - Petrol models
6   Cover plate for pedal holes
7   Cover plate for dipswitch hole
8   Rubber plug, redundant accelerator holes
9   Rubber grommet for demister holes
10  Rubber plug, redundant accelerator
stop holes
11  Mounting plate for pump
12  Tie bolt

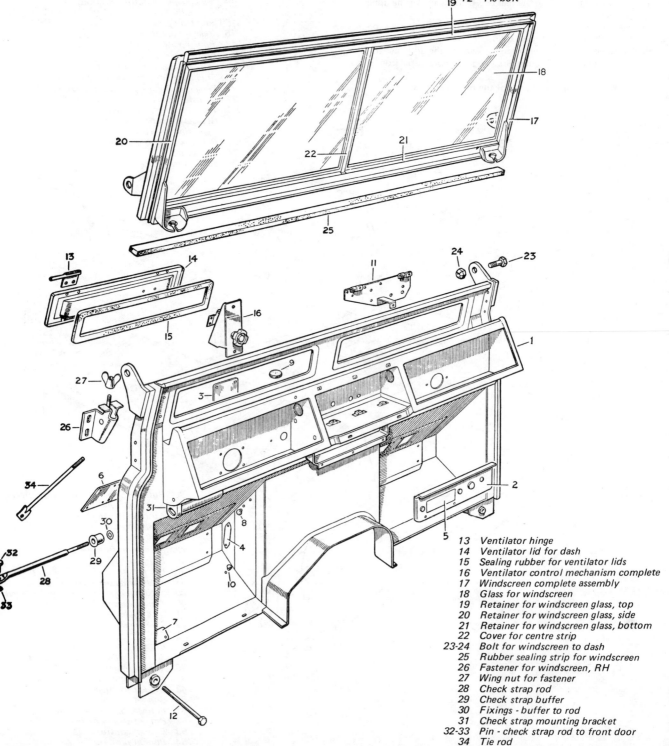

13  Ventilator hinge
14  Ventilator lid for dash
15  Sealing rubber for ventilator lids
16  Ventilator control mechanism complete
17  Windscreen complete assembly
18  Glass for windscreen
19  Retainer for windscreen glass, top
20  Retainer for windscreen glass, side
21  Retainer for windscreen glass, bottom
22  Cover for centre strip
23-24   Bolt for windscreen to dash
25  Rubber sealing strip for windscreen
26  Fastener for windscreen, RH
27  Wing nut for fastener
28  Check strap rod
29  Check strap buffer
30  Fixings - buffer to rod
31  Check strap mounting bracket
32-33   Pin - check strap rod to front door
34  Tie rod

## 11 Windscreen glass - renewal

1 Remove the windscreen wiper blade(s) as described in Chapter 10.
2 On earlier models, disconnect the wiper motor earth wire and remove the wiper motor from the screen. Refer to Chapter 10 if necessary.
3 Remove the screws from around the perimeter of the windscreen and prise off the glass retainers. Remove the glass.
**CAUTION: If the glass has been shattered, take great care when removing any remaining chips of glass from the windscreen frame.**
4 Before refitting a new glass apply a ½ in (12 mm) wide sealing strip around the outside of both sides of the glass. Refit the glass retainers and refit the glass using the reversal of the removal procedure.

## 12 Side doors - removal, refitting and adjustment

1 Disconnect the door check rod (photo).
2 Get an assistant to take the weight of the door and remove the four nuts and bolts securing the two hinges to the door. Lift the door away from the vehicle.
3 Refit the door using the reverse procedure.
4 Before attempting to adjust the door, refer to Fig. 12.5 and remove the hinge bolt cone, and spring and check them for wear. Obtain new ones if necessary.
5 Refit the hinge bolt, ensuring it is well lubricated and then adjust the hinge by tightening or slackening the bottom retaining nut. When the best setting is obtained, bend over the lockwasher.

12.1 Door check rod assembly

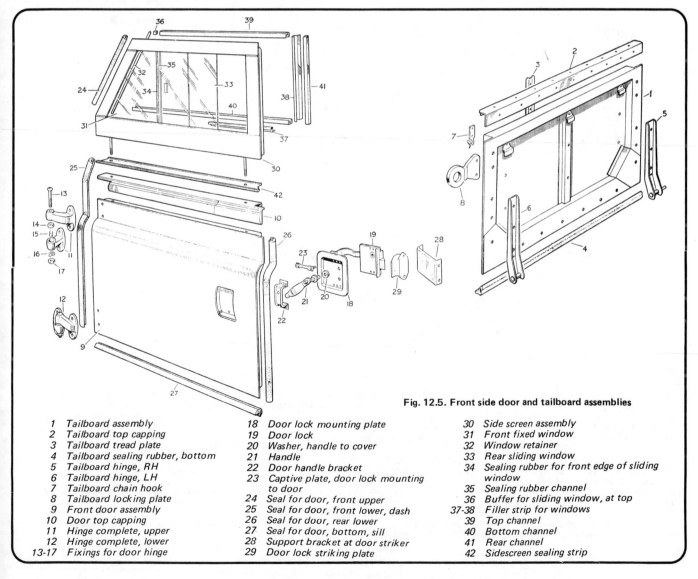

Fig. 12.5. Front side door and tailboard assemblies

| | | |
|---|---|---|
| 1 Tailboard assembly | 18 Door lock mounting plate | 30 Side screen assembly |
| 2 Tailboard top capping | 19 Door lock | 31 Front fixed window |
| 3 Tailboard tread plate | 20 Washer, handle to cover | 32 Window retainer |
| 4 Tailboard sealing rubber, bottom | 21 Handle | 33 Rear sliding window |
| 5 Tailboard hinge, RH | 22 Door handle bracket | 34 Sealing rubber for front edge of sliding |
| 6 Tailboard hinge, LH | 23 Captive plate, door lock mounting | window |
| 7 Tailboard chain hook | to door | 35 Sealing rubber channel |
| 8 Tailboard locking plate | 24 Seal for door, front upper | 36 Buffer for sliding window, at top |
| 9 Front door assembly | 25 Seal for door, front lower, dash | 37-38 Filler strip for windows |
| 10 Door top capping | 26 Seal for door, rear lower | 39 Top channel |
| 11 Hinge complete, upper | 27 Seal for door, bottom, sill | 40 Bottom channel |
| 12 Hinge complete, lower | 28 Support bracket at door striker | 41 Rear channel |
| 13-17 Fixings for door hinge | 29 Door lock striking plate | 42 Sidescreen sealing strip |

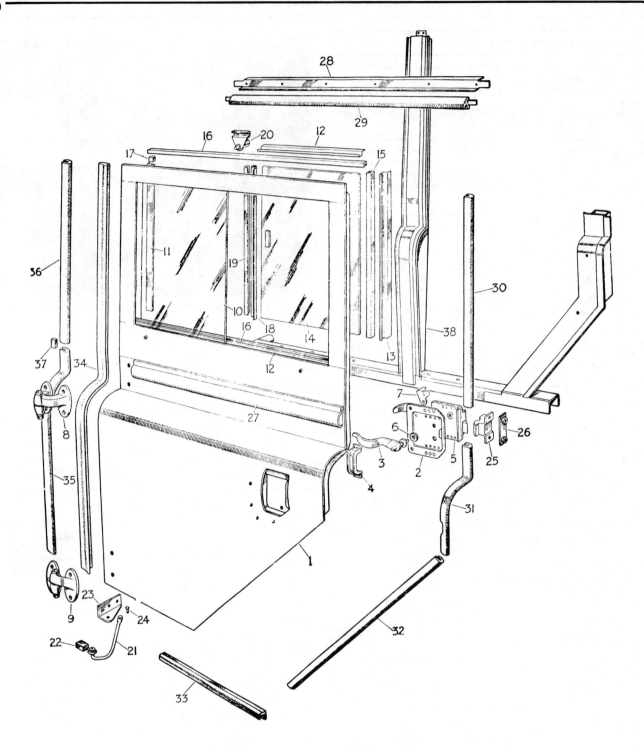

**Fig. 12.6. Rear door assembly (LWB Station Wagon)**

| | | |
|---|---|---|
| 1 | Rear side door assembly, LH | |
| 2 | Mounting plate for door lock | |
| 3 | Door handle complete, LH | |
| 4 | Bracket for door handle, outer mounting | |
| 5 | Door lock complete, LH | |
| 6 | Sealing washer, handle to cover | |
| 7 | Locking catch, LH | |
| 8 | Door hinge, upper LH | |
| 9 | Door hinge, lower LH | |
| 10 | Fixed window for sidescreen | |
| 11 | Retainer for sidescreen, fixed window | |
| 12 | Filler, top and bottom, for side screen | |
| 13 | Filler, rear, for sidescreen | |
| 14 | Sliding window with knob for sidescreen | |

15 Sliding light channel, rear
16 Sliding light channel, top and bottom
17 Buffer for sidescreen sliding window at top
18 Sealing rubber for sliding glass
19 Retainer for sliding glass sealing rubber
20 Sliding window catch
21 Rod for check strap, LH
22 Buffer for check strap, short
23 Door check bracket, LH, for rear side door
24 Clevis pin
25 Striking plate for rear side door locks
26 Nut plate
27 Waist moulding, rear side door, LH

28 Seal retainer for rear side door, LH top
29 Rubber seal for retainer
30 Door sealing rubber for upper vertical 'D' post
31 Door sealing rubber for lower vertical 'D' post, LH
32 Door sealing rubber for sloping 'D' post
33 Door sealing rubber at rear side sills, bottom
34 Door sealing rubber at 'C' post
35 Door sealing rubber at 'B' post, lower LH
36 Door sealing rubber at 'B' post, upper
37 Filler piece for 'B' post seal
38 Frame for front and rear side doors, LH

## 13 Side door windows - removal and refitting

### Sliding window

1 Push the sliding window to one side to gain access to the top glass channel retaining screws.
2 Remove the screws and lift out the top channel and sliding window. Remove the bottom channel if necessary.
3 Fit some new sealing strips to the window frame and refit the glass using the reverse procedure to that of removal.

### Fixed window

4 First remove the sliding window as described previously.
5 Remove the screw securing the front retainer, lift away the retainer and ease the glass out of the frame.
6 Fit some new sealing strips to the window frame and refit the glass using the reverse procedure to that of removal.

## 14 Door locks - removal, refitting and adjustment

1 Remove the door trim (later models only).
2 Remove the four securing nuts from the door lock (see photo) and remove the complete door lock and handle assembly.
3 The door locks cannot be repaired, and if damaged or broken a new lock assembly should be fitted.
4 Refit the door lock using the reversal of the removal procedure.
5 If the door rattles or will not shut correctly, slacken the two screws securing the striker plate to the door panel.
6 The striker should be positioned so that door draught excluders are just slightly compressed when the door is fully shut.

## 15 Rear tailgate - removal and refitting

1 Withdraw the tailgate securing keys and lower the tailgate.
2 Unhook both the tailgate support chains.
3 Remove the split pin and washer (or clip) from the right-hand hinge pin and with the help of an assistant slide the tailgate off the hinges.
4 Refit the rubber sealing strip if necessary and refit the tailgate using the reverse procedure to that of removal.

## 16 Dash panel - removal and refitting

1 Disconnect the battery earth terminal.
2 Remove the bonnet as described in Chapter 1.
3 Remove the front wings as described in Section 9 of this Chapter.
4 Remove the windscreen assembly (see Section 10).
5 Remove the front doors as described in Section 12.
6 Remove the front floor panels and transmission cover panel as described in Chapter 1.
7 Remove the split pin and nut securing the longitudinal arm to the steering box drop arm and, using Leyland tool No. 600590, remove

the balljoint from the drop arm (refer to Chapter 11 if necessary).
8 Disconnect the starter motor lead from the switch terminal.
9 Disconnect the high and low tension wires from the coil, and remove the oil pressure warning light lead from the switch on the side of the oil filter.
10 Disconnect the temperature gauge wire from the sender unit on top of the cylinder head.
11 Undo and remove the fluid outlet pipes from the clutch and brake master cylinders (refer to Chapter 9 if necessary).
12 Disconnect the clutch flexible hose from the bracket and rigid pipe on the dash panel.
13 Disconnect the throttle linkage and choke cable from the carburettor (see Chapter 3).
14 If a heater is fitted, drain the cooling system and remove the complete heater assembly (see Section 20).
15 Disconnect the leads from the rear of the dynamo (or alternator).
16 Disconnect the speedometer cable from the transfer box and release the cable from the clips securing it to the transfer box, chassis and flywheel housing (see Chapter 6).
17 Disconnect the horn and headlamp wires from the junction box on the dash panel.
18 Make a careful note of the position of each wire and then disconnect the main wiring harness snap connectors.
19 Remove the bolts securing the steering box support bracket to the dash panel.
20 Referring to Fig. 12.4, remove the two tie bolts, washers and nuts securing the dash panel to the chassis. Remove the nuts and bolts securing the sill panels to the dash panel.
21 Make a careful check that all electrical leads, brake pipes etc. are disconnected from the dash panel and then lift the complete panel assembly out of the vehicle.
22 Refit the dash panel using the reversal of the removal procedure. Refit the longitudinal arm to the drop arm with the front wheels in the straight ahead position. The brake and clutch systems will have to be bled as described in Chapters 5 and 9 respectively.

## 17 Cab assembly - removal and refitting

1 Remove the nuts and bolts retaining the front of the cab to the windscreen frame.
2 Remove the bolts securing the cab to the front mounting bracket (photo).
3 Remove the nuts and bolts securing the cab to the centre mounting brackets.
4 Remove the nuts retaining the cab to the rear hood sockets (photo).
5 Remove the nuts and bolts securing the rear mounting brackets to the body and lift off the complete cab assembly.
6 If required, remove the rear upper door section by undoing the nuts and bolts securing the stays to the side panel. Remove the split pins and withdraw the hinge pins. The door can now be lifted away from the rear of the cab.
7 Refer to Fig. 12.7 and 12.8 and renew any of the windows, window rubbers or sealing strips that have deteriorated.
8 Refit the cab assembly using the reverse procedure to that of removal.

14.2 Door lock assembly

17.2 Cab retaining bracket (forward)

17.4 Cab retaining bracket (rear)

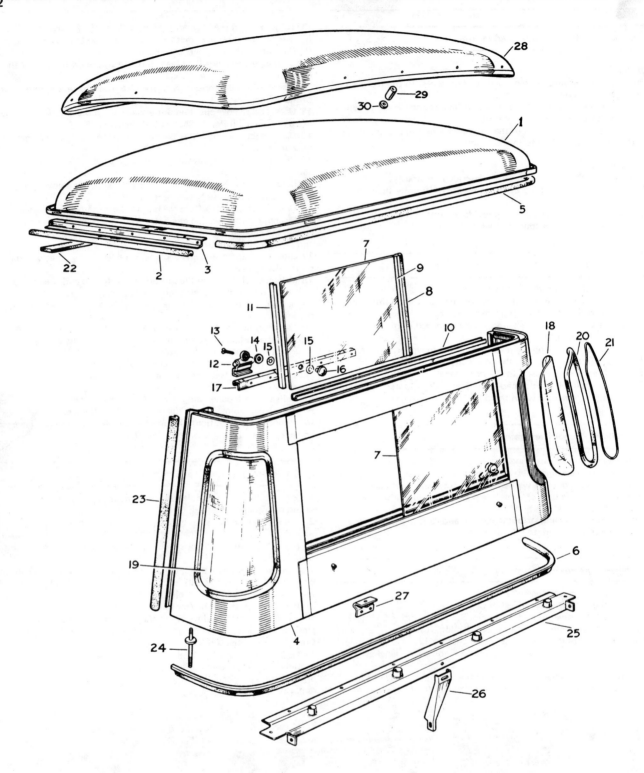

**Fig. 12.7. Drivers cab and tropical roof assembly**

| 1 | Cab roof |
| 2 | Sealing rubber, door top |
| 3 | Retainer for seal |
| 4 | Cab rear panel assembly |
| 5 | Rubber seal, roof to back panel, top |
| 6 | Rubber seal back panel to rear body |
| 7 | Sliding back light |
| 8 | Sealing rubber for back light |
| 9 | Channel for rubber |

| 10 | Channel, top and bottom } For back |
| 11 | Channel, sides } light |
| 12 | Back light catch |
| 13-16 | Fixings for catches |
| 17 | Runner for sliding back light catch |
| 18 | Cab quarter light, RH |
| 19 | Cab quarter light, LH |
| 20 | Weather strip } For quarter |
| 21 | Sealing strip } light |

| 22 | Sealing rubber, windscreen to roof |
| 23 | Sealing rubber, door side |
| 24 | Mounting stud |
| 25 | Mounting rail for cab |
| 26 | Mounting rail support bracket |
| 27 | Cab mounting distance piece |
| 28 | Cab tropical roof panel |
| 29 | Distance piece } Securing tropical roof |
| 30 | Rubber } panel to cab roof |

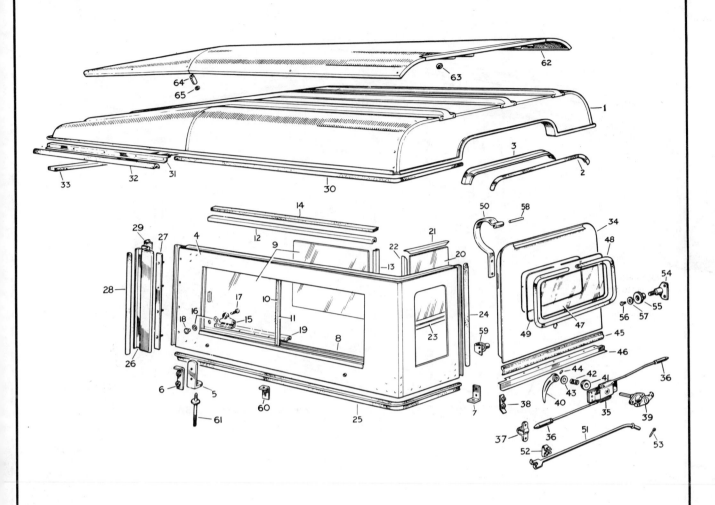

**Fig. 12.8. Estate wagon and rear door assembly**

1 Cab roof assembly
2 Rubber seal for roof, rear
3 Seal retainer for roof, rear
4 Side panel assembly, LH
5 Mounting bracket front
6 Nut plate - securing mounting bracket to body
7 Support bracket at tailboard
8 Drain channel complete for side windows
9 Glass for side window, sliding
10 Sealing rubber for sliding light
11 Channel for sliding light rubber
12 Channel for sliding light, top
13 Channel for sliding light, sides
14 Packing strip for top channel
15 Catch for sliding glass, front
16 Washer for catch
17 Screw fixing front catch
18 Tapped plate for catch
19 Runner for sliding catch
20 Glass for rear end window
21 Retainer for rear end glass upper LH

23 Retainer for rear end glass lower LH
24 Rubber seal for rear lid, side
25 Rubber sealing strip, lower edge to body
26 Capping for front door rear seal, LH
27 Stud plate - fixing cappings to side panel
28 Seal for front door, upper, side
29 Rubber seal at door pillar top and bottom
30 Rubber seal, roof to side
31 Seal retainer for door top, LH
32 Sealing rubber for door top
33 Sealing rubber, windscreen to roof
34 Rear lid assembly
35 Lock complete for rear lid
36 Bolt end for lock
37 Guide for rear lid lock
38 Nut plate
39 Handle for rear lid, outer, locking
40 Handle for rear lid, inner
41 Boss
42 Coil spring
43 Cup for coil spring       } Fixing handle
44 Locking pin

45 Rubber seal for rear lid, bottom
46 Retainer for bottom seal
47 Glass for rear lid
48 Weather strip for back light
49 Seal strip for weather strip
50 Hinge leaf for rear lid
51 Stay for rear lid, RH
52 Spring clip for rear lid stay
53 Split pin securing rear lid stay to support
54 Mounting bracket for stay support
55 Locking nut for mounting bracket
56 Screw       - Retaining locking nut
57 Plain washer
58 Pin for rear lid hinge
59 Socket for rear lid lock bolt, LH
60 Support bracket, centre, body side
61 Mounting stud - securing hard top to body
62 Tropical roof panel
63 Rubber washer - securing panel to roof at end of stiffener
64 Distance piece - Securing roof to
65 Rubber washer - panel at sides

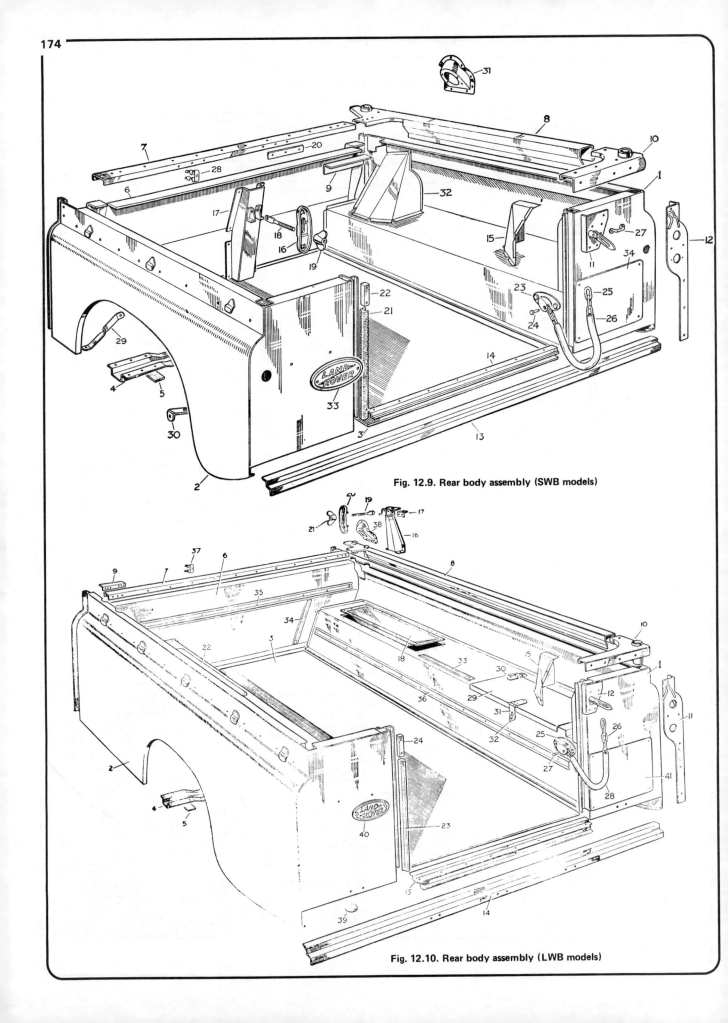

**Fig. 12.9. Rear body assembly (SWB models)**

**Fig. 12.10. Rear body assembly (LWB models)**

**Fig. 12.9. Rear body assembly (SWB models)**

1   Side and wheelarch complete RH
2   Side and wheelarch complete LH
3   Rear floor complete
4   Rear floor cross-member and pads
5   Rear floor cross-member mounting pad
6   Rear body front panel
7   Body front panel capping
8   Body top side capping
9   Corner strengthening angle
10  Hood socket complete, rear corner
11  Corner bracket and tailboard cotter
12  Rear protection angle
13  Rear mounting angle
14  Protecting strip at rear of floor
15  Cover panel for rear lamps
16  Spare wheel clamp
17  Clamp reinforcement bracket

18  Spare wheel clamp tie bar
19  Wing nut, fixing spare wheel clamp
20  Spare wheel rubbing strip
21  Tailboard sealing rubber
22  Tailboard rubber buffer
23  Tailboard chain bracket
24  Pin, securing tailboard chain to bracket
25  Tailboard chain
26  Sleeve for chain
27  Hood strap staple
28  Starting handle and jack handle clip
29  Rear wing stay, front
30  Rear wing stay, rear
31  Fuel filler cowl
32  Fuel filler cover plate
33  'Land-Rover' name plate
34  Registration plate

**Fig. 12.10. Rear body assembly (LWB models)**

1   Side and wheelarch complete RH
2   Side and wheelarch complete LH
3   Rear floor complete
4   Rear floor cross-member and pads
5   Rear floor cross-member mounting pad
6   Rear body front panel
7   Rear body front panel capping
8   Body top side capping
9   Corner strengthening angle
10  Hood socket complete, rear corner
11  Rear protection angle
12  Corner bracket and tailboard cotter
13  Protecting strip at rear of floor
14  Rear mounting angle
15  Rear lamp cover panel
16  Spare wheel mounting strengthening member
17  Nut plate
18  Spare wheel housing
19  Spare wheel clamp tie bar
20  Spare wheel clamp
21  Wing, nut, securing spare wheel clamp

22  Cover plate
23  Tailboard sealing rubber
24  Tailboard rubber buffer
25  Tailboard chain bracket
26  Tailboard chain
27  Clevis pin, securing chain to bracket
28  Sleeve for chain
29  Wheelarch box locker lid
30  Locker lid hinge
31  Locker lid hasp
32  Locker lid turnbuckle
33  Tread plate, wheelarch box top
34  Tread plate, vertical, front panel
35  Tread plate, horizontal, front panel
36  Tread plate for rear floor and wheelarch box sides
37  Starting handle and jack handle clip
38  Fuel filler cover plate
39  Rubber grommet, wheelarch, locker access hole
40  'Land-Rover' nameplate
41  Registration plate

## 18  Rear body section - removal and refitting

1   Remove the hood and sticks, or hard top, if fitted (see Section 17).
2   Remove the spare wheel and any other items of equipment that is stowed in the rear body.
3   On SWB models remove the seat cushions, on LWB models tilt the seat squabs forward.
4   Disconnect the fuel filler and breather hoses, referring to Chapter 3 if necessary.
5   Remove the bolts securing the rear body section to the seat base assembly.
6   Remove the bolts retaining the sill channel mounting brackets to the seat base and rear body.
7   Undo the nuts and bolts securing the rear sill panel to the body.
8   On SWB models only, remove the wing stays from the chassis members.
9   Undo the nuts and bolts securing the body to the rear crossmember mounting brackets.
10  Disconnect the wiring harness to the rear side and stop lights.
11  With the help of some assistants, lift the complete rear body section from the chassis.
12  Refit the rear body section using the reverse procedure to that of removal.

## 19  Heater system - general description

1   An interior heating system is available as an optional extra on all Land Rover models.
2   The earlier Smiths heater comprises a radiator/fan unit located below the instrument panel, (see photo) from which two flexible hoses lead up to demister ducts, one below each windscreen section. Engine coolant circulates around the heater matrix via inlet and outlet hoses and flaps on the heater unit enable the hot air flow to pass into the passenger compartment or be directed through the windscreen demist ducts.

3   A rheostat switch adjacent to the heater unit switches on the motor and controls its speed.
4   Later models have a more sophisticated system comprising a heater box and blower motor in the engine compartment, a water control valve and cable operated flaps that enable the hot air to be directed onto the screen or through foot level vents.
5   The water valve and flaps are controlled by two sliding knobs on the right of the instrument panel. The blower motor is controlled by an on/off switch on the front of the instrument panel.

19.2 Early type heater unit

## 20 Heater assembly (early type) - removal and refitting

1   To avoid air locks, first shut off the heater tap on top of the cylinder block and then drain the cooling system as described in Chapter 2.
2   From behind the heater unit, slacken the two hose clips and pull off the hoses from the heater inlet/outlet pipes.
3   Remove the two securing screws and lift off the demister hose junction box from the top of the heater unit (see Fig. 12.11).
4   Disconnect the heater motor feed wire at the snap connector.
5   Remove the three brackets securing the heater unit to the dash panel.
6   Lift out the heater unit from the vehicle.
7   The heater matrix can be flushed out by connecting a hosepipe to the inlet pipe on the heater unit (the left-hand pipe when looking at the front of the heater). Continue flushing until clear water emerges from the outlet pipe.
8   The heater motor is not repairable and if faulty should be renewed.
9   Refit the heater unit using the reverse procedure to that of removal. After refilling the cooling system run the engine and check the inlet and outlet hose connections for leaks.

## 21 Heater assembly (later type) - removal and refitting

1   From inside the cab, remove the screws securing the trim strip below the instrument panel and remove the strip. Lift the facia trim panel out of the bottom retaining clips and undo the two heater box lower retaining bolts (Fig. 12.12).
2   Drain the cooling system as described in Chapter 2 and from inside the engine compartment, remove the two hoses from the heater box.
3   Remove the four bolts securing the heater box to the dash panel, slacken the clip and pull off the large air inlet hose and lift out the heater box assembly from the engine compartment, (Fig. 12.13).
4   To remove the blower motor, first remove the battery earth terminal and then disconnect the two motor feed wires at the snap connectors.
5   From behind the facia trim panel removed previously, undo the four blower motor retaining screws.
6   Remove the top securing bolt from the rear of the wing panel and

manoeuvre the motor assembly out from under the wing lifting the wing panel up slightly to provide the necessary clearance.
7   The heater box matrix can be flushed out using the method described in Section 18.
8   The blower motor is not a repairable item, and if faulty should be renewed.
9   Refit the motor and heater box assembly using the reverse procedure to that of removal. If difficulty is experienced in refitting the air inlet seal over the motor inlet aperture, remove the inlet grille from the side of the wing and refit the seal through the hole in the wing (Fig. 12. 14).
10 After refilling the radiator check the heater box hose connections for leaks while running the engine.

## 22 Heater controls (later type) - removal and refitting

1   Remove the retaining screws and pull off the two heater control knobs.
2   Undo the two screws securing the control lever assembly to the end panel.
3   Remove the securing screws and withdraw the end panel and heater control lever assembly. To remove the control lever assembly from the vehicle slacken the clamps and grub screws securing the inner and outer control cables and withdraw the cables from the lever assembly (Figs. 12.15 and 12.16).
4   To adjust the cables, refit them to the lever assembly, and set the temperature control lever to the fully up position. Open the bonnet and check that the lever on the water control valve is fully closed. If it is not, slacken the locknut and screw on the water valve lever, push the lever to the closed position and tighten the cable retaining screw and locknut (Fig. 12.17).
5   Set the air flow lever fully up and looking through the air outlet grilles in the lower facia panel, (remove the grilles if necessary) check that the flaps are in the closed position. Adjust the inner cable, if required, by means of the grub screw on the control lever assembly.
6   Refit the heater control levers using the reversal of the removal procedure.

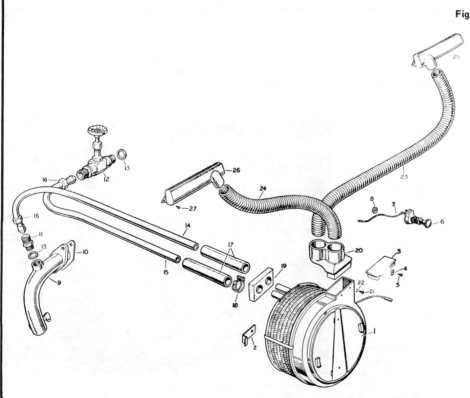

**Fig. 12.11. Heater components (early models)**

1   Heater
2   Bracket for heater
3   Blanking cap
4   Spire nut
5   Acme bolt
6   Switch for heater
7   Feed wire for heater
8   Grommet for heater leads
9   Inlet pipe for water pump
10  Joint washer for pipe
11  Reducing union for pipe
12  Valve for water supply
13  Joint washer for
    valve and union
14  Water outlet pipe
15  Water inlet pipe
16  Union nut for heater pipe
    to valve and union
17  Hose for water pipes
18  Clip for hose
19  Rubber seal for pipes
20  Junction box for
    demister tubes
21-22 Screws: junction box
    to heater
23  Tube for demister, RH
24  Tube demister
25  Nozzle for demister, RH
26  Nozzle for demister, LH
27  Drive screw fixing nozzle

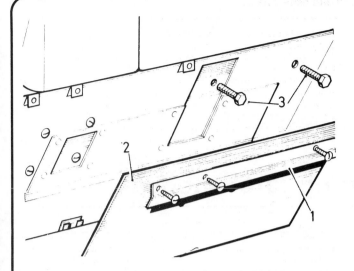

Fig. 12.12. Lower facia panel removed (later models)

1 Trim strip
2 Facia panel

3 Heater box securing bolts

Fig. 12.15. Heater control knobs and end panel (later models)

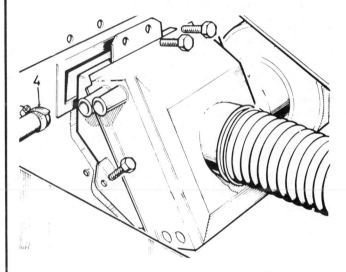

Fig. 12.13. Removing heater box assembly (later models)

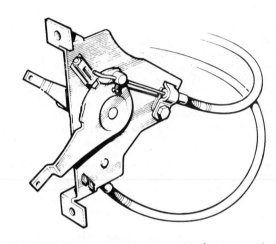

Fig. 12.16. Heater control lever assembly (later models)

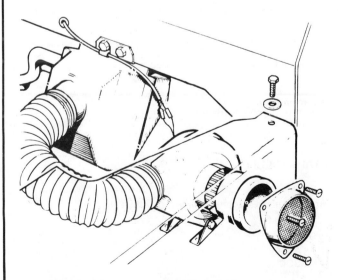

Fig. 12.14. Heater motor and intake grille (later models)

Fig. 12.17. Location of water control valve (later models)

# Chapter 13 Supplement:
# Revisions and information on later models

## Contents

## 1  Introduction

This supplement contains information which is additional to, or a revision of, material in the first twelve Chapters of this manual.

The Sections of this supplement follow the same order as the Chapters to which they relate. The Specifications are all grouped together for convenience, but they follow Chapter order.

It is recommended that before any particular operation is undertaken, reference be made to the appropriate Section(s) of this supplement. In this way, any change to procedure or components can be noted before referring to the main Chapters.

## 2  Specifications

*The following Specifications are supplementary to, or revisions of, those at the beginning of the preceding Chapters.*

### Engine
**Connecting rods**

| | |
|---|---|
| Big-end bearing running clearance ............................................ | 0.0007 to 0.0025 in (0.019 to 0.063 mm) |

**Crankshaft**

| | |
|---|---|
| Type ......................................................................................... | Five main bearing |
| Main bearing running clearance ................................................ | 0.0008 to 0.0022 in (0.020 to 0.055 mm) |

*All other dimensions are as given for the later type three bearing crankshaft*

**Flywheel**

| | |
|---|---|
| Minimum pressure face thickness ............................................. | 1.375 in (34.72 mm) |

**Valve timing**

| | |
|---|---|
| Cast crankshaft (engine serial No 36100001A) ......................... | Timing as given for three bearing crankshaft |
| Forged crankshaft (engine serial No 99100001A): | |
|     Inlet opens ........................................................................ | 16° BTDC |
|     Inlet closes ........................................................................ | 42° ABDC |
|     Inlet peak .......................................................................... | 103° ATDC |
|     Exhaust opens ................................................................... | 51° BBDC |
|     Exhaust closes ................................................................... | 13° ATDC |
|     Exhaust peak* .................................................................... | 109° BTDC |

*Where No 1 exhaust cam peak is 7° to the right of the camshaft keyway centre line viewed from the keyway end*

## Torque wrench settings

| | lbf ft | kgf m |
|---|---|---|
| Main bearing cap bolts: | | |
| Engine serial No 36100001A ............... | 85 | 11.5 |
| Engine serial No 99100001A ............... | 100 | 14 |
| Connecting rod cap nuts: | | |
| Engine serial No 36100001A ............... | 25 | 3.5 |
| Engine serial No 99100001A ............... | 32.5 | 4.5 |
| Flywheel bolts ............... | 100 | 14 |

## *Ignition system*
## Distributor

| | |
|---|---|
| Type ............... | Ducellier |
| Rotation ............... | Anti-clockwise at rotor end |
| Vacuum advance: | |
| Starts ............... | 4 in (102 mm) Hg |
| Finishes ............... | 12° at 18 in (457 mm) Hg |
| Dwell: | |
| Angle ............... | 57° |
| Variation ............... | ± 2° 30′ |
| No centrifugal advance below ............... | 900 rpm |
| Contact breaker gap ............... | 0.017 in (0.43 mm) |

## Ignition timing – Series IIA

| | |
|---|---|
| 7.0 : 1 compression ratio: | |
| 83 octane fuel ............... | 3° BTDC |
| 76 octane fuel ............... | TDC |
| 8.0 : 1 compression ratio: | |
| 85 octane fuel ............... | 3° BTDC |
| 90 octane fuel ............... | 6° BTDC |

## Ignition timing – Series III

| | |
|---|---|
| 7.0 : 1 compression ratio: | |
| 75 octane fuel ............... | TDC |
| 83 octane fuel ............... | 3° BTDC |
| 90 octane fuel ............... | 6° BTDC |
| 8.0 : 1 compression ratio: | |
| 85 octane fuel ............... | 3° ATDC |
| 90 octane fuel ............... | TDC |

## Spark plugs

| | |
|---|---|
| Series IIA: | |
| 7.0 : 1 compression ratio ............... | Champion N8 |
| 8.0 : 1 compression ratio ............... | Champion N8 |
| Series III: | |
| 7.0 : 1 compression ratio ............... | Champion N8 |
| 8.0 : 1 compression ratio ............... | Champion N12YC |
| Gap ............... | 0.030 in (0.76 mm) |

## *Gearbox – Series III vehicles, 1978 on*
## Main gearbox

| | |
|---|---|
| Type ............... | Four-speed and reverse with synchromesh on all forward gears |
| Gear ratios: | |
| Top ............... | 1 : 1 |
| Third ............... | 1.50 : 1 |
| Second ............... | 2.22 : 1 |
| First ............... | 3.68 : 1 |
| Reverse: | |
| Suffix 'A' type ............... | 3.887 : 1 |
| Suffix 'B' type ............... | 4.021 : 1 |

## Transfer gearbox

| | High | Low |
|---|---|---|
| Gear ratios: | | |
| Helical and spur gear type ............... | 1.15 : 1 | 2.35 : 1 |
| All helical type ............... | 1.53 : 1 | 3.27 : 1 |

## Overall gear ratios

| | High | Low |
|---|---|---|
| With helical and spur gear transfer: | | |
| Top ............... | 5.4 : 1 | 11.1 : 1 |
| Third ............... | 8.05 : 1 | 16.5 : 1 |
| Second ............... | 12.0 : 1 | 24.6 : 1 |
| First ............... | 19.88 : 1 | 40.7 : 1 |
| Reverse: | | |
| Suffix 'A' main gearbox ............... | 20.47 : 1 | 42.87 : 1 |
| Suffix 'B' main gearbox ............... | 21.6 : 1 | 44.31 : 1 |

| With all helical transfer: | **High** | **Low** |
|---|---|---|
| Top | 7.19 : 1 | 15.4 : 1 |
| Third | 10.81 : 1 | 23.1 : 1 |
| Second | 15.96 : 1 | 34.1 : 1 |
| First | 26.46 : 1 | 56.56 : 1 |
| Reverse: | | |
|     Suffix 'A' main gearbox | 27.87 : 1 | 59.76 : 1 |
|     Suffix 'B' main gearbox | 28.91 : 1 | 61.78 : 1 |

## Overdrive (optional)
| | |
|---|---|
| Type | Fairey, fully synchromesh |
| Ratio | 0.782 : 1 |
| Lubricant | SAE 90EP oil |

## Torque wrench settings
| | **lbf ft** | **kgf m** |
|---|---|---|
| Layshaft bolt (apply Loctite 601) | 50 | 7 |

*Propeller shaft*
| | |
|---|---|
| Shaft length: | |
|     Series III 109 in model (rear) | 41.062 in (1042.9 mm) |

*Front and rear axles -- 1980 on*
*Refer to Section 8 of this Chapter for full information on axle modifications and rationalisation*

## Hub endfloat
| | |
|---|---|
| Front hubs (with oil catcher) | 0.002 to 0.004 in (0.05 to 0.10 mm) |
| Rear hubs (with or without oil catcher) | 0.004 to 0.006 in (0.10 to 0.15 mm) |

## Hub oil seal recess
| | |
|---|---|
| Front and rear | 0.19 to 0.21 in (4.8 to 5.3 mm) from hub rear frame |

## Free wheeling hubs (optional)
| | |
|---|---|
| Type | Fairey |
| Hub lubrication: | |
|     Pre intermediate front axle shaft oil seal | Axle oil |
|     Post intermediate front axle shaft oil seal | Extreme pressure, lithium based grease |

## Torque wrench settings
| | **lbf ft** | **kgf m** |
|---|---|---|
| Hub oil catcher retaining bolts (apply Loctite 270) | 30 to 38 | 4.2 to 5.2 |
| Hub driving member retaining bolts | 30 to 38 | 4.2 to 5.2 |
| Wheel nuts | 75 to 85 | 10.3 to 11.7 |

*Braking system*
*Refer to Section 9 of this Chapter for full information on brake system modifications and rationalisation*

*Electrical system – Series III vehicles, 1978 on*
### Starter motor
| | |
|---|---|
| Type | Lucas 2M100 |
| Brush spring tension | 36 oz (1020 g) |
| Brush minimum length | 0.375 in (9.5 mm) |
| Commutator minimum thickness | 0.140 in (3.5 mm) |
| Armature maximum endfloat | 0.010 in (0.25 mm) |
| Light running current | 40 amp at 6000 rpm (approx) |
| Torque at 1000 rpm | 7.3 lbf ft (1.02 kgf m) with 300 amp |
| Lock torque | 14.4 lbf ft (2.02 kgf m) with 463 amp |

### Wiper motor
| | |
|---|---|
| Type | Lucas 14W single speed |
| Brush spring tension | 5.3 to 8 oz (150 to 250 g) |
| Brush minimum length | 0.190 in (4.8 mm) |
| Armature endfloat | 0.002 to 0.010 in (0.051 to 0.254 mm) |
| Armature winding resistance | 0.23 to 0.35 ohm at 60°F (16°C) |
| Current at 13.5V | 1.4 amp (max) with light running rack disconnected |

## Battery
| | |
|---|---|
| Rating | 55 amp/hour |

## Bulbs and units

| | |
|---|---|
| Sidelamps | Lucas 207, 12V, 5W |
| Stop, tail lamps | Lucas 308, 12V, 21/5W |
| Rear number plate lamps | Lucas 233, 12V, 4W |
| Warning light, brakes | Lucas 280, 12V, 1.5W |
| Warning light, flashers | Lucas 281, 12V, 2W |

## Torque wrench settings

| | lbf ft | kgf m |
|---|---|---|
| Alternator shaft nut | 25 to 30 | 3.5 to 4.2 |
| Starter motor through-bolts | 8 | 1.1 |
| Wiper blade drive adaptor bolts | 2.5 | 0.34 |

## Suspension and steering – Series III vehicles, 1978 on
*Refer to Section 11 of this Chapter for information on tyre sizes and pressures*

## Torque wrench settings

| | lbf ft | kgf m |
|---|---|---|
| Suspension shackle nuts and bolts | 60 to 70 | 8.3 to 9.7 |
| Front and rear leaf spring U-bolts | 58 | 8 |

## 3 Vehicle identification numbers – 1979 on

### Engine number prefixes
1 From November 1979, all engine numbers will have a three digit prefix denoting the particular engine specification. These prefixes are as follows:

| Prefix | Vehicle type | Compression ratio |
|---|---|---|
| 901 | 2286cc petrol | 8 : 1 |
| 902 | 2286cc petrol | 8 : 1 |
| 904 | 2286cc petrol | 7 : 1 |

The 902 prefix was introduced upon completion of the 901 range. An S prefix before the engine number indicates a service replacement item.

### Vehicle identification number (VIN)
2 From October 1979, all vehicles have a vehicle identification numbering system which replaces the previous chassis number. The identification plate and the position of the number on the chassis are shown in Figs. 13.1 and 13.2 respectively.
3 The following table relates to 2286cc petrol models for the UK market and shows the VIN replacement for the old chassis number prefix:

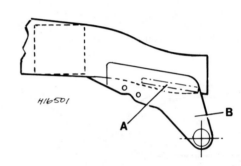

**Fig. 13.1 Vehicle identification number locations (Sec 3)**

A   VIN                          B   Front right-hand spring bracket

| Vehicle type | Old prefix | VIN prefix |
|---|---|---|
| 88 in Regular | 901 | LBAAHIAA |
| 88 in Half ton | 951 | LBBAHIAA |
| 88 in Station wagon | 921 | LBABHIAA |
| 109 in Station wagon | 931 | LBCMHIAA |
| 109 in Long | 911 | LBCAHIAA |
| 109 in One ton | 246 | LBDAHIAA |

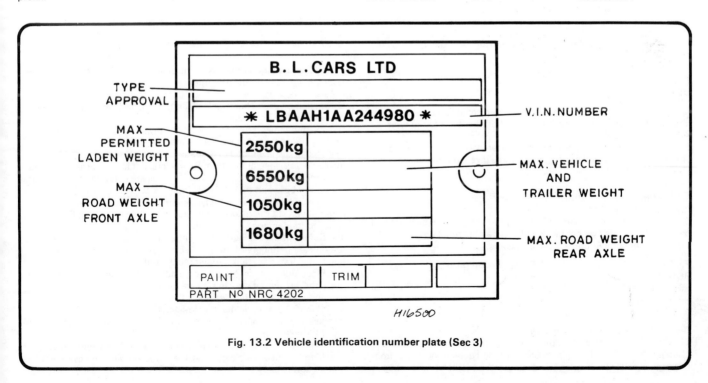

**Fig. 13.2 Vehicle identification number plate (Sec 3)**

## 4    Engine

### Cylinder head

1    From engine No 36400704, the new five bearing engine is fitted with an 'Elring' type cylinder head gasket. This gasket has a non-metallic base and is latex coated; it can be identified by its material composition and grey colour.

### Exhaust valves

2    From engine Nos 36100266 (8 : 1 compression ratio) and 36401012 (7 : 1 compression ratio), 'Tufrided' exhaust valves are fitted as standard. These valves can be used as replacements for the earlier type.

### Piston rings

3    From engine Nos 36111177 (8 : 1 compression ratio) and 36405395 (7 : 1 compression ratio), new piston rings have been introduced. Fig. 13.3 shows the new ring set which comprises two compression rings and an oil control ring. Note that the compression rings must be fitted with the marks 'T' or 'Top' facing the piston crown. These rings are fully interchangeable with the earlier type.

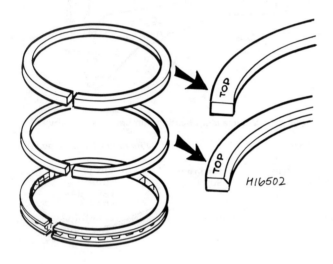

**Fig. 13.3 New type of piston ring set (Sec 4)**

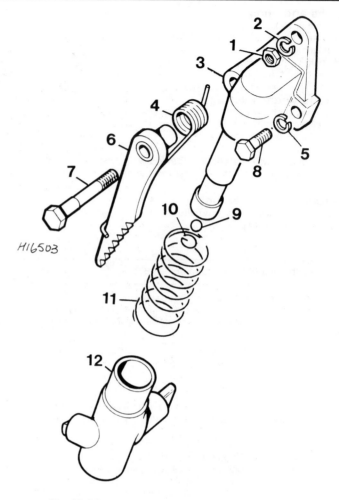

**Fig. 13.4 Later type of timing chain tensioner (Sec 4)**

| 1 | Nut | 7 | Pivot bolt |
|---|-----|---|-----------|
| 2 | Spring washer | 8 | Bolt |
| 3 | Body (piston assembly) | 9 | Ball |
| 4 | Ratchet spring | 10 | Retainer |
| 5 | Spring washer | 11 | Tensioner spring |
| 6 | Ratchet | 12 | Cylinder |

### Timing chain tensioner

4    From engine No 99100001A, the timing chain tensioner has been changed from the type shown in Fig. 1.22 of Chapter 1 to the type shown in Fig. 13.4.

5    This tensioner will give a slightly greater loading on the timing chain. The removal and refitting procedures given in Chapter 1 are unaffected.

### Five bearing crankshaft
#### Engine identification

6    The new five main bearing 2286cc petrol engine can be identified by the colour of its cylinder block which is painted red. Engine identification number prefixes are as follows:

| Prefix | Compression ratio |
|--------|-------------------|
| 36100001A | 8 : 1 |
| 36400001A | 7 : 1 |
| 99100001A | 8 : 1 |
| 99200001A | 7 : 1 |

#### Crankshaft rear oil seal – renewal

7    Refer to Chapter 1 and remove the engine, leaving the gearbox attached to the vehicle. Refer to Chapter 5 and detach the clutch from the engine. Refer to Chapter 1 and remove the flywheel. Alternative

methods of gaining access to the oil seal which do not involve engine removal are given in the aforementioned Chapters.

8    With the flywheel housing removed, discard both the housing O-ring and oil seal. Thoroughly clean the ring and seal housings and protect the flywheel housing from further contamination.

9    Examine the crankshaft journal for any damage which could destroy the seal lip. A guide which fits over the journal, thereby decreasing the likelihood of damage to the new seal during fitting, is available as a special tool from BL dealers. If it is not possible to obtain this tool, then ensure that the journal faces are completely smooth and the corner between them slightly radiused with no sharp edges. Smear the journal periphery with molybdenum disulphide grease. Alternatively, fit the guide and grease its periphery, having first checked for damage.

10    Before fitting the new oil seal into the flywheel housing, check that the outside periphery of the seal is clean and the seal location in the housing is free from burrs. Avoid touching the seal lip.

11    Place the flywheel housing on a flat work surface and carefully press the seal into it, the lip side leading. Keep the seal square to its housing and fit it so that its face is flush with, or a maximum of 0.020 in (0.50 mm) below, the housing face, see Fig. 13.7. If necessary, place a piece of wood across the seal and use a hammer to tap the seal home.

12    Press the new O-ring into its flywheel housing location, after checking for absolute cleanliness. Clean the housing and cylinder block mating surfaces.

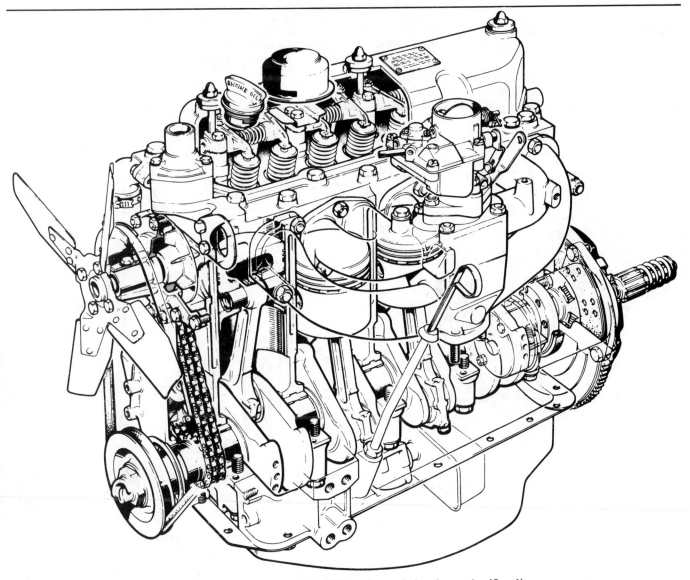

**Fig. 13.5 Sectional view of the 2286 cc five main bearing engine (Sec 4)**

13  Align the holes in the housing mating face with the dowels protruding from the cylinder block and carefully push the flywheel housing into position, taking care to observe that the seal lip passes smoothly over the crankshaft journal or its guide.

14  Using a soft-faced hammer, carefully tap around the flywheel housing to seat it against the cylinder block. Fit the housing retaining bolts and washers, finger tight, whilst renewing any flattened spring washers. If necessary, remove the seal guide. Fully tighten the housing retaining bolts, working in a diagonal sequence and tightening a little at a time to avoid distortion.

15  After having refitted the flywheel and clutch, smear the splines of the primary shaft and clutch centre with molybdenum disulphide grease. Refer to the Specifications of this Chapter for revised torque settings.

**Crankshaft – removal, examination and refitting**

16  To remove the crankshaft, refer to the appropriate Sections of Chapter 1 and carry out the following tasks:

> *Engine removal*
> *Sump removal*
> *Oil pump and filter removal*
> *Timing cover, gears and chain removal*
> *Clutch removal (Chapter 5)*
> *Flywheel and flywheel housing removal*
> *Pistons and connecting rods removal*
> *Crankshaft and main bearing removal (five bearings instead of three)*

17  Note any differences in specification before commencing the procedure for crankshaft and main bearing examination and renovation given in Chapter 1.

18  Check crankshaft endfloat by first locating the main bearing halves in the engine block and lubricating them with engine oil. Fit a thrust washer each side of the centre main bearing as shown in Fig. 13.8. The unplated side of each washer must face towards the bearing shell.

19  Position the crankshaft in the cylinder block. Set up a dial test indicator as shown in Fig. 13.9 and measure the crankshaft endfloat which should be 0.002 to 0.006 in (0.05 to 0.15 mm).

20  If crankshaft endfloat is incorrect then change the thrust washers to bring it within limits. Thrust washers are available in the following oversizes:

> *0.0025 in (0.06 mm)*
> *0.0050 in (0.12 mm)*
> *0.0075 in (0.18 mm)*
> *0.010 in (0.25 mm)*

To ensure the crankshaft remains centralised, variation of thrust washer thickness each side of the main bearing must not exceed 0.003 in (0.08 mm).

21  With endfloat correct, refit the crankshaft by first locating the bearing halves in their respective caps and then fitting the caps (1 to 4) over the crankshaft. Before fitting the cap retaining bolts note the following warning:

22 **Warning**: On engine Nos 36100001A and 99100001A it is essential that new bolts and washers are fitted. The bolts fitted to engine No 99100001A have plain washers whereas those fitted to engine No 36100001A have spring washers. Neither bolts nor washers are interchangeable.

23 Fit the retaining bolts through caps 1 to 4 and tighten, finger tight. Clean any old cork seal material from No 5 main bearing cap.

24 Prepare the two new cork T-seals for fitting between No 5 cap and the cylinder block by first chamfering their inner edge as shown in Fig. 13.10. Soak the seals in engine oil and fit them in the bearing cap.

25 BL supply guides which bolt to the cylinder block and prevent the seals from tearing on the block edge as the cap is fitted. If these guides are readily available, then ensure they are fitted parallel to the block edge. Photo 29.10 of Chapter 1 shows how a feeler gauge can be

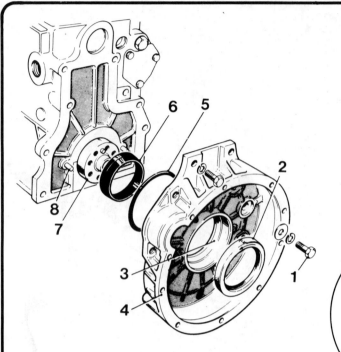

**Fig. 13.6 Flywheel assembly (five bearing engine) (Sec 4)**

| | | | |
|---|---|---|---|
| 1 | Retaining bolt | 5 | O-ring |
| 2 | Oil seal | 6 | Oil seal guide (special tool) |
| 3 | Seal housing | 7 | Crankshaft journal |
| 4 | Flywheel housing | 8 | Dowel |

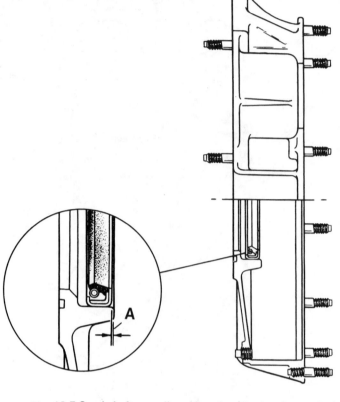

**Fig. 13.7 Crankshaft rear oil seal location (five bearing engine) (Sec 4)**

A    Maximum recess = 0.020 in (0.50 mm)

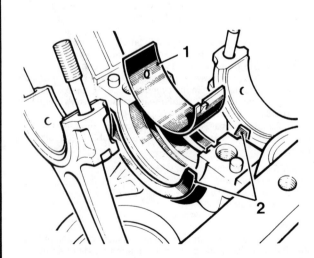

**Fig. 13.8 Positioning the crankshaft thrust washers (Sec 4)**

1    Centre main bearing shell          2    Thrust washers

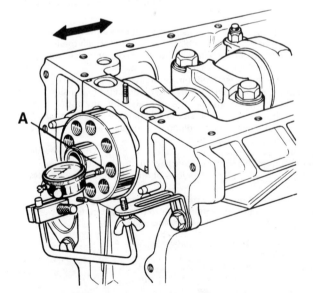

**Fig. 13.9 Measuring crankshaft endfloat (Sec 4)**

A    Dial test indicator contact point

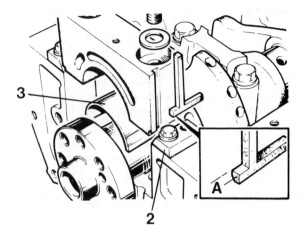

**Fig. 13.10 Fitting No 5 main bearing cap (Sec 4)**

A   Seal chamfer width =          1   No 5 main bearing cap
    0.016 in to 0.031 in          2   Seal guide (special tool)
    (0.40 to 0.80 mm)             3   Bearing shell

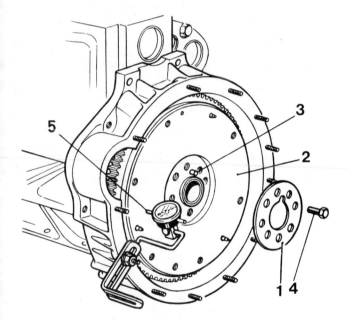

**Fig. 13.11 Measuring flywheel run-out (Sec 4)**

1   Reinforcing plate            4   Retaining bolt
2   Flywheel                     5   Dial test indicator contact
3   Dowel                            point

used to prevent tearing of each seal in the absence of guides.

26   Press No 5 cap fully home and fit its retaining bolts and washers, finger tight. Starting at the centre main bearing, evenly tighten the cap bolts to the specified torque loading.

27   It is necessary to allow for shrinkage of the cork T-seals after fitting. Ideally, fitting of the sump should be delayed for twelve hours and the seal ends then trimmed. If delay is not possible, trim the seal ends so that each one protrudes 0.03 in (0.8 mm) above the block face. The best way to do this is to place a close fitting washer of the correct thickness over each seal end and then trim off any surplus with a razor blade. Dab sealing compound over each seal end.

28   Reverse the dismantling procedure given in paragraph 16 whilst noting the following points:

29   Each connecting rod bolt has an eccentric head which locates in slots in the connecting rod. Check each bolt head is correctly located before tightening the cap nut to the specified torque loading.

30   Refer to the information contained in this Section for crankshaft rear oil seal renewal (it is advisable to renew this seal as a matter of course), fitting of the flywheel housing and fitting of the flywheel.

**Flywheel – removal, examination and refitting**

31   The flywheel fitted to the five bearing crankshaft differs from the earlier type in that it has a separate reinforcing plate which will become detached after removal of the flywheel retaining bolts. Otherwise, removal is as stated in Chapter 1.

32   In addition to the examination and renovation procedure given in Chapter 1, check the flywheel for run-out as follows.

33   Clean the flywheel and crankshaft mating faces, removing any burrs which can cause flywheel run-out. Check the dowel is placed correctly in the flywheel and crankshaft flange.

34   Fit the flywheel, reinforcing plate and retaining bolts. Tighten the bolts to the specified torque loading. Refer to Fig. 13.11 and attach a dial test indicator to the cylinder block so that its pointer rests on the flywheel at a point 4.5 in (114 mm) from the flywheel centre. Rotate the flywheel and check that run-out does not exceed 0.002 in (0.05 mm). If no cause for excessive run-out can be found then renew the flywheel.

---

## 5   Carburation

### Zenith tamperproof carburettor – idle adjustment

1   The idle adjustment screw of this carburettor is rendered 'tamperproof' by means of a locking ring surrounded by a protective shield. With the shield removed a special tool is needed to loosen the locking ring before the screw can be turned. The object of fitting both shield and ring is to discourage (and to detect) adjustment by unqualified or unskilled operators.

2   Before removing the shield, satisfy yourself that you are not breaking any local or national anti-pollution laws by so doing. If the vehicle is under warranty, be aware that you may be in breach of warranty conditions. Fit a new shield on completion where required by law.

3   Fig. 13.12 shows the special tool in use. Any attempt to carry out adjustment without this tool will result in damage to the screw, backing ring or carburettor. If the tool cannot easily be obtained then one will have to be manufactured from a length of steel tube of the appropriate bore and outside diameters.

4   It may be necessary to destroy the shield in order to remove it, do this very carefully. Ensure the special tool is a good fit in the locking ring and the screwdriver which passes through the tool is a good fit in the screw. On completion of adjustment, hold the screw whilst retightening the ring.

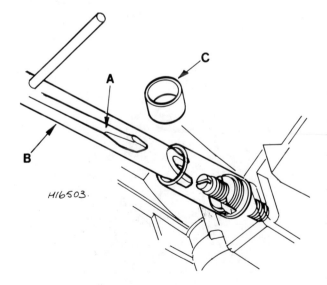

H16503

**Fig. 13.12 Adjusting idle on the Zenith tamperproof carburettor (Sec 5)**

A   Screwdriver              C   Shield
B   Special tool

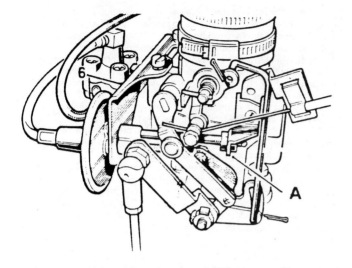

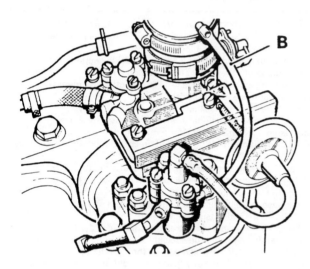

**Fig. 13.13 Adjusting the carburettor throttle prop (emission control system) (Sec 5)**

A    Vacuum unit adjusting rod        B    Atmospheric bleed pipe
     locknuts

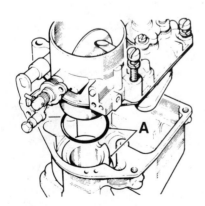

**Fig. 13.14 Checking carburettor top-to-base assembly seating (Sec 5)**

A    Venturi O-ring and location

### Carburettor throttle prop – adjustment (emission control system)

5    Commence adjustment of the throttle prop system by first running the vehicle for a minimum distance of 3 miles (5 km) to ensure that the engine reaches its normal working temperature.
6    It is now necessary to obtain an accurate tachometer and use it to determine that the engine is idling at 750 to 800 rpm.
7    Refer to Fig. 13.13 and loosen the locknuts which secure the vacuum unit adjusting rod to the carburettor bracket. Move the accelerator linkage so that engine speed rises to 2000 rpm, at the same time disconnecting the atmospheric bleed pipe from the air cleaner elbow and blocking the pipe end. Doing this retains the vacuum supply from the trigger valve, thereby ensuring that the throttle butterfly remains propped.
8    Now release the accelerator linkage, allowing engine speed to fall to the accelerator propped position. Turn the vacuum unit rod locknuts by equal amounts until engine speed reaches 1200 to 1250 rpm. Tighten the locknuts and reconnect the pipe to the air cleaner elbow, whereby the engine should return to its normal idling speed. Stop the engine and disconnect the tachometer.
9    Note that the above procedure is similar for all countries, but the setting speeds given are for UK and European vehicles only. Do not attempt to adjust the vacuum control valve, it is preset.

### Carburettor – fault diagnosis

10   Where the vehicle is operating in high ambient temperatures and an excessive rich mixture condition is experienced at idle which will not respond to normal mixture adjustment, then suspect incorrect seating of the carburettor top-to-base assembly around the venturi O-ring, see Fig. 13.14.
11   If the fitting of a new O-ring fails to effect a cure, then BL recommend carburettor replacement. Note that heavy fuel consumption may accompany the above fault.

---

**6    Ignition system**

---

### Ignition timing and fuel octane rating

1    Where it is necessary to run a vehicle on fuel which has a lower octane rating than that normally used, then avoid the risk of engine damage by ensuring that the ignition system is adapted as shown in the Specifications.

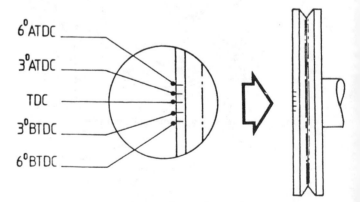

**Fig. 13.15 Ignition timing marks – 1980 on (Sec 5)**

### Ignition timing – 1980 on

2    In order to make reading of the ignition timing easier, vehicles from 1980 have a single timing pointer fixed to the front timing cover and a scale of five notches on the crankshaft pulley, see Fig. 13.15.

### Ducellier distributor

3    The Ducellier distributor supersedes the Lucas 45D4 type with which it is fully interchangeable.
**Contact breaker points – renewal**
4    Gain access to the points assembly by unclipping the distributor cup and then pulling the rotor arm from position. Remove the fixed contact after having released its securing screw.

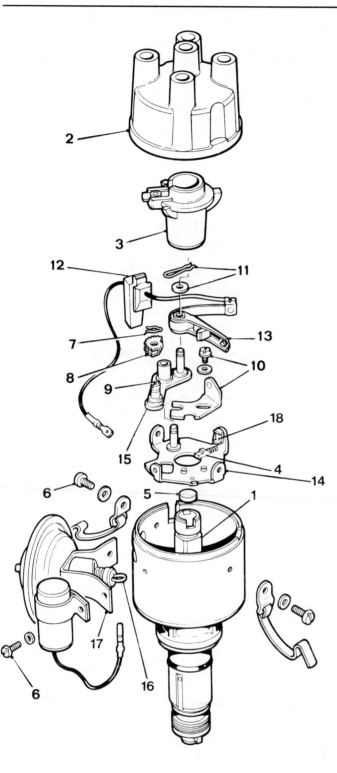

**Fig. 13.16 The Ducellier distributor (Sec 6)**

| | | |
|---|---|---|
| 1 | Cam | 10 | Fixed contact and screw |
| 2 | Cap | 11 | Clip and insulating washer |
| 3 | Rotor arm | 12 | Connector block |
| 4 | Pressure pad | 13 | Moving contact |
| 5 | Felt pad | 14 | Baseplate |
| 6 | Screws | 15 | Pivot plate |
| 7 | Clip | 16 | Vacuum operated link |
| 8 | Serrated cam | 17 | Vacuum unit |
| 9 | D-post | 18 | Spring guide |

5   Disconnect the suppressor lead from the connector block attached to the side of the distributor body. Disconnect the lead which runs from the connector block to the HT coil at the coil terminal.

6   Remove the moving contact retaining clip and the insulating washer. Lift the moving contact from its pivot, together with the connector block.

7   Fit the new points assembly by reversing the removal procedure, whilst taking care to fit the leaf spring plastic guide and the insulating washer correctly. Tighten the fixed contact securing screw finger tight.

8   Carry out a similar procedure to that given in Chapter 4 for contact breaker points adjustment, setting the breaker gap to that specified.

**Distributor — overhaul**

9   Using a similar procedure to that given in Chapter 4, remove the distributor from the vehicle.

10  Unclip the distributor cap. Pull away the rotor arm and dust cover and remove the felt pad from the rotor.

11  Disconnect the suppressor lead from the connector block. Remove the two screws and washers which retain the vacuum unit and suppressor and separate the suppressor from the distributor.

12  Detach the spring clip from the eccentric D-post. Mark the position of the serrated cam in relation to the spring seat of the vacuum operated link. Detach the cam and link from the D-post and separate the vacuum unit from the distributor.

13  Remove the fixed contact, after having released its securing screw and washer. Remove the moving contact retaining clip and the insulating washer. Lift the moving contact from its pivot, together with the connector block.

14  Mark the position of the baseplate in relation to the distributor body. Remove the plate retaining screws (those which also retain the cap clips), hold the pressure pad clear of the shaft and pull the plate from its position. Separate the baseplate and moving contact pivot plate.

15  Commence examination by checking the distributor shaft for excessive side-play which will obviously affect the breaker gap, causing it to fluctuate as the shaft turns. Excessive side-play will necessitate distributor renewal, although it may be possible for a competent engineer to insert bushes between the shaft and distributor body to take up any play. Renewal of the complete distributor is also recommended if the cam advance mechanism is damaged or worn.

16  Note that the distributor drive dog is designed so that it is loosely retained on the shaft, the float allowing for any misalignment. Do not mistake this float for excessive wear.

17  All other distributor components must be renewed if found to be damaged or excessively worn. Do not neglect to check the distributor cover for signs of tracking or cracks, clean the cover before doing this. Check and clean all electrical contacts, making sure the pick-up brush in the cap is not seized in its holder.

18  Reassembly is a reversal of the removal procedure, whilst noting the following points. Lubricate any pivot points and the pressure pad by lightly smearing them with a multi-purpose grease.

19  Realign any alignment marks made before component removal. If in doubt as to correct component location, refer to Fig. 13.16. Locate the moving contact spring in its guide.

20  On completion of reassembly, lubricate the felt pad of the rotor with a few drops of light machine oil. Lightly grease the rotor cam. Set the contact breaker gap, see paragraph 8, and refit the distributor to the vehicle.

**Dwell angle adjustment**

21  Setting the contact breaker gap by using feeler gauges must be regarded as a basic adjustment only. For optimum engine performance, the dwell angle must be checked. Dwell angle is the number of degrees through which the distributor cam turns during the period between the instance of closure and opening of the contact breaker points.

22  Checking dwell angle not only gives a more accurate setting of the contact breaker gap but also evens out any variations in the gap which could be caused by wear between the distributor shaft and body, or difference in height of any of the cam peaks.

23  Check the angle with a dwell meter, connected in accordance with the manufacturer's instructions. Note the specified dwell angle. Proceed by running the engine until it reaches normal operating temperature. Detach the pipe from the vacuum unit and allow the engine to idle. Check the dwell angle.

24  If the angle is incorrect, then stop the engine and adjust the points gap. Increase the gap if the angle is too large and reduce the gap if the

angle is too small. The dwell angle should always be adjusted before checking ignition timing.

**Dwell variation and vacuum advance adjustment**

25  If either of these adjustments is suspected of being incorrect (see Specifications) then refer the problem to your BL dealer who will have the necessary special tools and expertise at his disposal to effect accurate adjustment or to recommend component replacement

## Lucas sliding contact distributor

**Contact breaker points – renewal**

26  BL recommend that the contact breaker points fitted to this type of distributor are renewed every 25 000 miles (40 000 km), regardless of condition.

27  With the distributor cap and rotor arm removed, release the contact assembly retaining screw and lift the assembly clear of the baseplate. Detach the electrical connector from the spring. Before proceeding further, read the instructions on lubrication later in this Section.

28  Before fitting a new contact assembly, wipe the points with a petrol-soaked rag to remove their protective coating whilst observing the necessary fire precautions. Fit the electrical connector to the spring; black lead uppermost.

29  Align the peg of the contact assembly with the hole in the baseplate (see Fig. 13.17) and carefully push the assembly into position. Note that the sliding contact actuating fork must also locate over the peg.

30  Refit the assembly securing screw and washers, finger tight.

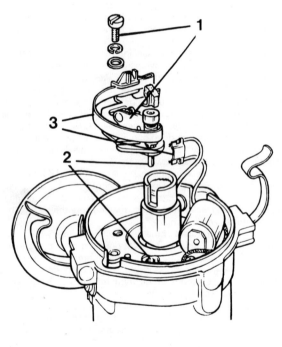

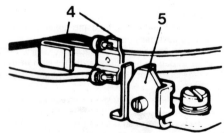

**Fig. 13.17 Fitting the Lucas sliding contact assembly (Sec 6)**

| | |
|---|---|
| 1   Contact breaker assembly and screw | 4   Connector fitment |
| 2   Peg and baseplate location | 5   Leaf spring location |
| 3   Electrical connector | |

Ensure that the contact leaf spring is located correctly in the insulation shoe.

31  Carry out a similar procedure to that given in Chapter 4 for adjusting the contact breaker gap to 0.014 to 0.016 in (0.36 to 0.40 mm). With all lubrication complete, refit the rotor arm and distributor cap.

**Lubrication**

32  BL recommend that the following procedure is carried out every 12 000 miles (20 000 km).

33  Clean the cam and lightly smear it with a multi-purpose grease. Smear a little grease on the underside of the heel actuator, on the actuator ramps, the contact breaker heel ribs, the peg and the actuator fork, see Fig. 13.18.

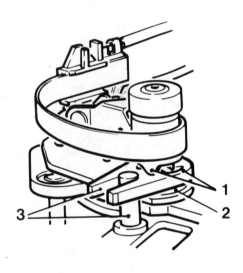

**Fig. 13.18 Lubricating the sliding contact assembly (Sec 6)**

| | |
|---|---|
| 1   Actuator ramps and breaker heel ribs | 3   Actuator fork and peg |
| 2   Heel actuator underside | |

34  Apply a few drops of clean engine oil to the felt pad beneath the rotor arm.

35  Every 25 000 miles (40 000 km), inject one or two drops of clean engine oil through the aperture in the baseplate and onto the automatic advance mechanism.

36  Before refitting the distributor cap, wipe its internal and external surfaces with a clean, dry piece of nap-free cloth whilst looking for signs of corrosion or tracking.

---

**7    Gearbox**

## Overdrive unit

1    BL fit the Fairey overdrive unit as an 'on-road economy option' to all County Station Wagon variants except the V8. If required, the unit can be purchased from the manufacturers and fitted by the owner, in which case full details for fitting should be supplied with the unit. Without doubt, fitting of the unit will result in a considerable saving of fuel gained by reduced engine speeds.

**Routine maintenance**

2    Lubrication for the overdrive unit is independent of the main and transfer gearboxes. Check the unit oil level every week, topping-up with the specified oil when necessary.

3    Drain and refill the unit after the first 500 miles (800 km) of use and thereafter every 6000 miles (9600 km).

4    Ensure that the selector linkage is kept lubricated.

**Running-in**

5    A new or rebuilt overdrive unit should be treated with the same care as exercised when running in a new or rebuilt engine. Drive the vehicle conservatively for at least 500 miles (800 km), taking care not to place any great strain on the unit.

## 8 Front and rear axles

### Axle rationalisation and modification – 1980 on

1   In order to reduce the number of axle types, some major modifications have been made and some components made common to all axles. The result has been to reduce the number of axle types to three.

2   The following components are common to all new axles and are fully interchangeable:

*Stub axles and bearing sleeves*
*Hub assembly*
*Hub driving member*
*Dual lip seal*
*Taper roller bearings*
*Hub nut cap*
*Hub cap O-ring*
*Locknuts and locking washers*

3   The major modifications made are as follows:

*New taper roller bearings (as Range Rover)*
*New dual lip hub seal*
*New intermediate front axle shaft seal*
*New oil catcher (except 88 in rear)*

4   88 in and 109 in vehicles will have identical front axle assemblies, the 88 in being uprated to 109 in specification. Oil catchers are fitted to the hubs and both vehicles are equipped with Rover differentials and 11 in (280 mm) diameter twin leading shoe brakes.

5   The 109 in rear axle is similar to the 88 in type except for the differential being of Salisbury design, the brake drums being of 11 in (280 mm) diameter and the oil catcher being fitted. The 88 in rear axle has a Land-Rover differential and 10 in (254 mm) diameter brake drums.

### Front axle hubs – servicing

6   Removal, examination and refitting of the front axle hubs is similar to that procedure given for servicing the wheel bearings in Chapter 8. Refer to Fig. 13.19 for the fitted position of each component and note the following points:

7   Before fitting the new oil seal, check its location in the hub for any damage which could in turn damage the seal. Check the housing is clean.

8   Liberally smear (do not pack) the cavity between the seal lips with a multi-purpose grease whilst taking care not to touch the seal lips. Obtain a length of metal tube (a socket is ideal) which has an overall diameter slightly less than that of the seal. Place the tube end against the four diametrically opposed pads on the seal face opposite its lipped side and use it to drift the seal home. Refer to Fig. 13.20 and recess the seal 0.19 to 0.21 in (4.8 to 5.3 mm) into the hub.

9   When fitting the bearing sleeve to the swivel housing, check the milled slot is at the bottom. Use a new joint washer and fit the backplate so that the drain hole is aligned with the milled slot, see Fig. 13.21.

10   When fitting the oil catcher to the backplate, coat its mating surface with sealing compound. Coat the threads of each retaining bolt with a locking compound, fit a serviceable spring washer to each bolt and fit and tighten the bolts to the specified torque loading. Tighten evenly and in a diagonal sequence to avoid distortion of the catcher.

11   Refer to the Specifications of this Chapter before checking hub endfloat. Note the torque wrench settings given for the driving member retaining bolts. Renew the hub cap O-ring if flattened or damaged.

### Rear axle hubs – servicing

12   The procedure for removal, examination and refitting of the rear axle hubs is similar to that given for servicing the wheel bearings in Chapter 8, with the additional information given in paragraphs 7 to 11 of this Section (where applicable).

13   Refer to Fig. 13.22 for the fitted position of each component. When refitting the circlip to the shaft end, check that it is not distorted and is a good fit in the shaft groove. If in doubt, renew the circlip.

### Differential pinion oil seal – renewal

14   Before fitting a new differential pinion oil seal to the Rover type axle, prevent the possibility of a repeat failure by carrying out the following checks:

15   Examine the old seal for signs of damage or uneven wear and if necessary, renew the flange.

16   Check that the axle has not been over filled with oil, which will cause the seal to blow. Check that the axle breather is not blocked. A blocked breather will cause axle pressurisation and must be cleaned or changed.

17   Lightly grease the outer periphery of the new seal before fitting; this will prevent the possibility of its tipping after fitment. BL state that satisfactory seal location can only be obtained by use of the appropriate special tool and that any attempt to use an alternative method of fitting will result in seal damage or misalignment. Ask your BL dealer about the possibility of borrowing or hiring a tool.

### Axle case remote breathers – fitting

18   Where persistent axle oil seal leakage is encountered and it is suspected that pressure within the axle casing is too high, then it is possible to reduce the pressure by fitting a remote breather system in place of the breather valve shown in Chapter 8. This system will be fitted to all later vehicles.

19   The remote breather system is fully interchangeable with the breather valve and no problems should be experienced when fitting. It is most important to route the breather tubes correctly so as to avoid excessive bending of the tubes and subsequent axle pressurisation, see Figs. 13.23 and 13.24.

### Free wheeling hubs

20   BL fit Fairey free wheeling front hubs as an option to all County Station Wagon variants except the V8. If required, units can be purchased from the manufacturers and fitted by the owner, in which case full details for fitting should be supplied with each unit.

**Lubrication**

21   After the axle rationalisation programme carried out in 1980 and the subsequent fitting of the intermediate front axle drift oil seal, free wheeling hubs can no longer rely on oil from the axle for lubrication. It is therefore necessary to ensure each hub is pre-lubricated with grease before fitting. Use a lithium based, extreme pressure grease. Remove each hub cover plate and apply 3 cc of grease to the splines inside the hub.

22   On pre 1980 vehicles, ensure correct hub lubrication by running the vehicle for 20 miles (32 km) in every 500 miles (800 km) with each hub set to its 4 x 4 position. Turn the hub end to select the correct position.

23   When carrying out adjustment of the wheel bearings, lightly smear the moving parts of each hub with a molybdenum disulphide based grease.

## 9 Braking system

### Brake modifications – 1980 on

1   In order to comply with legislation which requires front wheel locking to occur first under all laden braking conditions, some major modifications have been made to the braking system.

2   The first and most important modification is to the 88 in front axle, which is now equipped with 11 in (280 mm) diameter drums instead of the previous 10 in (254 mm) diameter type.

3   When servicing the braking system and ordering replacement parts of the same, take note of the following modifications:

**88 in single line system**

(a)   10 in front brake replaced by 11 in type. Backplate as 109 in
(b)   Larger diameter master cylinder. As 109 in (UNF threads)
(c)   Larger wheel cylinders at rear
(d)   Metric pipes and fittings, except on wheel cylinders

**88 in dual-line system**

(a)   10 in front brake replaced by 11 in type. Backplate as 109 in
(b)   Larger diameter master cylinder. As V8 type
(c)   Larger wheel cylinders at rear
(d)   Metric pipes and fittings, except on wheel cylinders
(e)   Pressure differential warning actuator (PDWA) valve now metric

**88 in dual-line system – Station Wagon, EEC pressure sensed**

As standard dual-line system (above) but with new pressure sensed PDWA

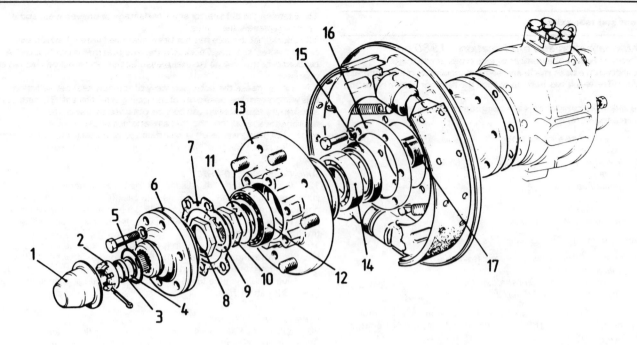

**Fig. 13.19 Front axle hub assembly – 88 in and 109 in vehicles, 1980 on (Sec 8)**

| | | | |
|---|---|---|---|
| 1 Hub cap | 6 Driving member | 10 Inner adjusting nut | 14 Inner roller bearing |
| 2 Castle nut | 7 Joint washer | 11 Keyed thrust washer | 15 Dual lipped seal |
| 3 Distance piece | 8 Outer lock nut | 12 Outer roller bearing | 16 Oil catcher |
| 4 Spirolox ring | 9 Lock washer | 13 Hub | 17 Bearing sleeve |
| 5 Hub cap O-ring | | | |

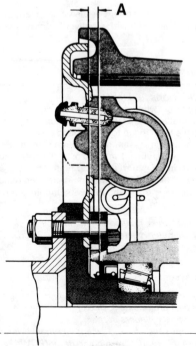

**Fig. 13.20 Fitting the front and rear axle hub oil seal (Sec 8)**

*A = 0.19 to 0.21 in (4.8 to 5.3 mm)*

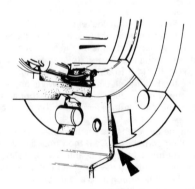

**Fig. 13.21 Aligning the drain hole and milled slot (except 88 in rear hub) (Sec 8)**

**109 in single line system**

(a)  *Metric pipes and fittings, except on wheel cylinders. Master cylinder connection remains UNF*

**109 in dual-line system**

(a)  *Larger diameter master cylinder. As V8 type*
(b)  *Metric pipes and fittings, except on wheel cylinders*
(c)  *Pressure sensed PDWA*
(d)  *System now basic fitment to all Station Wagons*

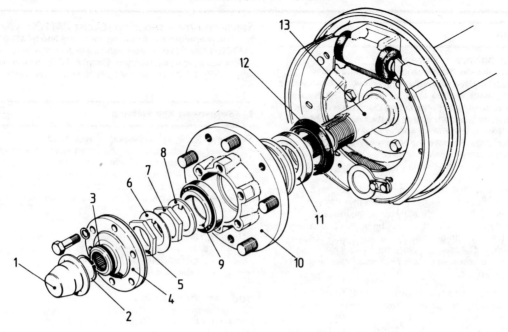

**Fig. 13.22 Rear axle hub assembly – 88 in vehicles, 1980 on (Sec 8)**

| | | | |
|---|---|---|---|
| 1 Hub cap | 5 Outer lock nut | 9 Outer bearing | 13 Bearing sleeve |
| 2 Circlip | 6 Lock washer | 10 Hub | |
| 3 Hub cap O-ring | 7 Inner adjusting nut | 11 Inner bearing | 109 in vehicles also have |
| 4 Driving member | 8 Keyed thrust washer | 12 Dual lipped seal | an oil catcher |

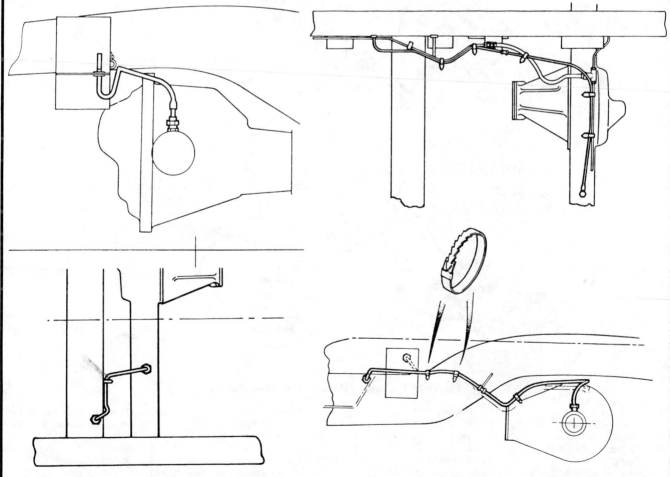

Fig. 13.23 Fitting the front axle case remote breather (Sec 8)

Fig. 13.24 Fitting the rear axle case remote breather (Sec 8)

## 10 Electrical system

### Low maintenance battery – storage

1    Ideally, batteries of the low maintenance type fitted to later vehicles should be disconnected when the vehicle is not in use for long periods. Ancillary equipment, such as electric clocks and the like, can reduce a battery to a state of half charge in less than twenty weeks.

2    Any attempt to maintain battery charge by starting the vehicle at regular intervals and leaving it to run for a short time will only accelerate battery discharge. Remove the battery and store it in a cool place. The self-discharge rate of a low maintenance battery will relate directly to the storage temperature, that is the lower the temperature, the less the loss.

3    If the vehicle is to be started after a long period of storage and the battery has been left connected, then it is important that the headlights are switched on for approximately thirty seconds before the battery voltage is checked, otherwise it will not be possible to obtain an accurate reading. Battery voltage should be at least 12.4 volts before starting is attempted. If possible, place the battery on a trickle charger for at least twelve hours. Any attempt at boost charging will appreciably shorten battery life.

### Water temperature gauge sender unit – identification

4    When investigating water temperature problems on later vehicles, check the colour of the insulating ring fitted beneath the spade connection of the sender unit. The colour of this ring should be beige; any other colour (black or white) will indicate that the wrong type of sender unit has been fitted.

### Starter motor – servicing (Lucas 2M100 type)

5    The procedure for removing, servicing and refitting the Lucas 2M100 motor fitted to later vehicles differs only in detail to that given for the Lucas M418G motor in Chapter 10. Before servicing the motor, refer to Fig. 13.25 and to the Specifications Section of this Chapter.

## 11 Suspension and steering

### Steering lock adjustment – warning

1    Under no circumstances should an attempt be made to improve the vehicle's turning circle by adjusting the steering lock stops on the axle. This will result in the steering rocker arm fouling the lock stops in the steering box, thereby subjecting the rocker arm to excessive loading under full lock conditions with the subsequent risk of component failure.

### Steering relay levers – adjustment (Series III)

2    Fig. 13.27 shows the revised angular relationship of the upper and lower relay levers. Refer to this figure when removing and refitting the relay unit, as detailed in Chapter 11.

### Body height variation

3    To check that the vehicle body height is within the acceptable limits, refer to Fig. 13.28 and measure the distance between each shackle pin centre and the ground. The vehicle must be unladen and parked on flat and level ground for any measurement to be relevant.

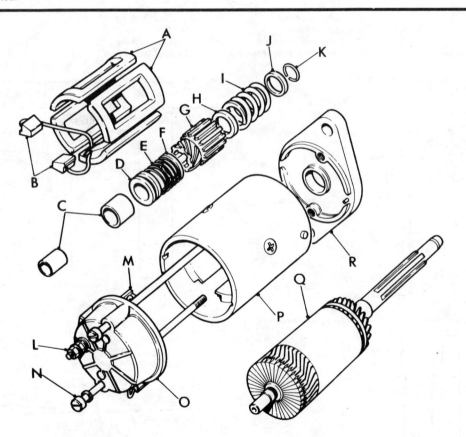

**Fig. 13.25 The Lucas 2M100 starter motor (Sec 10)**

| | | | | | | | |
|---|---|---|---|---|---|---|---|
| A | Field coils | F | Pinion collar | K | Circlip | O | Commutator end cover and |
| B | Field coil brushes | G | Pinion and screwed sleeve | L | Field coil input terminal | | brush box assembly |
| C | Bearing brushes | H | Washer | M | Earth brushes | P | Yoke |
| D | Spring retaining sleeve | I | Main spring | N | Through-bolt | Q | Armature |
| E | Spring | J | End collar | | | R | Drive end bracket |

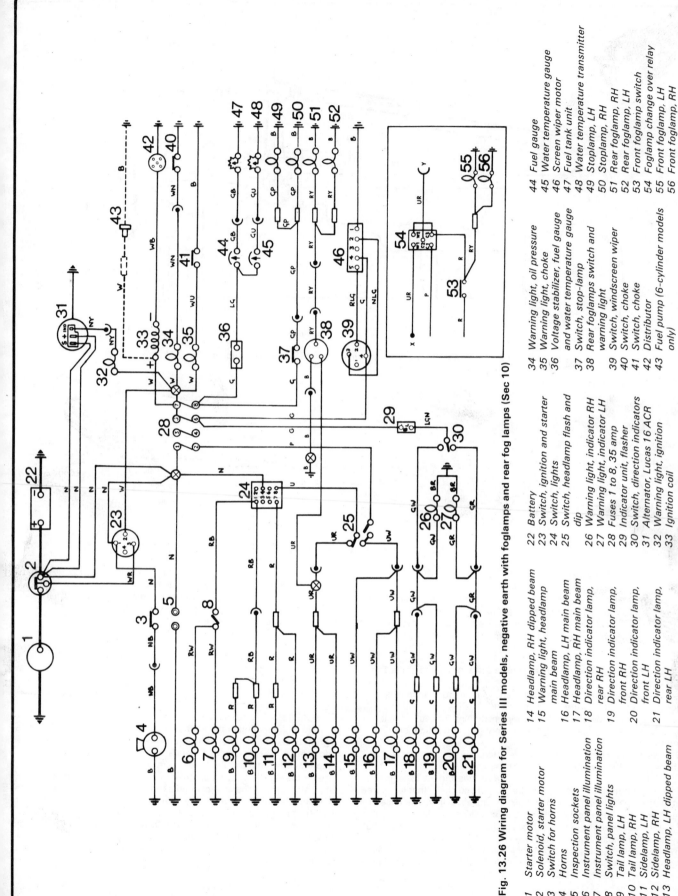

**Fig. 13.26 Wiring diagram for Series III models, negative earth with foglamps and rear fog lamps (Sec 10)**

1 Starter motor
2 Solenoid, starter motor
3 Switch for horns
4 Horns
5 Inspection sockets
6 Instrument panel illumination
7 Instrument panel illumination
8 Switch, panel lights
9 Tail lamp, LH
10 Tail lamp, RH
11 Sidelamp, LH
12 Sidelamp, RH
13 Headlamp, LH dipped beam

14 Headlamp, RH dipped beam
15 Warning light, headlamp
   main beam
16 Headlamp, LH main beam
17 Headlamp, RH main beam
18 Direction indicator lamp,
   rear RH
19 Direction indicator lamp,
   front RH
20 Direction indicator lamp,
   front LH
21 Direction indicator lamp,
   rear LH

22 Battery
23 Switch, ignition and starter
24 Switch, lights
25 Switch, headlamp flash and
   dip
26 Warning light, indicator RH
27 Warning light, indicator LH
28 Fuses 1 to 8, 35 amp
29 Indicator unit, flasher
30 Switch, direction indicators
31 Alternator, Lucas 16 ACR
32 Warning light, ignition
33 Warning light, ignition

34 Warning light, oil pressure
35 Warning light, choke
36 Voltage stabilizer, fuel gauge
   and water temperature gauge
37 Switch, stop-lamp
38 Rear foglamps switch and
   warning light
39 Switch, windscreen wiper
40 Switch, choke
41 Switch, choke
42 Distributor
43 Fuel pump (6-cylinder models
   only)

44 Fuel gauge
45 Water temperature gauge
46 Screen wiper motor
47 Fuel tank unit
48 Water temperature transmitter
49 Stoplamp, LH
50 Stoplamp, RH
51 Rear foglamp, RH
52 Rear foglamp, LH
53 Front foglamp switch
54 Foglamp change over relay
55 Front foglamp, LH
56 Front foglamp, RH

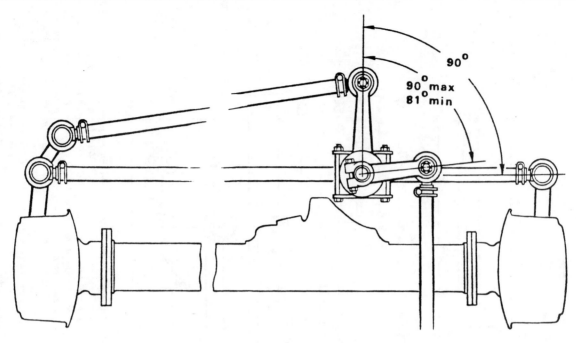

**Fig. 13.27 Positioning the steering relay levers (Series III vehicles) (Sec 11)**

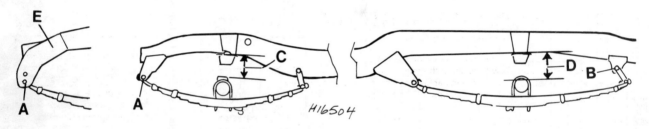

**Fig. 13.28 Checking body height variation (Sec 11)**

A    Front body height measuring point
B    Rear body height measuring point
C  =  4.41 in (112 mm) – 88 in basic and heavy duty suspension
       4.80 in (122 mm) – 88 in half ton
       4.72 in (120 mm) – 109 in basic and heavy duty suspension
       6.22 in (158 mm) – 109 in extended shackle

D  =  5.67 in (144 mm) – 88 in basic and heavy duty suspension
       5.59 in (142 mm) – 88 in half ton
       6.30 in (160mm) – 109 in basic and heavy duty suspension
       8.11 in (206 mm) – 109 in extended shackle
E      Detail of extended shackle

The acceptable variation between vehicle sides in body height is 1 in
(25.4 mm)
4    It has been found that apparent settling of the road springs is
generally a result of 'wind up' in the shackle bushes. Reference to
Fig. 13.28 will show the normal spring positioning for each vehicle
type. Before attempting to remove the springs for investigation, carry
out the following checks:
5    Check that the correct springs are fitted. The part number is
stamped on the lower face of one of the spring leaves.
6    With the vehicle weight taken off the springs and the vehicle
securely supported, remove each shackle pin and check that it is a free
fit in its mating threads or rubber bush inner sleeve. If not, then clean
the threads or bush sleeve to remove all corrosion and dirt.
7    Clean the ends of the inner faces of the shackle side plates so that
all traces of phosphating are removed.
8    Refit the shackle pins. Upon achieving the correct spring position,
tighten first the shackle pin and then its locknut to the specified torque.

Recheck the pins for security and allow the springs to take the weight
of the vehicle.

*Tyre sizes and pressures*
9    Since the writing of the main text of this Manual, BL have issued
a great deal of information which relates to tyre makes and sizes. This
information is being constantly updated and it is therefore
recommended that should there be any doubt as to the correct tyre
size for the vehicle in question, then advice should be sought from a
BL dealer. Let the dealer know under which circumstances the vehicle
is mainly used as this will greatly influence the choice of tyre.
10   BL state that any 88 in wheelbase vehicle fitted with 5.50 x 16
wheel rims can now be equipped with the Range Rover 205 x 16 tyres
which are designed to reduce rolling resistance and therefore increase
tyre life. Fitting these tyres will not affect steering lock or speedometer
accuracy.

# General repair procedures

Whenever servicing, repair or overhaul work is carried out on the car or its components, it is necessary to observe the following procedures and instructions. This will assist in carrying out the operation efficiently and to a professional standard of workmanship.

## Joint mating faces and gaskets

Where a gasket is used between the mating faces of two components, ensure that it is renewed on reassembly, and fit it dry unless otherwise stated in the repair procedure. Make sure that the mating faces are clean and dry with all traces of old gasket removed. When cleaning a joint face, use a tool which is not likely to score or damage the face, and remove any burrs or nicks with an oilstone or fine file.

Make sure that tapped holes are cleaned with a pipe cleaner, and keep them free of jointing compound if this is being used unless specifically instructed otherwise.

Ensure that all orifices, channels or pipes are clear and blow through them, preferably using compressed air.

## Oil seals

Whenever an oil seal is removed from its working location, either individually or as part of an assembly, it should be renewed.

The very fine sealing lip of the seal is easily damaged and will not seal if the surface it contacts is not completely clean and free from scratches, nicks or grooves. If the original sealing surface of the component cannot be restored, the component should be renewed.

Protect the lips of the seal from any surface which may damage them in the course of fitting. Use tape or a conical sleeve where possible. Lubricate the seal lips with oil before fitting and, on dual lipped seals, fill the space between the lips with grease.

Unless otherwise stated, oil seals must be fitted with their sealing lips toward the lubricant to be sealed.

Use a tubular drift or block of wood of the appropriate size to install the seal and, if the seal housing is shouldered, drive the seal down to the shoulder. If the seal housing is unshouldered, the seal should be fitted with its face flush with the housing top face.

## Screw threads and fastenings

Always ensure that a blind tapped hole is completely free from oil, grease, water or other fluid before installing the bolt or stud. Failure to do this could cause the housing to crack due to the hydraulic action of the bolt or stud as it is screwed in.

When tightening a castellated nut to accept a split pin, tighten the nut to the specified torque, where applicable, and then tighten further to the next split pin hole. Never slacken the nut to align a split pin hole unless stated in the repair procedure.

When checking or retightening a nut or bolt to a specified torque setting, slacken the nut or bolt by a quarter of a turn, and then retighten to the specified setting.

## Locknuts, locktabs and washers

Any fastening which will rotate against a component or housing in the course of tightening should always have a washer between it and the relevant component or housing.

Spring or split washers should always be renewed when they are used to lock a critical component such as a big-end bearing retaining nut or bolt.

Locktabs which are folded over to retain a nut or bolt should always be renewed.

Self-locking nuts can be reused in non-critical areas, providing resistance can be felt when the locking portion passes over the bolt or stud thread.

Split pins must always be replaced with new ones of the correct size for the hole.

## Special tools

Some repair procedures in this manual entail the use of special tools such as a press, two or three-legged pullers, spring compressors etc. Wherever possible, suitable readily available alternatives to the manufacturer's special tools are described, and are shown in use. In some instances, where no alternative is possible, it has been necessary to resort to the use of a manufacturer's tool and this has been done for reasons of safety as well as the efficient completion of the repair operation. Unless you are highly skilled and have a thorough under-standing of the procedure described, never attempt to bypass the use of any special tool when the procedure described specifies its use. Not only is there a very great risk of personal injury, but expensive damage could be caused to the components involved.

# Safety first!

Professional motor mechanics are trained in safe working procedures. However enthusiastic you may be about getting on with the job in hand, do take the time to ensure that your safety is not put at risk. A moment's lack of attention can result in an accident, as can failure to observe certain elementary precautions.

There will always be new ways of having accidents, and the following points do not pretend to be a comprehensive list of all dangers; they are intended rather to make you aware of the risks and to encourage a safety-conscious approach to all work you carry out on your vehicle.

## Essential DOs and DON'Ts

**DON'T** rely on a single jack when working underneath the vehicle. Always use reliable additional means of support, such as axle stands, securely placed under a part of the vehicle that you know will not give way.

**DON'T** attempt to loosen or tighten high-torque nuts (e.g. wheel hub nuts) while the vehicle is on a jack; it may be pulled off.

**DON'T** start the engine without first ascertaining that the transmission is in neutral (or 'Park' where applicable) and the parking brake applied.

**DON'T** suddenly remove the filler cap from a hot cooling system – cover it with a cloth and release the pressure gradually first, or you may get scalded by escaping coolant.

**DON'T** attempt to drain oil until you are sure it has cooled sufficiently to avoid scalding you.

**DON'T** grasp any part of the engine, exhaust or catalytic converter without first ascertaining that it is sufficiently cool to avoid burning you.

**DON'T** allow brake fluid or antifreeze to contact vehicle paintwork.

**DON'T** syphon toxic liquids such as fuel, brake fluid or antifreeze by mouth, or allow them to remain on your skin.

**DON'T** inhale dust – it may be injurious to health (see *Asbestos* below).

**DON'T** allow any spilt oil or grease to remain on the floor – wipe it up straight away, before someone slips on it.

**DON'T** use ill-fitting spanners or other tools which may slip and cause injury.

**DON'T** attempt to lift a heavy component which may be beyond your capability – get assistance.

**DON'T** rush to finish a job, or take unverified short cuts.

**DON'T** allow children or animals in or around an unattended vehicle.

**DO** wear eye protection when using power tools such as drill, sander, bench grinder etc, and when working under the vehicle.

**DO** use a barrier cream on your hands prior to undertaking dirty jobs – it will protect your skin from infection as well as making the dirt easier to remove afterwards; but make sure your hands aren't left slippery.

**DO** keep loose clothing (cuffs, tie etc) and long hair well out of the way of moving mechanical parts.

**DO** remove rings, wristwatch etc, before working on the vehicle – especially the electrical system.

**DO** ensure that any lifting tackle used has a safe working load rating adequate for the job.

**DO** keep your work area tidy – it is only too easy to fall over articles left lying around.

**DO** get someone to check periodically that all is well, when working alone on the vehicle.

**DO** carry out work in a logical sequence and check that everything is correctly assembled and tightened afterwards.

**DO** remember that your vehicle's safety affects that of yourself and others. If in doubt on any point, get specialist advice.

**IF,** in spite of following these precautions, you are unfortunate enough to injure yourself, seek medical attention as soon as possible.

## Asbestos

Certain friction, insulating, sealing, and other products – such as brake linings, brake bands, clutch linings, torque converters, gaskets, etc – contain asbestos. *Extreme care must be taken to avoid inhalation of dust from such products since it is hazardous to health*. If in doubt, assume that they *do* contain asbestos.

## Fire

Remember at all times that petrol (gasoline) is highly flammable. Never smoke, or have any kind of naked flame around, when working on the vehicle. But the risk does not end there – a spark caused by an electrical short-circuit, by two metal surfaces contacting each other, by careless use of tools, or even by static electricity built up in your body under certain conditions, can ignite petrol vapour, which in a confined space is highly explosive.

Always disconnect the battery earth (ground) terminal before working on any part of the fuel or electrical system, and never risk spilling fuel on to a hot engine or exhaust.

It is recommended that a fire extinguisher of a type suitable for fuel and electrical fires is kept handy in the garage or workplace at all times. Never try to extinguish a fuel or electrical fire with water.

## Fumes

Certain fumes are highly toxic and can quickly cause unconsciousness and even death if inhaled to any extent. Petrol (gasoline) vapour comes into this category, as do the vapours from certain solvents such as trichloroethylene. Any draining or pouring of such volatile fluids should be done in a well ventilated area.

When using cleaning fluids and solvents, read the instructions carefully. Never use materials from unmarked containers – they may give off poisonous vapours.

Never run the engine of a motor vehicle in an enclosed space such as a garage. Exhaust fumes contain carbon monoxide which is extremely poisonous; if you need to run the engine, always do so in the open air or at least have the rear of the vehicle outside the workplace.

If you are fortunate enough to have the use of an inspection pit, never drain or pour petrol, and never run the engine, while the vehicle is standing over it; the fumes, being heavier than air, will concentrate in the pit with possibly lethal results.

## The battery

Never cause a spark, or allow a naked light, near the vehicle's battery. It will normally be giving off a certain amount of hydrogen gas, which is highly explosive.

Always disconnect the battery earth (ground) terminal before working on the fuel or electrical systems.

If possible, loosen the filler plugs or cover when charging the battery from an external source. Do not charge at an excessive rate or the battery may burst.

Take care when topping up and when carrying the battery. The acid electrolyte, even when diluted, is very corrosive and should not be allowed to contact the eyes or skin.

If you ever need to prepare electrolyte yourself, always add the acid slowly to the water, and never the other way round. Protect against splashes by wearing rubber gloves and goggles.

When jump starting a car using a booster battery, for negative earth (ground) vehicles, connect the jump leads in the following sequence: First connect one jump lead between the positive (+) terminals of the two batteries. Then connect the other jump lead first to the negative (–) terminal of the booster battery, and then to a good earthing (ground) point on the vehicle to be started, at least 18 in (45 cm) from the battery if possible. Ensure that hands and jump leads are clear of any moving parts, and that the two vehicles do not touch. Disconnect the leads in the reverse order.

## Mains electricity

When using an electric power tool, inspection light etc, which works from the mains, always ensure that the appliance is correctly connected to its plug and that, where necessary, it is properly earthed (grounded). Do not use such appliances in damp conditions and, again, beware of creating a spark or applying excessive heat in the vicinity of fuel or fuel vapour.

## Ignition HT voltage

A severe electric shock can result from touching certain parts of the ignition system, such as the HT leads, when the engine is running or being cranked, particularly if components are damp or the insulation is defective. Where an electronic ignition system is fitted, the HT voltage is much higher and could prove fatal.

# Fault diagnosis

## Introduction

The vehicle owner who does his or her own maintenance according to the recommended schedules should not have to use this section of the manual very often. Modern component reliability is such that, provided those items subject to wear or deterioration are inspected or renewed at the specified intervals, sudden failure is comparatively rare. Faults do not usually just happen as a result of sudden failure, but develop over a period of time. Major mechanical failures in particular are usually preceded by characteristic symptoms over hundreds or even thousands of miles. Those components which do occasionally fail without warning are often small and easily carried in the vehicle.

With any fault finding, the first step is to decide where to begin investigations. Sometimes this is obvious, but on other occasions a little detective work will be necessary. The owner who makes half a dozen haphazard adjustments or replacements may be successful in curing a fault (or its symptoms), but he will be none the wiser if the fault recurs and he may well have spent more time and money than was necessary. A calm and logical approach will be found to be more satisfactory in the long run. Always take into account any warning signs or abnormalities that may have been noticed in the period preceding the fault – power loss, high or low gauge readings, unusual noises or smells, etc – and remember that failure of components such as fuses or spark plugs may only be pointers to some underlying fault.

The pages which follow here are intended to help in cases of failure to start or breakdown on the road. There is also a Fault Diagnosis Section at the end of each Chapter which should be consulted if the preliminary checks prove unfruitful. Whatever the fault, certain basic principles apply. These are as follows:

**Verify the fault.** This is simply a matter of being sure that you know what the symptoms are before starting work. This is particularly important if you are investigating a fault for someone else who may not have described it very accurately.

**Don't overlook the obvious.** For example, if the vehicle won't start, is there petrol in the tank? (Don't take anyone else's word on this particular point, and don't trust the fuel gauge either!) If an electrical fault is indicated, look for loose or broken wires before digging out the test gear.

**Cure the disease, not the symptom.** Substituting a flat battery with a fully charged one will get you off the hard shoulder, but if the underlying cause is not attended to, the new battery will go the same way. Similarly, changing oil-fouled spark plugs for a new set will get you moving again, but remember that the reason for the fouling (if it wasn't simply an incorrect grade of plug) will have to be established and corrected.

**Don't take anything for granted.** Particularly, don't forget that a 'new' component may itself be defective (especially if it's been rattling round in the boot for months), and don't leave components out of a fault diagnosis sequence just because they are new or recently fitted. When you do finally diagnose a difficult fault, you'll probably realise that all the evidence was there from the start.

## Electrical faults

Electrical faults can be more puzzling than straightforward mechanical failures, but they are no less susceptible to logical analysis if the basic principles of operation are understood. Vehicle electrical wiring exists in extremely unfavourable conditions – heat, vibration and chemical attack – and the first things to look for are loose or corroded connections and broken or chafed wires, especially where the wires pass through holes in the bodywork or are subject to vibration.

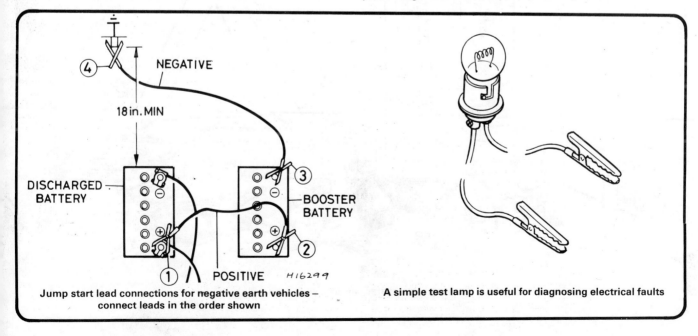

Jump start lead connections for negative earth vehicles – connect leads in the order shown

A simple test lamp is useful for diagnosing electrical faults

All metal-bodied vehicles in current production have one pole of the battery 'earthed', ie connected to the vehicle bodywork, and in nearly all modern vehicles it is the negative (–) terminal. The various electrical components – motors, bulb holders etc – are also connected to earth, either by means of a lead or directly by their mountings. Electric current flows through the component and then back to the battery via the bodywork. If the component mounting is loose or corroded, or if a good path back to the battery is not available, the circuit will be incomplete and malfunction will result. The engine and/or gearbox are also earthed by means of flexible metal straps to the body or subframe; if these straps are loose or missing, starter motor, generator and ignition trouble may result.

Assuming the earth return to be satisfactory, electrical faults will be due either to component malfunction or to defects in the current supply. Individual components are dealt with in Chapter 10. If supply wires are broken or cracked internally this results in an open-circuit, and the easiest way to check for this is to bypass the suspect wire temporarily with a length of wire having a crocodile clip or suitable connector at each end. Alternatively, a 12V test lamp can be used to verify the presence of supply voltage at various points along the wire and the break can be thus isolated.

If a bare portion of a live wire touches the bodywork or other earthed metal part, the electricity will take the low-resistance path thus formed back to the battery: this is known as a short-circuit. Hopefully a short-circuit will blow a fuse, but otherwise it may cause burning of the insulation (and possibly further short-circuits) or even a fire. This is why it is inadvisable to bypass persistently blowing fuses with silver foil or wire.

## Spares and tool kit

Most vehicles are supplied only with sufficient tools for wheel changing; the *Maintenance and minor repair* tool kit detailed in *Tools and working facilities,* with the addition of a hammer, is probably sufficient for those repairs that most motorists would consider attempting at the roadside. In addition a few items which can be fitted without too much trouble in the event of a breakdown should be carried. Experience and available space will modify the list below, but the following may save having to call on professional assistance:

*Spark plugs, clean and correctly gapped*
*HT lead and plug cap – long enough to reach the plug furthest from the distributor*
*Distributor rotor, condenser and contact breaker points*
*Drivebelt(s) – emergency type may suffice*
*Spare fuses*
*Set of principal light bulbs*
*Tin of radiator sealer and hose bandage*
*Exhaust bandage*
*Roll of insulating tape*
*Length of soft iron wire*
*Length of electrical flex*
*Torch or inspection lamp (can double as test lamp)*
*Battery jump leads*
*Tow-rope*
*Ignition waterproofing aerosol*
*Litre of engine oil*
*Sealed can of hydraulic fluid*
*Emergency windscreen*
*Worm drive clips*
*Tube of filler paste*

If spare fuel is carried, a can designed for the purpose should be used to minimise risks of leakage and collision damage. A first aid kit and a warning triangle, whilst not at present compulsory in the UK, are obviously sensible items to carry in addition to the above.

When touring abroad it may be advisable to carry additional spares which, even if you cannot fit them yourself, could save having to wait while parts are obtained. The items below may be worth considering:

*Throttle cable*
*Cylinder head gasket*
*Dynamo or alternator brushes*
*Fuel pump repair kit*
*Tyre valve core*

One of the motoring organisations will be able to advise on availability of fuel etc in foreign countries.

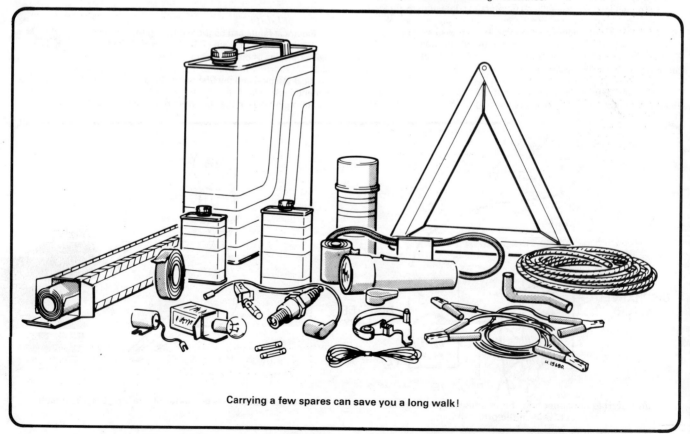

**Carrying a few spares can save you a long walk!**

## Engine will not start

### Engine fails to turn when starter operated
Flat battery (recharge, use jump leads, or push start)
Battery terminals loose or corroded
Battery earth to body defective
Engine earth strap loose or broken
Starter motor (or solenoid) wiring loose or broken
Automatic transmission selector in wrong position, or inhibitor switch faulty
Ignition/starter switch faulty
Major mechanical failure (seizure)
Starter or solenoid internal fault (see Chapter 10)

### Starter motor turns engine slowly
Partially discharged battery (recharge, use jump leads, or push start)
Battery terminals loose or corroded
Battery earth to body defective
Engine earth strap loose
Starter motor (or solenoid) wiring loose
Starter motor internal fault (see Chapter 10)

### Starter motor spins without turning engine
Flat battery
Starter motor pinion sticking on sleeve
Flywheel gear teeth damaged or worn
Starter motor mounting bolts loose

### Engine turns normally but fails to start
Damp or dirty HT leads and distributor cap (crank engine and check for spark)
Dirty or incorrectly gapped distributor points (if applicable)
No fuel in tank (check for delivery at carburettor)
Excessive choke (hot engine) or insufficient choke (cold engine)
Fouled or incorrectly gapped spark plugs (remove, clean and regap)
Other ignition system fault (see Chapter 4)
Other fuel system fault (see Chapter 3)
Poor compression (see Chapter 1)
Major mechanical failure (eg camshaft drive)

### Engine fires but will not run
Insufficient choke (cold engine)
Air leaks at carburettor or inlet manifold
Fuel starvation (see Chapter 3)
Ballast resistor defective, or other ignition fault (see Chapter 4)

## Engine cuts out and will not restart

### Engine cuts out suddenly – ignition fault
Loose or disconnected LT wires
Wet HT leads or distributor cap (after traversing water splash)
Coil or condenser failure (check for spark)
Other ignition fault (see Chapter 4)

### Engine misfires before cutting out – fuel fault
Fuel tank empty
Fuel pump defective or filter blocked (check for delivery)
Fuel tank filler vent blocked (suction will be evident on releasing cap)
Carburettor needle valve sticking
Carburettor jets blocked (fuel contaminated)
Other fuel system fault (see Chapter 3)

### Engine cuts out – other causes
Serious overheating
Major mechanical failure (eg camshaft drive)

## Engine overheats

### Ignition (no-charge) warning light illuminated
Slack or broken drivebelt – retension or renew (Chapter 2)

### Ignition warning light not illuminated
Coolant loss due to internal or external leakage (see Chapter 2)
Thermostat defective
Low oil level
Brakes binding
Radiator clogged externally or internally
Electric cooling fan not operating correctly
Engine waterways clogged
Ignition timing incorrect or automatic advance malfunctioning
Mixture too weak

**Note:** *Do not add cold water to an overheated engine or damage may result*

## Low engine oil pressure

### Gauge reads low or warning light illuminated with engine running
Oil level low or incorrect grade
Defective gauge or sender unit
Wire to sender unit earthed
Engine overheating
Oil filter clogged or bypass valve defective
Oil pressure relief valve defective
Oil pick-up strainer clogged
Oil pump worn or mountings loose
Worn main or big-end bearings

**Note:** *Low oil pressure in a high-mileage engine at tickover is not necessarily a cause for concern. Sudden pressure loss at speed is far more significant. In any event, check the gauge or warning light sender before condemning the engine.*

## Engine noises

### Pre-ignition (pinking) on acceleration
Incorrect grade of fuel
Ignition timing incorrect
Distributor faulty or worn
Worn or maladjusted carburettor
Excessive carbon build-up in engine

### Whistling or wheezing noises
Leaking vacuum hose
Leaking carburettor or manifold gasket
Blowing head gasket

### Tapping or rattling
Incorrect valve clearances
Worn valve gear
Worn timing chain or belt
Broken piston ring (ticking noise)

### Knocking or thumping
Unintentional mechanical contact (eg fan blades)
Worn fanbelt
Peripheral component fault (generator, water pump etc)
Worn big-end bearings (regular heavy knocking, perhaps less under load)
Worn main bearings (rumbling and knocking, perhaps worsening under load)
Piston slap (most noticeable when cold)

# Conversion factors

## Length (distance)

| | | | | | |
|---|---|---|---|---|---|
| Inches (in) | X | 25.4 | = Millimetres (mm) | X | 0.0394 | = Inches (in) |
| Feet (ft) | X | 0.305 | = Metres (m) | X | 3.281 | = Feet (ft) |
| Miles | X | 1.609 | = Kilometres (km) | X | 0.621 | = Miles |

## Volume (capacity)

| | | | | | | |
|---|---|---|---|---|---|---|
| Cubic inches (cu in; in$^3$) | X | 16.387 | = Cubic centimetres (cc; cm$^3$) | X | 0.061 | = Cubic inches (cu in; in$^3$) |
| Imperial pints (Imp pt) | X | 0.568 | = Litres (l) | X | 1.76 | = Imperial pints (Imp pt) |
| Imperial quarts (Imp qt) | X | 1.137 | = Litres (l) | X | 0.88 | = Imperial quarts (Imp qt) |
| Imperial quarts (Imp qt) | X | 1.201 | = US quarts (US qt) | X | 0.833 | = Imperial quarts (Imp qt) |
| US quarts (US qt) | X | 0.946 | = Litres (l) | X | 1.057 | = US quarts (US qt) |
| Imperial gallons (Imp gal) | X | 4.546 | = Litres (l) | X | 0.22 | = Imperial gallons (Imp gal) |
| Imperial gallons (Imp gal) | X | 1.201 | = US gallons (US gal) | X | 0.833 | = Imperial gallons (Imp gal) |
| US gallons (US gal) | X | 3.785 | = Litres (l) | X | 0.264 | = US gallons (US gal) |

## Mass (weight)

| | | | | | |
|---|---|---|---|---|---|
| Ounces (oz) | X | 28.35 | = Grams (g) | X | 0.035 | = Ounces (oz) |
| Pounds (lb) | X | 0.454 | = Kilograms (kg) | X | 2.205 | = Pounds (lb) |

## Force

| | | | | | |
|---|---|---|---|---|---|
| Ounces-force (ozf; oz) | X | 0.278 | = Newtons (N) | X | 3.6 | = Ounces-force (ozf; oz) |
| Pounds-force (lbf; lb) | X | 4.448 | = Newtons (N) | X | 0.225 | = Pounds-force (lbf; lb) |
| Newtons (N) | X | 0.1 | = Kilograms-force (kgf; kg) | X | 9.81 | = Newtons (N) |

## Pressure

| | | | | | |
|---|---|---|---|---|---|
| Pounds-force per square inch (psi; lbf/in$^2$; lb/in$^2$) | X | 0.070 | = Kilograms-force per square centimetre (kgf/cm$^2$; kg/cm$^2$) | X | 14.223 | = Pounds-force per square inch (psi; lbf/in$^2$; lb/in$^2$) |
| Pounds-force per square inch (psi; lbf/in$^2$; lb/in$^2$) | X | 0.068 | = Atmospheres (atm) | X | 14.696 | = Pounds-force per square inch (psi; lbf/in$^2$; lb/in$^2$) |
| Pounds-force per square inch (psi; lbf/in$^2$; lb/in$^2$) | X | 0.069 | = Bars | X | 14.5 | = Pounds-force per square inch (psi; lbf/in$^2$; lb/in$^2$) |
| Pounds-force per square inch (psi; lbf/in$^2$; lb/in$^2$) | X | 6.895 | = Kilopascals (kPa) | X | 0.145 | = Pounds-force per square inch (psi; lbf/in$^2$; lb/in$^2$) |
| Kilopascals (kPa) | X | 0.01 | = Kilograms-force per square centimetre (kgf/cm$^2$; kg/cm$^2$) | X | 98.1 | = Kilopascals (kPa) |

## Torque (moment of force)

| | | | | | |
|---|---|---|---|---|---|
| Pounds-force inches (lbf in; lb in) | X | 1.152 | = Kilograms-force centimetre (kgf cm; kg cm) | X | 0.868 | = Pounds-force inches (lbf in; lb in) |
| Pounds-force inches (lbf in; lb in) | X | 0.113 | = Newton metres (Nm) | X | 8.85 | = Pounds-force inches (lbf in; lb in) |
| Pounds-force inches (lbf in; lb in) | X | 0.083 | = Pounds-force feet (lbf ft; lb ft) | X | 12 | = Pounds-force inches (lbf in; lb in) |
| Pounds-force feet (lbf ft; lb ft) | X | 0.138 | = Kilograms-force metres (kgf m; kg m) | X | 7.233 | = Pounds-force feet (lbf ft; lb ft) |
| Pounds-force feet (lbf ft; lb ft) | X | 1.356 | = Newton metres (Nm) | X | 0.738 | = Pounds-force feet (lbf ft; lb ft) |
| Newton metres (Nm) | X | 0.102 | = Kilograms-force metres (kgf m; kg m) | X | 9.804 | = Newton metres (Nm) |

## Power

| | | | | | |
|---|---|---|---|---|---|
| Horsepower (hp) | X | 745.7 | = Watts (W) | X | 0.0013 | = Horsepower (hp) |

## Velocity (speed)

| | | | | | |
|---|---|---|---|---|---|
| Miles per hour (miles/hr; mph) | X | 1.609 | = Kilometres per hour (km/hr; kph) | X | 0.621 | = Miles per hour (miles/hr; mph) |

## Fuel consumption*

| | | | | | |
|---|---|---|---|---|---|
| Miles per gallon, Imperial (mpg) | X | 0.354 | = Kilometres per litre (km/l) | X | 2.825 | = Miles per gallon, Imperial (mpg) |
| Miles per gallon, US (mpg) | X | 0.425 | = Kilometres per litre (km/l) | X | 2.352 | = Miles per gallon, US (mpg) |

## Temperature

Degrees Fahrenheit = (°C x 1.8) + 32

Degrees Celsius (Degrees Centigrade; °C) = (°F - 32) x 0.56

*It is common practice to convert from miles per gallon (mpg) to litres/100 kilometres (l/100km), where mpg (Imperial) x l/100 km = 282 and mpg (US) x l/100 km = 235

# Index

Printed by
**J H Haynes & Co Ltd**
Sparkford  Nr Yeovil
Somerset  BA22 7JJ  England